英语专业系列教材

A COURSE IN ENGLISH-CHINESE TRANSLATION

FOURTH EDITION

英汉语篇翻译 （第四版）

李运兴 编著

清华大学出版社
北京

内 容 简 介

本书打破传统翻译教学中以语法为框架、以单个句子为基准的翻译训练模式,从语篇入手引导学习者领会翻译技能。本书注重译者的实际思维、决策过程,注重不同文体的翻译特点,注重培养在语篇翻译实践中多角度的思辨能力,使翻译技能的训练更贴近译者的实际操作过程。书中例文、例句丰富,讲解精练,富有启发性。本次修订融入了近年来翻译理论和教学的最新思考,对全书内容进行了校订、补充和深化。

本书适合翻译专业学生、其他专业高年级本科生及研究生使用。通过学习可掌握英译汉的基本原则和技能,进而独立翻译不同文体的英语原文。

本书配套的补充教学资源请在ftp://ftp.tup.tsinghua.edu.cn/上进行下载。

版权所有,侵权必究。举报:010-62782989,beiqinquan@tup.tsinghua.edu.cn。

图书在版编目(CIP)数据

英汉语篇翻译 / 李运兴编著. —4版. —北京:清华大学出版社,2020.6(2025.1重印)
英语专业系列教材
ISBN 978-7-302-53045-9

Ⅰ.①英… Ⅱ.①李… Ⅲ.①英语-翻译-高等学校-教材 Ⅳ.①H315.9

中国版本图书馆CIP数据核字(2019)第094447号

责任编辑:刘细珍
封面设计:子 一
责任校对:王凤芝
责任印制:沈 露

出版发行:清华大学出版社
网　　址:https://www.tup.com.cn,https://www.wqxuetang.com
地　　址:北京清华大学学研大厦A座　邮　编:100084
社 总 机:010-83470000　邮　购:010-62786544
投稿与读者服务:010-62776969,c-service@tup.tsinghua.edu.cn
质量反馈:010-62772015,zhiliang@tup.tsinghua.edu.cn
印 装 者:涿州市般润文化传播有限公司
经　　销:全国新华书店
开　　本:170mm×230mm　印　张:23.25　字　数:408千字
版　　次:2002年11月第1版　2020年6月第4版　印　次:2025年1月第4次印刷
定　　价:78.00元

产品编号:081490-01

第四版前言

自 2002 年出版以来,《英汉语篇翻译》历经第二版和第三版修订,至今已近 20 个年头了。现在推出第四版,以期进一步确立本教材的指导思想和学习路径,更新语篇素材,并更正个别疏漏之处,达到更精准有效地为翻译教学服务的目的。

"语篇翻译"的具体内涵是:1. 以语篇为准进行翻译操作,关注不同语言级层上翻译操作的特点;2. 语篇类型(text type)、交际功能与翻译策略和翻译方法密切相关;3. 语篇在一定的语境及互文关系中发挥交际功能。翻译策略的选择必须考虑翻译语境以及原文、译文与相关语篇的关联。在这一概念的指导下学习翻译,应突出两个基本意识:语篇意识和互文意识,绪论中将分两个单元结合翻译实践分别讨论。

翻译是一个过程,是"由原文引发的译文生成过程"(Neubert & Shreve 1992:43),是在某一翻译语境下通过译者与原文的互动而激活的信息转换能力的展现,一般可分为原文理解和译文表达两个阶段。本书在第二、三两章分别讨论这两个阶段出现的典型问题及应对原则和途径。

20 世纪七八十年代,德国学者 Reiss(1989;2000)移植德国心理学家 Karl Buhler 有关语言功能的观点,将语篇类型、功能和翻译方法联系了起来。Reiss 的模式表明了语言编码和交际功能之间的联系,凸显了译者操作的能动性,从而为翻译教学中的译文评价提供了一个可行的参照框架。本教材参照写作教学中的分类,按叙事、描写文体(第四章)和说明、论说文体(第五章)两大类分别讨论其翻译操作的规律和方法。至于前三版中涉及的应用文体翻译,新版予以删除。因为此类翻译是在掌握基本翻译技能的基础上,针对广告、法律等不同应用范畴的特定实践,应有专门教材加以指导。

全书体例为:翻译过程与语篇类型两大主线交错,原文语篇与译文语篇对照,并加上必要的注释,再聚焦其中一两个翻译问题展开讲解,旨在将语篇对照阅读与翻译技巧讲解融合起来,而不是各说各话地分立进行。第二章至第五章所附练习则针对本章内容提供更多练笔和思考素材。

第四版修订得到清华大学出版社领导和编辑的大力支持和指导,使用本书的师生亦提出许多宝贵的意见,在此深表谢意。

李运兴
2019 年 8 月

第三版前言

学习翻译的五种意识

谈到翻译教学，Delisle（1992，转引自 Lederer 2003：134）区分出两个概念：pedagogical translation 和 pedagogy of translations。前者指外语教学中把翻译作为一种教学方法——教学翻译，后者则指译员培训——翻译教学；前者把翻译作为手段，目的在于检验外语学习进展，提高词汇和语法方面的能力，教学活动围绕语言进行，基本不涉及语言外因素；而后者以翻译能力的培养为目的，语言只是实现跨语言和跨文化交际的一种手段，语言能力必须转化为跨语言交际能力才能达到培训目标。外语教学不是翻译教学，而是翻译教学的基础，只有外语和母语都达到了一定的水平，才能开始学习翻译。这正像一个运动员必须具备速度和耐力等基本身体素质后，才能参加马拉松训练。

但作为一本供学习者阅读的翻译教材的前言，我们想转换一下视角，从教转到学——学外语和学翻译有什么不同吗？这和教学翻译与翻译教学的区别有点关联。学外语可将翻译法作为一种手段，最终目标是掌握那种外语的词汇、语法，获得理解外语语篇和用外语语篇表达思想的口、笔头交际能力。而学习翻译旨在掌握跨语言、跨文化沟通技能，即帮助不同语言和文化群体间实现交际的技能。这要求除了语言能力（包括母语和外语）之外，还必须学习相关语言群体的文化，学习处理交际情景因素和交际参与者之间的关系。翻译学员学的是一种职业技能。要把翻译学好，必须注意加强以下五种意识。

首先，要培养职业伦理意识。虽然我们现在是在课堂里讨论翻译，做的是老师布置的翻译作业，译文的读者也只是老师和同学，但视野要透过教室的窗子，投向将来工作的社会。这不是假想，而是我们不久就会面对的现实。要强化这样的意识：我们的译文是按客户要求，译给不谙源语的译语读者读的，是读者了解源语信息的唯一或重要渠道，我们的工作决定着客户和读者间交际目的的实现。我们的客户可能是某个部门或某个人，读者可能是特定的人群或泛泛的某个社会群体。作为社会的、文化的人，他们有着各自的背景和要求，我们必须在翻译活动中认真考虑，译文要传递信息，要顾及交际效果，要承担审核责任，这就是我们的职业道德。我们的误解、误译、疏漏,对文化因素的处理,对转换技巧的使用,现在是个分数问题,但将来可是职业操守问题,甚至是法律问题。把作者的话歪曲了,篡改了,肯定会招致社会的批评、谴责,甚至造成严重政治、经济后果。正是出于这种考虑,我们在第三章中特别增加了关注翻译伦理问题的 Unit Nine。

其次,要强化交际意识。做翻译绝不能停留在语言层面,尽管我们读的确实是语符,译出来的也是语符。第一,要有语篇意识,这一点在第二章的 Unit One 中有更多讨论。语篇是交际功能的体现,它不等于其中语句的总和,也不单单是语句表层的意思,永远记住我们翻译的不是单个的句子或段落,而是一个有机的信息整体;语篇是在特定交际情境中发挥功能的,它的功能或效果最终要体现在交际者的关系中。原文作者在特定时间和空间里组句成篇,自有其意向或目的(这一点在第二章 Unit Two 中以"语篇的意向"为题讨论),译者不但要理解语篇的内容,还要领会作者的交际意向;第二,语篇本身也提供特定的语境,译者必须"看到"语篇所提供的一个个情景(第三章 Unit Three 有进一步讨论)。最后,要意识到翻译作为一种跨语言、跨文化的交际形式,其交际终端是译文的读者,必须考虑他们的文化背景和知识结构等因素。为此,译者有时要进行"解释性翻译",而从广义上来说,翻译就是译者对原文的一种释义过程(见新增的第五章 Unit Eight)。

第三,要加强文化意识。语言是文化的产物和积淀,语言运作于文化语境之中,没有了这个语境,语言符号就会失去交际意义。因此,必须强调和关注文化因素在翻译过程中的作用,这一点在第二章 Unit Four 中以"理解中的文化因素"为题讨论。我们看到,和所译语篇相关的文化因素在理解和表达中都起着关键作用,但还要进一步认识到,理解过程不是单纯的语符解码,而是用自己的语言能力加相关知识储备和原文进行沟通的过程,在这个过程中译者个人的知识结构和亲身经历都会发生作用。为此,我们在第二章专门增加了 Unit Five 来讨论"译者的知识和经验在理解中的作用"。

提到相关文化知识,我们自然想到如何获取的问题。其实途径很简单,可以从自己的生活经历中获取,更可以从其他的语篇资源那里获得。Chandler 说得对,"语篇不仅对其他语篇的构建至关重要,而且对经验的构建起着重要作用。我们对世界的了解很多来源于我们读过的书籍、报纸和杂志,来自于我们从电影、电视和收音机里看到或听到的。于是,不知不觉中生活就成了阅读各种语篇并被语篇所塑造的过程。"(Texts are instrumental not only in the construction of other texts but in the construction of experiences. Much of what we "know" about the world is derived from what we have read in books, newspapers and magazines, from what we have seen in the cinema and on television and from what we have heard on the radio. Life is thus lived through texts and framed by texts to a greater extent than we are normally aware of.）因此，要想成为一个合格的译者，必须博览群书并关注其他所有可能提供相关知识的信息来源。一种语言的全部语篇，在很大程度上就是那种语言所赖以生成和运作的文化。

　　第四，要强化互文意识。每一个语篇都存在于与其他语篇的关系中，每一个语篇都可能与先于它存在的语篇发生联系，也可能与后于它构建的语篇发生联系。原文语篇是源语语篇世界中的一员，构建中的译语语篇也将成为译语语篇世界中的一员。原文一方面是译文的源头，另一方面又假译文之功在译语环境中获得延续和再生。不管是原文还是译文，其构建和解读都受到其所在语篇世界的制约，也都影响和塑造着各自的语篇世界，为之做出种种贡献。互文性既可以从语篇类型的角度看，也可以从语篇和语篇间的关联的角度观察。

　　语篇类型可有不同的分法：按交际功能可分为以传达信息（informative）为主的语篇、以表达情感（expressive）为主的语篇、以劝诱、鼓动他人（operative）为主的语篇等，按体裁可分为小说、散文、论文等，按修辞目的又可分为叙事、描写、说明、议论等。不论如何分类，每一个语篇的构建和解读都是在同类语篇的成篇规范的制约下或在与同类语篇的互动中进行的。

　　至于语篇和语篇间的关系，新增加的第三章 Unit Eight 专门进行了讨论。译者在理解原文和构建译文时，要把原文放在它与有关源语语篇的关系中解读，也要把译文的构建置于与业已存在的有关译语语篇的关系中加以考虑。

　　第五，要加强技能意识。要认识到，了解了两种语言及其文化不一定就自然而然地成为合格的译者。双语能力和双文化素养只是成为一个好译员的基础和起始点。要做好翻译还必须在实践中加强技能的培养和精练。本书的大部分单元都在提供提高翻译技能的切入点。比如，第三章 Unit Two 讨论译者的具体操作；第四章 Unit Two 探讨了形合和意合问题、Unit Five 探讨了归化和异化问题；第五章 Unit Five 和 Unit Seven 谈信息焦点和连贯问题等。第三版还特别在第三章增加了 Unit Nine，沿着语篇连贯的思路进一步探讨了语篇形态问题。相信这些讨论会有利于培养翻译学习者的逻辑思维能力。

　　加强技能意识有一个十分有效的途径，那就是分析英汉两种语言和文化的差异。有了"异"的意识，自然就会意识到语际转换的必要，会努力寻求转换的方法，掌握转换的技巧。

　　以上五种意识，如果不是学习翻译特别需要具备的，也是相对于学习外语而言应特别强化的。相信大家通过学习本书，这几种意识会有所提高，为将来成为一名符合专业操守的翻译工作者打下坚实的基础，做好充分的能力和心理准备。

本书是在2003版《英汉语篇翻译》（第二版）的基础上修订的。新增加的六个单元和替换的三个单元体现了我们近年来对翻译理论和教学的最新思考，也是对第二版原有讲解项目的补充和深化。另外，对全书内容也进行了校订，增加了一些练习，改动了部分例句。

修订工作得到了清华大学出版社的大力支持，修订过程中得到南开大学外国语学院刘士聪和谷启楠两位资深教授的支持和指教，在此一并表示真诚的谢意。

引用文献

Chandler, D. *Semiotics for Beginners*. www.aber.ac.uk/media/Documents/S4B/sem0.9.html.

Lederer, M. 2003. *Translation: The Interpretive Model*. Manchester, UK & Northampton, MA: St. Jerome Publishing.

第二版前言

论语篇翻译教学

翻译教学的体系

按照 Holmes（1998；2000）的翻译研究体系，翻译教学（translator training）是翻译研究应用分支的重要组成部分；它本身又可以分为教学方法、测试技术和课程设计（teaching methods, testing techniques, curriculum design）三部分。如果将我们的研究视野聚焦到翻译教学上，那便会出现这样一幅细化的局部图表：

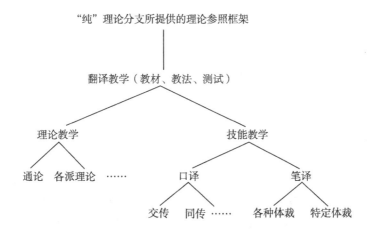

首先，所有教学活动必须自觉地在"纯"理论分支所提供的某种理论框架下进行，而"纯"理论分支中的描写范畴是沟通翻译教学和抽象理论原则的十分重要的环节，翻译教学能从描写语料库中汲取许多有用的材料。教师在理论的指导下制定教学大纲，编写教科书，制定实施教材的方法和建立反馈机制，还要制定出具有高信度和高效度的测试手段。可以看出，教师的理论素养在整个教学过程中起着关键作用。不懂理论的教师不是合格的教师，只能停留在师傅带徒弟的经验加实践的层次上。碰上徒弟悟性高，也是可以名师出高徒的。但对于大规模的译员培训，恐怕就很难高效地培养人才了。

翻译教学又可分为理论教学和技能教学两个分支。理论教学主要针对翻译专业（方向）的研究生，技能教学主要针对外语专业本科生。翻译专业的本科生（目前国内还很少）也应接受适当程度的理论培训。理论教学可包括通论、各派理论和翻译史等部分。技能教学是外语专业本科生必修课程，它的目的不是让学生了解系统的理论知识，而是培养从事翻译工作的技能。翻译实践按语篇方式（mode of discourse）可分为笔译和口译；口译又可分为交传和同传等。语篇类型的差异也使翻译活动呈现不同的特点，不同的语言对组也会出现不同的信息传译规律。这些都必须、也必然在翻译教学中体现出来，分门别类地加以对待。笔译和口译当然须分开教，英译汉和汉译英也不宜混为一谈，按不同语篇类型实施培训，如科技翻译、法律翻译，也已经有所实践。

理论教学可从"纯"理论分支中选取适用于教学对象和教学目的的材料，但技能教学分支就不能将理论分支的东西直接运用了。长期以来一直存在一个如何将理论与实践相结合的重要问题。

技能教学中的理论与实践的关系

关于翻译技能教学中理论与实践的关系或平衡问题历来受到国内外学者关注，《论翻译教学》（刘宗和主编）中有专栏讨论，Mona Baker 所编 *Routledge Encyclopedia of Translation Studies* 中 Didactics of translation 条目下亦将"教程设计中的理论和实践平衡"列为翻译教学诸论题的首位。我国学者所论涉及最多的是理论对翻译是否有用，与实践成怎样的比例合适等问题。我们觉得，理论与实践的关系不是一个简单的课时比例问题，翻译理论作为一个体系对翻译实践也并非有直接用途。罗进德（1997）说得对："课程的内容和方法应该有一个坚实可信的理论基础，或者说是让这样一个理论体系做后盾……就是让这样一个理论体系像一只'无形的手'，对教学的内容和方法进行幕后操纵。"Toury（1995：18）说得更有创见："……从翻译研究本身到它的任何一项实际应用间的过渡并不是直接完成的。从一个到另一个间的推导也更不是自动的。要实现这一过渡须遵循某些沟通法则（bridging rules）……"此外，Toury（1995：18）的另一个观点也很值得注意："……沟通法则肯定会因应用的类型不同而有所不同，而且，恐怕没有哪一项应用会只从翻译研究中汲取营养。"比方，翻译教学就会从教学法研究中获取理论支持和启示。

遗憾的是，Toury 并没有进一步阐述沟通法则如何确立以及包括什么内容。根据我们的理解和实际体验，建立沟通法则的关键是寻找理论原则和概念与实际翻译问题的接合面（interface）。技能教学中不能追求学生对翻译理论的全面或系统了解，学生所需要的是翻译的基本原则、策略和翻译技能要领。简言之，技能教学中的理论成分不应呈系统态势，而应是要点式、问题解决式的。这就要求教师对翻译实践有切实的、亲身的体验，对学生的翻译水平现状掌握确实的一手资料，从而发现翻译操作的焦点问题，再带着这些问题从翻译研究成果中寻求解决方案。这就是理论与实践的接合面。也就是说，这基本是一条从实际问题出发——寻求理论指导——制定教学指导原则的始于实践又终于实践的路径；而不是从理论出发制定指导原则，然后用于教学实践的演绎路径。

技能教材的编写

翻译教学中，教材编写显然是最重要、最关键的一环。它是翻译理论框架的具体体现，是实施教学方法的平台，也是制定测试方法的依据。不过，上文已说过，教材编写不仅是翻译理论框架的具体体现，还要结合教学法的有关原则才能编写出针对性强、易于有效实施的教材。

目前国内出版的翻译技能教材，大致可分为三类。传统语法框架、问题解决式框架和当代译论框架。第一种较为传统，基本没有当代译论的介入，如张培基等人的《英汉翻译教程》。第二种着眼于翻译操作中的实际问题，有当代译论的成分，但不明显，如范仲英的《实用翻译教程》。第三种有明确的理论介入，如柯平的《英汉与汉英翻译教程》和陈宏薇的《新实用汉译英教程》。但这种理论介入并不以系统介绍某译论体系为目的，而仍然呈现以翻译实践中常常遇到的典型问题为焦点的问题解决式倾向。因为，虽然技能教学要在"纯"理论分支所提供的某种理论框架指导下进行，却并不意味着理论介入越明显越好，越系统越好。从当前及今后的教学需要来看，后两种类型的教材均会有所需求，而第三类教材应该是发展的主导趋势。

语篇翻译教材

下面谈一谈以语篇分析理论为基本框架的教材——语篇翻译教材的编写。

"语篇翻译"这一术语是针对翻译实践提出的。总的含义是：以语篇为准进行翻译操作（translation operation）。具体内涵是：1）将译者的视野从字句扩展到句群、篇章等大于句的单位。凸显不同语言级层上翻译操作的特点。强调篇章——翻译任务所处理的语篇整体——是翻译操作的最终决策级层。2）语篇类型（text type）、交际功能与翻译策略、方法密切相关。3）语篇在一定的语境中发挥交际功能。翻译操作必须考虑翻译活动发生时译者所处的社会、文化环境，即翻译语境

(translation context)。

语篇翻译教材的理论支撑

语篇翻译教材的理论框架是语篇翻译研究,但绝不是把语篇翻译研究的成果一股脑地搬进教材中。教材编写者和教师必须结合翻译操作的焦点和翻译学习者常遇到的问题寻找和确定教材的理论支撑点:

1. 翻译不只是产品,更是一个过程。

早在1969年Nida(1969:33)就否定了在表层结构层次上借助所谓"中间语言"(go-between language)将源语直接转换为译语的一步式翻译模式(single-stage procedure),并根据Chomsky的转换生成语法提出了由分析(analysis)、转换(transfer)和重构(restructuring)三阶段组成的逆转换翻译模式(Munday 2001:39)。而20世纪七八十年代出现在德国的功能学派从翻译的目的出发,提出了翻译作为一种跨文化交际过程的循环模式(looping model)(Nord 1991:34-35):译者以翻译目的为出发点,对源语文化情景中的源语语篇进行分析,确定源语语篇与翻译活动有关的因素(translation-related elements),并按翻译目的的需要将源语信息进行传译(transfer),然后合成为译语语篇(TT synthesis),译语语篇在译语文化语境中实现翻译目的,于是便完成了跨文化交际的循环。另外,在源语文化和源语语篇间、译语文化和译语语篇间、在分析过程的步骤间、在源语语篇分析和译语语篇合成这两个步骤间,都可能出现局部的循环。Nord(1991:34-35)的这一循环模式将翻译活动置于特定的社会文化语境中,凸显了交际目的对译者决策的作用。

以上两个模式都提出了"转换"这一阶段,却未能对其进行详细阐述,未能赋予它实质性内容。倒是Bell(1991:45)的提法更为实在:他把翻译过程分为分析和合成两个阶段,在每个阶段中均存在三个不同的操作领域(areas of operation)——句法、语义和语用。译者在这三个领域中的分析原文和合成译文过程也就是进行语际信息传译的实质性过程。而这一过程的核心即Hatim所谓"能动的选择"(motivated choice):"语篇的生产者有他们自己的交际目的,并选择适当的词项和语法结构以达到这些目的。(Hatim 1990:4)"Neubert(1992:43)的话更加一语中的:"翻译过程是由语篇引发的语篇生成过程。""翻译过程是某一翻译情境下对翻译能力的激活。"那么,翻译教学中如何才能激活学生的翻译能力呢?学生的翻译能力又应包括哪些内容?这是必须结合翻译操作的具体情况和学生学习翻译的实际才能解答的问题。

教学实践表明，激活学生的翻译能力的关键在于强化（sensitize）其语篇意识。这包括三个层次上的基本知识的灌输：1）语篇是真正的交际单位，词语只是它的组成部分；2）语篇和语境密切相关；3）对语篇的功能、类型和结构的分析。

2. 语篇类型、功能与翻译方法密切相关。

20 世纪的七八十年代，德国学者 Reiss（1989；2000）移植德国心理学家 Karl Buhler 有关语言功能的观点，将语篇类型、功能和翻译方法联系了起来。Reiss 的模式表明了语言编码和交际功能之间的联系，凸显了译者操作的能动性，从而为翻译教学中的译文评价提供了一个可行的参照框架。

但 Reiss 的模式也遭到了一些批评，归纳起来主要有两个方面。一是如何确定语篇的功能和划分语篇的类型。Reiss 起初提出了四种功能和类型，即信息功能/语篇、表情功能/语篇、祈使功能/语篇和视听功能/语篇（informative text, expressive text, operative text, audiomedial text）。其中最后一种显然会与前三种有重叠和交叉。在讨论功能和翻译方法的关系时，Reiss 只谈及前三种。Nord（1997：44）在论及"以翻译为导向的语篇功能模式"时又加上了"应酬功能"（phatic function）。Newmark 谈到功能时又加上了"审美功能"和"元语言功能"，使功能总数达六种之多，但他重点讨论的仍是 Reiss 讨论的三种。

必须注意到，语篇功能的分类还有另一种与写作教程中的分类法类似的方法。如 Hatim（1990：153-158）就按议论语篇、说明语篇（包括描写和叙事——description, narration）和指令语篇（argumentative text type, expository text type, instructional text type），对翻译中的"语境焦点"（contextual focus）、"信息价值"（value）等问题进行了讨论。Bell（1991：204-205）也按"可赋予［语篇］的特定修辞目的（换言之，此语篇具有某一特定交际焦点——communicative focus）"区分出说明、议论和指令三种语篇类型，说明语篇包括描写、叙述、概念（descriptive, narrative, conceptual）三个次类，议论语篇包括明显和隐含（overt, covert）两个次类，指令语篇则包括可选择和不可选择（+option, -option）两个次类。Bell（1991：206）还特别强调了识别语篇类型的重要性："缺乏识别语篇作为某一特定形式的样本的能力（而这种形式本身就是某一特定语篇类型的象征），我们将无法决定如何去处理它；我们既无法理解也无法写作，说明白些，就是无法进行翻译。"

Reiss 遭到批评的第二个方面是：功能和翻译方法间是否存在 Reiss 所说的那样明确的对应关系。她声称的翻译方法在某一具体的翻译任务中可能会被打破。她的主要批评者 Koller 就例举过一个译者在译一篇"以内容为中心的"（content-centered）语篇时决定要以直译的方法传达瑞典官样文章韵味的实例，而按 Reiss 的模式"以内容为中心的"信息功能语篇应以传达事实为主，译文应是"平直文体"（plain prose）（Fawcett 1977: 107）。

我们认为，功能和译法间的规律性联系是确实存在的。但功能不是制定翻译策略和方法的唯一依据。译者有自己的翻译目的，发起人对译文也会提出特定要求，译文的功能也未必与原文相同。总之，翻译语境中的种种因素都会制约翻译策略的制定和翻译方法的选择。不过，归根结底，语篇类型绝不失为一个重要参数。

3. 语篇是一个级层体系，不同级层上有不同的翻译操作焦点。

早在 1965 年 Catford（1965: 6）就将系统语法中的级层（rank）概念引入了翻译理论，并讨论了发生在级层间的翻译转换——单位转换（unit-shift）问题。Newmark（1991: 66）论及系统语法在翻译研究中的应用时说："从译者的角度来看，我认为主要的描写单位（Halliday 体系的延伸）可构成这样一个级层体系：篇章、段落、句、小句、词组、词、词素。抽象地说，（如 Halliday 所言）哪个级层都不比另外的级层更重要，而在实践中，篇章是最后的仲裁，句是翻译操作的基本单位，而大部分的难题都集中在词汇单位，如果不是在词上的话。"当 Baker 和 Bell 将系统功能语法运用于翻译研究时，则更为系统地将级层的概念植入了他们的理论框架之中。Baker（1992）的 *In Other Words* 以对"对等"的讨论为主线，先后探讨了词汇、词组、小句及语篇各级层上翻译对等问题。Bell（1991）的 *Translation and Translating: Theory and Practice* 也同样结合各级层上翻译操作的特点进行了详尽的阐述。他们讨论的焦点问题总起来可概括如下：词汇级层主要讨论语义问题，如语义场、所指意义、内涵意义、命题、文化词汇的翻译、语际间的词汇非对等等问题；词组级层讨论搭配、成语翻译等问题；小句级层讨论及物性、语气和主位结构等；语篇级层则讨论衔接、连贯、语域、言语行为、合作原则等问题。这一理论框架涵盖了语义、句法和语用三大范畴，是教授翻译的一个既全面又便于操作的理论参照体系。

4. 语境

自从 Malinowski 从人类学视角提出语言的情景语境（context of situation）以

来，语境一直是语言学家所关注的课题。概括起来说，对语境的认识有两大派别。

一是系统功能语法的语境观：语境具体体现为以语篇范围、语篇体式和语篇方式（field, tenor, mode）为要素的语域分析。语境和语篇呈相互依赖关系。Hatim（1990；1997：22）将这一模式加以扩展，用于翻译研究，提出语境包括交际层面、语用层面和符号层面（communicative dimension, pragmatic dimension, semiotic dimension）。这三个层面决定着语篇的类型、布局和结构（text type, structure and texture）。如果说"系统功能语言学重视的是广义的文化语境和具体的情景语境"（朱永生，严世清2002：191）的话，那么语用学则是从认知的角度研究语境的，所以称为认知语境。语用学中，"语境是一种心理构成，是听话人对外部世界的设想的一个子集。"（Sperber & Wilson 1986：15）。Verschueren（1999：76-77）则把语境分为交际语境和语言语境两部分。交际语境包括物理世界、社交世界和心理世界，但"物理世界、社交世界和心理世界诸语境层面必须在语言使用者的认知过程中被激活的时候才能发挥作用"。因此，信息的发出者和接收者在交际语境中是起着至关重要的作用的。语言语境主要指衔接、互文性和线性序列（cohesion, intertextuality, sequencing）这些语篇自身的特质。

语篇翻译教学中，可取功能语言学模式，深化学生对文化语境和情景语境在语篇理解和构建过程中的作用。文化语境方面可强调翻译过程中对文化词语和文化形象的处理，以及不同文化对语篇结构和表达方式可能造成的影响。情景语境方面可强调情景对语篇意义的定义作用，还可引入语用学中Fillmore（1977）的情景和框架语义学（scenes-and-frames semantics）的核心概念情景（scene）和语言框架（linguistic frame）的概念。Fillmore给情景下的定义十分宽泛，除了通常意义上的可视情景外还包括其他任何储存在大脑里的生活经验；而框架则指"任何语言选择系统"，如词汇搭配和语法结构等。告诉学生在理解原文时调动大脑中储存的情景，并选择译语中最适宜的语言框架加以重现，是一种很有效的教学思路。

语篇翻译教材的设计

按上述理论支撑点设计的教材应呈多样化，这本教程只是一种已经和正在施行的方案而已。它的基本模式为：翻译过程（理解和表达）与语篇类型两大主线交错，原文语篇与译文语篇对照，每篇凸显一两个翻译问题。以双语语篇对照的形式编写的课本已不乏于坊间，如庄绎传编著的高自考教材《英汉翻译教程》和南开大学外语学院编写的英汉互译教材《英语翻译教程》。现在，值得进一步探索的问题是，如何使语篇对照的形式与语篇理论融合起来，使双语阅读得以在一个隐形的理论框架内进行（不是双语阅读 + 理论简介），对翻译实践产生切近要害的启示。本书尝试的做法是：1）结合翻译实际，明确理论支撑点，并以此为准确定要讨论的翻译操作焦点问题；2）所选语篇必须能凸显一、两个翻译操作焦点问题，并以这些问题为题展开阐述；3）所选练习须能配合上述焦点问题，让学生由理性至感性，进而对焦点问题产生更深的领悟。

语篇翻译教材的教学方法

教材的指导理论和设计本身其实已经包含了对教材实施方法的思考，已经设定了某些教学手段。与语篇翻译教材相适应的教学方法主要有三种：双语阅读法（bilingual reading）、讲评法（translation evaluation）和校改法（revision）。

语篇翻译教材的体例要求老师能指导学生从平行文本（parallel texts）的对照阅读中体会和领悟翻译操作的原则和要领。除课本上的材料外，还应为学生提供更多的平行语料，并指导他们自己收集有关语料，提示可能的语料来源、选择标准、阅读方法等，让他们独立阅读。此时，学生扮演着"学徒"的角色，跟着一个个的"师傅"体味翻译的难处和处理方法。培养学生的双语对照阅读的能力，指导他们根据个人情况确立起最有效的取人之长、为我所用的学习策略，将使他们终身受益。

自己动手是学习翻译的最重要的环节。翻译作业的选材当然要与课本密切配合，难易适当。此时，学生扮演着"工匠"的角色，亲手"打造"自己的产品——译文。而如何对学生的翻译练习进行讲评也就成了教学活动的重头戏。教师批改作业可用缩略词指明问题的类型，如理解失误（misun.）、选词不当（wdic）、连贯失调（cohr）、衔接不当（cohe）等，并要求学生进行修改，再次交来（实践证明：一次作业交两回，让学生经历翻译和修改两个过程，是十分有益的）。课上讲评最好将参考译文印发，紧密结合学生译文中出现的典型问题和本篇翻译焦点加以点评。并请学生对照参考译文发表自己的评论。

校改法指让学生修改他人的译文。译文质量应达到中等以上水平，具体说，基本理解失误很少，译文基本通顺达意。译文可从出版物或学生作业中选取。应能突出某个或某几个翻译问题。可让学生独立校改，也可取小组讨论、代表发言的形式。此时，学生的角色是"编辑"。他已不能按自己的思路进行翻译，不能将自己的译文一句一改地加于他人的译文之上，而必须尊重他人的译文，并认识到正确的译文绝不止一个，去体味别人的思路和译法，进而加深对翻译的本质的认识。

语篇翻译教材的测试

翻译测试有主观题和客观题。前者是传统测试方法，后者是近年来按标准化测试方法设计的诸如译文的正误判断和多项选择等类试题（徐莉娜 2001：445；宋志平 2001：435-436）。我们的语篇翻译教学仍使用较传统的测试方法，因为这种方法较为成熟，效度较高。虽然从理论上说信度差一些，但数十人的小规模考试阅卷人是同一个老师，信度并不成问题。常用的是两种题型：段落翻译和译文校改。

段落翻译考题的设计有两个重要原则：一是按叙事、描写、说明、议论和应用文体等分类选择不同文体的段落；二是为要求翻译的段落提供较充分的语境，这包括提供上下文和加注说明翻译的目的和译文预期读者群等情况。译文校改试题提供原文和译文对照片段，请考生进行校改。这类考题的设计除了考虑上述两条原则外，还要对校改的项目进行预控。校改项目可分为两类，一类是必须加以修改的理解失误——必改项，另一类是表达不确切、不通顺、不达意或文体方面的问题，对这类项目，不同的考生会做出不同的反应，因为不同学生在行文习惯、修辞偏好等方面自有其特质（idiosyncrasy）。因此，考生实际修改的项目会低于设计的修改项目数。校改题实际已经具有客观题的某些因素，但由于对非必改项目仍须由教师主观判定，所以还是有很大主观性的。

注：笔者还有"语篇翻译论"或"语篇翻译研究"的提法。指移植语篇分析、语义学、文体学等相关学科的理论以语篇视角对翻译活动进行描写、分析、归纳、抽象的翻译研究途径。其中对翻译操作的理解与本文所述相同。

引用文献

罗进德. 1997. 翻译教学门外谈. 外语研究（1）：62-65.
宋志平. 2001. 关于翻译测试的理论思考. 论翻译教学. 刘宗和主编. 北京：商务印书馆.
徐莉娜. 2001. 翻译测试探讨. 论翻译教学. 刘宗和主编. 北京：商务印书馆.
朱永生，严世清. 2002. 系统功能语言学多维思考. 上海：上海外语教育出版社.
Baker, M. 1992. *In Other Words*. London: Routledge.
Bell, R. T. 1991. *Translation and Translating: Theory and Practice*. London: Longman.
Catford, J. C. 1965. *A Linguistic Theory of Translation*. Oxford: Oxford University Press.
Fillmore, C. J. 1997. Scenes-and-frames Semantics. In A. Zampolli (ed.) *Linguistic Structures Processing*. Amsterdam: N. Holland.

Hatim, B. & Mason, I. 1990. *Discourse and the Translator*. London: Longman.

Munday, J. 2001. *Introducing Translation Studies*. London: Routledge.

Neubert, A. & Shreve, G. M. 1992. *Translation as Text*. Cleveland, Ohio: Kent State University Press.

Newmark, P. 1991. *About Translation*. Clevedon: Multilingual Matters Ltd.

Nida, E. A. & Taber, C. R. 1969. *The Theory and Practice of Translation*. Leiden: E. J. Brill.

Nord, C. 1991. *Text Analysis in Translation*. Amsterdam: Rodopi.

Reiss, K. 1989. Text types, translation types and translation assessment. In A. Chesterman(ed.), *Readings in Translation Theory*. Helsinki: Finn Lectura. pp. 105-115.

Reiss, K. 2000. *Translation Criticism: Potential and Limitations*. Translated by E. Rhodes. Manchester: St. Jerome and American Bible Society.

Sperber, D. & Wilson, D. 1986. *Relevance: Communication and Cognition*. Oxford: Blackell.

Toury, G. 1995. *Descriptive Translation Studies and Beyond*. Amsterdam: John Benjamins.

Verschueren, J. 1999. *Understanding Pragmatics*. London: Edward Arnold (Publishers) Ltd.

第一版前言

译者的具体操作似乎是在字、词和句子上进行的,但字、词、句的翻译不是孤立的,它们要受到其所在语篇的种种制约。译者的思维也绝不能只局限在字句上面。就句论句讲翻译,常常说不清,讲不透。因此,学习翻译必须把注意力从较低的语言层次扩展到段落和篇章这样一些较高的层次。语篇研究的某些成果也可以为翻译学习和研究提供有益的思考,帮助译者把对翻译活动的理解提高到一个新的水平。

本书的具体思路是:

一、强调语篇的整体性及层次性,把字、词、句的翻译纳入语篇这一大背景中,克服传统翻译学习中以词法、句法为框架、以单个句子为基准的模式。学习翻译,首先要培养语篇意识,即从大处(篇章和段落)着眼,小处(词和句)着手的翻译思路。为此,本书采取以语篇为基准的编排方式:每一单元的原文/译文都是独立或相对独立的一个篇章,这非常有利于翻译学习者从语篇的角度着眼体味翻译的种种原则、策略和技巧。在对翻译问题进行讨论时,本书力求兼顾语篇的词、词组、小句、句、段落、篇章等各个层次,而不是只讨论句子和词语的翻译。

二、强调翻译是一个动态的译者的思维和决策过程。翻译学习者应首先体会较为成熟的译者的思路和翻译原则,然后再学习他们的具体翻译方法和技巧。思路和原则较之具体翻译方法更具普遍性和指导性,因此也更是一个翻译学习者应该深刻领悟的。因此,本书一方面特别辟出原文的理解和译文的表达两个章节来集中从翻译过程的角度讨论有关问题,另一方面在探讨语篇各个层次的翻译问题时,特别注重对翻译思路的揭示和引导,力求通过有限的例子达到使读者能举一反三的目的。应指出,理解和表达作为两个章节,是为了便于编排、有所侧重,但在实际翻译过程中理解和表达并非必定是一前一后、泾渭分明的,它们是一个连续体,而且往往是表达基于理解,又可深化理解。

三、强调语篇由于文体不同在翻译策略及方法上造成的差异。在实际交际中,由于交际目的不同便形成了各种不同的文体,它们在选词、造句、谋篇等方面是有一定差异的。但本书不是研究文体的著作,不宜将文体分得很细。根据翻译学习的实际需要，我们分出叙述、描写类，说明、论说类以及应用类三大类型。而其中花大量篇幅讨论说明、论说类和叙述、描写类的各种翻译问题，应用类只是轻轻带过。因为前两大类，特别是说明、论说类，是具有普遍性的翻译问题十分集中的地方，学习者必须花大力气学习，而应用文的翻译大体只是个格式和用语的问题，只要在一般文字的翻译实践中打下坚实的基础，再加上一定的专业知识，应用文体的翻译问题是不难解决的。

四、翻译研究具有很强的交叉学科性质，同一个翻译问题往往可以从不同的角度（比如从语言学、信息论、美学、文化对比等角度）加以考察和探索；翻译实践中的一些操作技巧问题，也同样可以从不同侧面加以思考。比如，从句的翻译技巧可以从逻辑上考虑，也可以从句法结构上着眼，还可以从信息的线性排列上加以分析。因此，培养对同一翻译问题的多视角思考能力有助于翻译实践水平的提高。本书以语篇分析为框架尽量提供不同的视角，各章讲解内容力争散中有序。其目的不在为读者提供语篇理论体系，而是为翻译实践提供尽可能充实的思考材料。

基于以上思路，便形成了本书以语篇为框架，注重语篇交际功能，贴近译者实际思维、决策和操作过程的翻译学习模式。全书由序论及其他五个章节组成，每章又有若干单元，每个单元由原文篇章、译文篇章及注释、讲解几部分组成。原文和译文均经过5至10年的教学实践的应用，证明对翻译学习者有较强的启发及指导作用。每单元的注释针对译文的处理方法进行导向性点评。讲解部分则针对本单元译文中表现较为突出的翻译方法及策略进行较为详尽的阐发，以期学习者能从具体语篇的翻译中领悟翻译的决策过程。

本书的编写是在语篇研究理论的指导下进行的，但是我们同时也认识到，翻译实践不是理论研究，翻译学习者所需要的不是理论术语，而是理论指导下的实践，因此不宜用过多的理论和术语去干扰翻译学习过程。

翻译学习者使用本书应大体按下列方法进行：

一、通读原文语篇2~3次，查出生字，力求最大限度地理解原文。

二、将译文和原文对照阅读1~2遍，参考文后注释再研读1~2遍，以加深对原文的理解，琢磨译者的思路及译法，并结合自己的情况汲取有益的东西。

三、如果时间充裕，最好自己先把原文翻译一遍，再对照书中参考译文及注释研读。这样，收效会更大些。因为当个人的体验融入学习过程时，就会和他人的实践和经验发生碰撞和融合，大大促进学习的进程。

四、阅读讲解部分，领会翻译策略、思路及具体方法。对例句、例段仔细琢磨，力求能举一反三，指导自己的实践。注意：为节省篇幅，不少译例是以单个句子的形式出现的，但不要忘记它们都是选自一定的上下文的，切莫因句论句，关键是领悟其思路及方法。

五、书后附有少量翻译练习，并针对其翻译方法提出了一些问题，旨在促进思考，调动译者的主观能动性。学习者可先将原文翻译一遍，然后对照参考译文推敲、思考。

六、应特别强调培养学习者独立思考、亲自动手的能力。一方面要勤于翻译实践，笔耕不辍，因为没有3~5万字汉语译文的翻译体验，是谈不到对英汉翻译有任何真正的初步体会的；另一方面，还要有一种审视的眼光，不可人云亦云，对任何译文都应拿出自己的看法，既要虚怀若谷，对一切好的有用的东西兼收并蓄，又不能盲目崇拜，认为一切出版的东西就都是好的。

这本小书实属千虑一得，虽经长期使用，不足之处仍会不少。诚恳希望学习翻译、研究翻译教学的朋友们予以批评、指教。

作者 1997 年岁末
于东菊轩

目 录

第一章
绪论：怎样学习翻译

Unit One	Great Possessions	2
	讲解　译者的语篇意识	6
Unit Two	Why You Should Re-read *Paradise Lost* (Excerpts)	11
	讲解　译者的互文意识	15

小结 17

第二章
原文的理解

Unit One	Rules Every Achiever Knows	20
	讲解　词义和语境	23
Unit Two	How to Grow Old (Excerpts)	28
	讲解　一、对语篇结构的分析	31
	二、语篇的意向	33
Unit Three	The Good Teacher	36
	讲解　对原文句子结构的分析	40
Unit Four	The Whipping Boy	49
	讲解　理解中的文化因素	54
Unit Five	Republicans and Democrats (Excerpts)	59
	讲解　译者的知识和经验在理解中的作用	62

xxi

Unit Six	Caught in the Web of the Internet (Abridged)	65
	讲解　指代关系的理解	69

小结 74
练习 75

第三章
译文的表达

Unit One	How Dorothy Saved the Scarecrow (Excerpts)	80
	A Watering Place	82
	讲解　翻译中的文体问题	84
Unit Two	How Should One Read a Book?	88
	讲解　译者的具体操作	92
Unit Three	Bring on the Elites!	95
	讲解　一、语篇的语境	99
	二、翻译的标准	103
Unit Four	You Are What You Think	105
	讲解　一、主语 - 话题转换	108
	二、语法意义的翻译	110
Unit Five	Some Truths About Leadership	114
	讲解　一、四字词语的运用及"词组堆叠句"	118
	二、比较结构的翻译	123
Unit Six	For Some Victims of Crimes, the Fear Never Leaves	126
	讲解　一、表达角度及方式的转换	130
	二、译文的增益	133
Unit Seven	Think About It	136
	讲解　克服翻译体	141
Unit Eight	What's Right About Being Left-handed	146

	讲解 原文的不可译性	152
Unit Nine	For Better or Worse but Not for Lunch!	155
	讲解 互文性	158
Unit Ten	A Few Earthy Words (Excerpts)	163
	讲解 翻译伦理	167

小结 170
练习 171

第四章
叙事、描写文体的翻译

Unit One	Lambing Time	186
	讲解 英译汉中的意合趋势（总论）	190
Unit Two	Vanity Fair (Excerpt 1)	196
	讲解 一、英译汉中的意合趋势——时间序列问题	200
	二、英译汉中的意合趋势——叙事和描写的分立	203
Unit Three	The Page Turner (Excerpts)	206
	讲解 动词的翻译	210
Unit Four	Spring	215
	讲解 形象化语言及形象思维	219
Unit Five	Vanity Fair (Excerpt 2)	224
	讲解 形容词的翻译	228
Unit Six	Impulse (Excerpts)	232
	讲解 归化和异化	239

小结 243
练习 244

第五章
说明、论说文体的翻译

Unit One	The Energy Lesson	252
	讲解　译文逻辑连接的调整（一）	255
Unit Two	Politics and the English Language	259
	讲解　译文逻辑连接的调整（二）	263
Unit Three	Congress at Work	266
	讲解　一、外位成分的运用	272
	二、复合句的翻译	274
Unit Four	How Paper Shaped Civilization	277
	讲解　定语从句的拆译	281
Unit Five	Beauty (Excerpts)	288
	讲解　信息焦点的调整	293
Unit Six	About Electricity	297
	讲解　一、被动语态的翻译	300
	二、指代衔接与行文流畅	303
Unit Seven	The Jeaning of America	305
	讲解　译文的连贯	310
Unit Eight	Leafing Through Maple Lore	316
	讲解　解释性翻译	320
Unit Nine	The Origins of Modern Science (Excerpts)	322
	讲解　语篇形态	327

小结 334
练习 334

参考文献 343

第一章 绪论：怎样学习翻译

翻译是译者依据对原文信息及交际意图的理解，遵照特定翻译任务的要求，将原文用译语重新表达出来的过程。学习翻译就是要在老师的指导下去领会语际信息转换过程中的原则、规律和方法，以期掌握独立承担翻译任务的基本技能。学习的要领是导向正确、善于领悟、勤于实践。

选择适当的理论模式或观点，建立翻译教学的指导原则和路径，有利于教学的系统化，也有利于集中精力解决关键问题。要善于观察和思考两种语言在句法和行文等方面的异同，带着问题阅读双语对照语篇，善于发现和借鉴他人的经验和技巧，为我所用。翻译水平的提高全靠脑勤、手勤，即勤于阅读和勤于练笔。勤于阅读源语可增强理解原文的能力，勤于阅读译语可增强译文写作能力。译者的成功之路是错误和失败铺就的，尝试和摸索是必经之路，改正和改进是自我提高的关键词。

本章的两个单元将通过对两组英汉对照语篇的研读，谈一谈翻译学习中首先要树立的两个基本意识：语篇意识和互文意识。

Great Possessions

Aldo Leopold

[1]   One hundred and twenty acres, according to the County Clerk, is the extent of my worldly domain. But[1] the County Clerk is a sleepy fellow, who never looks at his record books before nine o'clock. What they would show at daybreak is the question here at issue.

[2]   Books or no books, it is a fact, patent both to my dog and myself, that at daybreak I am the sole owner of all the acres I can walk over.[2] It is not only boundaries that disappear, but also the thought of being bounded. Expanses unknown to deed or map are known to every dawn, and solitude, supposed no longer to exist in my county, extends on every hand as far as the dew can reach.[3]

[3]   Like other great landowners, I have tenants. They are negligent about rents, but very punctilious about tenures. Indeed at every daybreak from April to July they proclaim their boundaries to each other, and so acknowledge, at least by inference, their fiefdom to me.

[4]   This daily ceremony, contrary to what you might suppose, begins with the utmost decorum. Who originally laid down its protocols I do not know. At 3:30 a.m., with such dignity as I can muster of a July morning, I step from my cabin door, bearing in either hand my emblems of sovereignty, a coffee pot and a notebook. I seat myself on a bench, facing the white wake of the morning star. I set the pot beside me. I extract a cup from my shirt front, hoping none will notice its informal mode of transport. I get out my watch, pour coffee, and lay notebook on knee. This is the cue for the proclamations to begin.

[5]   At 3:35 the nearest field sparrow avows, in a clear tenor chant, that he holds the jackpine copse north to the riverbank, and south to the old wagon track. One by one all the other field sparrows within earshot recite their respective holdings. There are no disputes, at least at this hour, so I just listen, hoping inwardly that their womenfolk acquiesce in this happy accord over the status quo ante.[4]

[6]　Before the field sparrows have quite gone the rounds, the robin in the big elm warbles loudly his claim to the crotch where the ice storm tore off a limb, and all appurtenances pertaining thereto (meaning, in his case, all the angleworms in the not-very-spacious subjacent lawn).[5]

[7]　The robin's insistent caroling awakens the oriole, who now tells the world of orioles that the pendant branch of the elm belongs to him, together with all fiber-bearing milkweed stalks near by, all loose strings in the garden, and the exclusive right to flash like a burst of fire from one of these to another.

[8]　My watch says 3:50. The indigo bunting on the hill asserts title to the dead oak limb left by the 1936 drouth, and to divers[6] near-by bugs and bushes. He does not claim, but I think he implies, the right to out-blue all bluebirds, and all spiderworts that have turned their faces to the dawn.

[9]　Next the wren—the one who discovered the knothole in the eave of the cabin—explodes into song. Half a dozen other wrens give voice, and now all is bedlam. Grosbeaks, thrashers, yellow warblers, bluebirds, vireos, towhees, cardinals—all are at it. My solemn list of performers, in their order and time of first song, hesitates, wavers, ceases, for my ear can no longer filter out priorities. Besides, the pot is empty and the sun is about to rise. I must inspect my domain before my title runs out.[7]

[10]　We sally forth, the dog and I, at random. He has paid scant respect to all these vocal goings-on, for to him the evidence of tenantry is not song, but scent. Any illiterate bundle of feathers, he says, can make a noise in a tree. Now he is going to translate for me the olfactory poems that who-knows-what silent creatures have written in the summer night.[8] At the end of each poem sits the author—if we can find him. What we actually find is beyond predicting: a rabbit, suddenly yearning to be elsewhere; a woodcock, fluttering his disclaimer; a cock pheasant, indignant over wetting his feathers in the grass.

[11]　Once in a while we turn up a coon or mink, returning late from the night's foray. Sometimes we rout a heron from his unfinished fishing, or surprise a mother wood duck with her convoy of ducklings, headed full-steam for the shelter of the pickerelweeds. Sometimes we see deer sauntering back to the thickets, replete with alfalfa blooms, veronica, and wild lettuce.

More often we see only the interweaving darkened lines that lazy hoofs have traced on the silken fabric of the dew.

[12] I can feel the sun now. The bird-chorus has run out of breath. The far clank of cowbells bespeaks a herd ambling to pasture. A tractor roars warning that my neighbor is astir. The world has shrunk to those mean dimensions[9] known to county clerks. We turn toward home, and breakfast.

参考译文

广袤的领地

奥尔多·利奥波德

[1] 一百二十英亩，据沙县政府书记员的记载，就是我在这地球上的领地了。但书记员是个爱睡懒觉的家伙，上午九点之前从不会查看登记簿，所以他那些登记簿在拂晓时分能说明多少问题，倒是可以在此讨论讨论的。

[2] 登记簿看也罢，不看也罢，反正对我和我的狗来说，事实就是：拂晓时分，只要我能走到的地方，有多少英亩算多少英亩，就都是我一个人的领地。此时，不仅地界消失了，思维也没了羁绊。这片片相连的广袤大地，地契或地图并不知道，却为每个黎明所知晓。沙县人认为县内已不复存在的荒野幽居之地，此时正向四面八方延伸着，露水能洒多远这片荒野就有多大。

[3] 像其他大片土地的拥有者一样，我也有众多佃户。他们对租金不闻不问，却对租期斤斤计较。实际上从四月到七月，每个黎明他们都要宣告彼此的地界，而且，至少据我推测，也承认向我租借了土地。

[4] 这种例行的宣告仪式与你设想的不同，必以最隆重的礼仪开场。至于这些程序最初是谁制定的，我并不知道。凌晨三点半，我带着在七月的这个清晨所能拢聚的尊严，踏出我的小屋，手拿领地所有权标志——一把咖啡壶和一本笔记本。我在长凳上坐下，面对着启明星的白色轨迹。我把咖啡壶放在身边，从衬衣前襟里掏出一只杯子——希望没人会理会这种携带杯子的方式。我取出怀表，倒上咖啡，把笔记本放在膝上。这意味着宣告领地所有权的仪式就此开始。

[5] 三点三十五分，最近处的一只原野春雀展开喉咙，用清亮的男高音宣布他拥有北至河岸南至旧车道的那片短叶松林。接着在我听力所及范围内，其他春雀也

一个接一个用歌喉宣布了他们各自的领地。大家并无争执,至少此刻如此,因此我只需倾听,真心希望他们的女眷们能够默许对这种一贯的和谐状态的皆大欢喜的协议。

[6] 原野春雀的轮唱还没有停歇,大榆树上的知更鸟就婉转高歌,声称被冰暴折断树枝的那个树杈属于他,另加相关附属物(依他的情况,即指树下那片不大的草地上的所有蚯蚓)。

[7] 知更鸟持续的欢歌惊醒了那只黄鹂,他在告知黄鹂世界的伙伴们,那棵大榆树悬垂的树枝属于他,还有附近所有富含纤维的马利筋茎,以及花园里所有松垂的须茎。他还拥有专享特权,可以像出膛子弹一样在其间飞来飞去。

[8] 我的表显示三点五十分。小山上的靛蓝鹀宣称拥有 1936 年大旱留下来的那棵枯橡树的枝干,还有周围各类虫子和灌木。他并没有明言,但我想他在暗示,他有权让他的蓝色盖过所有蓝鸟和所有冲着曙光绽放的鸭拓草的蓝色花朵。

[9] 接下来轮到那只鹪鹩引吭高歌了,就是发现小木屋屋檐上节孔的那一只。六七只其他的鹪鹩也一起发声,一片嘈杂,混乱不堪。蜡嘴雀、打谷鸟、黄雀、蓝鸟、绿鹃、唧鹀、北美红雀都一展歌喉。我本想按照他们首曲的顺序和时间郑重列表,现在却踌躇不决,无法继续了,因为我的耳朵已无法分辨孰先孰后。再说,咖啡壶喝干了,太阳也即将升起。我必须在失去所有权之前巡视完我的领地。

[10] 我们立刻出发,我和我的狗,随意而行。狗儿对此起彼伏的歌声并不在意,对他而言,租用权限的证据不是歌声,而是气味。他觉得,任何大字不识的一团羽毛都能在树上弄出些噪音来。而他现在要做的,是把那些只能凭嗅觉才能阅读的诗行翻译给我,天知道那是些什么动物在夏夜里悄悄撰写的。不过在每首诗的结尾都可能看到那位作者——如果我们能找到他的话。而我们寻觅的结果往往出乎意料:一只兔子,突然要跑向别处;一只丘鹬,扇动着翅膀准备放弃此处的地盘;或是一只雄雉鸡,正为草地弄湿了自己的翅膀而懊恼不已。

[11] 偶尔,我们会惊起一只夜出觅食而迟归的浣熊或貂。有时候还会惊起一只正在捕鱼的苍鹭,或者惊动正带领一群幼鸟全速奔向梭鱼草丛躲藏的北美鸳鸯雌鸟。有时候,我们看到鹿群踱步回到灌木丛里,那里满目都是紫花苜蓿、婆婆纳,以及野莴苣。而更常见的,往往是一行行纵横交织的暗色蹄印,那是慵懒的动物在洒满露水的丝一般光滑的草地上留下的足迹。

[12] 我现在感受到阳光了。鸟儿的合唱已经停歇。远处牛铃响起,说明牛群正缓缓走向牧场。一部拖拉机轰鸣着,提醒我邻居已经起床劳作。世界已然回缩到县书记员们所了解的那种世俗维度。我们转身回家,去吃早饭。

注释

1. 注意连词 but 所连接的本段第一句和第二、三两句间的逻辑关系。第一句说的是登记簿记载的我的领地,但是,作者幽默地说,这个记载在凌晨是不算数的,凌晨我的领地可大了,有多大,听我给你说说。
2. 此句译文打破原句结构的束缚,将作者原意自然地再现出来。试比较:我就是我能漫步于其上的这片土地的唯一主人。
3. 句中 solitude 意为 a lonely or secluded place。Expanses unknown to deed or map are known to every dawn 的译文尽量保留了原文的修辞特点。其意为地契或地图上是看不出这片地域有多么寥廓的,只有黎明时分大自然才会展示出其本来的面貌。
4. 此段描述鸟儿们如何主张自己的领地权,作者用了拟人手法(he, womenfolk),汉译时不宜用"它"和"雌性伴侣",应保留原文的拟人修辞特点。
5. all appurtenances pertaining thereto 颇具法律语言的味道,译文也尽量用正式词语,以显幽默笔调。
6. divers 意为 several, various。
7. 句中的 title 指作者在凌晨时分的领地所有权,他觉得此刻他是不受土地登记簿的约束的,信步所及,一片和谐的生态乐园,非他莫属。
8. 此句如译成"现在他要把天知道是什么悄无声息的动物在夏夜涂写的气味诗行翻译给我"则嫌不够通达,现拆散来译,可凸显和上句的连贯性("气味"与"嗅觉"对应),意思也更明了。
9. mean dimensions 指人们对大地所有权的恣意分割,言外之意,浑然一体的生态世界才是自然界的本来面貌。

译者的语篇意识

  本文选自美国生态学家和环保人士奥尔多·利奥波德(Aldo Leopold)的名著 *A Sand County Almanac*(《沙乡年鉴》)。作者在这部散文集中描述了家乡威斯康星州 Sauk 县的自然态貌,倡导"土地伦理"观念,即人类必须承担起保护土地的责任。此书在其去世一年后由其子整理出版,被视为美国环保运动的开山之作,被译为多国文字,对全球环保事业做出了重大贡献。近年来我国坊间所见译本已足有一二十种。

　　下面我们循着注释所提出的思路，对原文和译文再进一步研读思考，看能得出哪些启示。

　　首先，按照注释1、3、7和9的提示思考，我们可看到文章的第[1]、[2]两个自然段以及注释7和9涉及的下文的两个句子存在紧密的语义关联，作者的行文意图一贯到底。

　　不妨结合近年出版的两个汉译本中的有关语段，将英语原文、本书译文以及两个汉译本中的译文（分别标为[a]和[b]）进行简要的对比分析。

1. One hundred and twenty acres, according to the County Clerk, is the extent of my worldly domain. But the County Clerk is a sleepy fellow, who never looks at his record books before nine o'clock. What they would show at daybreak is the question here at issue.

　　一百二十英亩，据沙县政府书记员的记载，就是我在这地球上的领地了。但书记员是个爱睡懒觉的家伙，上午九点之前从不会查看登记簿，所以他那些登记簿在拂晓时分能说明多少问题，倒是可以在此讨论讨论的。

   [a] 一百二十英亩，据沙县书记员所言，是我拥有的世俗疆域。但沙县书记员总是昏昏欲睡，上午九点之前从不浏览他的记录簿。而拂晓时分领地上展现的一切才是问题所在。

   [b] 根据沙乡书记官的说法，我拥有120英亩的领域。不过这个书记官是一个贪睡的家伙，在9点之前，他从来不查看记录簿。这些记录簿在凌晨所展示的内容，才是我们在这里将要讨论的问题。

2. Books or no books, it is a fact, patent both to my dog and myself, that at daybreak I am the sole owner of all the acres I can walk over. It is not only boundaries that disappear, but also the thought of being bounded. Expanses unknown to deed or map are known to every dawn, and solitude, supposed no longer to exist in my county, extends on every hand as far as the dew can reach.

　　登记簿看也罢，不看也罢，反正对我和我的狗来说，事实就是：拂晓时分，只要我能走到的地方，有多少英亩算多少英亩，就都是我一个人的领地。此时，不仅地界消失了，思维也没了羁绊。这片片相连的广袤大地，地契或地图并不知道，却为每个黎明所知晓。沙县人认为县内已不复存在的荒野幽居之地，此时正向四面八方延伸着，露水能洒多远这片荒野就有多大。

[a] 记录与否无关紧要，事实上，只有我与我的狗心知肚明，黎明时分我就是我走过所有地域的唯一主人。不仅仅地界消逝无踪，思维也没了羁绊。地契或地图上未知的广阔每个黎明都知晓，而荒野幽居之地，向来被认定在沙县已不复存在，却在露水洒落之处向四面八方蔓延。

[b] 不管有没有记录簿，对于我和我的狗来说，黎明时分，我就是我所走过的那些地方的唯一事实上的拥有者。这不仅意味着边界的消失，同时也意味着思想限制的消失。不为人或者地图所知晓的扩张行为，却为每一个黎明所熟知。而荒僻，我们原以为在我们的郡县已经不复存在，其实它却在朝着每一个方向不断延伸，一直扩张到露珠所能洒向的地方。

3. I must inspect my domain before my title runs out.
我必须在失去所有权之前巡视完我的领地。

[a] 我必须在失去资格之前巡视我的领地。
[b] 我必须在行使完主人职责之前去巡查我的领地。

4. The world has shrunk to those mean dimensions known to county clerks.
世界已然回缩到县书记员们所了解的那种世俗维度。

[a] 世界变得渺小，回归到沙县书记员所知的平庸维度。
[b] 世界又缩回到沙乡书记官所熟知的模式范围了。

先来看第 [1] 自然段。作者要表达的是：(1) 按人为的地契划分我的领地不算大；(2) 但凌晨时分展现的是大自然的原始状态，官方记载能说明什么！对第一层意思，[a]、[b] 两种译文均无体现；第二层意思两种译文都表达错了。

第 [2] 段开句紧承第 [1] 段提到的书记员 "never looks at his record books before nine o'clock" 的事实，所以 "记录与否无关紧要"（[a]）或 "不管有没有记录簿"（[b]）就都不贴切了。"Expanses unknown to deed or map are known to every dawn" 说的仍是第 [1] 段的官方记载和自然状态的土地之间的差别，两种译文均未译出其意，而 expanses 更不是 "扩张行为"（[b]）。

第 [9] 段中的 title 指作者在凌晨时分对广袤大地的所有权，太阳升起后他现时的所有权就作废了，因为按照书记官的记载他只拥有那 120 英亩土地。译文 [a] 的 "资格" 语焉不详，译文 [b] 的 "行使完主人职责之前" 更是不知所云。

第 [12] 段和第 [9] 段的语义关联十分明显，所谓 mean dimensions 就是登记簿上记载的领地界限，和大自然的浑然一体相对。"平庸维度"（[a]）尚可理解，"模式范围"（[b]）就不知所云了。

总体来看，[a]、[b] 两种译文未能准确传译原文信息，其症结在于译者对原文未能通篇考虑，缺乏语篇意识。

什么是语篇？语篇意识又是指什么？

所谓语篇，即在交际功能上相对完整和独立的，通常是大于句子的一个语言片段。它既可以是一部著作，也可以是一则通知或一首小诗。

翻译学习中我们可以把语篇看成是一个级层体系。最高级层叫作篇章——我们在一次翻译任务中处理的语篇的整体。它是由一个个段落组成，而段落又是由句子组成，句子又可分为一个个小句，小句里又有一个个的词组和词。重要的是，译者必须把要翻译的篇章当作一个有机整体来对待。篇章虽然是由一个个段落、一个个句子组成的，但大于一个个段落、一个个句子的总和，因为篇章不是语句的机械叠加，而是一种动态的组合，是作者交际意图的体现。翻译策略和技巧体现在每一个层次上都有一定的侧重点。在词及词组层次上主要是解决搭配问题；在小句及句子层主要是解决信息的解析、组合以及句子的构建问题，而在段落和篇章层次则主要解决小句及句子之间的逻辑连接问题。当然，在整个翻译过程中译者时时不能忘记语篇的文体特征和作者风格等是贯穿于各个级层之上的。如下图所示：

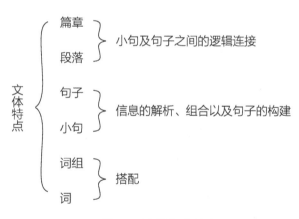

图 1.1 语篇文体特点

语篇意识就是在上述认识的基础上，进一步确立译词要译句中之词，译句要译段中之句，译段要译篇中之段，译篇要译交际中之语篇的翻译原则。这一原则的关键在于将语篇和情境融通于心，虽着手于字句却着眼于段落和全篇，永远将原文视为一个有机的词语衔接、语义连贯的信息整体。对此，上面对 [1]、[2]、[9]、[12] 自然段的分析已有初步讨论，第二章的 Unit One 中将有更多讨论。

语篇意识还强调对语篇交际目的和行文意向的认识。语篇是作者思想的文字载体，是用来和他人进行交际的。交际必有目的和行文意向。目的是作者企图达到的交际效果，意向是作者通过诸如选词、修辞、语气、文体等语言手段所要表达的思路和意图。本节原文 Great Possessions 的交际目的是展现沙乡的和谐生态原貌，唤起读者的生态环保意识。文章的选词和修辞都服务于这一目的，无不显示着作者的行文意图。如注释 4 和 8 涉及拟人和比喻修辞手段的应用，译者应尽力再现原文的修辞效果。试比较下面第 [10] 自然段中一个比喻句的译文，则更能凸显领悟作者行文意向的重要性。

5.   Now he is going to translate for me the olfactory poems that who-knows-what silent creatures have written in the summer night. At the end of each poem sits the author—if we can find him.

　　而他要做的，是把那些只能凭嗅觉才能阅读的诗行翻译给我，天知道那是些什么动物在夏夜里悄悄撰写的。不过在每首诗的结尾都可能看到那位作者——如果我们能找到他的话。

[a] 它将为我翻译不知道是哪只沉默的生物在夏夜用嗅觉写出的诗歌，诗作者就坐在每首诗的结尾处，如果我们能找得到它的话。

[b] 现在，它将用它的嗅觉为我诠释出它所了解的那些不为人知的生物所写的有关仲夏夜晚的无声的诗歌。每一首诗歌的结尾都署有作者的名字——如果我们能发现它的话。

这里作者将夜晚出没的动物比作诗人，是他们在黑暗中留下了自身气味的轨迹，写就了一首首气味诗歌。作者用了 he/him，显然汉语不宜用"它"来翻译；[a] 译文将 olfactory poems 译作"用嗅觉写出的诗歌"是对原比喻的误解，将 At the end of each poem sits the author 译作"诗作者就坐在每首诗的结尾处"，则把 sit（=to be in a particular place）译得太死板了，而 [b] 虽将其译为"署有作者的名字"，仍让读者费解。总之，这两种译文都未能再现原文比喻的修辞效果，妨碍了作者交际意向的传递。关于语篇意向问题，第二章的 Unit Two 中有更多的讨论。

　　最后，语篇的功能是交际，而译者是跨语言交际的接力者。这种语篇观要求我们要重视译德，即职业伦理问题。虽然我们现在是在课堂里讨论翻译，做的是老师布置的翻译作业，译文的读者也只是老师和同学，但视野要透过教室的窗子，投向将来我们所服务的社会。这不是假想，而是我们不久就会面对的现实。要强化这样的意识：我们的译文是按客户要求，服务于不谙源语的译语读者，是读者了解源语

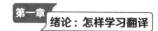

信息的唯一或重要渠道，我们的工作决定着客户和读者间交际目的的实现。我们的客户可能是某个部门或某个人，读者可能是特定的人群或泛泛的某个社会群体。作为社会的、文化的人，他们有着各自的背景和要求，我们必须在翻译活动中认真考虑这一点。译文要传递信息，要顾及交际效果，要承担审核责任，这就是我们的职业道德。我们的误解、误译、疏漏、对文化因素的处理、对转换技巧的使用，现在是个分数问题，但将来可是职业操守问题，甚至是法律问题。把作者的话歪曲了，篡改了，肯定会招致社会的批评、谴责，甚至造成严重的政治或经济后果。

总之，语篇意识包含对语篇的整体性、交际性的认识，以及作为跨文化交际参与者的译者的责任担当。

Why You Should Re-read *Paradise Lost* (Excerpts)

Benjamin Ramm

Clever Devil

[1]　When Milton began *Paradise Lost* in 1658, he was in mourning. It was a year of public and private grief, marked by the deaths of his second wife, memorialized in his beautiful *Sonnet 23*, and of England's Lord Protector, Oliver Cromwell, which precipitated the gradual disintegration of the republic.[1] *Paradise Lost* is an attempt to make sense of a fallen world: to "justify the ways of God to men", and no doubt to Milton himself.

[2]　But these biographical aspects should not downplay the centrality of theology to the poem. As the critic Christopher Ricks wrote of *Paradise Lost*, "Art for art's sake? Art for God's sake". One reason why Milton is read less now is that his religious lexicon—which sought to explain a "fallen" world—itself has fallen from use.[2] Milton the Puritan spent his life engaged in theological disputation on subjects as diverse as toleration, divorce and salvation.

[3]　The poem begins with Satan, the "Traitor Angel", cast into hell after rebelling against his creator, God. Refusing to submit to what he calls "the Tyranny of Heaven", Satan seeks revenge by tempting into sin God's precious creation: man. Milton gives a vivid account of "Man's First Disobedience" before offering a guide to salvation.

[4]　Ricks notes that *Paradise Lost* is "a fierce argument about God's justice" and that Milton's God has been deemed inflexible and cruel. By contrast, Satan has a dark charisma ("he pleased the ear") and a revolutionary demand for self-determination. His speech is peppered with the language of democratic governance ("free choice", "full consent", "the popular vote")—and he famously declares, "Better to reign in Hell, than serve in Heaven". Satan rejects God's "splendid vassalage", seeking to live:

> *Free, and to none accountable, preferring*
> *Hard liberty before the easy yoke*
> *Of servile Pomp.*[3]

[5]　Nonconformist, anti-establishment writers such as Percy Shelley found a kindred spirit in this depiction of Satan ("Milton's Devil as a moral being is… far superior to his God", he wrote). Famously, William Blake, who contested the very idea of the Fall, remarked that "The reason Milton wrote in fetters when he wrote of Angels & God, and at liberty when of Devils & Hell, is because he was a true Poet and of the Devil's party without knowing it".

[6]　Like Cromwell, Milton believed his mission was to usher in the kingdom of God on earth. While he loathed the concept of the "divine right of kings", Milton was willing to submit himself to God in the belief, in Benjamin Franklin's words, that "Rebellion to Tyrants Is Obedience to God".

[7]　Although discussion of *Paradise Lost* often is dominated by political and theological arguments, the poem also contains a tender celebration of love. In Milton's version, Eve surrenders to temptation in part to be closer to Adam, "the more to draw his love". She wishes for the freedom to err ("What is faith, love, virtue unassayed?"). When she does succumb, Adam chooses to join her: "To lose thee were to lose myself". He says:

> *How can I live without thee! How forego*
> *Thy sweet converse, and love so dearly joined,*

To live again in these wild woods forlorn?
Should God create another Eve, and I
Another rib afford, yet loss of thee
Would never from my heart.

参考译文

为什么要重读《失乐园》？

本杰明·拉姆

聪明的魔鬼

[1] 1658 年弥尔顿开始创作《失乐园》,此刻的他正深陷哀痛之中,这哀痛既有家庭的也有国家的。这一年,弥尔顿的第二任妻子去世,他写了凄美的《十四行诗之二十三》寄托哀思;同年,英国护国公奥利弗·克伦威尔逝世,加速了共和国的逐步解体。《失乐园》试图理解那个失落的世界:"证实上帝处置人类的方式的正当性",当然这也包括对他自己的处置。

[2] 但这些与作者生平相关的因素不应淡化这部长诗的神学内核。正如评论家克里斯托弗·里克斯在评论《失乐园》时所言,"为艺术而艺术吗?是为上帝而艺术"。弥尔顿的作品现在鲜有人读的原因之一是他试图用宗教语汇来解释"失落的"世界,而这些语汇已不为大家所使用。作为清教徒,弥尔顿将一生都投入到神学论辩之中,话题涉及诸如宽容、离婚、救赎等,十分广泛。

[3] 长诗以撒旦开篇,这个"叛徒天使"在反抗他的造物主上帝后被打入地狱。但他拒绝屈服于他所谓的"天堂暴政",于是便设法迷惑上帝所创造并珍爱的人类,诱其犯下原罪,对上帝进行报复。弥尔顿在指明获救之路之前,生动描述了"人的首次抗命"。

[4] 里克斯指出,《失乐园》是"一场关于上帝之公正的激辩",弥尔顿笔下的上帝被描绘得僵死而残忍。相比之下,撒旦则颇具黑暗魅力("他的话悦耳动听"),还提出了自己决定命运的革命性主张。他的话语充斥着许多民主理政的词汇("自由选择""一致同意""全民投票"),他还喊出了著名的口号:"宁为地狱王,不做天堂奴"。撒旦拒绝做上帝的"显赫的奴仆",他要追求自己的生活:

自由自在，对谁都不负责，与其

做奴隶而显赫，羁轭中求舒服，宁可

辛劳而自由。

[5]　不信奉国教、反体制的作家们，比如珀西·雪莱，在弥尔顿刻画的撒旦身上找到了精神认同。（雪莱写道："弥尔顿笔下的魔鬼作为道德之身……远远高出他所塑造的上帝"。）众所周知，威廉·布莱克曾对"失落"这一提法表示质疑，他说，"弥尔顿写天使和上帝时束手束脚，写魔鬼和地狱却挥洒自如，其原因在于，他是个真正的诗人，不知不觉中做了魔鬼的同党"。

[6]　和克伦威尔一样，弥尔顿相信他的使命是在人世间开创一个上帝的王国。他虽然憎恶"王权神授"的观念，但却甘愿服从上帝，因为他相信，用本杰明·富兰克林的话说，"对暴君的反抗就是对上帝的顺从"。

[7]　虽然有关《失乐园》的研讨多以政治和神学为主导，但这部史诗也包含着对爱的温情赞颂。在弥尔顿的描述中，夏娃之所以屈从于诱惑，其中一个原因是她想与亚当更亲近些，"得到他更多的爱"。她期盼着犯错误的自由（不经受考验，何来信念、爱情和美德？）当夏娃抵挡不住诱惑时，亚当选择和她一同受罚："失去你就是失去我自己"，他说道：

没有你我怎么能生活？怎能舍弃

你亲密的谈话，和血肉相连的爱情，

又孤单寂寞地生活在这些荒林里？

即使上帝再创造个夏娃，我又

提供根肋骨，因失去你而造成的这一创伤

绝不会从心头消失。

注释

1. 这个长句的信息被分解放在译文的两个句子中：主句与原文第一句话合在一起，构成译文的第一句；从属部分 marked by..., and of..., which... 译为两句，分别叙述两个人物的逝世及相关情况。
2. 原文句中插入的定语从句融合到译文全句结构中去了。试比较：……他的试图用以解释"失落的"世界的宗教词汇已经不再使用了。
3. 以上两个段落涉及《失乐园》的内容及部分诗行。汉译《失乐园》有多种版本，此处译文系根据金发燊的译本稍作调整后纳入现译文中的，第七段的译文同此。

讲解

译者的互文意识

Why You Should Re-read Paradise Lost 原载于 BBC，本单元只选了其中的一节。这是一篇关于《失乐园》的文章，要阅读和翻译这篇文字当然要对这部著名的史诗有所了解：读过原诗并参阅过有关介绍和评论。文中还引用了《失乐园》中的诗句，而其汉译版本就有五六种。译者须考虑是自译还是选用某一个版本，以及选用哪一个版本。这里又牵涉对不同译本的选择问题。也就是说，翻译活动不仅涉及原文本身，还有和它相关的语篇，这往往能组成一个语篇网络。这个网络也是一个知识网，是译者理解和翻译原文的知识支撑和语言来源。这体现了语篇的一个重要特性——互文性。

什么叫互文性呢？

语篇不是孤立的，总是和其他语篇有着各种各样的关联。这种关联可以是由于语篇类型相同或主题相同或相关而产生的；也可以是由于评论、回应、引用或模仿其他语篇而产生的。每一语篇都可能与先于它存在的或与它同时或后于它构建的语篇发生关联。就翻译活动而言，原文语篇是源语语篇世界中的一员，构建中的译语语篇也将成为译语语篇世界中的一员。原文一方面是译文的源头，另一方面又假译文之功在译语环境中获得延续和再生。不管是原文还是译文，其解读和构建都受到它们所在语篇世界的制约，也都影响和塑造着各自的语篇世界，为之做出种种贡献。语篇间这种跨时空、跨文化的关联，这种互生、互动的动态交织便是译者眼中的互文性。

翻译活动就发生在这样的互文网络中，而且这不单是语言层面上的网络，还更是知识层面的网络。如 Chandler 所说，Texts are instrumental not only in the construction of other texts but in the construction of experiences. Much of what we "know" about the world is derived from what we have read in books, newspapers and magazines, from what we have seen in the cinema and on television and from what we have heard on the radio. Life is thus lived through texts and framed by texts to a greater extent than we are normally aware of.（"语篇不仅对其他语篇的构建至关重要，而且对经验的构建起着重要作用。我们对世界的了解很多来源于我们读过的书籍、报纸和杂志，来自我们从电影、电视和收音机里听到或看到的。于是，生活在比我们觉察到的更大的程度上就成了阅读各种语篇并被语篇所塑造的过程。"）现代社会中，人人都处于语篇交织成的信息网络中，问题是你是否用心去汲取网络

带给我们的语言的和知识层面的营养。作为一个译者，必须自觉地不断增加在语言和知识上的积累。而这种积累无不源于阅读。我们常说，学好英语一定要读一读莎士比亚，读一读《圣经》，因为这些经典语篇常会出现在各类文章之中，是英语语篇互文网络中不可或缺的经纬线。

上面的讨论使我们看到，不但如本章 Unit One 的讲解部分所指出的那样，语篇内部各句段有机交织共同发挥交际功能，语篇的外部关联也同样重要。原文的意义不仅出自对其自身的解析，还出于对其与相关语篇的关联的认识；译文的构建不仅在于自身的用词造句，还在于其是否能在译语同类语篇之中适存。这种认识就是学习翻译过程中必须反复强调的互文意识。

语篇的互文性时时提醒我们，要广读英语来保证准确理解，要广读汉语来提高写作水平。也就是说，学翻译要以阅读为起点，建立互文意识的途径是广泛阅读。不读，何谈理解；不读，何谈写作。而理解不准，写作不精，又何谈翻译。千万不要以为理解原文只靠细心研读原文本身就够了，也不要满足于我们目前运用母语的能力，还要不断阅读，力求提高汉语表达水平。强调英、汉语单语阅读以提高译者整体语言水平，而非只从双语对照阅读中寻求翻译技巧的积累，是翻译培训中凸显互文意识的具体体现。

翻译学习中，教师常会总结出一些翻译技巧。其实所谓翻译技巧，说到底就是译者的选词、构句、谋篇等行文选择。写作水平越高，选择余地越大，越能得心应手地找到最大限度地再现原文词语、句法、修辞、风格特点的表达方法。阅读汉语为构建汉语译文提供语言资源。译散文、小说，就要多读散文、小说；译论说文，就要多读汉语的论说文。要保证熟悉译语不同体裁、题材的各类语篇，保证具有写作此类语篇的能力。每个译者的阅读经验有所不同，写作能力和行文倾向也各异，所以同一篇原文经不同译者之手会产生出不同的译文。

许多翻译学者都强调写作能力的重要性。Chesterman & Arrojo (2000) 说："强化译者的写作意识，因为这关乎他们在不同文化间建立种种联系的重大责任。"Pattison（2007）报告过以写作提升翻译能力工作坊的经验，他指出"教育机构已经认识到，原创写作在翻译培训和职业发展中占有重要一席"。Schrijver（2016）说："鉴于翻译的语篇构建属性（text-productive nature），很显然译者应具备目的语的语篇构建能力。"Newmark（1995）早就非常明确地指出，"译者"即是"写作者"，并且要具有相当高的不同文体的写作水平。他说："我认为，译者的主要特质就是他们是写作者；他们能针对不同的语域——写实的或是抒情的，普及性的或是专业性的，正式的或是通俗的——写出明晰、简洁而优雅的文字。"

互文意识其实也是一种文化意识，因为一种语言的全部语篇就几乎是其所在文化的全部表述。当然，文化的表述还有其他形式，比如绘画、雕塑、服饰、建筑等，但这些在很多情况下也都是用语言表述的形式呈现的。语言就是文化，语言产生于文化之中，又促进着文化的发展，支持着文化的运作。语言不是文化的全部，但没有了语言，文化将不复存在。

小结

学习翻译的过程中，要不断深化自己的语篇意识和互文意识，努力积累语言资源和拓展互文视野，加强跨文化交际参与者的使命感和责任感。说得具体一些，起步阶段要做到以下几点：

（1）不要逐字死译，要分析上下文，翻译语境中的词、语境中的句。

（2）不要忽视基本语法分析，要对英语语篇各级层分清析透，避免基础层次上的误解误译。

（3）不要一律沿袭英语的行文逻辑，要按汉语写作的用词、构句、谋篇规范，组织句子和段落，建构连贯通达的语篇。

（4）不要对英语原文似懂非懂就急于动笔翻译，要全篇通读，融汇于心，再动笔。为此，要多读英语各类语篇，以提高英语解读能力。

（5）不要盲目相信自己的母语表达能力，要多读汉语，在英语的比照下加深对汉语的认识，不断增强各类语篇和话题的写作能力。

第二章 原文的理解

翻译的第一步是理解，理解要从建立语篇意识开始。所谓语篇意识，从翻译操作的层面上说，就是对语篇进行从宏观到微观的全面分析和理解。宏观指与语篇有关的社会-文化背景、语篇的整体结构、作者意图；微观指句子结构分析、词义的确定、指代关系的识别等。

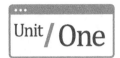

Rules Every Achiever Knows

[1] In October 1982, a 25-year-old woman finished the New York City Marathon. No big deal—until you learn that Linda Down has cerebral palsy and was the first woman ever to complete the 26.2-mile race on crutches. Down fell half a dozen times, but kept going until she crossed the finish line, 11 hours after she started. Her handicap limited her speed but not her determination.

[2] Henry W. Longfellow[1] once wrote: "Great is the art of beginning, but greater is the art of ending." How nice it would be if we all had a genie who could help us finish what we begin. Unfortunately, We don't. But what we do have is a dynamic called discipline[2]—which extracts a high price. Following one of Paderewski's performances, a fan said to him, "I'd give my life to play like that." The brilliant pianist replied, "I did."

[3] Accomplishment is often deceptive[3] because we don't see the pain and perseverance that produced it. So we may credit the achiever with brains, brawn or lucky break, and let ourselves off the hook because we fall short in all three. Not that we could all be concert pianists just by exercising enough discipline. Rather, each of us has the makings of success in some endeavor, but we will achieve this only if we apply our wills and work at it.

[4] How can we acquire stick-to-itiveness? There is no simple, fast formula. But I have developed a way of thinking that has rescued my own vacillating will more than once. Here are the basic elements:

[5] **"Won't" power.** This is as important as will power. The ancient Chinese philosopher Mencius said, "Men must be decided on what they will not do, and then they are able to act with vigor in what they ought to do."[4]

[6] Discipline means choices. Every time you say yes to a goal or objective, you say no to many more. Every prize has its price. The prize is the yes; the price is the no. Igor Gorin, the noted Ukrainian-American baritone, told of his early days studying voice. He loved to smoke a pipe, but one day his

professor said, "Igor, you will have to make up your mind whether you are going to be a great singer, or a great pipesmoker. You cannot be both." So the pipe went.

[7] **Delayed gratification.**[5] M. Scott Peck, M. D., author of the best-seller *The Road Less Traveled*, describes this tool of discipline as "a process of scheduling the pain and pleasure of life in such a way as to enhance the pleasure by meeting and experiencing the pain first and getting it over with".

[8] This might involve routine daily decisions—something as simple as skipping a favorite late-night TV show and getting to bed early, to be wide awake for a meeting the next morning. Or it might involve longer-term resolves. A young widow with three children decided to invest her insurance settlement in a college education for herself. She considered the realities of a tight budget and little free time, but these seemed small sacrifices in return for the doors that a degree would open. Today she is a highly paid financial consultant.

[9] The secret of such commitment is getting past the drudgery and seeing the delight. "The fact is that many worthwhile endeavors aren't fun," says one syndicated radio and TV commentator. "True, all work and no play makes Johnny a dull boy. But trying to turn everything we do into play makes for terrible frustrations, because life—even the most rewarding one—includes circumstances that aren't fun at all. I like my job as a journalist. It's personally satisfying, but it isn't always fun."

参考译文

成功者的守则

[1] 1982年10月，一个25岁的姑娘跑完了纽约市马拉松赛的全程。这没什么了不起——可是当你了解到琳达·道恩患有大脑性麻痹，是第一位拄着双拐跑完26.2英里的女性的时候，你就会改变想法了。道恩摔倒了五六次，但仍坚持不懈，一直跑到终点。这时她已跑了11个小时。残疾限制了速度，但不能减弱她的决心。

[2] 19世纪美国著名诗人亨利·瓦兹沃思·朗费罗曾写道："善始固然伟大，善终更为伟大。"如果能有一位神灵帮助我们去完成业已开始的事情，那该多好呀！只可惜，我们没有。但是，我们却拥有一种叫作自律的动力——它要求我们付出

很高的代价。听完帕德雷夫斯基的演奏，一个音乐迷对他说："要是能弹得像您这样，我宁愿付出整个生命。"这位卓越的钢琴家答道："我已经付出过了。"

[3] 成就常常有误导作用，因为它会使我们看不到成功背后的艰难困苦和坚韧不拔的精神。于是我们常会把别人的成就归功于人家脑子灵，身体壮或者运气好，而以我们不具备这三个条件为自己开脱。不是说我们只要严格要求自己就都能成为独奏钢琴家；而是说我们每个人都具备在某一方面取得成功的基本条件，不过只有下决心，坚持不懈才能达到目标。

[4] 怎样才能做到坚持不懈呢？简单快捷的公式是没有的。但我已总结出一套思想方法，使我不止一次地克服了意志动摇的毛病。其要点如下：

[5] **"不为"的毅力**。"不为"与"有为"同等重要。中国古代哲学家孟子说过："人有不为也，而后可以有为。"

[6] 自律就意味着有取有舍。每当你选定了一个目标，也就同时放弃了其他许多目标。每项成绩的获得都有它的代价。成绩来自你的所取，代价就是你的所舍。著名乌克兰裔美国男中音歌唱家伊戈尔·戈林曾谈起他早年学声乐的事。他喜欢抽烟，可是一天教授对他说："伊戈尔，你得下决心，要么做个大歌唱家，要么做个大烟鬼。两者不可兼得。"于是，他舍弃了烟斗。

[7] **先苦后甜**。医学博士M·斯科特·佩克写了一本题为《较少有人走过的路》的畅销书。他把这种自律的方法描述为"对生活中苦与乐的一种安排：先去吃苦，苦尽甜来，欢乐倍增。"

[8] 这可能只涉及日常小事的安排。比如这么一个简单的决定：你爱看的电视节目很晚才能演，为了次日上午开会头脑清醒，只好早点上床睡觉。也许会涉及较为长期的目标。一位带着三个孩子的年轻寡妇决定用保险金去上大学。她考虑过经济拮据、时间紧张这些现实问题，但较之学位将为她开启的扇扇大门，这些只是小小的牺牲而已。如今她已是一位收入颇丰的金融顾问了。

[9] 做出这种抉择的诀窍在于，要越过艰辛看到欢乐。"实际上，许多值得为之一搏的事并没有什么乐趣，"一位为多家电台和电视台撰稿的评论家说道，"确实，只会工作不会玩儿，约翰变成笨小孩儿。然而，把我们做的每件工作都当成愉快的游戏，就会招致悲惨的失败，因为生活，即便是最富成果的生活，也有全然没有乐趣的时候。我喜欢我的记者工作，它让我感到满足，但也并非总是趣味盎然的。"（喻云根译）

注释

1. 朗费罗何许人也？英美读者可能很熟悉，但中国读者却未必知道。因此，译者点明其身份，以便译语读者理解。
2. discipline 切莫译为"纪律"。其义应根据上下文确定，可参阅带英语解释的字典，如 Longman 对此词的释义为：training of the mind and body to produce obedience and self-control。
3. deceptive 不宜译为"欺骗性的"，而应取 misleading 义（见 *Longman Dictionary of Contemporary English*）。
4. 遇有引用中文原著英译文的情况，最好查出出处，转抄原句。如有困难，则应注明是据英语转译，或不用引号。
5. Delayed gratification 不宜直译为"延迟的喜悦"。这是下面几段的小标题，要参照下文内容，须译得概括、达意。

讲解

词义和语境

  Peter Newmark 曾仿照 John Donne 的著名诗句说："No word 'is an island entire to itself'."。一个词在词典里似乎只是一个孤立的词条，只有几个"死"意义，可一旦用于具体的语篇当中，就会"活"起来，因为它们被纳入了特定的语境之中。什么是语境？词语的语境指其被使用时所处的上下文以及具体情境和文化背景。按 Peter Newmark 的说法，"Visibly and linguistically, words are put into context by their collocations, their grammatical functions and their position in the word order of a sentence. Outside language, invisibly and referentially they are within a context of a real or imagined situation, a cultural background, a topic and a shared experience with the reader."。这里，Newmark 谈及词语被语境化的四个方面：一是被搭配或组合、语法功能以及其在语符系列中的位置所语境化；二是被某一真实的或虚构的情境所语境化；三是被特定的文化背景所语境化；四是被某一话题或作者与读者共享的经验所语境化。第一种使词语语境化的因素也就是我们常说的上下文，是可见的语言想象，而第二至第四种语境化因素不一定很直观地存在于文字表面，但可以从上下文所显示的交际场合、交际对象等推而知之。

  翻译过程中确定一个词语的意义，一定要注意分析上下文等语境因素，推想出其使用的具体情境。比如，广告中说 Next time you want a lift, pick Vivarin（Vivarin 是一种片剂，可冲成饮料，一片中含有两杯咖啡的咖啡因含量），这里的 lift 就是 feel happier 的意思，意即要提神，请用 Vivarin。而新闻中说 They have moved fifty tons of food to the village in a single lift，那就是 an upward movement of sth.，意即他们一次就向那个村子运去了五十吨食品。当你在商场问朋友 Do you want to take the lift or use the stairs? 时，你当然是问他要坐电梯还是走楼梯。诚然，这些词在词典里自有基本释义和对应词，但将这些基本意义激活的是这个词语所在的语境。本单元注释 2、3 和 5 都涉及词义的确定，请用心体会译者是如何根据上下文进行翻译的。再观察下面译例：

1. (1) Mike Findlay got the flying bug early.
   迈克·芬德利从小就对飞行情有独钟。

   (2) He wanted to go to flying school instead of university. He bugged his parents about it all the time.
   他愿意上飞行学校而不愿上大学。为此，他总是在父母面前软磨硬泡。

   (3) They (the police) arrested the bug-eyed pair and led them away.
   警察逮捕了惊讶得瞠目结舌的两个劫机者，随即把他们带走。

   这三个译例均选自名为 The Guy Who Loved to Fly（作者：John Ryan）的短文，bug 一词出现在三种不同的语境中，译文自然也便随上下文而定了。

2. After the Thanksgiving dinner, when Mike was taking his mother-in-law home, his car stalled on a railroad track. The old lady got excited and begun to give orders from the back seat.
   在吃完感恩节大餐后，麦克送他的岳母回家。他的车在铁轨上熄火了，老太太很激动，在后座上开始发号施令。

   mother-in-law 一词词典的释义有"岳母；婆母"，而在具体的语境中当然只能选其一，依据就是上下文。

3. ...and we appear to talk exclusively about people we know who have been committed to mental hospitals, about people we know who have been booked on drunk driving charges, and about property, particularly about property, land, price per acre and C-2 zoning and assessments and freeway access.
   ……在他看来我们好像尽在谈熟人，哪个被送进了精神病院，哪个被控酒后驾车。还谈财产，特别是地产、土地和地价，C-2 区制规划及评估，还有高速公路的出入口，等等。

原文中 property 前后紧跟着用了两次，却分别译为"财产"和"地产"，因为第一次用是泛指，与 people 相对；第二次用是特指，是和其他几个财产项目并列的。

4. The torpedo bombers skimmed low, launching their missiles from just fifty feet off the calm surface of the water. Once these torpedoes hit the water, they drive along under their own power.

鱼雷轰炸机低低掠过，在距平静的水面仅五十英尺的高度发射鱼雷。这些鱼雷一旦进入水中就靠自身动力向前推进了。

句中 missile 一词很容易误译为"导弹"。这一段谈的是鱼雷攻击目标的情况，missile 是 torpedo 的上位词，意为"投射出的武器"（any weapon projected at a target）。

5. I knew my Bible, especially the marital parts, in which I took deep interest. I had read the Bible through many times under the eye of one particular aunt. I knew a lot about matrimony from that. But Uncle Amos had me puzzled. He had broken no commandments. All his marriages were open and above-board. He wasn't like the patriarchs who didn't always wait for one wife to go before another came.

我对《圣经》很熟，对有关婚娶的章节尤感兴趣，在一位爱挑剔的姑妈的监督之下曾多次通读，从中学到许多有关婚姻的清规戒律。但艾默大叔却令我困惑。他没有触犯任何一条戒律，每次婚姻都是公开的，光明正大的，不像那些道貌岸然的人，妻子还好好的，就又勾搭上了别的女人。

原文中 patriarch 一词本意为：① the father or ruler of a family or tribe；② a person regarded as the founder or father of a colony, religion, business, etc.；③ a man of great age and dignity；④ the oldest individual of a class or group；⑤ a bishop。这是一篇回忆录，表达了作者对一位平凡而善的长辈的思念。本段谈论大叔在婚姻问题上的处世态度，可以说词典上列出的词意没有一个是完全切合这一上下文的。译者以上下文为依据，认为该词系指那些威严的长辈，且带贬义，故有上述译文：那些道貌岸然的人。

6. …In 1991, one of the most eventful years of this century, the world witnessed the dramatic and transforming impact on those events of live television by satellite. The very definition of news was rewritten—from something that has happened to something that is happening at the very moment you are hearing it. …

These shots heard, and seen, around the world appeared under the aegis of the first global TV news company, Cable News Network. ...

……1991年，本世纪最多事的年份之一，世界目睹了卫星现场直播电视对这些事件所产生的影响，连新闻定义本身也被改写了——从已发生的事改为收看电视时正在发生的事。……

这些全世界都听到都看到的枪声，是在第一家全球性电视新闻公司，即有线新闻电视公司（CNN）的主持下出现的。……

上面译例包括了两个自然段的关键语句。第二自然段把 shots 译为"枪声"是否得当？单从这一句译文的词语搭配来看，就已能发现问题。枪声可听到，但怎么能看到呢？其实，shots 一词是和上一段中所提到的现场直播电视节目相呼应的，应译为"电视实况转播镜头"。

我们看到，词义的理解和翻译不仅关乎一个句子，还影响着整个句群或段落的语义衔接和逻辑连贯。如何在译文中构建连贯的语义链，是译者必须认真考虑的。以本单元原文的第六自然段为例。这一段的首句 Discipline means choices 点明了主题，然后作者对主题进行阐述，并用一个简短的例子加以说明。阐述主题的几个句子结构简单，逻辑环环相扣。请将下面译文和本单元原文加以对照：

纪律就是说它有选择性，每当你肯定一个目标或对象的时候，你同时也否定了更多的目标。每种奖励都有它的代价，肯定的是奖励，否定的是代价。

此译的症结是：句对句的机械翻译，忽视了句群的整体性。其实原文脉络是很清楚的，这几句都围绕主题展开，choice—yes—no 构成一条明晰的词汇链。所以在我们的参考译文中便使用了"有取有舍—选取—舍弃—所取—所舍"等交际功能相近的词语，围绕"取"与"舍"阐发主题，句子间的关系便连贯流畅了。

再看下面一段译例：

7. One of the things we have to understand about Japanese society is its gender structure, a structure similar to what the United States had in the 1950s. Women do all the domestic labour. Men are in the factories and shops and they're working long hours, but they don't do much work when they come home. They don't take care of children, they don't do housework, cooking, etc. In the U.S., there are both men and women in the work force and both men and women at home. Japanese workers may work longer in the marketplace, but you have to calculate the total amount of work that people do to figure out how hard people are working and how much leisure time they have.

我们必须了解日本社会的一个特点，那就是它的性别结构，类似于美国二十世纪五十年代的结构。妇女包揽全部家务劳动，男人到工厂、商店上班工作时间很长，但回到家里就不干多少活了。他们不管看孩子，不做家务事，不做饭，等等。<u>在美国，有很多男人和女人都在劳动大军之列，也有都在家里的。日本工人可能在市场里工作的时间较长</u>，但是我们在估算人们工作的辛苦程度以及他们有多少闲暇时间时，必须把整个工作量都计算进去。

仔细对照原文，不难发现有两处意义失去连贯的地方（见译文划线部分）。第一处，作者讨论的是美、日性别结构差异，更具体地说，即男人是否干家务。怎么会突然提到"有很多男人和女人都在劳动大军之列，也有都在家里的"？是夫妻双双失业吗？第二处，只说日本工人在"市场"里工作时间长，与上文"男人到工厂、商店上班"也不相符。很显然，译文脱离了其所在的上下文，与这一段中的其他句子不能连贯成篇。本段主旨是美、日性别结构的区别：日本是男人工作，女人管家务；而美国是男女都工作，也都管家务。作者在谈到男女社会分工时运用了两组词语：

(1)   (2)
in factories and shops   do domestic labour
in the work force   take care of children
in the marketplace   do housework, cooking, etc.
                               at home

一旦将上下文连起来，词义就明了了：第一组词与"上班"有关，按照这一思路 marketplace，也就不再是"市场"，而是"工作地点"（上文所说的工厂、商店等）。第二组词与"做家务"有关，于是，at home 便不是"在家里"，而是"做家务"。这样，两处划线部分便可分别改译为：

在美国，男女都参加工作，也都从事家务劳动。

日本工人可能在工作单位劳动时间较长，但我们在估算人们的劳动强度和闲暇时间多少时，必须把全部劳动都算在内。

Peter Newmark 在谈到词义时说过这么两句耐人寻味的话："A common mistake is to ignore context. A not uncommon mistake is to make context the excuse for inaccurate translation."。的确，成也语境败也语境，上下文等语境因素对词义的理解至关重要，除了个别词语（如某些科技词语）之外，几乎所有词语都是受语境因素制约的，诚如语言学家 J. R. Firth 所言："Each word when used in a new context is a new word."。

How to Grow Old (Excerpts)

[1] As regards health, I have nothing useful to say since I have little experience of illness. I eat and drink whatever I like, and sleep when I cannot keep awake. I never do anything whatever on the ground that it is good for health, though in actual fact the things I like doing are mostly wholesome.

[2] Psychologically there are two dangers to be guarded against in old age. One of these is undue absorption in the past. It does not do to live in memories, in regrets for the good old days, or in sadness about friends who are dead. One's thoughts must be directed to the future, and to things about which there is something to be done. This is not always easy; one's own past is a gradually increasing weight. It is easy to think to oneself that one's emotions used to be more vivid than they are, and one's mind more keen. If this is true it should be forgotten, and if it is forgotten it will probably not be true.

[3] The other thing to be avoided is clinging to youth in the hope of sucking vigour from its vitality. When your children are grown up they want to live their own lives, and if you continue to be as interested in them as you were when they were young, you are likely to become a burden to them, unless they are unusually callous. I do not mean that one should be without interest in them, but one's interest should be contemplative and, if possible, philanthropic,[1] but not unduly emotional. Animals become indifferent to their young as soon as their young can look after themselves, but human beings, owing to the length of infancy[2], find this difficult.[3]

[4] I think that a successful old age is easiest for those who have strong impersonal interests involving appropriate activities. It is in this sphere that long experience is really fruitful, and it is in this sphere that the wisdom born of experience can be exercised without being oppressive.[4] It is no use telling grown-up children not to make mistakes, both because they will not believe you, and because mistakes are an essential part of education.[5] But if you are one of those who are incapable of impersonal interests, you may find that your life will be empty unless you concern yourself with your children

and grandchildren. In that case you must realize that while you can still render them material service, such as making them an allowance or knitting them jumpers, you must not expect that they will enjoy your company.

[5] Some old people are oppressed by the fear of death. In the young there is a justification for this feeling. Young men who have reason to fear that they will be killed in battle may justifiably feel bitter[6] in the thought that they have been cheated of the best things that life has to offer. But in an old man who has known human joys and sorrows, and has achieved whatever work it was in him to do, the fear of death is somewhat abject and ignoble. The best way to overcome it—so at least it seems to me—is to make your interests gradually wider and more impersonal, until bit by bit the walls of the ego recede, and your life becomes increasingly merged in the universal life. An individual human existence should be like a river—small at first, narrowly contained within its banks, and rushing passionately past boulders and over waterfalls. Gradually the river grows wider, the banks recede, the waters flow more quietly, and in the end, without any visible break, they become merged in the sea, and can painlessly lose their individual being.[7] The man who, in old age, can see his life in this way, will not suffer from the fear of death, since the things he cares for will continue. And if, with the decay of vitality, weariness increases, the thought of rest will be not unwelcome. I should wish to die while still at work, knowing that others will carry on what I can no longer do, and content in the thought that what was possible has been done.

参考译文

怎样才能活得老

[1] 谈到健康问题，我就没有什么可说的了，因为我没怎么生过病。我想吃什么就吃什么，想喝什么就喝什么，眼睛睁不开了就睡觉，从来不为对身体有益而搞什么活动，然而实际上我喜欢做的事大都是有助于促进身体健康的。

[2] 从心理方面来说，到了老年，有两种危险倾向需要注意防止。一是过分地怀念过去。老想着过去，总觉得过去怎么好怎么好，或者总是为已故的朋友而忧伤，这是不妥的。一个人应当考虑未来，考虑一些可以有所作为的事情。要做到这一点是不大容易的；自己的经历就是一个越来越沉重的包袱。人们常常会对自己说，我过

去感情多么丰富，思想多么敏锐，现在不行了。如果真是这样的话，那就不要去想它，而如果你不去想它，情形就很可能不是这样了。

[3] 另一件需要避免的事就是老想和年轻人待在一起，希望从青年的活力中汲取力量。孩子们长大之后，就希望独立生活，如果你还像他们年幼时那样关心他们，你就会成为他们的累赘，除非他们特别麻木不仁。我不是说一个人不应当关心孩子，而是说这种关心主要应该是多为他们着想，可能的话，给他们一些接济，而不应该过分地动感情。动物，一旦它们的后代能够自己照顾自己，它们就不管了；但是人，由于抚养子女的时间长，是难以这样做的。

[4] 我认为，如果老年人对于个人以外的事情怀有强烈的兴趣，并参加适当的活动，他们的晚年是最容易过得好的。在这一方面，他们由于阅历深，是能够真正做得卓有成效的，也正是在这一方面，他们从经验中得出的智慧既可以发挥作用，又不致使人感到强加于人。告诫成年的子女不要犯错误，那是没有用的，一来他们不听你的，二来犯错误本身也是受教育的一个重要方面。但是如果你这个人对于个人以外的事情不发生兴趣，就会感到生活空虚，除非你老惦记着儿孙。在这种情况下，你可要明白，虽然你还可以在物质方面给他们以帮助，比如给他们零用钱，或者为他们织毛衣，但你绝不要指望他们会喜欢跟你做伴。

[5] 有些老年人因怕死而惶惶不安。年轻人有这种情绪是情有可原的。如果青年人由于某种原因认为自己有可能在战斗中死去，想到生活所能提供的最美好的东西自己全都无法享受，觉得受了骗，因而感到痛苦，这是无可指责的。但是对老年人来说，他经历了人生的酸甜苦辣，自己能做的事情都做到了，怕死就未免有些可鄙，有些不光彩了。要克服这种怕死的念头，最好的办法——至少在我看来——就是逐渐使自己关心更多的事情，关心那些不跟自己直接有关的事情，到后来，自我的壁垒就会慢慢消退，个人的生活也就越来越和宇宙的生命融合在一起了。人生好比一条河，开头河身狭小，夹在两岸之间，接着河水奔腾咆哮，流过巨石，飞下悬崖。后来河面逐渐展宽，两岸离得越来越远，河水也流得较为平缓，最后流进大海，与海水浑然一体，看不出任何界线，从而结束其单独存在的那一段历程，但毫无痛苦之感。如果一个人到了老年能够这样看待自己的一生，他就不会怕死了，因为他所关心的一切将会继续下去。如果随着精力的衰退，日见倦怠，就会觉得长眠未尝不是一件好事。我就希望在工作时死去，知道自己不再能做的事有人会继续做下去，并且怀着满意的心情想到，自己能做的事都已做到了。（庄绎传译）

注释

1. contemplative 未按词典意义译为"沉思的",philanthropic 也没有照词典对号入座译为"慈善的"或"仁爱的"。译者根据上下文提供的具体情景,灵活再现了源语作者的交际意图。
2. infancy 一词的理解也应依据上下文。如译成"人类由于对婴儿哺育的时间长",似对 infancy 理解过于狭窄。从上下文看,作者指的是孩子能独立生活前的那段时间,译为"抚养子女的时间"是妥当的。这与注释 1 一样都体现了译者对原文交际意图的揣摩和理解。
3. 请对照这一句的原文和译文。译文句式采取突出主题的方法,即"动物,……;但是人,……",这可达到层次清晰、重点突出的行文效果。试比较下面一种译文:"动物在其小动物可以独立生活时,就对他们比较冷淡;但人类由于对婴儿哺育的时间长,很难做到这点。"
4. 原文是强调句式,"it is in this sphere that..."用了两次。译文用"在这一方面……也正是在这一方面……"再现了原文的逻辑层次。
5. 对原文两个并列的状语从句"both because..., and because...",译文用"一来……,二来……"译出。纵观注 4、注 5 所涉及的这一部分译文,可看出译者很注重也很精于保持和再现原文的行文层次和脉络。
6. justifiably feel bitter 未译为"有理由感到痛苦"或"理所当然地感到痛苦",而是把副词 justifiably 拆译成一个小句。
7. 此处未译为"毫无痛苦地失去了它单独的存在",而是采取了与注 6 所说相同的拆译方法。

讲解

一、对语篇结构的分析

翻译的操作过程可分为原文理解、译文表达、校对修改三个阶段。其中原文理解是基础。

对原文的理解一般应采取由宏观至微观的方法。译者要通读原文,最少两至三遍,抓住原文的主旨,析清原文的层次,并体会其运用语言的特点和风格。这便是宏观分析,也就是对原文的整体认识。其次要对文章中的节或段落进行结构分析,认清其逻辑推进层次。每个段落也是一个微型的篇章,它有自己的主题及层次,它们的有机组合便构成整篇文章。对段落中的字句,特别是难懂字句的分析和理解,也是至关重要的。这里应特别强调,字句的分析一定要放在段落,乃至整个篇章这个更大语言单位的背景下去进行。

这样，我们就完成了从整个篇章到段落的层次分析。不过实际上，这种分析不是单向的。先把握全篇的主旨、行文层次，目的是为段落分析提供可靠的、明晰的导向，而段落的分析反过来又可加深对宏观结构的认识。译者需要对段落与段落之间的关系、段落与全篇之间的关系进行反复思考，直到认识清楚了全篇的层次才能动笔进行翻译。

翻译的三个阶段也不是截然分开的，表达阶段和校对阶段还会出现始料不及的某些理解问题。但在动笔之前，仍有必要析清原文的结构。这样可以避免译文表达走弯路，不会事倍功半。初学翻译的人往往会急于求成，看一句翻一句，或读完一段就翻译一段。这好比没画图纸就盖房子，盖到哪儿算哪儿，到头来可能发现少盖了一间，或门窗弄错了位置，弄得前功尽弃。必须记住，虽然我们下笔处译出的是一个个句子，但它们不是孤零零的句子，每个句子都是嵌在篇章这一个大背景中的有机成分。

下面我们以本单元原文为例，进行一次语篇结构分析。

这篇文章是英国哲学家罗素（Bertrand Russell）的名篇。这里略去了原文的第一自然段。第一自然段的作用主要是解题，第一句话为：In spite of the title, this article will really be on how not to grow old, which, at my time of life, is a much more important subject.（题目虽然这样写，实际上本文所谈的却是人怎样才可以不老。对于像我这样年纪的人来说，这个问题就更是重要得多了。）很明显，"人怎样才可以不老"便是全篇主旨。接着，作者从身体健康、心理健康、对死亡的态度等方面分别阐述了自己对老年生活的看法，逻辑层次清晰，语言生动精练。下面列出全篇的结构层次（阿拉伯数字系本单元原文中段落序号，不含已删去的第一自然段）：

1. 健康问题；
2 和 3. 心理上的两种错误倾向；
4. 老年人应对个人以外的事情怀有强烈的兴趣；如何对待子女；
5. 对死亡的正确态度。

很明显，本文各层次之间是一种并列关系。当然，各层次间也是有联系的。比如，第 5 自然段中再一次提到第 4 自然段中应"对个人以外的事情怀有强烈兴趣"的观点，并结合对待死亡问题做了进一步阐述。

厘清了全篇的结构之后，还应对较长的、重要的段落进行分析，认清行文脉络，弄清楚各句之间是如何连在一起组成连贯语篇的。

比如，第 4 自然段 I think that... It is in this sphere..., and it is in this sphere...

It is no use..., both because..., and because... 这三个句子所表现的"观点 + 分析"的逻辑推进层次。再比如第 5 自然段，先批评某些老年人的怕死心理，然后用类比方法生动形象地说明只有将自我融入社会才能泰然面对生命终结的道理。

对原文进行语篇结构分析是译者的一项基本功。译者分析原文的方法与一般读者不尽相同，因为读者只需获得原文信息，而译者还要在此基础上将原文信息用译语再表达出来。译者的理解是以表达为目的的。忽视原文的语篇结构无疑会影响译文的质量。下面为大家提供第 3 自然段末和第 4 自然段前几句的另一种译文，请对照本单元的参考译文并参照注解 3、4 和 5 加以研读对照，看看哪种译文在语篇层次上更清晰些。

……我不是说对他们漠不关心，而是要设身处地多为他们着想，如果有可能的话，对他们要本着善心，但不要太感情用事。动物在其小动物可以独立生活时，就对他们比较冷淡，但人类由于对婴儿哺育的时间长，很难做到这一点。

我想多寄兴趣于不涉及个人感情的事物上，并从事适宜的活动的人，其晚年就最易于过得比较惬意。他们在这方面长时间积累的经验就能够富有成果；而他们在经验中产生的智慧也就可以发挥作用而不会成为累赘。叫成年的孩子不要犯错误是没有用的。因为他们根本不信你的话，而且，犯错误本身就是教育的重要组成部分……

很显然，上述译文在逻辑层次上不如参考译文明晰。其原因何在？最根本的一点就是译者对原文的逻辑推进层次注意不够。其中最明显的一个例子是第 4 自然段第二句，原文用 It is in this sphere that..., and it is in this sphere that... 的句式来层层递进地阐发老年人的优势，参考译文用了相应的"在这一方面，……，也正是在这一方面……"来再现原文的行文层次，而这也正是上面所引用的第二种译文的不足之处。

二、语篇的意向

交际过程中语篇承载着信息，也承载着作者的交际意向——包括要表达怎样的思想、心情和态度，想在读者身上产生怎样的效果，造成怎样的印象，等等。作者在构建语篇时会把自己的交际意向用语言符号表达出来。作者的意向存在于自己的大脑中，是抽象的，是转瞬即逝的，是读者无法直接了解的。但是，作为其意向载体的语篇就要具体、稳定多了。正是通过作者的遣词造句、谋篇布局等手段，读者才得以体味出作者想要达到的思想和交际意图（参阅本单元注释 1 和注释 2）。

怎样从作者的文字编码中体会其交际意图呢？主要有以下几个方面：一是词汇搭配；二是句子结构；三是标点符号的运用；四是印刷格式。非常规的词语搭配和特定句式均可表明作者试图达到的修辞效果；而标点和格式这些规范性很强的语篇特征也会传达出作者的意图：感叹号的情感意义自然不同于句号，而一个小小的逗号也可造成不同的语气。黑体、斜体、大写等都体现着作者的不同意图。当然，除了这些，还必须从语篇的角度，认清作者谋篇布局的章法，体味作者字里行间的用心。请看下面两例：

1. The gods, they say, give breath, and they take it away. But the same could be said—could it not?—of the humble comma. Add it to the present clause, and, of a sudden, the mind is, quite literally, given pause to think; take it out if you wish or forget it and the mind is deprived of a resting place. Yet still the comma gets no respect. (Pico Iyer: *In Praise of the Humble Comma*)

   人都说老天爷把气赐予生灵，又把气夺走。不过这话用在小小的逗号上，何尝不是如此？给现成的句子加上个逗号，脑子里真会突然停下来想想；若随意去掉，或忘了它，就剥夺了脑子休息的空间。尽管如此逗号仍然不受人尊重。

   译者未能领会作者的意图：用当前的小句为例，说明逗号的作用。这个意图是通过两个手段来表达的：一是用 the present clause 表明作者要以现在这个句子为例；二是灵活地使用标点符号。一个小句里频加逗号，另一句一气呵成没有标点。这两点译者显然都忽略了。下面的改译运用词汇和标点手段再现了原文意图：

   ……给现在这个句子，加几个逗号，于是，突然，脑子一下，就真的，能停下来，思考了；但如果你不愿意加逗号或是忘了加那么脑子就被剥夺了休息的空间。……

2. They care! They simply are eaten up with caring. They are so busy caring about Fascism or Leagues of Nations or whether France is right or whether marriage is threatened, that they never know where they are. They certainly never live on the spot where they are. They inhabit an abstract space, the desert void of politics, principles, right and wrong, and so forth. They are doomed to be abstract. Talking to them is like trying to have a human relationship with the letter x in algebra. (D. H. Lawrence: *Insouciance*)

   这是 Lawrence 的一篇散文。作者在旅馆的阳台上与左邻右舍的欧洲游客交谈，发现他们对眼前的大自然和人熟视无睹，却对政治、社会等抽象话题津津乐道。Lawrence 认为现代人生活的可悲之处正在于此。这段文字写出了作者对那几个游客的反感和贬斥。比较下面几个译文，看哪一个能更好地再现作者的这种意图：

[a] 他们关心！他们简直已经被关心所销蚀。他们是如此之忙于关心法西斯，关心国联，关心法国是否有理，关心婚姻制度是否受到了威胁，以至于从来意识不到身处何地。他们肯定地并不生活在他们所在之地。他们存活在一个抽象的空间，一个政治、原则是非等等的荒无所有的空洞之境。他们摆脱不了抽象的厄运。同他们谈话就像试图用代数里的 x 符号来培养人际关系。

[b] 他们事事关切！他们几乎被关切心所吞噬。他们关心法西斯主义，关心国际联盟，关心法国是否正确，或人们的婚姻是否受到了威胁。他们关心这儿，关心那儿，就是不知道自己身处何地。他们显然没生活在自身所在的地方，他们生活在一片抽象的空间中，一片由什么政治、原则，什么是非善恶之类组成的荒漠的空间中。他们注定走向抽象，与他们交谈无异于试图和代数里的 x 建立一种人与人之间的关系。

[c] 他们关心！他们满肚子都是关心。他们忙于关心法西斯主义，国家联盟，法国有没有理，婚姻有没有受到威胁。从来就不知道自己的处境。他们自然从不生活在现有的地方。他们居住在抽象的空间，居住在政治、原则、对错等荒野的虚空。跟他们谈话就像试图跟代数符号 x 发展人际关系。

译文 [b] 和 [c] 似比译文 [a] 对作者意图的体现更为明显些，这种效果来自遣词也来自造句。译文 [b] 中的划线部分对作者意图有凸显作用，译文 [c] 简洁的句式，也颇有助于再现原文语篇的意向。

3. The French usually have two courses for entertaining: a starter (entree) and a main course will be enough. It is quite common for us Chinese to treat 6 people to 6 dishes and one soup, and we can consume them all, whereas at a French dinner we can also eat our fill.

法国人请客，通常只需做两个菜：一个头盘，一个主菜，就够了。我们中国人请客，六个人吃六个菜加一个汤，是很平常的。那么多菜我们都能吃下去，而吃他们的，也跟他们一样，能吃得非常饱。

译文为达到连贯已经做了增益处理，但怎样才能使译文达到真正的连贯呢？这就要体会作者的意向，抓住"中国人请客菜多，法国人请客菜少"这两个对立的事实。划线部分可改为：那么多菜我们都能吃下去，而法国人请客，菜虽少，我们也一样能吃饱。

The Good Teacher[1]

[1] For many of these teachers-to-be, the image of the ideal teacher they carried with them into their pre-service course was of one who did not simply "teach" in the sense of "passing on" or quickening skills, knowledge and facts, but one who would "make a difference", "touch lives": one for whom pupils' cognitive and affective development was paramount, but for whom such development needed to take place within what might be called a fundamentally pastoral mode of pedagogy.[2] For these novice teachers, the teacher they envision eventually becoming is a carer, nurturer and role model as much as an "educator" in the narrower sense of the word, one whose modus operandi[3] is characterized by personal "performance" and student admiration along the lines described by Harris and Jarvis in their finding from their own research with student teachers that "the cultural images dominating the minds of intending teachers are those of charismatic individuals who have changed the lives of those with whom they work."[4]

[2] There is nothing wrong, of course, about teachers being remembered or about new teachers wanting to emulate the ways and styles of teachers whom they have previously experienced as successful themselves. Nor, on the evidence of the testimonies of the teachers and students involved in the projects on which this book is based,[5] would many prioritize the charismatic, enthusiastic, caring, inspirational conceptualization of the good teacher to the extent of ignoring or refuting other, less obvious qualities and skills that a successful teacher might require.[6] We might also agree that at a time when technicist models of teaching appear (certainly, to the student teachers we spoke to) to be holding centre stage, the more intuitive, spontaneous, collaborative aspects of teaching need celebrating more than ever. As Hartley poignantly asks: "Where is the pleasure for the teacher in this emerging and empowered charisma-free zone called the 'competent' classroom?... What now is the pedagogical relationship when contract replaces trust?" —reminding us of Woods' timely reminder that teaching is, very often, "expressive and emergent, intuitive and flexible, spontaneous and

emotional."[7]

[3] There are, however, difficulties with the notion of the charismatic subject, one of which I have already alluded to and which emerges when student teachers are asked to elaborate on their recollections of good teaching. While it is not uncommon for them to recite qualities such as a sense of humour, a commitment of fairness, good communication skills or infectious enthusiasm for the subject area, these are often expressed in the very vaguest of terms, suggestive of an over-reliance on notions of "personality" and a corresponding under-reliance on matters of technique—something which can prove both very dangerous and very unhelpful to practitioners setting out on[8] their teaching careers. There is, certainly, seldom reference in these accounts (explained partly, perhaps, by their "invisibility" as far as the school-student may be concerned) to such things as planning, preparation, classroom management skills or assessment of students' work and progress. As Rousmaniere et al. have observed in this connection:[9]

> Often the stories that we remember and tell about our own schooling are not so much about what we learned, but how we learned and with whom. There are stories about teachers we loved, teachers we hated and those we feared.

[4] Always, in such stories, the emphasis is on the teacher as personality, and always the implication is that good teachers are "born" rather than "made", that their qualities are somehow inherent and perhaps even inherited.

[5] An additional difficulty[10] is immediately apparent: If the identified qualities of good teaching are inherent, what hope does the student teacher who selfperceives as charismatically deficient have of acquiring them, or of even knowing how to acquire them?[11] And how might the student teacher's own teachers contribute to the achievement of such a difficult goal? As Dalton observes, the spectre[12] of the charismatic teacher often has the unfortunate effect of making life very difficult for student teachers when, in the classroom situation, they discover that they cannot emulate, or be instantly respected in the manner of, the only truly effective teacher they can remember from their own school days. One reason for this, I would suggest, is that the attempted emulation of such role models is typically based on a simple misunderstanding—"charisma" is innate. In reality, however, while a

teacher's "charisma" may appear to be embodied in and to "emanate from" the teacher, it is in essence an attribute that is conferred upon the teacher by their students. (This is what Zizek and others, after the psycho-analyst Jacques Lacan, have referred to as the "transferential illusion", whereby a quality that one invests in another object appears to reside, intrinsically, in the object itself.)

参考译文

好 教 师

[1] 许多即将成为教师的人在进行岗前培训时，心中就已经勾勒出好教师的形象，他们认为好教师不是简单的"教"，也就是所谓的"传递"或者说迅速地传授技能、知识和事实，而应该能够"产生巨大影响""触及生命"：对一个好教师来说，学生的认知和情感发展至关重要，而这样的发展需要在以所谓田园式教学模式为基调的情景中进行。在准教师的心目中，教师不仅是狭义上的"教育者"，还应该是对学生施以关怀和进行培育的人，是学生的楷模。他们还认为教师的普遍特征是"展现"自我和赢得学生的敬仰，就像哈瑞斯和加沃斯对实习教师们进行研究后所描述的那样："准教师心目中占主导地位的文化意象是那些有超凡魅力的人，他们改变了受教育者的人生。"

[2] 当然，有些教师被人们记住，有些新教师刻意效仿自己以前见过的成功教师的风格或授课方式，这些都无可厚非。而根据对参与有关研究项目（本书即是根据这些项目编写的）的师生们的调查，他们中的许多人也没有过分强调个人魅力、热情待人、关心他人、善于鼓舞人心等优秀教师的特质，从而忽视了成功的教师还需要具备的而没有受到广泛关注的其他素质和技巧。我们还认为，当技术型教学模式（当然是在我们所调查的实习教师眼里）占据了中心舞台的时候，那种更凭借直觉、更朴实自然、更强调合作性的教学模式比以往任何时候更应该受到大家的重视。就像哈特里尖锐地指出的那样："在这个被称为'达标'教室的、不靠个人魅力的新兴场所，教师的乐趣何在？……现在，合同取代了信任，教与学的关系又是怎样的呢？"这使我们想到伍斯的及时提醒：教学通常是一种"自我表达且即兴而发，要凭直觉并灵活变通，还要不矫不饰而富于情感"。

[3] 然而，"人格魅力"这个概念理解起来还有诸多问题。其中一个问题前面我已经提过，当要求实习教师回忆什么是他们心目中的优秀教学模式并进行详细说明

时，问题就产生了。如果他们机械地列出诸如幽默感、主持公道、良好的沟通技巧或者是对所教学科怀有感人至深的热情等品质作为答案的话，那一点儿也不奇怪，但上述品质常常表述得很模糊，似有过分强调"人格"，而过分忽视教学技巧之嫌——这对刚刚走上讲台的教师的发展有百害而无一利。当然，他们很少提及（部分原因可能是在校学生还"看不到"这些东西）诸如编写教案、备课、对课堂的掌控技巧以及对学生作业和进步的评估等因素。儒斯迈尼尔等人就此评论道：

通常，我们对自己学生时代的记忆和讲述不是学了什么，而是怎么学和跟哪位老师学的。有许多关于老师的故事，包括我们喜欢的老师、讨厌的老师和惧怕的老师。

[4] 这些故事通常强调教师的个性特征，言外之意好教师是"天生的"而不是"培养的"；他们的品质是与生俱来的，甚至可能是遗传的。

[5] 另一个问题也就随之而来：如果好教师的品质是天生的话，那么，那些意识到自己缺乏个人魅力的师范生还有什么希望获得这些品质，甚至只是了解一下获得这些品质的途径呢？师范生的老师们又将怎样帮助自己的学生实现这个难以达到的目标呢？据达尔顿观察，做一个极具个人魅力的教师的念头，其影响常常是负面的，这给实习教师的课堂教学带来重重困难。实习教师发现，他们无法模仿记忆中那些教学效果极佳的教师，也不能像那些老师那样马上赢得学生们的敬爱。究其原因，我认为这种试图模仿榜样的行为恰恰是基于一种错误的认识，即"魅力"是与生俱来的。然而事实上，虽然教师的"魅力"体现或"发散"于他们自身，但从根本上来说，那所谓的"魅力"是学生赋予教师的。（这就是继心理学分析家杰奎茨·拉坎之后，兹载克等人提出的"让渡的幻觉"，即某人将某种品质归结到某人身上，而看起来，这个品质却像是那个人所固有的。）

注释

1. 本文节选自 Alex Moore 于 2004 年出版的教育学专著 The Good Teacher: Dominant Discourses in Teaching and Teacher Education 的第三章。文章句式繁复，逻辑性强，注意析清文章脉络，构建流畅清晰的汉语译文。
2. 这是一个比较复杂的句子，下面是它的主干结构：
   ...the ideal teacher (whom)...was of one who..., but one who...
   one for whom..., but for whom...within what...
   主语 teacher 带有一个定语从句（whom 省略），表语部分的 one 带有由 who 引导的两个定语从句，冒号后的同位语 one 又带有两个由 whom 引导的定语从句，在最后一个定语从句中又有一个由 what 引导的介词（within）宾语从句。

3. modus operandi：做法；行为方式。即：mode of operation; a way of behaving or doing something that is typical of a person or group。
4. 这又是一个复杂句式，要像对上一个句子那样析清主句和各个从句间的关系，这里不再重复，但有必要指出一点：finding 和下文由 that 引导的直接引语是同位语关系。
5. 定语从句 on which this book is based 如果译为定语，那译文有可能是这样的："根据参与成为本书编写基础的有关研究项目的师生们的表述，……"。显然，汉语中定语太长，读起来拗口，意义也表达不清楚。此处将其译为一句话放在括号中，是翻译定语从句的一种可取的方法。
6. Nor...would many prioritize...to the extent of ignoring or refuting... 相当于：Many would not prioritize...so much that they ignore or refute...
7. 此处的三对形容词不宜机械地直接选取英汉词典中的汉译，而要结合上下文选择最贴切的词语灵活处理。
8. set out on...：开始立业；开始从事工作。即：to start doing or working on something in order to achieve an aim。
9. et al. = and other people；in this connection = in this context。
10. 这里的 difficulty 要和第三自然段的 There are, however, difficulties with the notion of the charismatic subject, ... 联系起来，指"人格魅力"这个概念所带来的问题。
11. 注意分析这个长句的句法，其表达的语义关系为：what hope of acquiring them does the student teacher...have, or what hope of even knowing how to acquire them does the student teacher...have?
12. spectre：something that is seen in the mind and may happen in the future, especially when it may cause fear.

 讲解

对原文句子结构的分析

运用基础英语学习阶段所学到的语法知识对原文句子结构进行语法分析是原文理解过程的重要组成部分。一般来讲，由于外语学习比母语习得更依赖于语法体系，所以在译者头脑中，外语语法呈显性（explicit）而母语语法是隐性的（implicit）。这就使语法在原文理解过程中显得尤为重要了。但我们不是说译者要对每个句子都刻意进行一番语法分析，语法分析在大多数情况下都是在下意识中进行的，但遇到长句或较特殊、较复杂的结构时译者就要有意识地仔细分析了。本单元原文是论说文体，句法结构较复杂，比如注释 2、4、6、11 所涉及的句子。囿

囵吞枣势必造成莫名其妙的大错。翻译实践中，由于结构分析失误造成的误译并不少见。请看下面两例：

1. Near Kitty Hawk. North Carolina, in 1903, the Wright brothers managed to urge their motorized kite some 120 feet into a gust off the sea that might have elevated a barn door.

  1903年，在美国北卡罗来纳州基蒂霍克市附近，莱特兄弟借着海滨一阵强风，成功地使他们的机械动力飞机飞行了约120英尺，飞行高度也就是高过一扇谷仓门。

  句中划线的定语从句修饰的是gust，所以正确的翻译应该是：莱特兄弟迎着能把一扇谷仓门掀起来的强劲海风，驾着他们的机械大风筝飞行了120英尺。

2. When a complicated word processor attempts to double as a desktop publishing program or a kitchen appliance comes with half a dozen attachments, the product is bound to be unwieldy and burdensome.

  如果一台复杂的文字处理机想具有台式出版程序系统两倍的功能，或一台厨房用具配有五六种附件，那么这种产品就必然笨重累赘。

  译文或是忽略了介词as，或是误解了double as 的意义。正确的译文应当是：如果一台复杂的文字处理机想兼有桌面出版程序系统的功能。

  下面分几类情况举例说明。

  一般来说，谓语的识别是不会出错的。但在有修饰成分干扰的情况下，也要防止谓语识别上的错误。请分析下面译例：

3. He held it (her hand) but an instant, and in his fear of being too demonstrative, swerved to the opposite extreme, touching her fingers with the lightness of a small-hearted person.

  他握住了那手，然而只那么一瞬间，由于担心自己的感情过于外露，使事情突然走向另一个极端，因此，这个小心翼翼的人只是轻轻地碰了一下她的手指。

  译者未能认清 swerved 是与 held 并列的谓语，有关部分可改译为：……便完全改变了做法，只是小心翼翼地碰了碰她的手指。

4. The brain needs its antioxidants—powerful chemicals that disarm free radicals, the harmful molecules created when the body coverts food into energy and breaks down toxic substances.

  大脑需要抗氧化剂——一些强有力的、能够消除自由基伤害力和分解有毒的化学物质，自由基是身体在将食物转化为能量时所产生的有害分子。

上述译文将 breaks down toxic substances 看成是 chemicals 的谓语,而正确的分析是 when 引导的从句中主语 body 有两个谓语——coverts 和 breaks down。本句可改译为:大脑需要抗氧化剂——就是一些强有力的、能够消除自由基的化学物质。自由基是身体在将食物转化为能量和分解有毒物质时所产生的有害分子。

一般情况下,动词或非限定性动词与其宾语的关系也无需刻意分析,系表结构也一目了然,但有时在动、宾或系、表之间插入了其他较长的成分,就要特别留意了。如:

5. Their voices had been to him (William), lying there on the carpet with his head wrapped in his arms, indistinguishable.

注意句中的系表结构为:had been indistinguishable to him. 可译为:威廉趴在地毯上,两臂抱头,听不清他们在说什么。

6. One should, therefore, be extremely cautious about projecting onto the conception of the "modern" popular and casually arrived at notions that have not been systematically tested empirically.

注意析清下列动宾搭配关系:…projecting…popular and casually arrived at notions onto the conception of the "modern". 全句可译为:因此,我们必须十分谨慎,不要把虽然流行但却未经系统实证而随便得出的观点加在"现代性"这一概念上。

7. Any species capable of producing, at this earliest, juvenile stage of its development—almost instantly after emerging on the earth by any evolutionary standard—the music of Johann Sebastian Bach, cannot be all bad.

注意 producing…the music of Johann Sebastian Bach 这一动宾结构,全句可译为:任何一个物种,在其进化的初始阶段(依任何进化标准看,都几乎是刚刚在地球上出现)就能产生出像巴赫这样的音乐作品,就不能说是糟得一塌糊涂的。

句中的定语、状语、同位语等修饰成分也必须分析清楚,否则也极易造成翻译失当或失误。请分析下面几个译例:

8. But owing to the constant presence of air currents, arranging both the dust and vapour in strata of varying extent and density, and of high and low clouds which both absorb and reflect the light in varying degrees, we see produced all those wondrous combinations of tints and those gorgeous ever-changing colours.

不过，由于不断出现气流，把尘埃与水汽分层排列，广度不均，密度各异，加上高低空常有云层，不同程度地吸收并反射阳光，我们这才看到各种奇异的色调斑驳陆离，诸多绚丽的色彩变化万千。

须特别注意分析 and of high and low clouds... 在上文的语法关系：它与 of air currents... 并列，均为 the constant presence 的定语；而并非与 of varying extent and density... 并列，做 strata 的定语。下面的译文就未能认清这种关系：

由于大气中时时存在着气流，使尘埃与水蒸气形成范围与密度不等的空气层，形成不同程度地吸收并反射阳光的高空或低空的云层……

另外，主句中 see produced sth. 应为 see sth. produced 之倒置语序，也应识别出来。

9. [Why is this enormous increase in population taking place?] It is really due to the spread of the knowledge and the practice of what is coming to be called Death Control. [You have heard of Birth Control? Death Control is something rather different...]

中间一句的译文是：其原因确实在于知识的普及及那种将被称作"死亡控制"的实践活动。

为提供上下文，本句前后各引用了几个句子。很明显，of what is coming to be called Death Control 作为定语，既修饰 the practice，也修饰 the knowledge，因此可改译为：其原因确实在于被称作"死亡控制"的有关知识的普及及有关实践的开展。

10. And most men manage to protect themselves from injury so far as is needed to keep both ears. Whereas trees cannot protect themselves from the loss of branches.

大多数人都设法保护自己免受伤害，甚至力求保护两耳完好无损。然而树木却不能保护自己不掉树枝。

这句话把树枝和人的耳朵加以比较：人能保护耳朵，而树却不能保护自己的枝叶。上述译文说人们"甚至力求保护两耳完好无损"，似乎"保护耳朵"成了一种非分之想。译者显然把状语 so far as is needed to keep both ears 理解错了。这句话可直译为：在保证两只耳朵不受伤害方面，大部分人都是能做到的。可改译为：保护耳朵不受伤害是大部分人都能做到的，而树木却无法保护自己的枝杈。

11. It is more difficult to deal with the self-esteem of man as man, because

we cannot argue out the matter with some non-human mind.

　　而作为人类的人的自尊心就更难对付了，因为我们不能用某种非人类的意识去辩论这一点，以求得结论。

　　原文中的 as man 作状语修饰 deal with。另外，argue out 也不是"辩论"，而是"说清楚"，故可改译为：作为人，要讨论人类的自大心理就更加困难了，因为我们不具有某种非人类的头脑，无法把这个问题讲清楚。

12. There is a vulgar notion that Hardy's novels show man as puppet in a world dominated by Fate, a gross exaggeration; but they do show, in poignant detail, the impact of creeping industrialization and concomitant social change on traditional agrarian communities and their way of life.

　　有一种庸俗的看法认为，哈代的小说把人描绘为被命运主宰的世界的傀儡，是一种夸张；但这些小说的确以深刻细腻的笔触显示日益发展的工业化的影响和传统农业社会中随之而来的社会变革及其生活方式。

　　译文将 their way of life 与 concomitant social change on traditional agrarian communities 看作并列结构，造成译文错误。应认清句中词语的正确搭配关系，即：the impact of A and B on C and D。译文可改为：……但这些小说的确以深刻细腻的笔触描写了潜移默化的工业化和随之而来的社会变革对传统农业社会及其生活方式所造成的影响。

13. Finding a common set of positions that will accommodate so many viewpoints is not an easy task, and much of their work is being coordinated on EcoNet.

　　鉴于不易找到公共场合来容纳如此众多的观点，他们就使用生态网进行大量工作。

　　此译将 finding 误认为状语，译文大错。可改为：寻求能满足如此众多观点的共同立场可不是一件容易事，因此大部分工作都是在生态网上进行的。

14. The world's fastest class of computers, supercomputers are used by scientists and engineers to perform tasks requiring huge numbers of calculation...such tasks as designing airplane wings, forecasting the weather and building nuclear weapons.

　　科学家与工程师使用这类世界上运算速度最快的计算机——超级计算机来完成任务，需要大量计算的工作，例如机翼设计、天气预报和核武器制造等任务。

译文未能正确表达 requiring... 分词短语作定语修饰 tasks 这一语法关系。可改译为：科学家与工程师使用这类世界上运算速度最快的计算机——超级计算机，来完成需要进行大量计算的工作……

15. The first two aluminizing processes are used on mild and low-alloy steels. They increase the resistance to hot oxidation and give some protection against corrosion. This can give them a useful life at 600°C–800°C for considerable periods, provided the conditions are freely oxidizing... The third process is generally applied to nickel alloys to increase the hot-corrosion resistance where free oxidizing conditions do not exist or where there is a sulphur-bearing atmosphere.

最后一句的译文是：第三种处理法常用于镍合金以提高其抗热腐蚀性，处理时没有自由氧化条件或者有含硫的空气。

据此汉译文推断，译者是把状语从句（where...）当作谓语动词（is applied）的修饰语来理解的。这两个状语从句是否可能修饰不定式 to increase 呢？要判断这里的修饰关系，单看这个句子本身还不够。所以，上面原文引用了与此句相关的处于同一个自然段的几个句子，以便从语篇的角度分析句中状语从句的所属关系。由于有了较充分的上下文，问题就一目了然了。这一段谈论的是三种渗铝处理法（aluminizing process），前两种方法可使被处理部件在自由氧化条件下，在 600°C~800°C 高温中延长使用寿命。而"第三种处理法常用于镍合金，以提高其在没有自由氧化条件或在含硫空气中的抗热腐蚀性"。也就是说，状语从句应从属于不定式 to increase。

16. The creations of a small coterie of malicious hackers who invent toxic software for the sheer deviltry of it, viruses are short strings of software code that have three properties:...

计算机病毒系一小撮存心不良的黑客所为，这些人纯属为了搞恶作剧而编造有毒软件。病毒是短行的软件代码，具有以下三个特征：……

这句话的前半部分很长，却只是 viruses 的同位语。上述译文在析清结构的前提下，采用了拆译的方法，将同位语部分译为一个句子。

某些特殊的句式，如倒装、强调句等，也要仔细辨清，以免造成误译，如：

17. Less visible, but probably more important, are the thousands of ways industry has put electric energy to work.

45

然而可见的却不多，更重要的是工业领域已广泛地用电能做功。

此译似乎没注意到，less visible 和 more important 同是被倒装了的表语，可改译为：不大为人所知，但或许更为重要的，是工业中运用电能的种种途径。

18. That the big, sober carpenter loved Hetty Arthur had no idea.
    至于这个严肃的大个子木匠爱着海蒂，阿瑟却一点儿也没想到。

19. Yet what it was that she must cover up she never knew.
    但是要遮掩什么，她压根儿就不知道。

20. It was with difficulty that I could bring myself to admit the identity of the wan being before me with the companion of my boyhood.
    我好不容易才使自己相信，面前这位面色苍白的人和我童年时代的伙伴确系一人。

    本句中还须特别注意 the identity of...with... 这一搭配。

21. It was the manner in which all this, and much more, was said—it was the apparent heart that went with his request—which allowed me no room for hesitation.
    是他讲这些话——还有另外好多话——时的态度，还有他提出这些要求时那显而易见的一片诚心，使我毫不犹豫的余地。

22. Never a night passed when we were both in London that we did not telephone, no matter how late.
    我们俩在伦敦的时候，不论时间多晚，每晚必通电话。

    如：

23. And if the rhetoric of his (Rudy Giuliani) introduction to the *Life* volume is not Churchillian, his leadership during the darkest hours, as captured in many images throughout these books, certainly was.
    如果说他为《生活》画册所作序言的修辞缺乏丘吉尔的文学才华的话，那他在纽约最黑暗时刻所显示的领导才能，正如这些画册中的许多画面上所捕捉到的那样，无疑再现了丘吉尔般的将帅才华。

    对于原文中省略的成分也必须认清，以保证译文表达清楚明确。注意原文最后的省略现象：...certainly was (Churchillian)。

24. Watching what you eat might help avoid a heart attack, even cancer. But keep you quick-minded? Amazingly, research shows that the very processes that clog your heart's arteries and cause cancerous changes in your cells also damage the delicate communication network in your brain. All of a sudden, there is new meaning to the "eating wisely".

注意你吃的东西可能有助你避免心脏病发作，甚至癌症。

但是，要保持你才思敏捷吗？令人吃惊的是，研究显示，正是堵塞你的心脏动脉和在你细胞中引起癌症变化的这些过程，同时也损坏你大脑中精密的通信网络。突然间，"明智地吃东西"这句话又有了新意。

划线部分应理解为：But, (might watching what you eat) keep you quick-minded? 译文对省略部分应有所补充：但食物也能帮你保持头脑灵活吗？

25. He was about to give a student a zero for his answer to a physics question, while the student claimed he should receive a perfect score and would if the system were not set up against the student.

他正要给一个学生的物理题打零分，而那学生却说他应该得满分，而且考试不能与学生为敌。

显然，译者没有析清原文中的省略成分：...and would (receive a perfect score) if the system were not set against the student. 故译文划线部分应改为：还说假使考试不与学生为敌的话，他是能得满分的。

26. This subject—the death of the city of New York—continues to be disinterred by those of us who should know better.

这个话题——纽约城的衰亡——还在被我们这些对纽约比较熟悉的人们谈论着。

原句结尾处省略部分补充完整应为：who should know better than to disinter it。可改译为：……仍在被我们这些人谈论着，而我们本不应再这么做了。

27. "There are sharks sleeping at the bottom," said the guide, flashing an impish grin. "Let's wake them up." In a riot of scuba bubbles, tourist and guide plunged 110 feet into an underwater cavern. And, true to his words, the guide darted through the gloom, chasing sleek five-foot-long shadows. Not to worry. In the spectacular undersea world off Palau, the sharks are as laid back as the local residents. And who wouldn't be? Slung across the Pacific 800 miles southwest of Guam, the string of islands—eight inhabited,

200 or more still unpopulated—make up one of those increasingly rare commodities, a Pacific paradise.

"水下的鲨鱼正在睡觉呢，"导游做了个鬼脸笑着说，"让我们去把它们叫醒。"随着潜水呼吸器咕噜咕噜的水泡声，旅游者和导游潜入了水下一百一十英尺深的一个洞口。导游的话不假，他飞快地穿过阴暗的水层，去追逐那光滑的有五英尺长的一个个黑影。不用担心，在帕劳区水下世界的壮丽景观中，鲨鱼犹如当地居民一样自由自在，但谁不担心呢？遍布在关岛西南八百英里海域的一系列岛屿——八百个有人居住，两百或更多的岛屿仍荒无人烟——构成了一片越来越珍贵的宝地，一个位于太平洋中的乐园。

原文划线部分究竟省略了什么？据上述译文推测，译者认为完整的句子应该是：And who wouldn't be worried? 然而，语法分析告诉我们，省略的只能是 laid back。另外，从整段的上下文看，译成"谁不担心呢"也使译文失去了逻辑上的连贯。有关部分可改译为：……在帕劳区水下世界的壮丽景观中，鲨鱼犹如当地居民一样悠哉悠哉，又有谁不会如此（悠哉悠哉）呢……

28. Well, that's what some in the literary establishment believe. They also say he (Tolkien) drew the maps in his books to compensate for his lack of literary skills. But as with *Harry Potter* author J. K. Rowling and popular children's English writer Enid Blyton—much to the annoyance of the literary crowd which found these authors' works trivial and lacking in craft—it didn't prevent Tolkien from being successful. But why?

这就是文学界的一些人的看法。他们还说，他在书上画地图是用来弥补其文学技巧上的贫乏。与此相仿，文学圈里的人对于《哈利·波特》的作者J·K·罗琳和著名的英语儿童文学作家伊妮德·布莱顿的作品也是颇有微词——认为这些作家的作品均为平凡之作且缺乏文学技巧——既然如此，托尔金又是怎样走上成功之路的呢？

最后的问句省略了什么？完整的问句应该是：But why (didn't it prevent Tolkien from being successful)？可直译为：但它为什么未能阻止托尔金取得成功呢？结合上下文，可改译为：……但正像被文学界斥为平庸无味、缺乏技巧的《哈利·波特》的作者J·K·罗琳和著名英语儿童文学作家伊妮德·布莱顿一样，这些指责并未阻止他取得成功。这又是为什么呢？

The Whipping Boy[1]

[1] Should anyone much care whether an American boy living overseas gets six vicious thwacks on his backside?[2] So much has been argued, rejoined and rehashed about the case of Michael Fay, an 18-year-old convicted of vandalism and sentenced to a caning in Singapore, that an otherwise sorry little episode has shaded into a certified International Incident, complete with intercessions by the U.S. head of state. An affair that sometimes sounds—on the editorial pages—equivalent to the abduction of Helen of Troy has outraged American libertarians even as it has animated a general debate about morality East and West and the proper functioning of U.S. law and order[3]. The Trojan war this is not: The wooden horse is in America's citadel.[4]

[2] Which, to all appearances, is what Singapore wanted. The question of whether anyone should care about Michael Fay is idle: Though Singapore officials profess shock at the attention his case has drawn, they know Americans care deeply about the many sides of this issue. Does a teenager convicted of spraying cars with easily removed paint deserve half a dozen powerful strokes on the buttocks with a sopping-wet bamboo staff? At what point does swift, sure punishment become torture? By what moral authority can America, with its high rates of lawlessness and license, preach to a safe society about human rights? Isn't the shipshape and affluent little city-state molded by Lee Kuan Yew a model of civic virtues?

[3] Not quite the game of Twenty Questions[5], but close enough. The caning sentence has fascinated many Americans who had never heard of Singapore and perhaps could not tell Southeast Asia from Sweden on a map. It has concentrated minds wondrously on an already lively domestic debate over what constitutes a due balance between individual and majority rights. Too bad Michael Fay has become a fulcrum for this discussion. Not only does he seem destined to be pummeled and immobilized by an instrument of ordeal, but the use of Singapore as a standard for judging any other society, let alone the cacophonous U.S. is fairly worthless.

[4]　To begin with, Singapore is an offshore republic that tightly limits immigration. Imagine crime-ridden Los Angeles, to which Singapore is sometimes contrasted, with hardly any inflow of the hard-luck, often desperate fortune seekers who flock to big cities. Imagine in the same way Jakarta or Shanghai. Beyond that, Singapore began its life as a British colony designed to serve as a shipping, administrative and financial center[6]. Today it is a highly skilled society without the urban sprawl and rural poverty that afflict larger nations. An analogue might be Manhattan incorporated as a republic between the Battery and 96th Street, with its own flag, armed forces and immigration controls.

[5]　Even without its government's disciplinary measures, Singapore more than plausibly would be much the same as it is now. An academic commonplace today is that the major factor determining social peace and prosperity is culture—a sense of common identity, tradition and values. The house that Lee built is 76% ethnic Chinese, a people with one of the most self-disciplined cultures in the world. Prizing family, learning and hard work, overseas Chinese have prospered wherever they have settled.

[6]　And America's?[7] Don't ask. Unlike Singapore, though, the U.S. today is a nation in search of a common culture, trying to be a universal society that assimilates the traditions of people from all over the world. Efforts to safeguard minority as well as individual rights have produced, as Lee charges, a gridlock in the justice system. America is not the pandemonium portrayed in the shock-addicted mass media. But its troubles stem more from the decay of family life than any government failures. Few societies can afford to look on complacently. As travel eases and cultures intermix, the American experience is becoming the world's.

[7]　Singaporeans have every right to be proud of their achievements. Does that mean Michael Fay must be caned? A letter writer to the *New York Times* advised that "six of the best", as he suffered at an English public (that is, private) school, might cure all that ails American youth. Comparing Fay's sentence to a headmaster's paddling is fatuous—but then, as John Updike once noted, old boys of Eton and Harrow can often "mistake a sports car for a woman or a birch rod for a mother's kiss".[8] The pain from flaying with wet rattan, as it is done in Singapore, can knock a prisoner out cold.

[8]　The circumstances of this affair—evidently no Singaporean has ever been punished under the Vandalism Act for defacing private property—suggest that Singapore has used Fay as an unwilling point man in a growing quarrel between East and West about human rights. Several large Asian countries, China among them, argue that the U.S. has no business criticizing their own, equally legitimate values. But Japan stresses majority rights too. So does Hong Kong. Neither is watering its economic miracle with the blood from a bamboo cane.

参考译文

替 罪 羊

[1]　一个生活在海外的美国青年，屁股上要恶狠狠地挨六鞭，人们应该对此大为关注吗？十八岁的迈克尔·费伊在新加坡犯了破坏公物罪，被判笞刑。人们对此案争来吵去，无休无止，使本来一个不幸的小插曲演变成一桩名副其实的国际事件，最后以美国总统出面调解而告终。报刊社论有时把这个事件说得如同海伦被劫到特洛伊城一样，美国的自由之士亦极为震怒，甚至引起了一场关于东西方道德及美国法律与秩序的适当功能的大辩论。不过现在发生的可不是当年的特洛伊木马之战，因为木马在美国的城堡中。

[2]　从种种迹象来看，这正是新加坡想要达到的目的。人们是否应该关注迈克尔·费伊这个问题是没有意义的。尽管新加坡官员声称，此案引起如此广泛的关注，他们感到十分震惊，但他们明白，美国人所深深关注的是这一事件所引发的诸多方面的思考：一个十几岁的少年把一种易擦洗的涂料喷到别人的汽车上，是否就该用沾湿的竹鞭在他屁股上狠狠抽上六下？迅速有效的惩罚做到何种程度就会演变为折磨？无法无天、自由无度的美国，在道德上有什么资格就人权问题对一个井然有序的社会说三道四？这个李光耀一手缔造的干净整洁、富足殷实的城市国家难道不是文明和公民道德的楷模吗？

[3]　这并非要和大家做二十问那样的游戏，不过确实也很难回答。笞刑引起了许多美国人的关注，而这些人可能从未听说过新加坡这个国家，甚至在地图上连东南亚和瑞典都分不清。个人权利和大多数人的权利如何平衡，这是美国国内一直激烈争论的问题。现在，费伊的笞刑又一次不可思议地使人们关注起这个问题。可怜的费伊成了当前这场争论的焦点。一方面，他要被施以重刑，卧床数日；另一方面，把

新加坡作为判断任何其他社会——尤其是观念纷杂的美国社会——的标准，也是毫无价值的。

[4] 首先，新加坡是一个岛国，严格限制移民。只需想象一下，如果罪犯充斥的洛杉矶（人们有时把它和新加坡相比照）没有了那些涌进大城市的命运潦倒、求财心切的亡命徒，会变得怎么样？雅加达或上海，如果没有了那些涌入城市的财迷心窍的人，是不是也会平静得多？另外，新加坡起初只是一块英国殖民地，要建成造船管理和金融中心。如今，它已是一个技术发达的国度，而且没有困扰大国的城市无限蔓延、农村贫困化的种种问题。可以把新加坡比作纽约曼哈顿自巴特利公园至九十六街的一片地区。它自成一统，自立共和，挂自己的国旗，有自己的军队，也有自己的移民政策。

[5] 即使没有政府的严格管治，新加坡也完全可能和现在差不多。现在学术界的一般看法是，决定社会安宁和繁荣的主要是文化因素—— 一种对身份、传统和价值的共识。李光耀建立的这个国家，居民有百分之七十六是华裔，而华人文化是世界上最强调严于律己的文化之一。海外华人重视家庭、学识和勤奋，走到哪里都兴旺发达。

[6] 那么美国的犯罪率如何呢？不须问，与新加坡不同，美国正在寻求一种共同文化，力图同化来自世界各地的各种不同文化传统，建立一个兼收并蓄的社会。正如李光耀所批评的，对个人和少数人权利的保护导致了法律体系中的弊病。美国社会并非如耸人听闻的大众媒介所描述的那样，乌七八糟、鬼魅横行。它的问题的症结在于家庭生活的败落，而不是政府管理不力。对这种情况，几乎没有哪个社会能得意扬扬地冷眼旁观。旅游的便利，文化的交流，都使美国的经历正在变成全球的体验。

[7] 新加坡完全有资格为自己的成就感到自豪。但是，这难道就意味着费伊必须遭受鞭笞之苦吗？纽约《时代周刊》收到的一封读者来信说道，这"绝妙的六鞭子"——正如他在一所英国公立（应该是私立）学校所尝过的那样——可以治愈美国青年的一切顽疾。把费伊的笞刑和英国校长的体罚相提并论是荒唐的，但正如约翰·厄普代克曾经说过的，伊顿和哈罗公学的毕业生常常"把跑车当成女人，把木棍当成母亲的吻"。像新加坡这样的沾水竹条的抽打，是足以把犯人疼昏过去的。

[8] 显然，还没有哪个新加坡人因为弄脏别人的物品受《破坏公物惩治法》之苦，

遭受什么惩罚。费伊事件说明，新加坡在东西方关于人权的日趋激烈的争论中，有意把费伊当成了一个焦点人物，尽管这个美国小伙子并不甘心情愿。包括中国在内的几个亚洲大国都说美国无权批评它们同样合法的价值观。日本同样强调大多数人的权利，但它却没用竹鞭下的鲜血去浇灌自己的经济繁荣之花。

注释

1. the whipping boy: [historical] a boy brought up together with a young prince and required to take the punishment for the latter's misdeeds. (*Webster's New World College Dictionary*, Fourth Edition) 这是发表在 1994 年 4 月 25 日 *Time* 上的一篇署名文章。评论的是由一次不大不小的毁坏他人财物的事件所引发的美国和新加坡之间的政治争端。翻译此文应对那次事件的有关情况有所了解。可查阅那一时期的报刊资料。这次事件导致的两国间的外交战从一个侧面生动地反映了东西文化价值观念上的冲突。
2. 这个长问句如何翻译为好？第 2 段也有几个问句，不过要好译一些。可参阅第五章 Unit Three 注释 7。
3. 以上两句，结构比较复杂，须仔细分析，认清基本信息单位，然后依照汉语行文逻辑关系的需要，重新组织原文的信息。
4. 要了解 Helen of Troy、the Trojan war 等有关文化背景知识，可查阅一下有关资料。the Trojan war 是希腊神话中希腊人与特洛伊（Troy）人之间长达 10 年之久的战争。起因是特洛伊王子 Paris 诱走了 Menelaus 国王的妻子 Helen。希腊人为夺回 Helen 便远征特洛伊，但该城久攻不下，于是便造一木马，内藏精兵，佯装溃败，将马弃于城外。特洛伊人误将此马作为战利品拖入城内，于是中计。文中说报界有人将 Fay 比作被劫的 Helen of Troy，但本文作者认为，这并非木马之战，因为不是美国声讨新加坡，而是新加坡将了美国一军，向美国价值观发起了挑战。
5. the game of Twenty Questions 之意不可妄自臆断，可查阅有关资料或找一位美（英）国人问一问。这是美国的一种传统的室内游戏（parlor game），游戏者争相回答有关历史人物、体育事件、娱乐等方面的问题，看谁能最先答完。这里的含义是：普通美国人要想了解在文化传统上与美国相去甚远的新加坡的价值观是很难的。
6. 以上两个以 imagine 打头的句子如何译出？怎样才能使语气更为连贯？
7. 注意省略成分的分析及翻译。
8. 未查到此引语的出处，sports car、birch rod 与 woman、mother's kiss 风马牛不相及，此处讥讽将鞭刑作为一种文明社会的法律，逻辑混乱、荒唐可笑。20 世纪 50 年代的美国，sports car 是富裕的中产阶级的象征，人们常用描写女性的字眼（如 shapely、curvy extension，甚至 voluptuous）描写汽车。

讲解

理解中的文化因素

参阅本单元注解 1、4、5、8 我们可以清楚地看到，对一篇文章的理解不仅仅是一个语言解码的问题，它更是对一种文化的解读（第三章 Unit Three 的讲解部分有关文化语境的讲解和译例也涉及同样的问题）。一个合格的译者不仅要有语言能力，还要具有对相关文化的深刻了解，并具有一定的理解能力和表达能力。

文化是一个十分宽泛的概念，一般认为包括社会系统、思想意识系统、技术-经济系统和语言系统（social system, ideational system, techno-economic system, linguistic system）四大部分。社会系统包括社会制度、行政体制、教育体制、历史、风俗等方面；思想意识系统包括宗教、哲学、信仰、价值观等方面；技术-经济系统包括科学技术和经济诸领域的理论、运行模式等；语言系统则指语音、文字、语法、词汇、修辞规范等方面。语言是文化的重要组成部分，与其他三个系统共同构成一个民族的文化，但它与其他三个系统又有着明显的区别，那就是，其他三个系统在很大程度上要借助语言才能表达和存在。语言既是文化的载体，也是文化的组成部分；语言反映文化的演变，又受到文化因素的制约。语言和文化相辅相成，互为依存，不可有须臾的分割。Susan Bassnett 的一个比喻非常贴切：Language, then, is the heart within the body of culture, and it is the interaction between the two that results in the continuation of life-energy. In the same way that the surgeon, operating on the heart, cannot neglect the body that surrounds it, so the translator treats the text in isolation from the culture at his peril.（因此，文化是身体，语言就是心脏，而正是这两者的互动才产生了连续不断的生命能量。医生给心脏动手术不能无视整个身体，同样，译者把语篇和文化割裂开来也是在铤而走险。）

因此，学习语言必须同时关注与这种语言相关联的文化，一个好的译者不仅仅要具有跨语言的交际能力，还必须具备跨文化的交际能力。翻译实践中，要时时将对源语语篇的理解放在源语文化的大背景上进行，平时多多积累，译时勤问（尤其应向以源语为母语的人士请教）、勤查（手边应备有百科全书等资料）。下面这个句子出自 2000 年第 12 届韩素音青年翻译奖竞赛的英译汉原文和译文（见《中国翻译》2000/1、6）：

About midday on June 30, while Manara was dying in the hospital, Garibaldi was galloping across the Tiber to the Capitol, whither the Assembly of the Roman

Republic had summoned him to attend its fateful session. （6月30日，大约中午时分，马纳拉在医院里生命垂危的时候，加里波第正策马越过台伯河，朝卡匹托尔奔去。他奉罗马共和国议会之召，去那里参加决定共和国命运的会议。）

该次竞赛的评审者在评析文章中指出，文章的难度来自两个方面：一是语言陷阱；二是有些细节的背景资料不好查找。为了析清 the Capitol 的所指，评审者参阅了包括 Academic American Encyclopedia、Encyclopedia Americana、Encyclopedia Britannica 在内的多达15种参考书，最后才排除了"朱庇特神殿""卡匹托尔山"等不当译名，定为"卡匹托尔"，并加译注说明此系"卡匹托尔山上接近山顶处的卡匹托尔广场及广场周围建筑物的总称"。由此我们可清楚地看到，译者与作者的语言沟通在很大程度上其实是文化沟通。下面这些译例进一步说明文化因素在语言理解中的重要性。

1. "It's easy to pass laws that are tough on sex offenders. It makes big political points," he says, "but we are really starting to see some Draconian measures being taken."

他说："通过一些对性犯罪比较强硬的法令是容易的，在政治上也很必要。但我们真正看到的却是一些过分严厉的法规正在被加以实施。"

Draconian 一词源于 Draco，是古雅典的立法者，他编制的雅典第一部成文法以严酷著称。

2. John F. Kennedy Jr.'s father was John F. Kennedy, the American President who has had the most impact on the psyche of America in the late 20th century. That impact was due not only to the "Camelot" mythology which an optimistic administration under Kennedy put in place in the 1960's, at the heart of the Cold War, but because of the dark-hued tragic stamp put on his short reign by his assassination in 1963.

小约翰·F·肯尼迪的父亲就是在20世纪后期对美国人的心灵影响最大的美国总统约翰·F·肯尼迪。肯尼迪总统之所以会有如此巨大的影响，不仅是因为他领导下的一个乐观的政府在20世纪60年代"冷战"关键阶段适时地推出"肯尼迪盛世"的神话，而且是由于他1963年遇刺身亡而打在他短暂执政时期上的暗色调悲剧印记。

Camelot（卡米洛）原指传说中英国亚瑟王宫廷所在地。此处背景为20世纪60年代，美国报刊用以指肯尼迪总统当政时期，亦指任何充满激情、理想和文化高度发展的时期。Cold War 首字母大写专指第二次世界大战后为争夺世界霸权的美苏"冷战"时期。

3. Sundials have long been beautifully crafted but now some innovative Western sculptors are creating dramatic new variations on the theme, such as a vertical or wall dial for a modern courtyard setting. Bold colourful sun designs or simple minimalist wall plaques are available, and there is even a water fountain dial where the water jet replaces the gnomon (finger) as marker of time.

　　日晷长期以来一直是造型漂亮的一道工艺；而今，锐意创新的西方雕刻家又在这一主题上独辟蹊径，创造了风格、造型奇异多姿的日晷，诸如用于现代庭院环境的立式或壁式日晷。有明快多彩的太阳图案设计或微型简易的壁匾日晷；甚至还有喷泉式日晷，用喷出的水柱代替晷针来标记时间。

　　minimalism 是美术术语，一般译为"最简单派艺术"或"极简抽象派艺术"。该派艺术家主张用极少的色彩、极少的形象，简化画面，去除干扰主体的不必要的东西。译文划线部分可改为：有明快多彩的太阳图案设计或极简抽象派风格的壁匾日晷。

4. In New York, the Spice Girls went on David Letterman's *Late Show* on TV to publicize their debut album which went to No.1 in America—outperforming the performance of the Beatles in the 1960s.

　　在纽约，辣妹们上大卫·莱特曼主持的电视节目《最新秀》为自己的首张专辑做宣传。该唱片在美国居销量榜首——超过了20世纪60年代的甲壳虫乐队。

　　Late Show 是美国著名节目主持人 David Letterman 主持的每天23:00电视新闻结束后播出的午夜节目，应改译为《午夜秀》。

5. The music that accompanies the famous author's entrance is a calculated touch among this so civilized group of 50-odd fans gathered for afternoon tea of club sandwiches, little cakes and a large injection of literary class.

　　陪伴这位著名作家进入大厅的音乐是经过精心安排的，这里已聚集了50多位彬彬有礼的热心读者，将和他共享由俱乐部特制的三明治、小甜点和浓厚的文学气息组成的下午茶。

　　club sandwiches 是三明治的一种，由三片或更多片面包夹着鸡肉、火腿、熏肉、生菜、番茄、蛋黄酱等。常译为"总会三明治"（而不是"由俱乐部特制的三明治"），如需要可加译注。

6. There are as many kinds of essays as there are human attitudes or poses, as many essay flavors as there are Howard Johnson ice creams.

散文种类之多,犹如人的姿态,而散文风格韵味之多则犹如霍华德·约翰逊食品店的冰淇淋。

Howard Johnson 是美国一家旅馆、餐饮连锁店,以冰淇淋品种繁多著称。

7. But the more we standardize wages, hours and prices, the more we insist upon social security for everybody, the more we compel two and two to make four everywhere, the more people will take to the greyhound tracks and the football pools. For it is when two and two miraculously make five that the heart leaps up at last. It is when money looks like manna that we truly delight in it.

然而我们越使工资、工时和价格标准化,越要为人人谋求社会保障;越要处处强制实行二加二等于四,那么人们就越发沉迷于跑狗场和足球赌博。因为,只有当二加二奇迹般地等于五时,才能使人欣喜若狂。只有当钱像上帝赐予的神粮一样,我们才会体味到其中的乐趣。

the greyhound tracks 和 the football pools 是两种赌博形式,前者指赛狗,后者指赌足球赛的输赢;manna 出自《圣经》,指古以色列人经过荒原时得到的天赐的食物。

8. All this was cut off by the fatal shears of that abstract word *Fascism*, and the little old lady next door was the Atropos who cut the thread of my actual life this afternoon.

所有这种联系都被那个抽象的名词"法西斯主义"像一把无情的剪刀一样给剪断了。而隔壁的瘦老太就像希腊神话中的女神阿特罗波斯一样,把我整个下午的真实生命之线割断了。

此句摘自 D. H. Lawrence 的名篇 *Insouciance*。句中 all 指上文所描述的作者与眼前的现实景物之间的联系。当时作者在旅馆的阳台上欣赏山坡上的景色,而隔壁的住客却大谈政治,他因此有感而发。Atropos 是希腊神话中命运三女神之一:Clotho 编织生命之线;Lachesis 量其长度;而 Atropos 则割断之。

9. It is easy to take this subculture, this minority group, the teenagers, and read our characters and future in them as though they were tea leaves.

把青少年这个亚文化群,这个少数派,看成是一些能预卜未来的因素,并很容易在他们身上看到我们的性格和未来。

tea leaves 指杯中的茶叶渣,据说通过观察茶叶渣的分布可预测未来。

10. The first point about chores is that they are repetitive. They come every day or whereabouts, and once done they require after a certain time to be done again. In this regard a chore is the very opposite of a "happening"—that strange sort of event which a few years back was so much in fashion. For a happening was in essence unrepeatable; it came about in ways no one could predict, taking form from vaporous imaginings or sudden impulse. Chores, by contrast, can be foreseen in advance; for better or worse, I know that tomorrow I must be reenacting the same small round of ritualistic deeds; and they arise, moreover, from practical necessities, not from poetic flights.

家务事的第一个特点是反反复复。几乎天天都有,做完之后,过一定时间又要重做一遍。在这个意义上,家务事与几年前盛行的"即兴剧"里的表演可正好相反。"即兴剧"里表演的事儿根本就不会再重复,事先谁也不知要演什么,全凭想象或心血来潮。与之相反,家务事是可预见的,不论喜不喜欢,我知道明天肯定还要干这同样的烦琐的例行公事。另外,家务事来自实际需要,而不是一时兴起。

此段中的 happening 系指美国曾十分流行的一种戏剧表演形式,常是即兴的,观众亦可参与,表演的动作荒唐、可笑,之间也并无联系。此处以这种戏剧形式的偶发和不可预知性与家务活儿进行对比,形成强烈反差。

Republicans and Democrats (Excerpts)[1]

Barack Obama

[1]   It was Bill Clinton's singular contribution that he tried to transcend this ideological deadlock,[2] recognizing not only that what had come to be meant by the labels of "conservative" and "liberal" played to Republican advantage, but that the categories were inadequate to address the problems we faced. At times during his first campaign, his gestures toward disaffected Reagan Democrats could seem clumsy and transparent (what ever happened to Sister Souljah?[3]) or frighteningly coldhearted (allowing the execution of a mentally retarded death row inmate to go forward on the eve of an important primary). In the first two years of his presidency, he would be forced to abandon some core elements of his platform—universal health care, aggressive investment in education and training—that might have more decisively reversed the long-term trends that were undermining the position of working families in the new economy.

[2]   Still, he instinctively understood the falseness of the choices being presented to the American people. He saw that government spending and regulation could, if properly designed, serve as vital ingredients and not inhibitors to economic growth, and how markets and fiscal discipline could help promote social justice. He recognized that not only societal responsibility but personal responsibility was needed to combat poverty. In his platform—if not always in his day-to-day politics—Clinton's Third Way went beyond splitting the difference. It tapped into the pragmatic, nonideological attitude of the majority of Americans.

[3]   Indeed, by the end of his presidency, Clinton's policies—recognizably progressive if modest in their goals—enjoyed broad public support. Politically, he had wrung out of the Democratic Party some of the excesses[4] that had kept it from winning elections. That he failed, despite a booming economy, to translate popular policies into anything resembling a governing coalition said something about[5] the demographic difficulties Democrats were

facing (in particular, the shift in population growth to an increasingly solid Republican South) and the structural advantages the Republican enjoyed in the Senate, where the votes of two Republican senators from Wyoming, population 493,782, equaled the votes of two Democratic senators from California, population 33,871,648.

[4] But that failure also testified to the skill with which Gingrich, Rove, Norquist, and the like were able to consolidate and institutionalize the conservative movement. They tapped the unlimited resources of corporate sponsors and wealthy donors to create a network of think tanks and media outlets. They brought state-of-the-art technology to the task of mobilizing their base, and centralized power in the House of Representatives in order to enhance party discipline.

[5] And they understood the threat Clinton posed to their vision of a long-term conservative majority, which helps explain the vehemence with which they went after[6] him. It also explains why they invested so much time attacking Clinton's morality, for if Clinton's policies were hardly radical, his biography (the draft letter saga, the marijuana puffing, the Ivy League intellectualism, the professional wife who didn't bake cookies, and most of all the sex) ?[7] proved perfect grist for the conservative base. With enough repetition, a looseness with the facts, and the ultimately undeniable evidence of the President's own personal lapses, Clinton could be made to embody the very traits of sixties liberalism that had helped spur the conservative movement in the first place. Clinton may have fought that movement to a draw, but the movement would come out stronger for it—and in George W. Bush's first term, that movement would take over the United States government.

参考译文

共和党和民主党（节选）

巴拉克·奥巴马

[1] 比尔·克林顿的杰出贡献，在于他力图超越这种意识形态僵局。他不仅认识到诸如"保守派""自由派"这样的标签到头来只会对共和党有利，他还认识到这样的划分对解决当前面临的问题于事无补。第一次竞选中，他对离经叛道的里根派民

主党人的姿态可能显得有些笨拙和直白（索尔嘉妹妹究竟怎么样了？），抑或有些冷酷无情（一个重要的初选日前夕他批准处决了一名有精神障碍的死刑犯）。在总统任期的头两年里，他不得不放弃了竞选纲领中的一些核心内容——比如，全民医疗保险，对教育和培训的大力投资，而这些政策本可能决定性地扭转新经济中长期以来有损劳动家庭地位的倾向。

[2]　另外，他还直觉地认识到，提供给美国人民的种种选择都是错误的。他看到，政府的开支和调控如果规划得当应该成为促进经济增长的重要因素，而不是阻力。他还看到，市场和财政制度有助于保证社会公正。他认识到，战胜贫困不仅是社会的责任，也是个人的责任。在他的竞选纲领中——如果不是在日常施政中的话——克林顿的第三条道路确实超越了一味强调分歧的做法，从而迎合了美国大多数民众务实和不拘泥于意识形态的态度。

[3]　的确，在他任期届满的时候，克林顿的政策——尽管目标低调，但显然成绩不菲——已获得广泛的民众支持。政治上，他摒弃了民主党那些曾阻碍该党赢得选举的过激做法。至于尽管经济一片繁荣，克林顿却未能将合乎民心的政策演变为类似于执政同盟之类的东西，只能说明民主党人所面临的人口分布上的不利因素（特别是人口增长向共和党日趋强势的南部的迁移），以及共和党在参议院中的结构优势。参议院中，来自只有493,782个公民的怀俄明州的两位参议员的选票与来自拥有33,871,648个公民的加利福尼亚州两位参议员的选票在效力上竟是同等的。

[4]　但是，克林顿建立执政同盟的失败也验证了金里奇、罗夫、诺奎斯特等人使保守运动得以加强和制度化的运作技巧的高明。他们利用企业赞助人和富豪捐助人的无限资源，建立了智囊和媒体网络。他们运用最新技术发动其支持者，并在众议院中推行集权以强化党内纪律。

[5]　另外，他们也明白，想长期保持保守派多数的局面，克林顿是个严重威胁。这就解释了他们为什么那么卖力地反对克林顿。也解释了他们为什么花费那么多时间去攻击克林顿的道德缺陷，因为如果说克林顿的政策并不激进，那他的生活经历（逃避兵役、吸食大麻、常青藤名校的教育背景、不会做家务地职业夫人，还有最致命的性绯闻）无疑就成了保守势力发难的绝好素材。通过不断地重复，添枝加叶，再加上总统本人某些无可否认的过失，克林顿就可能被当成当年促发保守运动的六十年代自由派种种特征的代表。克林顿可以和保守派打个平手，但那只会使保守派卷土重来，变本加厉——而且在乔治·W·布什的第一个任期中，保守派将主导整个美国政府。

注释

1. 本文节选自奥巴马《无畏的希望》(*The Audacity of Hope*)的第一章 Republicans and Democrats。
2. this ideological deadlock 指上文提到的非此即彼、非友即敌的二元对立的政治观点。
3. Sister Souljah 是美国著名黑人说唱(rap)音乐人和社会活动家,曾因发表有关种族言论而招致批评。克林顿在1992年的竞选活动中为了争取中间选民,对与民主党关系密切的索尔嘉妹妹的观点进行了批驳。但这样做也有疏远该党盟友和基本选民的风险。从此之后,美国政治生活中凡是某位政治家为了政治目的涉及他和他的政党的极端个人或观点的批驳就被称为索尔嘉妹妹时刻(Sister Souljah moment)。
4. excesses 按2002版 *Macmillan English Dictionary for Advanced Learners* 的解释,指 any behavior that you consider wrong because it is too extreme。
5. say something about... =to show indirectly what someone or something is like,比如:The accident showed something about the poor management of the company.
6. go after 根据2002版 *Macmillan English Dictionary for Advanced Learners* 的解释,指 to try to catch or stop someone 或 to try to arrest or punish someone,此处可译为"对着干""反对",不是"追随"的意思。
7. 这里说的是克林顿几个授人以柄的地方。和注解3提到的有关索尔嘉妹妹的情况一样,译者必须具备一些相关的背景知识,不然就无法正确理解并用译语清晰表达。the draft letter saga 指越战期间克林顿逃避兵役的事,他曾给负责后备军官训练队的霍尔姆斯上校写过一封信,申诉了他对越战和服兵役的态度;the marijuana puffing 指的是克林顿被指责年轻时曾吸食大麻的事;the Ivy League intellectualism 指的是克林顿在常青藤名校耶鲁大学的教育背景;the sex 指的是人们关于克林顿包括和莱温斯基的关系在内的一系列性丑闻。这也成了保守派和反知性主义(anti-intellectualism)者的抨击对象。就连其夫人的女强人形象 the professional wife who didn't bake cookies 也难逃被揶揄攻击的命运。这些相关知识在理解原文的过程中起着重要作用,在译文表达中也必不可少。不然只按字面意思翻译,便会令人不知所云。比如将 the marijuana puffing 译为"有关大麻的言论",或将 the draft letter saga 译为"信笺草稿的长篇故事"等就会严重扭曲原文信息。

 讲解

译者的知识和经验在理解中的作用

Wayne K. Hoy 和 Cecil G. Miskel 在2007出版的 *Educational Administration: Theory, Research, and Practice* (eighth edition) 中指出:已有知识在很大程度上决定着我们在获取新信息过程中关注什么,感知什么,学习什么,记忆和遗忘的又是

什么。知识不仅仅意味着以往学习之所得,也将指导新鲜信息的获取。心理学家曾做过一个实验。将一些高中生按阅读能力和对棒球的了解程度分为四组:阅读能力强且棒球知识强的;阅读能力强而棒球知识弱的;阅读能力弱而棒球知识强的;阅读能力弱且棒球知识弱的。然后让他们阅读同一篇有关棒球比赛的文章,并测试他们的理解和记忆情况。结果发现,对棒球的了解在理解中起到了关键作用:阅读能力弱而棒球知识强的不但比阅读能力强而棒球知识弱的得分高,甚至和阅读能力强且棒球知识强的学生不相上下。

这说明语篇信息并非是存在于语篇中的客观实体,没有读者的加工,语篇并不自动生成意义。只有当读者以自己的固有知识能动地去对语篇进行加工时,意义才会产生。意义是读者以自己对世界和人类的固有知识对语篇进行解读即释义的结果。理解是语言能力和百科知识共同发挥作用的认知过程,理解绝不是简单的语言解码过程。因此,要成为一名合格的译者,必须不断积累和丰富自己的知识储备,并在接受了一项翻译任务后进行充分的翻译前和翻译过程中相关资料查阅工作。本单元注释3和7都集中说明了获得原文相关背景知识的必要性和重要性。再看下面译例:

1. It's tempting to politicize the memory of a day so full of personal and national honor, too easy to allude to the wars of our times as if they naturally mirrored World War II. <u>The iconic starkness of the forces that met on the beaches of Normandy</u> makes that temptation all the greater. But beyond the resemblance of young soldiers dying in wars 60 years apart, there is no analogy, and that is something we must remember today as well.

这是发表在2004年6月6日《纽约时报》上纪念诺曼底登陆60周年的文章片段。作者指出,美国现在进行的战争和当时的诺曼底登陆是风马牛不相及的。整段的翻译,尤其是划线的句子,需要译者具备相关知识,知道那是以美国为首的同盟国和德国法西斯的一场决战,决定着"二战"的走向,也决定着人类的命运。请参照下面译文:

今天我们回忆起那一天,很容易将其政治化,因为那一天充满了个人的光荣和国家的荣耀。我们很容易将它和今天的战争联系起来,仿佛我们今天进行的战争自然可以和"二战"同日而语。<u>在诺曼底海滩上交锋的两股势力象征着壁垒分明的善恶对峙</u>,这就更诱人想做这种联想。但是,与"二战"相比,60年后正在进行的战争除了在牺牲年轻的战士之外,并没有任何相似之处。时至今日,我们必须牢记这一点。

译文划线部分没有按照原文字面译为"在诺曼底海滩上相遇的各种力量的象征性对比",而是"两股势力"和"善恶对峙",这不只是措辞的问题,而是在相关知识的导向和支持下的行文。有经验的译者不放过任何语言细节,旁人也许觉得无关紧要,他们却不遗余力地查找有关知识,精益求精地构建译文。又如下例:

2. There are no roads that can take us here. Not even the network of overgrown logging roads will lead us to this pristine place. We travel by boat, across miles made long by open Pacific water, to tuck ourselves behind the reefs and swells into the safety of this Vancouver Island harbour.

我们到这里来没有公路可走。就连草木丛生的伐木运输网也通不到这个仍保持着原生态的地方。我们通常乘船,要渡海二十多英里,由于是在太平洋海域航行,路途显得格外漫长。驶过礁脉,穿过涌浪,就来到了隐蔽其后的这个温哥华岛的港湾,进入了安全的水域。

看过汉译文,我们是否会想到,句中 mile 的复数的汉译竟也需要相关知识的支撑。译者谷启楠教授说"原文中的 miles,数量不定,不好译。参阅同一位作者写的另一篇文章"Learn from Earth and Ocean"得知,他们是从温哥华岛西海岸中部的托菲诺镇乘船去伊尤苏克的。又根据其他资料,从托菲诺镇到赫什奎亚特港大约有 23 英里,到伊尤苏克还要再远一点。据此将 miles 译成"二十多英里"。(参阅《中国翻译》2007(1):85)

以上译例说明,所谓理解就是译者运用自己的语言能力加相关知识对原文的解读过程。语言能力不够会造成重大理解错误,但只强调语言分析能力而忽视有关知识的作用,会造成更为重大甚至荒唐可笑的错误。

除了知识积累,译者本人的经历也会对原文理解过程和译文构建过程产生影响。朱乃长在他英汉对照的《小说面面观》的第 114 页,批评一个 1990 年出版的译本将 wolf 译为"色鬼"的重大错误:

3. The gulf that separates Man Friday from Batouala may be paralleled by the gulf that will separate Kipling's wolves from their literary descendants two hundred years hence,...

"星期五"同巴杜亚拉之间的悬殊,可以和吉普琳笔下的色鬼同二百年以后他们在文学作品中的子孙之间将要形成的悬殊相提并论……

造成这种错误的原因,朱教授没有分析。我们推想,译者很可能受到周围社会环境的影响:翻译此书时,文学作品中的"色狼"形象已是十分常见。于是,译者便以自己的所见所闻代替了源语作者使用这个词语的语境。

这种情况多半是无意识的，还有一种情况是译者有意用自己的经验干预译语的表达。据说"二战"时作为战地记者曾深入英伦三岛进行战地报道的翻译家萧乾，在翻译《战争风云》的过程中就借用了不少的亲身经历，为此书增色不少。（据《金陵晚报》2004年11月23日）另外，王宪明在研究了严复所译《社会通诠》后正确地指出，其译文"其实是掺杂了东方中国的翻译者的思想在其中"（参阅《语言、翻译与政治》，2005：18）。严复翻译西方政治社会学方面的著作，其个人的直接、间接经验和思想意识无一不在选题、增删、注解等方面进行干预。他的译文是典型的原文思想和译者思想、翻译意图相结合的产物。

Caught in the Web of the Internet (Abridged)

[1]　It's the equivalent of inviting sex addicts to a brothel or holding an Alcoholics Anonymous (AA) meeting at the pub.[1] Internet addicts tired of their square-eyed, keyboard tapping ways[2] need look no further than the Web for counselling. There is now an online counselling service at www.relate.org.nz for Internet obsessives. Just e-mail the details of your Internet-induced crisis and help comes direct to your inbox. The new breed of cybertherapists see nothing strange about offering help through the very medium that is swallowing their clients' free time and splitting their marriages.

[2]　Sue Hine, of Relationship Services, says: "Internet obsession has become a more noticeable problem over the last 18 months. At least this is an area addicts are familiar with and they'll be able to use it as a tool to overcome their obsession." Nor do experts worry that the Relate Website might become a favourite—a place to spend hours online in the name of Internet therapy. Dependency is always a risk with any form of counselling. There are various strategies we can adopt to keep that in perspective,[3] says Hine.

[3]　Though some may regard Internet addiction as another dubious ailment dreamed up to keep therapists in work, Relationship Services[4] says the problem is real.

[4]   Internet usage is up to four-and-a-half hours on the Web each week, compared to three-and-a-half hours a year ago. Therapist Robin Paul says there tend to be two scenarios. Some people meet through chatrooms and fall in love. It's like having an affair, then they meet and it's like a whirlwind honeymoon. It's devastating for the person left behind and quite often it has no real foundation.

[5]   The second scenario is that a person starts spending more and more time on the Net. They may not meet someone else but they don't spend any time with their partner and of course the relationship suffers.

[6]   Such stories may appear to be almost urban legends, so ashamed are Internet addicts and their partners. After all, who wants to admit they have a 100 a day habit (e-mails, that is) or are somehow less alluring than a piece of hardware? But in America, which has long had a love affair with both therapy and the Net, these stories are common.

[7]   "I guess I was a typical example of someone hooked on the Internet," says Parker, who now spends just an hour a day online. "I was coming home at lunchtime to get on the computer. At 6 p.m. I'd feed my son and put him to bed but all the time I was going backwards and forwards to the computer. Then I'd stay up until 5 a.m.or 6 a.m., typing away 'chatting' on my computer screen all night."

[8]   "I learned from my experience with romance on the Net that people aren't always what they seem. The guy I met, for example, was very nice but also quite mixed up. The trouble is you get lonely housewives talking to someone and they think, 'This guy sounds nice compared to what I've got.'"

[9]   But I don't think anyone who is married or in a sound relationship should really be spending hours talking to someone else and ignoring their nearest and dearest. While Parker provided her own therapy by putting her experiences down on paper, she recommends others take up the online counselling offer, or log off from the World Wide Web gradually.

[10]   Computer whizz Steve Phillips grins at the mention of Internet Addiction Disorder (IAD)—he's been there, done that. Now 28, and a seven-year veteran on the Internet, he spends a mere 10 to 15 hours for entertainment on the Web each week. A few years ago, when he was in the

grip of his addiction, that was the amount of time—10 to 15 hours—he spent online each day.

[11] The habit started hitting hard[5] when he finished his studies in the big city and moved back home. Without the support of a school paid computer, he racked up hundreds of dollars in Internet-related toll bills. The huge expense, followed by a few months offline while he searched for a job, was the wake-up call he needed.

[12] The Internet is definitely addictive but if you can keep it in control it has advantages, too. Using it can be a steep learning curve so it helps you become very quick at learning. Also there is a huge demand for people in the field of Information Technology (IT) and hours on the Internet are great training.

参考译文

沉迷因特网（删节）

[1] 在网上提供戒除网瘾咨询服务就好比邀好色之徒去妓院，或在酒馆里举行"嗜酒者互戒协会"（AA）会议。对眼盯屏幕手敲键盘感到厌烦而无力自拔的网迷们只须在网上便可得到咨询了。现在有一种为网迷开设的网上咨询服务，网址是 www.relate.org.nz。你只需把上网引发的"危机"详情用电子邮件发出去，就会在你的信箱中收到帮助信息。提供咨询的媒介是网络，而吞噬网迷们的时间、拆散他们的婚姻的也恰恰是这个网络，但这些新型的网络治疗专家们对此并不感到有什么奇怪。

[2] "关系服务"网站的苏·海因说："最近18个月中，上网成瘾已经成为一个更为突出的问题。怎么说网站也是网迷们熟悉的地方，他们能把它作为戒掉网瘾的工具来使用。"专家们也并不担心上服务网站会成为网迷们的新嗜好——以网络治疗为名整天待在上面。任何形式的咨询服务都有产生依赖性的危险。海因说，我们可以采取各种策略处理好治疗和依赖性的问题。

[3] 尽管有人质疑沉迷因特网是否真是一种病症，认为那只是假想出来以保住治疗专家们的饭碗的，但关系服务网站认为这个问题确实存在。

[4] 一年前，因特网的使用率为每周3.5小时，而现在达到了4.5小时。治疗专家罗宾·保罗说，沉迷于因特网有两种常见的情况。有些人在聊天室相识并坠入爱河。这就像有了暧昧关系，然后约会，度过一段旋风般的蜜月。被抛弃的一方在感情上

会受到极大的打击,而这种网上恋爱通常没有现实基础。

[5]　另一种情况是:有些人把越来越多的时间耗费在因特网上,他们也许没有网上情人要见面,可也不愿花时间去陪伴自己的爱人,夫妻关系当然会因此受到伤害。

[6]　诸如此类的情形简直成了一个个都市传奇,那些痴迷于因特网的网民们以及他们的配偶都感到难以启齿。毕竟,谁也不愿意承认他们有每天收发 100 封电子邮件的习惯,或者承认自己竟然还不如一台电脑有吸引力。然而,对于美国这样一个与心理治疗和网络结缘已久的国家来说,此类故事屡见不鲜。

[7]　"我想我曾经是个典型的网迷,"帕克说,现在她每天只上网 1 小时,"那时我每天午饭时回家上网。下午 6 点我给儿子喂点吃的,安排他睡觉,但此间我也不时地再去敲两下电脑。随后,我会在网上待到清晨 5 点或 6 点,不停地敲打键盘'聊天',通宵达旦。"

[8]　"我的网上浪漫史让我明白了,人们并不总像他们表现出来的那样。例如,我曾认识一个网友,他很讨人喜欢,可脑子有点糊涂。问题是,有些家庭主妇难耐寂寞,和别人聊上了,就会想:'与我的那位比起来,这家伙听起来还不错呀。'"

[9]　可我认为,对于已婚的或者伴侣关系良好的人来说,实在不应该把大量的时间耗在与别人聊天上,而把自己至爱至亲的人冷落在一旁。帕克通过把自己的经历写成文章的方式治疗了网络沉迷症,她建议别人可以接受网上咨询服务,或者逐步地疏远网络。

[10]　计算机高手史迪夫·菲利普笑着提及网络沉迷症(IAD)——他自己就是个网迷,自有体味。他今年 28 岁,是一个有 7 年网龄的老手,现在他每周只上网玩 10~15 个小时。几年前,他上网成瘾,难以自拔,每天在网上耗费的时间就达 10~15 个小时。

[11]　菲利普的上网习惯难以为继,是在大城市念完书,回到家中之后。由于不能再使用学校付费的电脑了,他要支付几百美元因特网服务费。这笔巨大的费用使他适时地警醒了。在随后的几个月中,他去找工作,不再上网。

[12]　因特网的确容易让人着迷,但如果你能把握分寸,也会获益良深。使用因特网可以提升你的学习曲线,有助于你快速获取知识。另外,信息技术(IT)领域需要大批人员,经常使用因特网无疑是个很好的自我培训。

注释

1. 文章开篇的第一个词就是代词 it。代词常常指代前文出现过的名词或词组，也可指代下文的某个名词或词组，这里便是后一种情况。请仔细阅读下文，确定其所指，并参阅讲解部分的有关说明。
2. tired of their...ways 即"对他们自己的……行为方式感到厌烦了"之意。
3. keep...in perspective=to judge and handle sth. properly as it is related to other things。句中代词 that 指的是上文的 dependency。
4. Relationship Services 和上文的 Relate Website 都是指第一段中提到的新西兰网站 www.relate.org.nz。
5. hit hard=to have a bad effect on。这里指网络痴迷的恶习开始显示出更严重的后果——上网费用要自己支付，而他无能为力。

讲解

指代关系的理解

代词是语篇中的重要衔接手段，英语中代词的使用频率比汉语要高。英语中的代词常无须译出，但也常还原成其所指名词在汉译中再现，这就要求译者对代词的指称有一个清晰的理解。代词可以用来指代前文的名词（词组），叫作"前指照应"（anaphoric reference），也可指代下文的名词（词组），叫作"后指照应"（cataphoric reference）。后指照应有时不仅仅是一个词或词组，也可能是一句话，一个事实。例如：Perhaps I shouldn't tell you this, but when I was young I had hair down to my waist! 句中 this 所指其实就是 When I was young I had hair down to my waist 这个事实。

本单元原文第一个词就是代词 it，它的所指当然只能在下文中寻找。这种指代关系会增加理解和翻译的难度。不妨先读一读下面一段发表过的译文：

上网成瘾如同邀约好色的人逛妓院，或者在小酒馆里举行"嗜酒者互戒协会"（AA）会员集会。网迷们疲劳地盯着显示屏，敲击着键盘，只想通过万维网寻求咨询。现在有一种为网迷开设的网上咨询服务，其网址是 www.relate.org.nz。你只需把上网引发的"危机"详情用电子邮件发出去，就会从你的信箱中直接收到帮助信息。新式的计算机治疗专家认为，通过网络寻求帮助并不奇怪，正是它吞噬着网迷们的时间，而且危及他们的婚姻。

上述译文将此代词还原为"上网成瘾"，而正确的理解应该是 it=online counselling service。可以看到，对这个代词的解读不仅涉及本句的理解，还和

"...need look no further than..." 以及 "...offering help through the very medium that is swallowing their clients' free time and splitting their marriages." 两个句子在语义和逻辑上有着密切联系。因此，不是"只想通过……"，而是"只需……便……"。网络治疗专家们不奇怪的也不是"通过网络寻求帮助"，而是"提供咨询的媒介是网络，而吞噬网迷们的时间、拆散他们的婚姻的也恰恰就是这个网络"，也就是"救人也网络，害人也网络"的意思。我们无法推断，是代词的理解影响了译者对全段的理解，还是对下文的理解影响了对代词所指的定夺。恐怕是两者兼而有之。这个译例说明，代词虽小，也万万忽视不得。

再请仔细阅读下面译例，析清代词的所指，并注意它们在译文中的表达：

1. I dislike war not only for its dangers and inconveniences, but because of the loss of so many young men any of whom may be a Newton or an Einstein, a Beethoven, a Michelangelo, a Shakespeare, or even a Shaw. Or he may be what is of much more immediate importance: a good baker or a good weaver or builder. If you think of a pair of combatants as a heroic British St. Micheal bringing the wrath of God upon a German Lucifer, then you may exult in the victory of St. Micheal if he kills Lucifer, or burn to avenge him if his dastardly adversary mows him down with a machine-gun before he can get to grips with him. In that way, you can get intense emotional experience from war. But suppose you think of the two as they probably are: say, two good carpenters taken away from their proper work to kill one another. That is how I see it; and the result is that, whichever of them is killed, the loss is as great to Europe and to me. In 1914, I was as sorry for the young Germans who lay slain or mutilated in no man's land as for the British lads who lay beside them, so I got no emotional satisfaction out of the war. It was to me a sheer waste of life. (Bernard Shaw: *As I See It*)

我不喜欢战争，这不仅仅是因为它会带来危险和麻烦，还因为它让好多年轻人丧了命，而他们当中说不定哪一个就会成为又一个牛顿、爱因斯坦、贝多芬、米开朗基罗、莎士比亚或是萧伯纳；或许他们现在就是非常有用的人，如优秀的面包师、织工或建筑工人。设想一下，假如英勇的英国士兵圣·迈克尔正义愤填膺地与德国鬼子卢瑟福交战，如果圣·迈克尔杀了卢瑟福你自然会欣喜若狂，而当你看到圣·迈克尔还未来得及和德国鬼子交手就被机枪扫倒，你又肯定会怒火中烧，誓报此仇。于是你体会到战争带给你的强烈震撼；但如果你转念想一想他们可能的身份，比方说，被强拉到这里相互厮杀以前他们本是两个善良的木匠，又会怎样？我就是这样想的。在我看来，无论谁死，结果都是对欧洲以及我本人的一大损失。

1914年，当我看到年轻的士兵横尸疆场，无论他是德国人还是英国人，我都会感到难过。从战争中我根本得不到任何满足。对于我来说战争就是浪费生命。

　　划线句子中有两个人名（St. Micheal 和 Lucifer），还有六个第三人称代词（包括 he、him、his），只有最后一个（him）指的是 Lucifer。在译文中这些代词有的被还原为其所指代的名词，有的则略去未译。

2. Two things are outstanding in the creation of the English system of canals, and they characterize all the Industrial Revolution. One is that the men who made the revolution were practical men. Like Brindley, they often had little education, and in fact school education as it then was could only dull an inventive mind. The grammar schools legally could only teach the classical subjects for which they had been founded. The universities (there were only two, at Oxford and Cambridge) also took little interest in modern or scientific studies; and they were closed to those who did not conform to the Church of England.

　　在修建英国的运河网的过程中，有两点是非常突出的，而这两点也正是整个工业革命的特点。首先，发动这场革命的都是些实干家。同布林德雷一样，他们一般都没有受过什么教育。事实上，当时那种学校教育也只能扼杀人的创造性。按规定文法学校只能讲授古典学科，这些学校的办学宗旨本来就是如此。大学（当时只有两所，一所在牛津，一所在剑桥）对现代的或科学的学科也不怎么感兴趣；这两所大学还把不信奉英国国教的人关在门外。

　　注意译文中划线的名词词组，原文中与它们相应的都是代词 they，而译文中均被还原成了其所指代的名词。这在英译汉中是常见的。

3. We need a vantage-post, for the novel is a formidable mass, and it is so amorphous—no mountain in it to climb, no Parnassus or Helicon, not even a Pisgah. It is most distinctly one of the moister areas of literature—irrigated by a hundred rills and occasionally degenerating into a swamp. I do not wonder that the poets despise it, though they sometimes find themselves in it by accident. And I am not surprised at the annoyance of the historians when by accident it finds itself among them.

　　我们需要一个有利的地位，因为小说是一个不容易对付的庞然大物。它又是那么扑朔迷离，叫人难以捉摸。这里没有高山可供攀援：没有帕纳萨斯山或者赫利孔山，甚至没有一座像毗斯迦那样的山峦。它显然是文学领域里面一个比较潮湿和泥泞的地区——上百条小河流淌其间，有时候还会沦为一片沼泽。诗人对它嗤之以鼻，我并不觉得奇怪，尽管有时他们也会发现自己纯属偶然地涉足其间。而当历史学家发现小说偶尔也闯进了他们的领域，因而感到恼恨，我也不会惊讶。

这段原文中有 6 个 it 和 1 个 itself，都指 the novel。译文将这些代词还原为相应的名词，行文流畅准确，对最后一句中的 it 和 itself 的处理尤其值得学习借鉴。

从以上几个译例可看出，代词在译文中常常被还原为名词或略去不译。再如下面一个简短的译例：

4. It had been damaged; when he lifted it, he heard something clink feebly inside. He set it back on the ground.

那东西摔坏了。他拿起来，听见里面叮当直响，就又放回地上。

原文的三个 it 在译文中有一个转译为名词"那东西"，另两个未译出。但如果英语中代词的使用具有明显的修辞意图，那么为了使译文取得同样的效果，代词可以照译。如：

5. The sparkling of the water around him (a fish) and the sound of it cascading over the creek bed made me weak and I woke suddenly, convulsed. I knew the fish. I knew the place. I set out immediately.

它周围的水，噗噜噗噜地冒着气泡，水声一阵阵传到小河河底，让我浑身发软，我一阵痉挛，突然醒了。我知道这种鱼。我知道那地方。我立刻向那里走去。

该句选自一篇题为"Drought"的散文，作者以感人的笔触叙说了河流即将枯竭、鱼儿奄奄一息的景象，表现了对自然的深情至爱〔参阅《中国翻译》2001（1）：65〕。这段连用三个以代词 I 打头的短句，以体现作者心情的急切和忧虑。译者照样以三个"我"为主语的句子相对。

英语人称代词基本形式只有 8 个，加上格的变化也不过二十几个，但它们在语篇中的衔接作用却是十分重要的，绝对不可掉以轻心。请观察下面译例中的理解失误之处，从中汲取经验。

6. Cary Sloane's body was found next morning on the lower shelf of a pillar of Queensboro Bridge. In the darkness and in his excitement he had thought that it was the water flowing black beneath him, but in less than a second it made no possible difference—unless he had planned to think one last thought of Edna, and call out her name as he struggled feebly in the water.

第二天早上，卡里·斯隆的尸体在昆斯波罗桥桥墩下面的一个架子上被发现了。一方面因为是在黑暗中，一方面也因为他太激动，<u>他以为水黑黑地在他下面流</u>

过，可是不到一秒钟，这就不可能有什么不同了——除非他打算再最后想念一下埃德娜，并且在水中软弱无力地做最后挣扎的时候呼唤她的名字。

此译文忽视了"he had thought that it was the water..."中代词 it 的所指，致使译文读起来令人感到莫名其妙，读者会问："不同"之处在哪里？而原文说得很清楚，it 指的是上句话中的 the lower shelf of a pillar，也就是说黑暗中 Cary 误将桥墩上的架子当成了水面，于是冲着架子跳下去，结果是摔死，而不是淹死。死这一点是相同的，不同的是摔死是立即死亡，淹死还会挣扎一会儿，最后想念一下心上人。指代关系搞清了，译文划线部分就可改为：……他误以为那桥墩架子就是脚下流过的黑乎乎的河水……

7. To parliamentarians trained in British terminology, "the government" means the cabinet: a group of the legislature's own members, <u>chosen by it</u> to devise public policies, to manage the legislature's major activities, and to exercise executive powers.

对于那些受英国术语熏陶的议员们，"政府"指的是内阁，是立法机构本身的一批成员，由内阁任命来制定公共政策，对付议会的重大活动并行使权力。

按此汉译，内阁是由内阁来任命的，岂不荒唐？问题出在对原文中 it 的理解上。实际上 it 代替的是 legislature，而不是 cabinet。故划线部分应改译为：由立法机构任命……在英国执法机构内阁和立法机构议会密切相关，而不像美国那样相互分立。英国下院多数党领袖就是内阁成员。

8. The primary use of crystallization is purification of a single compound, as opposed to separation and isolation of two or more compounds in a mixture. The latter can sometimes be accomplished by fractional crystallization in which successive crops of crystals of different composition are collected from the solution and then further recrystalized. This approach to separation, however, is far less efficient than chromatography and is not widely used.

与分开和隔离混合物中两种或两种以上的化合物不同，结晶的基本用途是对单一化合物的提纯。后者有时用部分结晶的方法完成，其中一连串的不同成分的晶粒可从溶液中收集，然后再结晶。然而用此法分离效率比色谱法低，所以没有广泛应用。

原文 latter 指的是 separation and isolation of two or more compounds。译文将原文第一句中的叙述顺序颠倒了，可是 latter 仍照译为"后者"，依译文的叙述顺序，"后者"乃是"对单一化合物的提纯"。这样一来所指关系完全颠倒了。可改译为：结晶的基本用途不是分开和隔离混合物中两种或两种以上的化合物，而是对单一的化合物进行提纯。前者有时可用部分结晶法完成，即从溶液中依次收集晶粒，然后再结晶。然而这种分离方法效率比色谱法低得多，所以没有广泛使用。

9. ...a ranking government official declared last week that Japan's high-definition television system...had been technologically outdistanced by advances in the U.S. and might have to be scrapped. "The global trend is digital," said Akimasa Egawa, a director general at the Minister of Posts and Telecommunications, adding that the government would reach a decision in the coming months on whether to throw its support to an all-digital system, as pursued in the U.S. and Europe...

Caught off guard, the major Japanese electronics companies and NHK,...responded with indignation. Egawa bowed to the hostile reaction and toned down his remarks at a press conference the following day, explaining that he had only meant to suggest that eventually Japan had to go digital, though for the time being the government would continue to support the present system.

While the swift about-face demonstrated the power of the Japanese electronics industry, there was little chance that it would prevail...

我们要研究的是上述段落中最后一句的译文。为提供充分的语境，引用了上文的两个自然段的大部分内容，最后一句的译文是：他的态度迅速向后转，表明日本电子工业势力强大，在这种情况下，他的建议几乎没有奏效的可能。

按照这个译文，it 指的是 "Egawa 的建议"，但据上文 Egawa 并未提出什么建议。其实，it 指的是 the power of the Japanese electronics industry。故可改译成：他的态度的突然转变，固然说明日本电子工业势力强大，但日本电子工业继续保持优势的可能性是很小的。

小结

理解的过程是译者发挥自己的语言能力和文化能力与原文（源语作者）进行沟通的过程。本章的 6 个单元从以下几个方面探讨了对理解过程的认识。

首先，语言的交际单位是语篇，而不是孤立的句子。因此，译者所面对的首先是语篇，而不是句子。译者必须把语篇看作一个整体，语句是这个整体的有机组成部分，对语句的理解必须在语篇这个整体框架内进行。

第二，语篇的意义不是语句的简单叠加。孤零零的语句不按照一定的逻辑和思

维模式组织起来,就无法完成交际任务。而一旦组织起来了,就不再是互不关联的语言单位。作者如何组句成篇,他的意图何以体现,文脉如何发展——这些也都是译者要分析和理解的重要内容。

第三,对语篇意义的理解不只是对语言编码的解析,还更是对有关文化因素的认同和理解。语篇好比一棵树,只有扎根于相应的文化土壤中才具有生命力。要理解这棵树就不能不了解其生长土壤、环境和气候。要做一个合格的译者,就要阅读大量有关源语文化的书籍资料,为翻译工作增加文化储备。

第四,理解过程的主体是译者,是译者与作者之间能动性的对话。而要做到能动地与作者对话,译者仍须大量阅读包括各类文体在内的原文资料,以尽量缩短自己和源语读者间的差距——不仅是语言水平上的差距,还有语用和文化背景知识上的差距。只有读透吃准原文,从源语读者的角度去理解和思考,才能成为一个合格的译者。

 练习

1. 翻译下列段落。

Translators will always use bilingual dictionaries alongside other reference materials, and therefore need to be aware of the limitations as well as the strengths of the bilingual dictionaries; they must know their way around them and how to use them efficiently, and need to keep them up to date. I believe, however, that in the training translators receive, learning to "release words from the unconscious memory hold" plays a crucial part; as linguists, we have a capital of words, collocations and phrases that is often much larger and richer than we give ourselves credit for, and bilingual dictionaries need to be approached as tools in helping us to exploit this resource rather than as replacements for it. There could also be instances when the bilingual dictionary may not be the translator's best friend and "intelligent guessing" may be a complementary or even an alternative, and better, strategy—not, clearly, where the bilingual dictionary has a good range of renderings but certainly where, for whatever reason, the equivalents on offer to the bilingual dictionary user are inadequate.

⚠ 提示

注意句子结构的分析。

2. 翻译下列短文。

A Game of Cards[1]

[1] Ever since I was old enough to read books on philosophy I have been intrigued by the discussions on the nature of man. The philosophers have been debating for years about whether man is primarily good or primarily evil, whether he is primarily altruistic or selfish, cooperative or competitive, gregarious or self-centered, whether he enjoys free will or whether everything is predetermined[2].

[2] As far back as the Socratic dialogues in Plato[3], and even before that, man has been baffled about himself. He knows he is capable of great and noble deeds, but then he is oppressed with the evidence of great wrongdoing.

[3] And so he wonders.[4] I don't presume to be able to resolve the contradictions. In fact, I don't think we have to. It seems to me that the debate over good and evil in man, over free will and determinism, and over all the other contradictions[5]—that this debate is a futile one. For man is a creature of dualism. He is both good and evil, both altruistic and selfish. He enjoys free will to the extent that he can make decisions in life, but he can't change his chemistry or his relatives or his physical endowments—all of which were determined for him at birth. And rather than speculate over which side of him is dominant, he might do well to consider what the contradictions and circumstances are that tend to bring out the good or evil, that enable him to be nobler and a responsible member of the human race[6]. And so far as free will and determinism are concerned, something I heard in India on a recent visit to the subcontinent may be worth passing along. Free will and determinism, I was told, are like a game of cards. The hand that is dealt you represents determinism. The way you play your hand represents free will[7].

[4] Now where does all this leave us?[8] It seems to me that we ought to attempt to bring about and safeguard those conditions that tend to develop the best in man. We know, for example, that the existence of fear and man's inability to cope with fear bring about the worst in him. We know that what is true of man on a small scale can be true of society on a large scale. And today the conditions of fear in the world are, I'm afraid, affecting men everywhere. More than twenty-three hundred years ago, the Greek

world, which had attained tremendous heights of creative intelligence and achievement, disintegrated under the pressure of fear. Today, too, if I have read the signs correctly in traveling around the world, there is great fear. There is fear that the human race has exhausted its margin for error[9] and that we are sliding into another great conflict that will cancel out thousands of years of human progress. And people are fearful because they don't want to lose the things that are more important than peace itself—moral, democratic, and spiritual values.

[5]　The problem confronting us today is far more serious than the destiny of any political system or even of any nation. The problem is the destiny of man: first, whether we can make this planet safe for man; second, whether we can make it fit for him. This I believe—that man today has all the resources[10] to shatter his fears and go on to the greatest golden age in history, an age which will provide the conditions for human growth and for the development of the good that resides within man, whether in his individual or his collective being[11]. And he has only to mobilize his rational intelligence and his conscience to put these resources to work. (Norman Cousins)

⚠ 提示

1. 分析整篇短文的结构，作者是用什么方法阐明自己观点的。写出简短提纲。
2. 注意分析此长句结构，以及六对意义相对的词语的确切含义。句中 he 用以指代 man，这种指代关系下文出现多次，怎样译为好？
3. 查阅有关资料，大致了解 Plato 与 Socrates 其人其事。
4. 这一短句具有怎样的语篇功能（在句子或段落的连贯上有怎样的作用）？
5. 怎样理解这个词？
6. 注意分析此句结构。
7. 注意作者的类比（analogy）手法。
8. 参照提示 4，同样注意这一短句具有怎样的语篇功能。
9. 怎样理解 exhausted its margin for error 的意义？
10. 这一段中的 resources 一词如何理解？
11. 注意分析 whether in his individual or his collective being 与其他句子成分的语法关系。

第三章 译文的表达

如果说原文理解是译者调动自己的知识储存与作者沟通的过程，那么，译文表达就是译者运用自己的译语写作能力将这种沟通的成果具体化为语码的过程了。理解是翻译的关键，但理解准确只能保证原文信息不被严重扭曲，不出现重大误译，并不意味着准确的理解必然产生高质量的译文。本章就将针对译文构建中的一些关键问题进行探讨。首先，要明确翻译的标准，而对翻译标准的认识也要基于明确的语篇意识——语篇有不同的文体，在特定语境中发挥其作用，译者的操作也有不同的层次。所以，本章前三个单元先讨论了这三个问题，之后才提出翻译的标准。其次，译者必须对汉语的行文特点，特别是与英语有明显差异的那些方面，有明晰的了解和把握，以保证译文的通顺达意。为此，Unit Four 至 Unit Seven 专门探讨了译文构建中的一些关键问题。第三，必须认识到，翻译作为一种信息传递过程，必有所失，有些信息甚至根本无法传递给译语读者。这就是不可译性，或可译性的限度（见 Unit Eight）。第四，还必须认识到，原文是源语语篇世界中的一员，构建中的译文将成为译语语篇世界中的一员，因此必须把原文和译文都放在和其他相关语篇的关系中加以处理，Unit Nine 就讨论了这个互文性问题。最后，要在把握好翻译标准的基础上进一步强化职业道德意识，Unit Ten 将做具体探讨。

How Dorothy Saved the Scarecrow (Excerpts)[1]

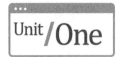

[1]　She bade her friends goodbye, and again started along the road of yellow brick. When she had gone several miles she thought she would stop to rest, and so climbed to the top of the fence beside the road and sat down. There was a great cornfield beyond the fence, and not far away she saw a Scarecrow, placed high on a pole to keep the birds from the ripe corn.[2]

[2]　Dorothy leaned her chin upon her hand and gazed thoughtfully at the Scarecrow. Its head was a small sack stuffed with straw, with eyes, nose, and mouth painted on it to represent a face. An old, pointed blue hat, that had belonged to some Munchkin, was perched on his head,[3] and the rest of the figure was a blue suit of clothes, worn and faded, which had also been stuffed with straw. On the feet were some old boots with blue tops, such as every man wore in this country, and the figure was raised above the stalks of corn by means of the pole stuck up its back.

[3]　While Dorothy was looking earnestly into the queer, painted face of the Scarecrow, she was surprised to see one of the eyes slowly wink at her. She thought she must have been mistaken at first, for none of the scarecrows in Kansas ever wink; but presently the figure nodded its head to her in a friendly way. Then she climbed down from the fence and walked up to it, while Toto[4] ran around the pole and barked.

[4]　"Good day," said the Scarecrow, in a rather husky voice.

[5]　"Did you speak?" asked the girl, in wonder.

[6]　"Certainly," answered the Scarecrow. "How do you do?"

[7]　"I'm pretty well, thank you," replied Dorothy politely. "How do you do?"

[8]　"I'm not feeling well," said the Scarecrow, with a smile, "for it is very tedious being perched up here night and day to scare away crows."

[9]　"Can't you get down?" asked Dorothy.

[10]　"No, for this pole is stuck up my back. If you will please take away the

pole I shall be greatly obliged to you."

[11] Dorothy reached up both arms and lifted the figure off the pole, for, being stuffed with straw, it was quite light.

[12] "Thank you very much," said the Scarecrow, when he had been set down on the ground. "I feel like a new man."

[13] Dorothy was puzzled at this, for it sounded queer to hear a stuffed man speak, and to see him bow and walk along beside her.

参考译文

救出了稻草人（节选）

[1] 她向朋友们说了声"再会"，就沿着黄砖铺砌的路又动身了。她赶了好几里路，想停下来休息，就爬到路旁栅栏的小凳上坐下来。栅栏那边是一大块玉米地，不远处，只见一个稻草人高挂在竹竿上，监视着鸟儿，不让它们飞近成熟的玉米。

[2] 多萝西一只手托着腮，呆呆地凝视着稻草人。他的头是一只小布包，塞满了草杆，上面画着眼睛、鼻子和嘴巴，装成了一个脸儿。头顶上扣的是一顶破旧的蓝帽子，尖顶，不定是那个芒奇金人曾经戴过的。身上穿的是一件蓝色的旧衣服，已经褪了色，身体里面也塞满了草。套在脚上的是一双蓝布面的旧靴子，在这个地方，好像每一个人都穿这样的鞋子。一根竹竿戳入他的背部，这家伙就被高高地吊起在玉米地上面了。

[3] 多萝西正认真地注视着稻草人那张奇特的画出来的脸，突然吃惊地看见他一只眼睛正一闪一闪地向她眨着。起初，她想自己一定是弄错了，因为在堪萨斯州稻草人可不会眨眼睛。但眼前这个家伙却明明在友好地向她点着头。于是她从栅栏上爬下来，走过去。这时候淘淘在稻草人四周跑着、吠着。

[4] "你好啊！"稻草人说，声音有几分嘶哑。

[5] 小女孩不解地问道："是你在讲话吗？"

[6] "当然，"稻草人说，"你好啊！"

[7] "谢谢你，我很好，"多萝西很有礼貌地说，"你好吗？"

[8] "我觉得不舒服，"稻草人微笑着说，"整天整夜地被吊在这里吓唬小鸟，真是

烦死了。"

[9] 多萝西问:"你能下来吗?"

[10] "不能,因为竹竿儿插在我的后背上。如果你替我抽掉它,我将非常感谢。"

[11] 多萝西伸出两只手臂,把他从竹竿上端抽出来,里面塞的是草,是十分轻的。

[12] 稻草人被放在了地上,他说:"多谢了,我觉得自己像一个新生的人了。"

[13] 听一个稻草人说话,看他鞠躬,还在她身旁走动,实在是一件奇怪的事,多萝西觉得十分惊异。

注释

1. 这是儿童文学名著 The Wonderful Wizard of OZ (作者 L. Frank Baum) 第三章的一个片段。讲的是一个叫多萝西的小女孩被旋风刮到一个奇异美丽的国度——奥兹国,为了重返家乡,她必须到翡翠城去找魔法师奥兹帮忙。在去翡翠城的路上,她首先遇到并解救了稻草人。
2. 注意译文的文体风格:结构简明,朗朗上口,面对一群小朋友娓娓道来。climbed to the top of the fence beside the road and sat down 译成"就爬到路旁栅栏的小凳上坐下来",是按照原著的插图译出的。插图上画的是矮矮的木头栅栏,上面有类似梯凳似的东西。to keep the birds from the ripe corn 译成"监视着鸟儿,不让它们飞近成熟的玉米"。将信息拆散,正是讲故事的口气。
3. had belonged to 表示"曾经属于",也就是别人戴过的;Munchkin 是奥兹国的居民;perched 一词不译成"戴"而译成"扣"更为生动些。
4. Toto 是多萝西所喜爱的一条小狗的名字。

A Watering Place

Hayden

The Warwickshire Avon falls into the Severn here, and on the sides of both, for many miles back, there are the finest meadows that ever were seen.[1] In looking over them, and beholding the endless flocks and herds, one wonders what can become of all the meat[2]! By riding on about eight or nine miles farther however, this wonder is a little diminished; for here we come

to one of the devouring WENS: namely, CHELTENHAM, which is what they call a "watering place", that is to say, a place to which East India plunderers, West India floggers, English taxgorgers, together with gluttons, drunkards, and debauchees of all descriptions, female as well as male, resort, at the suggestion of silently laughing quacks, in the hope of getting rid of the bodily consequences of their manifold sins and iniquities[3]. When I enter a place like this, I always feel disposed to squeeze up my nose with my fingers. It is nonsense, to be sure; but I conceit that every two-legged creature, that I see coming near me, is about to cover me with the poisonous proceeds of its impurities. To places like this come all that is knavish and all that is foolish and all that is base; gamesters, pick-pockets, and harlots; young wife-hunters in search of rich and ugly and old women, and young husband-hunters in search of rich and wrinkled or half-rotten men, the former resolutely bent, be the means what they may, to give the latter heirs to their lands and tenements[4]. These things are notorious; and, Sir William Scott, in his speech of 1802, in favour of the non-residence of the Clergy, expressly said, that they and their families ought to appear at watering places, and that this was amongst the means of making them respected by their flocks! Memorandum: He was a member for Oxford when he said this[5]!

参考译文

温泉胜地

海 顿

　　华立克夏的爱望河在此处流入色纹河，两河沿岸若干英里水草丰美，前所未见。草地上牛羊成群，沿途不断。看着这景色，这牛羊，心想这些好肉可作多少用途，不禁感到神奇。但是再向前骑八九英里，这神奇之感就破灭了；原来我们已到达一个毒瘤似的害人地方，名叫却尔特能，所谓温泉胜地是也。这地方充满了东印度的劫掠者、西印度的奴隶主、英国的税吏、吃客、酒鬼、淫棍，各色各样，男女俱全。他们听了一些窃窃暗笑的江湖郎中的鬼话，以为在做了多少丑事之后，一身孽障，可以到此一洗而净！我每次进入这等地方，总想用手指捏住自己的鼻子。当然这话没有道理，但我一看见这儿任何一个两腿畜生向我走来，实在觉得他们肮脏不堪，像是一有机会就要将他们的毒疮传染给我似的！来这地方的都是最恶劣、最愚蠢、最下流的人：赌鬼，小偷，娼妓，一心想娶有钱的丑老婆子的年轻男子，一心想嫁有钱的满脸皱纹、半身入土的老头子的年轻女人，这些少夫幼妻为了便于继承产业，不惜一切手段，坚决要为这些老妇衰翁生男育女！这等丑事，尽人皆知。然而威廉·司各特爵士在 1802 年演讲，明白主张牧师不必定居教区，而应携眷到温泉游览，据说这样反而能得到他们教区子民的尊敬云云。查此人作此语时，官任代表牛津城的国会议员！（王佐良译）

注释

1. the finest meadows that ever were seen 译作"水草丰美，前所未见"，摆脱原文结构羁绊，灵活而得体。
2. 这一句拆译成两句。先将 endless flocks and herds 译为单独一句，再译原句中其余部分。
3. 注意析清此句的语法结构，a place 后所跟定语从句（to which...）中谓语动词为 resort, resort to 意为"常去某地"。译者在处理此句时采用了拆译方法。at the suggestion of... 和 in the hope of... 两个介词短语被拆译成一个句子，译得十分自然、畅达。
4. 注意句中 former 和 latter 的所指，former 指 young wife-hunters 及 young husband hunters；latter 指 rich and ugly and old women 和 rich and wrinkled or half-rotten men。译文分别译为"少夫幼妻"和"老妇衰翁"，译得精确而洗练。
5. 原文结尾颇为奇特，直译为"备忘录：他讲这话时，任牛津城议员"。译文用故作公文腔调的措辞，译出了讥讽、针砭的内涵。

讲解

翻译中的文体问题

　　语言的交际单位不是单个的句子，而是语篇。语言在交际过程中由于其使用范围、场合和交际参与者的不同而形成不同的文体。新闻报道语篇显然有别于法律文献，叙事语篇也不同于政论语篇，正式发表的讲演和朋友的私下交谈自然也会有显著区别。掌握一门语言，不仅意味着掌握它的词语搭配和句法，也意味着掌握根据不同交际目的、交际场合和交际对象组句谋篇的技能。句子的衔接、语义的连贯、文体的适切，这些都是达到交际目的必不可少的因素。

　　翻译的目的是用译语语篇在译语语境下再现源语语篇的交际功能，译语语篇也必须遵守相应文体组句谋篇的一些原则。下面我们就谈一下文体的适切问题。

　　各种文体都有一些各自常用的词语，这既包括专业术语，也包括专业术语以外的一些体现文体特色的词语，如政论文中多用庄重大词，而儿童文学作品则多用小词；科技文体中用词严谨、词义明确，而抒情散文、诗歌中往往会出现意义相对模糊的词语。

不同的文体，其句式也有不同之处。论说文一般句子较长，结构较复杂；新闻报道则结构简明，信息密度大；科技文章多出现被动语态，而童话、神话则多用简单句。

不同文体的语篇结构也不同：叙事文体通常以时间顺序组句成篇；描写语篇通常以空间顺序为主线；论说语篇则主要以逻辑层次的安排来布局谋篇。

对原文语篇的这些文体特征，译者必须了如指掌，以作为构建译语语篇的重要参照。

先来看看本单元中的两篇原文及译文。

第一篇译文引自我国著名儿童文学家陈伯吹所译《绿野仙踪》，为适应翻译教学需要稍有改动。童话当然是给儿童读的，原文文字浅显、流畅、生动。译文也要适合我国儿童的阅读水平。陈伯吹创作过许多儿童文学作品，且写有儿童文学专著，深知自己的读者的喜好和要求。《绿野仙踪》中一些稍微偏僻的字都注了发音，显然考虑十分周到。陈伯吹的译文总的来看用词通俗易懂，句式简洁明快，很好地保持了原作的文体风格，读起来同样清新、流畅，如同面对膝前的孩子们娓娓而谈。与此形成对照的是 *A Watering Place*。这是一篇游记，夹叙夹议，"既有随笔小品的情致，又有政论文的锋利"文章措辞严谨，句式凝重、繁复，王佐良的译文用词洗练，不时运用文言文的典雅句式，同样传达了原文的文体风格。试想，用《绿野仙踪》的风格译 *A Watering Place*，或以《温泉胜地》的句式去译 *The Wonderful Wizard of OZ*，那后果会怎样呢？

一个好的译者，不仅要准确传达原文的基本信息，还要传达其文体风格特征。因此，译者必须领会原文在用词、句法等方面的特征，并熟悉译入语相应文体的有关特征。

下面是关于美国球星 Michael Jordan 的一篇报道中的一句话及其译文：

1. After three championships with the Chicago Bulls, a second gold medal with the U.S. team at the 1992 Olympics, and all the accolades the game can bestow, Jordan felt his motivation slipping away.

在芝加哥公牛队打球得三次冠军，在美国队打球于1992年奥林匹克运动会获得第二枚金牌，并获得篮球所能给予的一切荣誉之后，乔丹说他打球的动力在消退。

这句话表面并未译错，译文也还算通顺。但如果译者能注意到相应的汉语文体特征——这里主要是指用词上的特征，这个句子是可以译得更好的，如可译为：在加盟芝加哥公牛队连获三冠，入主美国队于1992年再获奥运金牌，并囊括篮球运动各项殊荣之后，乔丹觉得自己打球的动力已日渐消退。

下面一句选自一封外贸信函：

2. We acknowledge receipt of your enquiry of August 2, asking us to make you a firm offer for 500 dozen Tiantan Brand men's silk shirts in various sizes and colours, for September shipment to Odense.

我们收到了你们8月2日的来函，你们要求我们就500打各种尺寸各种颜色的天坛牌男绸衬衣做出报价，于9月运抵奥登赛。

这个译文也没错，但不符合外贸函件的文体要求：一是要用外贸术语；二是要简明达意，表达准确无误。试对照下面译文：8月2日询盘收悉。贵方要求我方报出实盘：500打各种尺码、各种颜色的天坛牌丝绸男衬衫，9月装船，欧登赛交货。

再看下面几段原文和译文，特别注意其文体特点。

3. The popular views about the government's ability and effectiveness to sustain prosperity have shifted over time; there seems to be an increasing tolerance for unemployment and moderate inflation. There is a detectable shift from an exaggerated view about the potency of so-called Keynesian tools to a far-reaching agnosticism about their ability to produce, in an uncertain world, a sustained full employment growth without intolerable price and balance-of-payments instabilities. At present, the opprobrium falls on policies which are blamed for retardation in the rates of economic activity, disharmonious growth, and the combined evils of slump and inflation, but which are erroneously identified as Keynesian economics.

随着时间的推移，人们对政府在维持繁荣方面的能力和效率所持的观点已有所改变；对失业和适度的通货膨胀的忍耐性似乎也在增强。目前，对所谓凯恩斯理论的作用所做的过高估计已显而易见地为一种影响深远的不可知论所代替，人们怀疑这种理论是否能够在这个动荡不安的世界中使就业情况持续地、全面地好转，而不致引起物价的过度上升及支付平衡的波动。目前，谴责的矛头都指向政府各项政策。人们指责这些政策妨碍了经济的发展，引起了增长比例的失调，导致了滞胀（停滞和通货膨胀）交织症。然而，人们却将这些政策错误地同凯恩斯主义经济理论等同起来。

上述原文选自题为"Macroeconomic Theorizing and the Instability of Post-Keynesian

Capitalism"的一篇论文。本段由三个句子组成。后两个句子结构较复杂：第二句中用作各种修饰语的介词短语很多；第三句中有两个定语从句。译文表达体现出一种"解析—重组"过程，即首先对原文进行结构分析，认清逻辑层次，然后在不受原文结构束缚的情况下，构建出逻辑清晰、疏散铺排、层层推进的汉语句子。原文主从分明、环环相扣的句子结构被化整为零，成为一个个按逻辑顺序铺排的分句（如第二句的翻译），也可以把某个成分译为单独的一句话（如第三句的翻译）。在用词上自然也要力求正式、简明、准确。

4. Awiyao reached for the upper horizontal log which served as the edge of the head-high threshold. Clinging to the log, he lifted himself with one bound that carried him across to the narrow door. He slid back the cover, stepped inside, then pushed the cover back in place. After some moments during which he seemed to wait, he talked to the listening darkness.

"I'm sorry this had to be done. I am really sorry. But neither of us can help it."

The sound of the gangsas beat through the walls of the dark house, like the muffled roar of falling waters. The woman who had moved with a start when the sliding door opened had been hearing the gangsas of she did not know how long. The sudden rush of the rich sounds when the door opened was like a sharp gush of fire in her. She gave no sign that she heard Awiyao, but continued to sit unmoving in the darkness.

阿威伸手够住一人多高、当作门槛的横木，双手握紧，一纵身跳上狭窄的小门。他把门拉开，走进去，又把门关好。他似乎要等什么似的站了一会儿，才对着黑暗中的人说。

"我很遗憾非这么做不可。是真的。可我们谁也没法子。"

锣声透过这幽暗的小屋的墙壁传进来，如同沉闷的瀑布声。刚才的开门声使屋里的女人吓了一跳。她一直在听锣声，自己也不知听了多久。门一开响亮的锣声涌了进来，她心里像激起了一团火。她好像没听见阿威进来，仍旧呆坐在黑暗中。

此段选自题为 *Wedding Dance* 的一篇短篇小说，描写一个叫 Awiyao 的小伙子不得不离开心上人，和另一个姑娘举行婚礼的凄凉场景。句子相对较短，动词（包括非谓语动词）出现频率颇高。这正是叙述文体的特点。译文选词平易，句式明快，注重对动词的选择，力求再现原文淡雅的风格。

5. Article XIV

Section 1. All persons born or naturalized in the United States, and subject to the jurisdiction thereof, are citizens of the United States and of the State wherein they reside. No State shall make or enforce any law which shall abridge the privileges or immunities of citizens of the United States; nor shall any State deprive any person of life, liberty, or property, without due process of law; nor deny to any person within its jurisdiction the equal protection of the laws.

第十四条

一、凡出生或归化于合众国并受其管辖之人，皆为合众国及其所居之州的公民。无论何州，不得制定或施行剥夺合众国公民之特权或特免的法律；亦不得未经正当法律程序前，使任何人丧失其生命、自由或财产。并且对于该州管辖区内之任何人，皆不得拒绝给予法律上平等的保护。

这是法律文件。句子结构刻板，用词正式，属于超正式文体（或所谓 frozen style）。译文亦体现了浓重的书面语特点。

How Should One Read a Book?

Virginia Woolf

[1]   It is simple enough to say that since books have classes—fiction, biography, poetry—we should separate them and take from each what it is right that each should give us.¹ Yet few people ask from books what books can give us. Most commonly we come to books with blurred and divided minds, asking of fiction that it shall be true, of poetry that it shall be false, of biography that it shall be flattering, of history that it shall enforce our own prejudices.² If we could banish all such preconceptions when we read, that would be an admirable beginning. Do not dictate to your author: try to become him. Be his fellow-worker and accomplice.³ If you hang back, and reserve and criticize at first, you are preventing yourself from getting the fullest possible value from what you read. But if you open your mind as widely as possible⁴, then signs and hints of almost imperceptible fineness,

from the twist and turn of the first sentences, will bring you into the presence of a human being unlike any other. Steep[5] yourself in this, acquaint yourself with this, and soon you will find that your author is giving you, or attempting to give you, something far more definite. The thirty-two chapters of a novel—if we consider how to read a novel first[6]—are an attempt to make something as formed and controlled as a building:[7] but words are more impalpable than bricks; reading is a longer and more complicated process than seeing. Perhaps the quickest way to understand the elements of what a novelist is doing is not to read, but to write; to make your own experiment with the dangers and difficulties of words.[8] Recall, then, some event that has left a distinct impression on you—how at the corner of the street, perhaps, you passed two people talking. A tree shook; an electric light danced; the tone of the talk was comic, but also tragic; a whole vision, an entire conception, seemed contained in that moment.

[2]　But when you attempt to reconstruct it in words, you will find that it breaks into a thousand conflicting impressions.[9] Some must be subdued; others emphasized; in the process you will lose, probably, all grasp upon the emotion itself. Then turn from your blurred and littered pages to the opening pages of some great novelist[10]—Defoe, Jane Austen, Hardy. Now you will be better able to appreciate their mastery. It is not merely that we are in the presence of a different person—Defoe, Jane Austen, or Thomas Hardy—but that we are living in a different world. Here, in Robinson Crusoe, we are trudging a plain high road; one thing happens after another; the fact and the order of the fact is enough. But if the open air and adventure mean everything to Defoe they mean nothing to Jane Austen. Hers is the drawingroom, and people talking, and by the many mirrors of their talk revealing their characters. And if, when we have accustomed ourselves to the drawingroom and its reflections, we turn to Hardy, we are once more spun around[11]. The moors are round us and the stars are above our heads. The other side of the mind is now exposed—the dark side that comes uppermost in solitude, not the light side that shows in company. Our relations are not towards people, but towards Nature and destiny. Yet different as these worlds are, each is consistent with itself. The maker of each is careful to observe the laws of his own perspective, and however great a strain they may put upon us they will never confuse us, as lesser

writers so frequently do, by introducing two different kinds of reality into the same book.[12] Thus to go from one great novelist to another—from Jane Austen to Hardy, from Peacock to Trollope, from Scott to Meredith—is to be wrenched and uprooted; to be thrown this way and then that.[13] To read a novel is a difficult and complex art. You must be capable not only of great finesse of perception, but of great boldness of imagination if you are going to make use of all that the novelist—the great artist—gives you.

参考译文

怎样读书？

弗吉尼亚·伍尔夫

[1] 书既然有小说、传记、诗歌之分，就应区别对待，从各类书中取其应该给予我们的东西。这话说来很简单。然而很少有人向书索取它能给我们的东西，我们拿起书来往往怀着模糊而又杂乱的想法，要求小说是真实的，诗歌是虚假的，传记要吹捧，史书能加强我们自己的偏见。读书时如能抛开这些先入之见，便是极好的开端。不要对作者指手画脚，而要尽力与作者融为一体，共同创作，共同策划。如果你不参与，不投入，而且一开始就百般挑剔，那你就无缘从书中获得最大的益处。你若敞开心扉，虚怀若谷，那么，书中精细入微的寓意和暗示便会把你从一开头就碰上的那些像山回水转般的句子中带出来，走到一个独特的人物面前。钻进去熟悉它，你很快就会发现，作者展示给你的或想展示给你的是一些比原先要明确得多的东西。不妨先来谈谈如何读小说吧。一部长篇小说分成三十二章，是作者的苦心经营，想把它建构得如同一座错落有致、布局合理的大厦。可是词语比砖块更难捉摸，阅读比观看更费时、更复杂。了解作家创作的个中滋味，最有效的途径恐怕不是读而是写；通过写亲自体验一下运用文字的艰难险阻。回想一件你记忆犹新的事吧。比方说，在街道的拐弯处遇到两个人正在谈话。树影婆娑，灯光摇曳，谈话的调子喜中有悲。这一瞬间似乎包含了一种完整的意境，全面的构思。

[2] 可是当你打算用文字来重现此情此景的时候，它却化作千万个互相冲突的印象。有的必须淡化，有的则应加突出。在处理过程中你可能对整个意境根本把握不住了。这时，还是把你那些写得含糊杂乱的一页页书稿搁到一边，翻开某位小说大师，如笛福、简·奥斯汀或哈代的作品来从头读吧。这时候你就能更深刻地领略大

师们驾驭文字的技巧了。因为我们不仅面对一个个不同的人物——笛福、简·奥斯汀或托马斯·哈代,而且置身于不同的世界。阅读《鲁滨逊漂流记》时,我们仿佛跋涉在旷野大道上;事件一个接一个;故事再加上故事情节的安排就足够了。如果说旷野和历险对笛福来说就是一切,那么对简·奥斯汀就毫无意义了。她的世界是客厅和客厅中闲聊的人们。这些人的言谈像一面面镜子,反映出他们的性格特征。当我们熟悉了奥斯汀的客厅及其反映出来的事物以后再读哈代的作品,又得转向另一个世界。周围茫茫荒野,头顶一片星空。此时,心灵的另一面被揭示出来:不是聚会结伴时显示出来的轻松愉快的一面,而是孤独时最容易萌生的忧郁阴沉的一面。和我们打交道的不是人,而是自然与命运。虽然这些世界截然不同,它们自身却浑然一体。每一个世界的创造者都小心翼翼地遵循自己观察事物的法则,不管他们的作品读起来如何费力,却不会像蹩脚的作家那样,把格格不入的两种现实塞进一部作品中,使人感到不知所云。因此,读完一位伟大作家的小说再去读另一位的,比如说从简·奥斯汀到哈代,从皮科克到特罗洛普,从司各特到梅瑞狄斯,就好像被猛力扭动,连根拔起,抛来抛去。说实在的,读小说是一门困难而又复杂的艺术。要想充分享用小说作者(或称为伟大的艺术家)给予你的一切,你不仅要具备极高的感受能力,还得有大胆的想象力。

注释

1. 此句译成两句,先译 to say that...,后译主句。表达的顺序正好倒过来,但在信息传达功能上是和原句等值的,在和下文的连贯上也是得体的。与下列译文对照一下,就更能体会到此译文的连贯了:说来容易,既然书有各种各样——小说、传记、诗歌——那我们就应该把它们分门别类,并且各按其类来汲取每本书理应给予我们的内容。然而,很少人读书时想过书本能提供些什么问题。
2. 此句中的 come to、divided、ask of、true false、flattering、prejudices 等词语的意义看似不难,但实际翻译起来是颇费思索的,必须反复推敲其在上下文中的含义才能找到确切的对等词语。
3. 以上两句,译者是合在一起译的。请注意 dictate、become him、fellow-worker 及 accomplice 等词语的对等词的推敲。
4. open your mind as widely as possible 译为"敞开心扉,虚怀若谷"两个四字词语,词义贴切,也符合原文的语体特点。
5. steep 本义"浸泡",译文根据汉语表达习惯译为"钻进去",即"钻研"。
6. 这个插入的状语从句被提到前面译成单独的一句。这样处理使译文层次分明,行文连贯。
7. 此句中的 attempt、formed、controlled 都不是难词、大词,但在此文中却不好译。必须依据上下文仔细体味其含义。

8. 此句中 elements of what a novelist is doing、make your own experiment with、dangers and difficulties of words 都是不大好译的短语。译文准确、地道，值得体味。另外，译文全句十分流畅，最后一个分句加进"通过写"三个字，达到了贯通文气的效果。
9. 此句中的 reconstruct it、breaks into a thousand conflicting impressions 都是必须将字、词融入上下文仔细揣摩才能译得贴切的。试对照下面只顾字义不顾上下文的生硬译文：但当你企图用词语重建它的时候，你会发现它破碎成成千个相互冲突的印象。
10. 此句是祈使语气，译文用两个分句，译得贴切达意。
11. we are once more spun around 理解为"我们转而面对另一个迥异的世界"，是准确的。而如译为"当我们习惯于这个客厅及其中闪烁多姿的映象以后又转而去阅读哈代，那我们又会晕头转向"，就欠妥贴了。
12. 此句中 by introducing two different kinds of reality into the same book 是修饰 confuse 还是 do，只从这一句是很难判断的。唯一的解决办法是根据上下文推断。此句中的 reality 指的就是前面几句中的 world。每一位文学大师都创造一个独特的、不同于他人的世界（consistent with itself）。所以，可以有把握地说，by introducing... 修饰的是 do，即只有 lesser writers 才会把两类不同的世界混杂于一本书中。
13. 注意译文对 ...is to be wrenched and uprooted 和 to be thrown this way and then that 中的暗喻形象是如何处理的。对照下面译文：因此，从一位伟大的小说家到另一位——从简·奥斯汀到哈代，从皮科克到特罗洛普，从司各特到梅瑞狄斯——我们都要经受一场脱胎换骨、离乡背井的痛苦，被扔过来又赶过去。

讲解

译者的具体操作

翻译的具体操作是在两个层次上进行的。一是词句层，也就是像作文一样的遣词造句过程。译者在这一层次上所思考的主要是词义的确定及句式的安排。注释 2、4、5、7、8、9 所涉及的基本属于此类操作。但译者只在句以下的层次上进行思考是不够的。因为有时会把原文的一句拆成两句（注释 1、6、10），有时又会把原文的两句合译为一句（注释 3），有时一个词、一个结构的意义并非在本句的范围内就能解决（注释 12），必须放在更大的语言单位中去分析思考。这就需要译者在句以上的语篇层次上进行操作，不仅要考虑一个句子，还要顾及几个句子，整个段落，以至整篇文章。这道理也正和作文一样，光遣词造句是不够的，还必须善于连句成篇，句与句之间的结构衔接、意义连贯也是保证译文质量的重要环节。仔细阅读上面译文，不仅要体味译者在选词造句上的精妙，也要综观语篇层次上意义的

连贯和流畅,作为自己翻译实践的借鉴。

以第一自然段最后几句为例(自 Recall, then, some event that left an impression on you... 开始),译文在句子安排上和原文是有差别的:首先,断句不一样;其次,原文连接词 perhaps 插在句子中间,译文将其译为"比方说"放在句首;另外,原文最后一句主语是 vision 和 conception,译文主语改为"这一瞬间"(相对于原文状语 in that moment)。这些变动不只是简单的句子结构变动,而是保证了在更高层次上的语篇连贯,使译文读来文通理顺,毫无翻译的斧凿之痕。下面再观察几个译例,请特别注意译者在词句层和语篇层的具体操作。

1. Earlier in the day we had a tussle over the words "mug" and "water". Miss Sullivan had tried to impress it upon me that "mug" is mug and that "water" is water, but I persisted in confounding the two. In despair she had dropped the subject for the time, only to renew it at the first opportunity.

那一天我们已经为 mug 和 water 这两个词纠缠过一番了。沙利文小姐想让我知道 mug 就是 mug(有柄杯),water 就是 water(水),可是我老把这两个词搞混。她没有办法,只好暂时放下这个话题,等有机会再说。

原文 in despair 是"绝望"的意思。但此处讲的只是老师对"我"感到失望而已,照词典上的意义译就太重了,故只译为"没有办法"。

2. Scientists now know that great quakes...like the one that devastated San Francisco in 1906...are the product of multiple ruptures of geological faults and that the trigger setting off the chain reaction can be a very local failure.

现在科学家们知道,大地震,比如 1906 年使旧金山遭受严重破坏的大地震,是地质断层在多处裂开所引起的,而最初引发这一连锁反应的可能只是一个局部地区出现的问题。

根据上文此句 failure 一词指的是地层的断裂,所以不能译为"失败"。

3. "My husband and I were liberal people—giving the benefit of the doubt to everyone, bending over backwards to be fair," she recalled.

"我和丈夫都很宽厚,总觉得大家都是好人,总是尽量做得公正,"她说。

the benefit of the doubt 本是法律术语,意为在证据不足的情况下先假定无罪。在此处则指对周围人的行为均作善意解释和理解。译文根据上下文及口语的语体特点译成"觉得大家都是好人",准确而得体。

译者不但要考虑意义的准确,也要考虑逻辑的连贯。请观察下面各例:

4. He wanted to join the Chinese Communist Party in Berlin, he would study and work hard, he would do anything he was asked to do but return to his old life, which had turned to ashes beneath his feet.

他要求加入中国共产党在柏林的党组织,他一定会努力学习和工作,只要不再回到旧的生活里去——它已经在他的脚下化为尘埃了,派他做什么工作都行。

上述译文没有错误,但连贯性差,上下文有些不连贯。可改译如下:……一定会努力学习和工作,派他做什么工作都行,只要不再回到旧的生活里去——那种生活已经在他的脚下化为尘埃了。

5. The people were there and the land—the first dazed and bleeding and hungry, and, when winter came, shivering in their rags in the hovels which the bombings had made of their homes; the second a vast wasteland of rubble. The German people had not been destroyed, as Hitler, who had tried to destroy so many other peoples and, in the end, when the war was lost, themselves, had wished.

人民还在那里,土地也还在那里。但人民都茫茫然,流着血、挨着饿,当冬天到来时,他们在被炸成断垣残壁的破屋中,穿着破烂的衣服不停地打着哆嗦;土地则一片荒芜,瓦砾成堆。曾经企图毁灭其他许多民族的希特勒,在战争最后失败的时候也想要毁灭德国人民,但与他的愿望相反,德国人民并没有被毁灭。

对照原文可发现译者在行文上做了不少变动:first 和 second 所指代的名词(people 和 land)被复原,最后一句的重心也做了调整(将主句 The German people had not been destroyed 放在译文最后)。这些变动顺应了汉语的行文规范和习惯,使译文条理清晰,流畅自然。

6. When I reached the age of twelve I left the school for ever and got my first full-time job, as a grocer's boy. I spent my days carrying heavy loads, but I enjoyed it. It was only my capacity for hard work that saved me from early dismissal, for I could never stomach speaking to my "betters" with the deference my employer thought I should assume.

我十二岁那年就永远离开了学校,并且找到了全职工作干,最初是在一家食品杂货店里当伙计。我整天扛很重的货物,干得倒也挺带劲。要不是能干重活,我早就给辞退了。因为老板想要我毕恭毕敬地跟那些"上等人"说话,这样干,我实在受不了。

原文最后一句译得有些逻辑失调,请比较下面经过逻辑调整的译文:……可是

老板想要我毕恭毕敬地跟那些"上等人"说话,我实在难以做到,要不是能干重活,我早就给辞退了。

译者在词汇及句子两个层次上的操作可以这样加以概括:译者翻译的不是词典上的词(照词典上列出的对应词译),而是上下文中的词;不是孤零零的句子,而是有机地组合成语篇的句子。

Bring on the Elites![1]

Joel Stein

[1] I went to a better college than you did. That does not make me a better person[2] than you. It does, however, make me smarter, more knowledgeable, more curious and more ambitious. So, in a lot of ways, better.

[2] Though that may seem obvious, we in the academic elite don't bring up stuff like this often, because the income gap between us and everyone else has ballooned grotesquely, and we feel bad about it. Plus, as technology removes barriers to entry, the nonacademic elite has come to believe that because anyone can do anything, we are all equally skilled at everything. Bloggers opine about world politics on TV alongside members of the Council on Foreign Relations. On YouTube, $100 million studio movie clips go up against guys crying over rainbows. More appalling, people demand that I read their e-mails, since I expect them to read my columns. This is like arguing that LeBron James has to play one-on-one with every NBA fan. In that analogy, I am LeBron James and the e-mail author is the NBA fan. I explain this only because you went to such a bad college.[3]

[3] The idea that we're all equally qualified is so widely accepted that when interviewing Vice President Joe Biden on the *Today* show about the nomination of Elena Kagan to the Supreme Court, Matt Lauer said, "Here's how the current bench will look. Five of the current Justices will be graduates of Harvard Law School. Three will be graduates of Yale Law School. Another will have gone to Yale Law School but graduated from Columbia...Doesn't it

sound a little elitist to you?" Undoubtedly, spell-check sounds a little elitist to you when an hour of your news program is anchored by Hoda Kotb and Kathie Lee Gifford.[4]

[4] I had assumed the Supreme Court was one of the places that needed to be elitist. Being a Supreme Court Justice isn't like being a community-college student or a *Huffington Post* columnist. The court is one of the few institutions in which people have to do some elite thinking. Have you ever read the Constitution? Of course you haven't: It's boring as hell. It's for nerds. It contains sentences like "No Bill of Attainder or ex post facto Law shall be passed". Now try to use that sentence to explain why gays should or shouldn't get married. You can see why you'd have to go to Yale Law for this.

[5] This isn't the first time someone has made the antielitist argument about the court. When G. Harrold Carswell, a man who apparently could not spell either of his own names, was nominated by Richard Nixon, Senator Roman Hruska defended him by saying, "Even if he were mediocre, there are a lot of mediocre judges and people and lawyers. They are entitled to a little representation, aren't they, and a little chance?" I'm guessing Hruska was one of those kids who actually put his Little League participation trophy on top of his dresser.[5]

[6] The difference is that when Hruska said that, everyone immediately made fun of him, and Carswell lost the nomination. Forty years later, Lauer sounded reasonable. Even the Vice President didn't try to talk him out of it. We have elevated common sense above learned reason. Magazine editors and network executives make writers cut references and words they think most people won't know—even though everybody has Wikipedia. We are becoming a country that believes the rich have earned their money but the well educated have not earned their intellectual superiority. This leads to a nation that idolizes Kardashians[6].

[7] Antielitism is a cancer waiting to metastasize in any democracy and one that Alexis de Tocqueville worried about for the U.S. Why do I bring this up? Because in any argument of any kind, elites always quote Tocqueville.[7]

[8] Yes, it's unfair that so much of our future is determined by what we did in high school, as if we were some Soviet Olympic team. But until we come up with a better system, if I have brain surgery, I want it done by a doctor

who went to an amazing medical school. Just like I want my Brazilian jujitsu instructor to have a red belt, my prisoners of war to be rescued by a Navy Seal and my technical-support phone operator to speak passable English. In fact, I wish more jobs had clear forms of elitism. Specifically, building contractors.

[9] Teaching our children that we're all equally valuable, it turns out, was a stupid message. We have to go back to keeping the scores of kids' games and giving trophies only to the ones who win. I lost almost every game I played, and I didn't mind. You know why? Because I knew I'd be going to a better college than the other kids.

参考译文

力挺精英！

[1] 本人当年上的大学比你的好。虽然这并不会使我的人品比你强，但的确让我变得更聪明，更有知识，更具求知欲，也更雄心勃勃。可以说，在很多方面，确实比你更强些。

[2] 尽管这一点显而易见，但我们这些身处学术精英圈子的人并不会经常提起这种话题，因为我们与其他职业的收入差距已经大得有些荒唐，我们颇感愧疚。此外，由于科技发展消除了进入学术领域的壁垒，那些非学术领域的精英们已经开始相信，既然只要想做人人都可以做，那我们在各个方面也就都拥有同样的能力了。博客写手可以在电视节目里与美国外交关系委员会成员大谈世界政治。在YouTube上，斥资1亿美元的大片片断，只落得和面对彩虹大哭的镜头一起播放。更不像话的是，很多人要求我阅读他们的电子邮件，因为我希望他们阅读我的专栏。这就等于要求勒布朗·詹姆斯必须和每一个NBA球迷都来场一对一的比赛。在这个比喻里，我就是勒布朗·詹姆斯，而那些电子邮件的作者就是NBA球迷。别怪我在这儿饶舌，谁让你当年上的是那么糟糕的一所大学呢。

[3] 人人资格均等的想法已被普遍接受，就连《今日》节目主持人马特·劳尔就埃伦娜·卡根被提名为最高法院法官一事采访副总统拜登时，也这样说道："看来最高法院的构成将是这样的：五名毕业于哈佛大学法学院，三名毕业于耶鲁大学法学院。另外一个读过耶鲁，但最终毕业于哥伦比亚大学……你难道不觉得这有点太精英化了吗？"说来也是，如果你看的新闻节目有整整一个小时都让郝姐·寇碧和凯希·李·吉福德这样的娱乐名嘴来主持，那么你就会觉得，就连电脑文档的拼写检

查也都带上精英味道了。

[4] 我一直认为,最高法院就是一个需要精英化的地方。出任最高法院法官,可不同于当个社区大学的学生或《赫芬顿邮报》的专栏作家。最高法院是人们必须从事精英化思考的为数不多的机构之一。你读过宪法吗?你当然没读过:那东西无聊透了。是给书呆子读的。那里面尽是这样的句子:"不得通过任何褫夺公权的法案或追溯既往的法律。"现在,你不妨试着用这个句子来说明一下同性恋者到底是应该还是不应该结婚的理由。这下你就会明白,你得先去念念耶鲁大学法学院了吧。

[5] 这已经不是第一次有人针对最高法院发表反精英主义言论了。当那位显然连自己的名和姓都拼不对的G·哈罗德·卡斯韦尔被尼克松总统提名为最高法院法官时,参议员罗曼·赫鲁斯卡曾经辩解说:"就算他是个平庸之辈,可实际上平庸的法官、公民和律师也多得很。难道他们就没资格拥有自己的代表,获得一点机会吗?"这话让我不禁觉得,这个赫鲁斯卡准是那种连少年棒球联盟参赛纪念品都摆在小柜子上炫耀的孩子。

[6] 所不同的是,当年赫鲁斯卡的话一说出口,就立即招来一片嘲笑讥讽,卡斯韦尔最终也没通过提名。可四十多年后,劳尔的这番话听起来却似乎颇有道理,就连副总统本人也没有让他收回的意思。我们已经把常识摆到了学识之上。杂志编辑和网络主管要求作者删去那些他们认为大多数人看不懂的说法和词语,而实际上人人都可上网查查维基百科呀。我们正在变成这样的一个国家:人们相信,富人已经挣到属于自己的钱,而受过良好教育的人却未能赢得自己的智力优势。这么一来,难怪举国上下都疯狂崇拜起卡戴珊三姐妹那样的低俗影视形象啦。

[7] 反精英主义是民主社会中随时都会扩散的恶性肿瘤,也是当初阿历克西·德·托克维尔担心美国会出现的情况。为什么我会提到这一点呢?因为不管辩论到什么话题,精英们总爱引用托克维尔的话。

[8] 是啊,我们的未来在如此大的程度上是由我们上中学时的表现决定的,这不公平,就像苏联的奥运代表队一样。但是,在我们能建立一个更好的体制之前,假如我要做脑部手术,我还是希望主刀医生是某所顶尖医学院的高才生。我还希望,找巴西柔术教练要有红腰带的,解救战俘的任务最好派海豹突击队去实施,技术支持的电话接线员的英语也要过关。说实话,我希望有更多的行业都能由精英主导,特别是建筑承包业。

[9] 这样看来,告诉我们的孩子人人都具有同等价值只是一种愚蠢的说教。我们必

须一如既往把孩子们参与的比赛的结果记录下来,并只向那些获胜者颁发奖品。尽管我小时候几乎每赛必输,可我并不在乎。你知道这其中的原因吗?因为我当时就知道,我将要就读的大学比其他孩子的都要好。

注释

1. 反精英主义一直是美国文化传统的一部分,在奥巴马竞选、当选以及随后的全球金融危机中,反精英主义的声音更是十分强烈,以致奥巴马和希拉克都对自己的常青藤名校背景有意回避。本文却力主精英之道,可以说是反其道而行之,曾招致不少批评和热议。文章标题可有如下选择:《力挺精英!》《敢论精英!》《为精英鼓劲!》。《英语文摘》和译言网都刊有汉语译文,可对照阅读,其汉译标题分别为《提升精英!》和《精英挑大梁》。
2. 此处 person 有 personality 之意。
3. 这里注意译出作者的语气。
4. 注意这句话的讽刺味道:新闻节目是严肃的黄金档节目,如果允许郝妲·寇碧和凯希·李·吉福德这样的大众娱乐节目名嘴来主持,那大众的品位岂不太低了,就连最普普通通的拼写检查恐怕也会被称作精英化了,还有什么不能贴上精英化的标签呢?
5. 要理解这句话,如同注释 4 所涉及的句子一样,都需要相关的背景知识。Little League 是小学生的棒球比赛,连参赛纪念品都拿来显摆的孩子显然没得过什么重大奖项,既无能力又有点虚荣。同样,这个罗曼·赫鲁斯卡虽身为参议员,却也无甚高明,胡言乱语而已。译文中加了"炫耀"二字,意为明确这种含义。
6. Kardashians 指的是美国 2007 年首映的电视连续剧 *Keeping up with the Kardashinas* 中的三姐妹,其形象浅薄而庸俗。
7. Alexis de Tocqueville(1805—1859)是法国作家和政治家。1831 年曾赴美国考察,著有《美国的民主》一书,对美国的政治制度进行了剖析。

讲解

一、语篇的语境

语境指的是语篇在构建和解读过程中所涉及的有关语篇本身的语言知识以及和语篇相关的语外知识的总和。语篇中的各个句子无论在意义上还是在逻辑上都是有机地联系在一起的,同时这些句子也和语篇构建和解析时的情境和文化背景密切关联,因为只有这样才能有效地传达信息。

要认识与原文语篇相关的语境因素,并保证译文行文在语境等层面的连贯性,译者应注意如下三类语境因素。

一是语言语境（linguistic context），亦称上下文（co-text）。这指的是语篇自身的结构衔接及逻辑连贯。译者一定要将原文通读几遍，将原文各句段融会贯通，在头脑中形成一个脉络清晰的整体。具体的翻译过程中，先要保证词语译得准确，每个段落中句子安排得当，文气贯通，逻辑明晰，再注意更为宏观的段与段间的连接及全文的流畅。

现在请观察下面一个翻译实例：

1. I was thrilled by my correct reading of the dance, yet my feelings could hardly compare to those of the Danish and West German scientists when, in August 1988, they first put an imitation bee on a comb in a darkened hive, directed it by computer, and realized they were "talking" to real bees.

虽然我为自己正确解释蜜蜂的舞蹈而激动万分，但是，我的心情却难以同那些丹麦和西德的科学家的心情相比。当1988年8月这些科学家第一次将一只人工仿制的蜜蜂放到遮黑的蜂箱的蜂巢上，利用计算机控制它做动作，这时科学家们意识到，他们竟然同真蜜蜂"交谈"上啦。

原文是由一句话组成的一个自然段，语义连接很紧密。译文把状语从句拆开，在汉语中单立为一个句子。这种译法是可取的。但同时也带来了译文行文连贯的问题。上述译文中的两句话衔接不够紧密，代词"这些""这时"的所指也未能和上文呼应，致使行文松散，文气不能贯通。试比较下面译文，并仔细思考上下文的连贯问题：

我为自己能正确地解释蜜蜂的舞蹈而激动万分，但是，我的心情却难以同当年那些丹麦和西德的科学家们相比。1988年8月，那些科学家们第一次将一只人工仿制的蜜蜂放到遮黑的蜂箱的蜂巢上，并利用计算机控制它做动作，科学家们意识到，他们竟然同真蜜蜂"交谈"上啦。

这个译文与原译文相比并没有多大变动，只不过增加了"当年""并"两个词，把"这些"改成了"那些"，并进行了少许文字调整，但这种变动却体现出译者的语言语境意识。

二是情景语境（situational context），这指的是语篇所涉及的具体场景、参与者等。不把语言符号和它们所表现的客观世界联系起来，这些语言符号也就失去了意义，无法传递连贯的信息。

首先，要了解文章发表时的具体情况或背景，同样的话语在不同的场合和背景下呈现出来，意义会有很大区别。比如在翻译"Bring on the Elites!"之前，了解一下文章发表的背景（见注释1）对把握整篇文章的主旨和语气以及标题的翻译都是非常必要的。

另外，语篇所描述的真实的或虚拟的场景体现着语符和现实场景间的联系，需要译者对相关情景有所了解，能够联想出现实世界中的类似情景细节，以便用译文将其再现。请看下面一例：

2. Our hosts hovered over us. Did we like the caviar? How was the Khachapuri (a kind of bread)? Why weren't we eating more roast chicken? We were finally saved from certain *crise de foi* by Aleksandro, just before the shashlik arrived.

这一段描写的是一个美国人访问苏联的格鲁吉亚时应邀参加一个家庭宴会的情景，hover over 一词描述了主人在餐桌旁热情招待的情景，几个问句表达了主人对客人的热情关照，而所谓"信念危机"只是由于主人的热情使客人应接不暇，有些窘迫而已。试调动自己的有关经验，构想这段文字所描绘的场景，并比较下面两种译文：

[a] 主人在我们周围走动着。我们喜欢鱼子酱吗？面包怎么样？我们为什么不多吃些烤鸡？在烤肉串端上来之前，我们终于被亚利山德罗从信念危机中解救出来。
[b] 赫尔来兹一家人一直在我们身边照应着。喜欢不喜欢鱼子酱呀？咖查普利（一种面包）好不好吃呀？为什么不多吃点烤鸡呀？问得我们不知如何回答才好。直到快上最后一道菜烤肉串时，亚历山德罗才给我们解了围。

显然，译文 [b] 更贴近类似情景的汉语表达习惯和方式，更能唤起译语读者对有关情景的联想。

再观察下面一个译例：

3. Neil, the new chairman of the Bury St. Edmunds branch of the National Front, called me at home from a pay phone in a pub. It looked likely that he would get approval for me to come along to their disco party. The date for the party had been fixed—Saturday, the 14th of April. Could I make it? He would meet me at the station.

英国民族阵线党伯里圣埃德蒙兹支部的新主席叫尼尔。他用一个啤酒店的公用电话往我家里打电话。看来他能为我争取得到许可来参加他们的迪斯科派对。派对的日期已定在4月14日星期六。我能来吗？他将到车站接我。

以上译文只是一种文字对应，失去了情景上的连贯。这说明译者未把这段文字与相关的情景挂上钩。可将后两句改为：

......看来他能为我争取得到许可，让我去参加他们的迪斯科舞会。舞会的日期已定在 4 月 14 日星期六。他问我能去吗？还说他将到车站去接我。

三是文化语境（cultural context），即语篇所涉及的文化、社会背景。原文语篇是在源语社会、文化背景下产生和传播的，而其译文要在译语的社会、文化背景下传播。这就要求译者去充当跨越两种文化的桥梁作用：首先他要设身处地，从源文文化语境的角度理解原文；然后，他还要从译语文化语境着眼，将原文信息重新表述为能为译语读者接受和理解的连贯语篇。

拿本单元的翻译来说，就特别需要译者了解有关的社会文化背景，注释 4、5、6 特别凸显了有关背景知识对理解原文和构建译文的重要性。译者可借助译注向自己的读者提供必要的背景信息，也可在译文行文中提供必要提示。

再请阅读下面短文：

4. There may never have been another baseball con man like Dizzy Dean, the great St. Louis Cardinals pitcher, who often used the sport for his own amusement. One day the New York Giants put runners on first and second with two out, and Dean intentionally walked Hughie Critz to load the bases. It seemed like a dumb move as the dreaded Bill Terry, the last National Leaguer ever to hit 400 was next up.

But Dean walked down from the mound and confronted Terry at the plate. "Bill," he said, "I'm sorry to do this to you, but I promised a girl I'd strike you out with the bases loaded."

And he did—on three pitches.

再没有像迪恩这样善于捣鬼的棒球运动员了。他是圣路易斯队的投球手，常常在比赛中为自己寻求乐趣。一次，纽约巨人队的跑垒队员已占领了一垒和二垒，两名队员出局。迪恩故意投出四个坏球保克里茨上垒。这一招看来很蠢，因为下一个击球手是上届全国联赛打满 400 分的名将比尔·特里。

可迪恩从投球踏板走到本垒上的比尔面前，说："比尔，对不起啦。我已经答应了一个姑娘，要在你们队员已经上垒的情况下，把你三球击下。"

他说到做到——投出三个好球比尔都未能接到，按规则比尔三击不中只能出局。

不少读者看了这段文字可能都感到有些不知所云。这并非是你的英语不好，而是你不了解有关的文化背景知识：棒球的基本常识。换句话说，理解的障碍不是语言问题，而是文化问题。译者如果想传达原文信息，就得自己先查看有关材料读懂原文，翻译时可采取加注或在译文字里行间增添解释性文字的办法（参阅第三章

Unit Six 的讲解部分）。以上译文便采取了后一种方法。如仍不足以充分传达原文信息，那恐怕只能靠中文读者自己去查看有关资料了。

二、翻译的标准

什么样的译文是合格的译文，好的译文？不同历史时期的翻译工作者实际上一直在自觉不自觉地遵循着某种标准。

在我国，100 多年前的翻译家严复在他翻译的《天演论》（1898）的"译例言"中提出了译事的三字标准"信、达、雅"。后世翻译工作者虽不乏争论，但基本上将之奉为圭臬，力求信达，沿袭至今。20 世纪 80 年代张培基等编写的《英汉翻译教程》将其重新措辞为"忠实、通顺"四个字，并赋予新的解释。"忠实"指完整而准确地表达原作的内容和保持原作的风格；"通顺"指译文语言通顺易懂，符合规范。这也一直是指导我国翻译教学的标准。1990 年版的《高等学校英语专业英语教学大纲》，1994 年版的《高校英语专业八级考试大纲（试行本）》以及 2000 年版的《高等学校英语专业英语教学大纲》在谈到翻译标准时也同样强调了这两个原则——"忠实于原意，语言通顺""忠实原意，语言流畅"和"准确、流畅"。

在西方，Alexander Fraser Tytler 在 1797 年提出过翻译的三条原则：(1)译文须完全再现原文的意义；(2)译文的写作风格须和原文一致；(3)译文须和原文一样自然流畅。20 世纪 50 年代以来逐渐形成的西方现代翻译研究对以忠实为核心的传统的翻译理念提出过不少质疑，并产生了一些新的认识和理论。20 世纪 60 年代，Eugene A. Nida 提出"动态对等"的概念，认为译语读者对译文的反应应与源语读者对原文的反应基本相同。他还以《圣经》的翻译为例主张译文不仅要传达原文的信息，还应实现其表达感情和鼓动他人的功能。因此他给翻译下的定义是："Translating consists in reproducing in the receptor language the closest natural equivalent of the source-language message, first in terms of meaning and secondly in terms of style."（翻译就在于用接受语重新写出源发语信息的最贴切而自然的对等语，首先在意义上，其次在风格上。）。对我们来说，这个定义有如下几点值得注意：(1)所谓 equivalent 是与 identity 相对而言，译文与原文是意义与意义的对等，而非字句形式上的等同；(2) equivalent 前面有两个修饰语 closest 和 natural，这就是说，可能有两个及两个以上的译文与原文在意义上很相近，译者要选择最相近的，而且译文应自然流畅；(3)当翻译过程中意义和形式发生矛盾时，意义对等应优先于形式对等。20 世纪 70 年代，德国的翻译学者 Katharina Reiss 提出语篇类型和翻译方法之间的关系。她认为不同的语篇交际功能要求使用相应的翻译方法：以传达信息（informative）为主要功能的语篇（如科技文章、新闻报道）的翻译应确保译文的准确性；以表达作者情感（expressive）为主要目的的语篇（如散文、诗歌）的翻译应注重审美价值的再现；而以号召、鼓动或给予读者指令（operative）为主要目的的语篇（如宣传材料、广告、使用手册）的翻译应能在译语读者身上体现出相应的效果。80年代Katharina Reiss和她的同事Hans J. Vermeer又共同提出了翻译的"目的论"（skopos theory），进一步提出翻译的目的决定翻译方法的观点。译者根据翻译的目的以及翻译活动发生时的社会文化因素确定自己的翻译方法，而且译者的交际目的可能不同于源语作者。这种理论突出了译者在跨文化交际过程中的重要作用。

那么，关于翻译标准的讨论对我们的翻译实践有什么启示呢？第一，翻译是一种跨文化交际活动，语言是文化的重要组成部分，但不是全部。翻译操作不仅发生在语言层面，也发生在与所译的语篇有关的文化层面——社会／文化因素、作者的思想意识、翻译的目的等都会对语言层面的操作产生影响和制约。因此，译者必须明确为何译，为谁译，才能知道怎么译。第二，为实现不同的交际目的，语篇是有不同类型的。不同语篇类型的翻译标准和方法应有所区别。第三，文化制约和交际目的等因素归根结底都要落实到译者对语篇的操作上。原文语篇的信息必须在最大程度上加以再现——这种"忠实"虽然受到文化及交际语境的制约，也会因译者在解读能力和思想意识上的个体差别，或时间、空间因素的影响而有些不好把握，但某一时期、某一地域、某一文化背景下的一群读者面对同一语篇在很大程度上是能达成共识的。这便是"忠实"的基础。第四，译文须自然流畅。这也是评价译文的重要标准，因为不合乎译语文化和语言规范的译文一般来说很难达到交际目的。

基于上述理解，并结合翻译学习的实践，可将翻译标准概括为：好的译文应该最大限度地再现原文信息和文体特点，合乎译语文化、语言规范，实现交际目的。

以本章的Unit Two和Unit Three两个单元的译文为例。Unit Two的原文以生动、练达的笔触告诉读者如何理解、体味并与作者共享艺术世界之精妙。翻译此文的目的是向中国读者介绍这一英语名篇的深邃思想，给人以启迪。译文理解准确，注意再现原文的文体特点，语言精练，句式严谨，形象表达得体、达意。Unit Three的原文是*Time*上的一篇专题文章，面对当前美国的反精英主义的浪潮，语句犀利尖刻，针砭嘲讽，译文应尽可能传达出这种风格，并适当介绍有关社会背景知识，加强中文读者对美国时政的了解。

 # You Are What You Think

[1]   Do you see the glass as half full rather than half empty? Do you keep your eye upon the doughnut, not upon the hollow?[1] Suddenly these cliches are scientific questions, as researchers scrutinize the power of positive thinking.

[2]   A fast-growing body of research—104 studies so far, involving some 15,000 people—is proving that optimism can help you to be happier, healthier and more successful; pessimism leads, by contrast, to hopelessness, sickness and failure, and is linked to depression, loneliness and painful shyness. "If you could teach people to think more positively," says psychologist Craig A. Anderson of Rice University in Houston, "it would be like inoculating them against these mental ills."

[3]   "Your abilities count," explains psychologist Michael F. Scheier, "but the belief that you can succeed affects whether or not you will." In part, that's because optimists and pessimists deal with the same challenges and disappointments in very different ways.

[4]   Take, for example, your job. In a major study, psychologist Seligman and his colleague Schulman surveyed sales representatives at the Metropolitan Life Insurance Co. They found that the positive-thinkers among longtime representatives sold 37percent more insurance than did the negative-thinkers. Of newly hired representatives, optimists sold 20percent more.

[5]   Impressed, the company hired 100 people who had failed the standard industry test but had scored high on optimism. These people, who might never have been hired,[2] sold 10 percent more insurance than did the average representative.

[6]   How did they do it? The secret to an optimist's success, according to Seligmann, is in his "explanatory style". When things go wrong the pessimist tends to blame himself. "I'm no good at this," he says, "I always fail." The optimist looks for loopholes. He blames the weather, the phone connection,

even the other person. That customer was in a bad mood, he thinks. When things go right, the optimist takes credit while the pessimist sees success as a fluke.

[7]　Craig Anderson had a group of students phone strangers and ask them to donate blood to the Red Cross. When they failed on the first call or two, pessimists said, "I can't do this." Optimists told themselves, "I need to try a different approach."

[8]　Negative or positive, it was a self-fulfilling prophecy. "If people feel hopeless," says Anderson, "they don't bother to acquire the skills they need to succeed."

[9]　A sense of control, according to Anderson, is the litmus test[3] for success. The optimist feels in control of his own life. If things are going badly, he acts quickly, looking for solutions, forming a new plan of action, and reaching out for advice. The pessimist feels like fate's plaything and moves slowly. He doesn't seek advice, since he assumes nothing can be done.

[10]　Optimists may think they are better than the facts would justify and sometimes that's what keeps them alive. Dr. Sandra Levey of the Pittsburgh Cancer Institute studied women with advanced breast cancer. For the women who were generally optimistic, there was a longer disease-free interval, the best predicator of survival. In a pilot study of women in the early stages of breast cancer, Dr. Levey found the disease recurred sooner among the pessimists.

参考译文

事在人为

[1]　盛有半杯水的杯子，你是否只看到它有水的一半，而不管那没水的一半？空心的面包圈，你是否只盯着那圈面包，而不去理会那个空心？这些老生常谈的问题，在研究人员考察积极思维的作用时，却突然具有了科学意义。

[2]　有关研究与日俱增，至今已有 104 项，涉及大约 15,000 人。研究结果表明，乐观能使人更愉快、更健康，事业也更有成就；相反，悲观则导致失望、疾病和失败，并造成沮丧、孤独和令人痛苦的怯懦等心理问题。休斯敦市莱斯大学的心理学

家克雷格·A·安德森说:"如果能教会人们以更积极的方式去思考,那就等于给他们接种了预防这类心理疾病的疫苗。"

[3] 心理学家米切尔·F·施歇尔解释说:"你的能力固然是重要的,但有无必胜的信心将决定你是否能成功。"其中部分原因是,对同样的挑战和挫折,乐观者和悲观者的处理方法截然不同。

[4] 就拿人们的工作表现来说吧。心理学家赛里曼和同事舒尔曼对大都会人寿保险公司的销售人员做过一次重要的调查,发现工作年龄较长的销售人员中,积极思维的人比消极思维的人的推销额高37%;新雇用的销售人员中,乐观派也多推销出20%。

[5] 该公司对调查结果十分重视,雇用了100名在标准招工测试中名落孙山、但在乐观测试上得分颇高的人。这些本来不会有人雇用的人,却比一般销售人员多推销出10%。

[6] 他们是如何成功的呢?据赛里曼的分析,乐观者成功的秘诀在于他"解释问题的方式"。事情不顺利时,悲观者总是责怪自己,说:"这事我干不了,总是失败。"而乐观的人却为自己找借口:埋怨天气,责怪电话,甚至归咎于对方,认为是那个客户心情欠佳。事情顺利时,乐观者认为是自己的功劳,而悲观者认为只是侥幸成功。

[7] 安德森要一组学生打电话给素不相识的人,请他们为红十字会献血。打了一两个电话没能成功,悲观的学生便说"这事我干不了",而乐观的学生却安慰自己说,"我再换个法儿试试"。

[8] 无论采取消极的还是积极的态度,都是对能否实现自己的目标的一种预示。安德森说:"如果人们感到无望,他们就不会去设法学习成功所需要的技能了。"

[9] 按照安德森的说法,对事物的驾驭能力,是事业能否成功的试金石。乐观者自信能驾驭生活。如果事情不顺利,他就立即采取行动,寻求解决办法,制订新的行动计划,并主动求教于他人。悲观者则觉得自己只是命运的玩物,行动迟缓,也不向别人求教,因为他认为一切都无济于事。

[10] 乐观的人认为他们比事实所能证明的还要好,而有时候,正是这种信念才使他们得以存活下去。匹兹堡癌症研究所的桑德拉·里维博士对患晚期乳腺癌的妇女进行过研究,发现如果患者心态总的来说较为乐观,那么其发病间隔期就比较长,而这是存活的最好征兆。在对早期乳腺癌患者的初步研究中,里维博士发现情绪悲观的患者疾病复发较快。(喻云根译)

注释

1. 这两个问句的翻译，在结构上有较大变化，都是采取先将话题提出然后再设问的句式。
2. 应特别注意 might never have been hired 所表达的语法意义。不可译成"这些可能从未就业过的人"。
3. 此句的 litmus test 没有直接译为"石蕊试验"。这是因为考虑到读者接受可能会有困难，不如"试金石"这一比喻更为汉语读者所熟悉。

讲解

一、主语 - 话题转换

本文开头两句的译文在结构上与原文有较大差异（参阅注释1）。这涉及英语和汉语在句子结构上的一个重要区别。英语构句以 SV(O) 为框架，主谓一致是构句的基本要素。而汉语由于没有严格意义上的形态，其主语和谓语间的关系和英语有很大差别。请看下面几句话：

这药吃了准好。
家里的事不用你管，有我呢。
我的法语看报很吃力。
这茶才喝出点味儿来。

这类句子的谓语和主语的关系是一种陈述与被陈述，说明与被说明的关系，而不必有动作上的支配关系。正如赵元任先生在《汉语口语语法》中所说，"主语和谓语的关系可以是动作者和动作的关系。但在汉语里，这类句子的比例是不大的……因此在汉语里，把主语和谓语当作话题和说明来看待，比较适合。"这也就是说，英语的主谓具有明确的形式结构特征，而汉语的主谓则主要是一种语义上的结合。这样，在英译汉过程中有时便需要重新确立汉语的主语，以顺应汉语"话题+说明"的信息结构。请观察下面几个典型的译例：

1. He got his haberdashery at Charvet's, but his suits, his shoes and his hats in London.

    普通的服饰买自夏费商店，可衣服鞋帽总要在伦敦买。

2. You don't grow the grain you eat and you don't make the clothes you wear.

    你吃的粮食不是你自己种的，你穿的衣服也不是你自己做的。

3. The girl was used to this kind of dialogue for breakfast and more of it for dinner.

这类话不仅早餐有，午餐也有，这姑娘早就习惯了。

4. The constant sunshine and mild climate of southern California made it an ideal site for shooting motion pictures.

　　加利福尼亚州南部阳光充足，气候宜人，是拍摄影片的理想场所。

5. Tact must be used in requesting permission.

　　征求同意，应注意方式方法。

6. Mere chance seemed to determine who lived and who died.

　　究竟谁死谁活，似乎只由一种偶然性决定。

7. We prattle about scientific discoveries, but we have made scant use of them for our benefit.

　　科学上的新发现我们谈了不少，但怎样利用它们为我们服务却做得很不够。

8. We used a plane of which almost every part carried some indication of national identity.

　　我们驾驶的飞机几乎每一个部件上都有国籍的某种标记。

9. I thought about that quotation from Emerson for a long time, and until my heart healed, I left it where my mother had written it.

　　这句引自艾默生的话我琢磨良久，并把母亲写的这句话一直留在那儿，直到我的心灵创伤得以愈合。

10. (But I never stopped imagining who the anonymous giver might be...) My mother contributed to these imaginings.

　　（但是，我对匿名送花人的猜测从未停止过……）冒出这许多遐想，有我母亲的一份功劳。

11. I do not pretend that the conversation I have recorded can be regarded as verbatim reports. I never kept notes of what was said on this or the other occasion, but I have a good memory for what concerns me, and though I have put this conversation in my own words they faithfully represent, I believe, what was said.

　　书中人的谈话，我并不要假充是逐字逐句的记载。在这种或其他的场合下，人家的谈话我从不记录下来。可是，与我有关的事我记得很清楚。所以，虽则是我写的，敢说能忠实地反映他们的谈话。

109

可以看出：英译汉时常常是将英语句子中的宾语转换为汉语句子中的话题，有时也会将其他成分进行话题转换，这要视上下文及汉语表达的需要而定。

12. Scientists are studying synesthesia because they believe it may help explain how the human mind takes in and deals with information from the world outside it. The condition first was reported by an English doctor more than one hundred years ago. Since then, scientists have found many different kinds of synesthesia. They say the two most common kinds are sounds and tastes that produce colored pictures in the mind.

[a] 科学家们正在研究联觉，因为他们认为牵连感觉有助于解释人脑是怎样摄取和处理来自外部世界的信息的。一百多年前，一位英国医生首次报道了这种牵连感觉。自此之后，科学家们又发现许多不同类型的牵连感觉。他们说，两种最常见的牵连感觉是声音和味道在头脑中产生出彩色图像。

[b] 科学家们正在研究通感，认为研究通感有助于揭示人脑是怎样摄取和处理信息的。通感现象一百多年前一位英国医生就曾经研究过。一百多年来，科学家们又发现了许多情形各异的通感现象，并且指出：两种最常见的通感现象是听觉牵连和味觉牵连，声音和味道会使头脑中浮现出彩色图像。

注意译文中划线部分对整段译文连贯性的影响。译文 [a] 划线句为"状语 + 主语 + 谓语"句式，译文 [b] 为"话题 + 评论"句式。读者读到译文 [a] 划线句，他对下文的预期是英国医生在一百多年前做了些什么，而下文讲的其实仍是"牵连感觉"，这就破坏了译文在读者头脑中的连贯性。译文 [b] 用"通感现象"做话题，顺理成章地引出了下文的内容。

二、语法意义的翻译

如注释 2 所示，语法意义常常容易被忽略，从而造成误译。翻译中必须注意英语中通过形态变化所表示的意义。这包括名词的复数形式、动词的时态及虚拟形式等。汉语由于缺乏相应的语法手段，须用词汇手段再现原文的语法意义。

名词复数所表达的意义并非都要着意加以再现，汉语无复数形式变化，在很多情况下上下文可将复数概念衬托得十分清楚。但有时为了修辞的目的，适当的词汇手段就显得很有必要了。

1. ...on clear evenings the church corner rang till late with the shouts of coasters.

……每逢星月之夜，教堂转角处，滑雪人总是笑语喧哗，常到半夜。

2. No white person or persons shall be permitted to settle upon or occupy any portion of the territory, or without the consent of the Indians to pass through the same area.

凡白人，无论是一人或多人，均不得在本地区内任何部分定居或将其占有，未经印第安人同意，亦不得穿越本地区。

3. They drove into the country, where the houses were all of wood and all new and where the washbasins and bathtubs were very commodious, and in the morning her signora showed her the machines and how to work them.

他们驱车进入乡间，那儿全是崭新的木头房子，洗脸盆和浴缸十分宽绰。第二天早上，她的女主人就给她看这种机那种机，还教她如何使用。

至于动词的不同形态所表达的语法意义，虚拟形式一般是要用适当的词汇手段加以翻译的，时态则只有在具有明显的时间对照意义时才有必要刻意表达出来，一般情况下上下文已足以将时间序列表达清楚。

4. It was dark and it would have been difficult to recognize anyone, but because one of them, walking toward the corner, had a dachshund on a leash, it could have been Trencher.

天很黑，本来很难认出人来，但因为走向街角的那个人手中牵着一只猎獾狗，所以那可能就是特连卓尔。

5. ...but the old one (a hippopotamus) fifty times heavier than the baby, and might easily, such is the consistency of her alarming barrel, be full of lead.

而这老的就又比这小的重五十倍了，要是按那滚圆躯体的密度来说，和灌了铅的也差不多。

6. Even if they had any appetite, the sixteen-pound turkey would have looked almost like new when they had eaten their fill.

即便他们食欲不错，而且吃到饱得不能再吃，那只十六磅重的火鸡看起来也几乎原封未动。

注意这个句子的含义：事实上他们胃口不大好，火鸡又十分之大，所以就更像没人吃过一样了。试对照下面的不当译文：尽管他们有食欲，当他们吃饱的时候，十六磅的火鸡就像是新的一样。

7. "I loved fighting with Bill Fulbright. I'm quite sure I always lost, yet he

managed to make me think I might have won."

"我过去很喜欢和比尔·福布赖特争论。我确信我常输给他,但是他有办法让我以为我也许赢了。"

这是克林顿在阿肯色大学为参议员福布赖特塑像揭幕时说的话。上面译文中"让我以为我也许赢了"未把 might have won 的虚拟语气译出,试比较下面译文:我很喜欢和比尔·福莱特争论。我明白我肯定会输,但是他有办法让我以为我也许能赢。

8. [The letter came by the first post, and after breakfast I rang up Roy. As soon as I mentioned my name I was put through to him by his secretary.] If I were writing a detective story I should immediately have suspected that my call was awaited, and Roy's virile voice calling hallo would have confirmed my suspicion. No one could naturally be quite so cheery so early in the morning.

假如我现在写的是一部侦探小说,就会这么写:我怀疑当时罗伊正在等我的电话,而他接电话时那精神饱满的语气更证实了我的怀疑。这么一大早接电话却如此高兴,是不大合情理的。

此段引自 Maugham 的 *Cakes and Ale*。未提供译文的句子放在方括弧内,作为必要的上下文。句中的虚拟语气 were writing 是针对"现在"的,should have suspected 和 would have confirmed 都是针对"过去"的。其含义是:我现在写的不是侦探小说,也就不必把当时的情况说得那么玄乎了。下面的译文忽略了虚拟语气所表达的语法意义,可进行对照推敲:如果我在写一个侦探故事的话,我马上就会怀疑罗伊正在等候我的电话,而罗伊拿起话筒后一上来的那种精神饱满的语气更足以使我肯定我的怀疑。没有人一大清早接别人电话时自然地就会这样兴高采烈。

9. She is a good girl. I've been meaning to suggest keeping her on…
   她是一个好姑娘,我一直想建议把她留下……

10. [This was the best entomological lesson I ever had—a lesson whose influence has extended to the details of every subsequent study;] a legacy the professor had left to me, of inestimable value, which we could not buy, with which we cannot part.

    这是教授留给我的无价宝,当时用金钱买不到,现在也绝不能丢掉。

句中的时态（had left...could not...cannot...）形成了鲜明的对照，所以应该用词汇手段加以表达。试对照下面缺乏"时间感"的译文：这也是教授留给我的遗产，其价值无法估量，也并非拿钱能买得到，也是我们割舍不了的。

11. I can still feel the agony of not being invited to a party that almost everyone was going to. But I also recall the ecstasy of being plucked from obscurity at another event to dance with a John Travolta look-alike.

有一次聚会几乎人人都参加了，而我却没受到邀请，我至今仍能感到当时的痛苦。而在另一次聚会上一个酷似约翰·特拉瓦尔特的人把不引人注目的我请了出来与他共舞，我现在也还能感受到当时那激动、喜悦的心情。

原文中主句谓语动词为现在时，从句中为过去时，其他从属成分中（being invited.../being plucked...）也含有过去时态意义，与主句谓语动词形成对照，翻译时应以词汇形式再现。下面一例同样有现在时与过去时的对照问题：

12. ...There is a housing project standing now where the house in which we grew up once stood, and one of those stunted city trees is snarling where our doorway used to be. This is on the rehabilitated side of the avenue. The other side of the avenue—for progress takes time—has not been rehabilitated yet and it looks exactly as it looked in the days when we sat with our noses pressed against the windowpanes, longing to be allowed to go across the street. The grocery store which gave us credit is still there, and there can be no doubt that it is still giving credit. The people in the project certainly need it—far more, indeed, than they ever needed the project.

……眼前是一片新建筑群，我们童年时代的老屋原来就在这儿。原来的屋门口，现在一棵矮墩墩的树长得枝盘叶绕。这是重建过的一侧。路的另一边——发展总是要时间的——还没重建，还跟从前一样。那时我们趴在窗前向外张望，鼻子都贴到玻璃上了，巴不得能获准到对面去玩。原来老赊账给我们的杂货店如今还在，而且显然仍在赊账。住在这些新房子里的人现在一定需要这家店铺——胜过他们当初对重建工程的需要。

Some Truths About Leadership

[1] After leaving the university, I spent nearly five years researching a book on leadership. I travelled around America spending time with 90 of the most effective, successful leaders in the nation—60 from corporations and 30 from the public sector. My goal was to find these leaders' common traits, a task that required more probing than I had expected.[1] For a while, I sensed much more diversity than commonality among them. The group included both rational and intuitive thinkers; some who dressed for success and some who didn't; well-spoken, articulate leaders and laconic, inarticulate ones; some aggressive types and some who were the opposite.[2]

[2] I was finally able to come to some conclusions, of which perhaps the most important is the distinction between leaders and managers: leaders are people who do the right thing; managers are people who do things right. Both roles are crucial, but they differ profoundly. I often observe people in top positions doing the wrong[3] thing well.

[3] After several years of observation and conversation, I defined[4] four competencies evident to some extent in every member of the group: management of attention, management of meaning, management of trust, and management of self.[5] The first trait apparent in these leaders is their ability to draw others to them, not just because they have a vision but because they communicate an extraordinary focus of commitment. Leaders manage attention through a compelling vision that brings others to a place they have not been before.[6]

[4] One of the people I most wanted to interview was Leon Fleischer, a child prodigy who grew up to become a prominent pianist, conductor, and musicologist. I happened to be in Colorado one summer while Fleischer was conducting the Aspen Music Festival. Driving through downtown Aspen, I saw two perspiring young cellists carrying their instruments, and I offered them a ride to the music tent. As we rode I questioned them about Fleischer. "I'll tell you why he's so great," said one. "He doesn't waste our time."

[5] Fleischer agreed not only to be interviewed but also to let me watch him rehearse and conduct music classes. I linked the way I saw him work with that simple sentence, "He doesn't waste our time." Every moment Fleischer was before the orchestra, he knew exactly what sound he wanted. He didn't waste time because his intentions were always evident.

[6] So the first leadership competency is the management of attention through a set of intentions or a vision, not in a mystical or religious sense but in the sense of outcome, goal, or direction.[7]

[7] The second competency is management of meaning. To make dreams apparent to others and to align people with them, leaders must communicate their vision. Communication and alignment work together.

[8] The third competency is management of trust. Trust is essential to all organizations. The main determinant of trust is reliability, what I call constancy. When I talked to the board members or staffs of these leaders, I heard certain phrases again and again: "She is all of a piece." "Whether you like it or not, you always know where he is coming from, what he stands for." A recent study showed that people would much rather follow individuals they can count on, even when they disagree with their viewpoint, than people they agree with but who shift positions frequently.

[9] The fourth leadership competency is management of self, knowing one's skills and deploying them effectively. Management of self is critical; without it, leaders and managers can do more harm than good.[8]

[10] Leaders know themselves; they know their strengths and nurture them. The leaders in my group seemed unacquainted with the concept of failure. What you or I might call a failure, they referred to as a mistake. I began collecting synonyms for the word failure mentioned in the interviews, and I found more than 20: mistake, error, false start, bloop, flop, loss, miss, foulup, stumble, botch, bungle[9]—but not failure. One CEO told me that if she had a knack for leadership, it was the capacity to make as many mistakes as she could as soon as possible, and thus get them out of the way. Another said that a mistake is simply "another way of doing things". These leaders learn from and use something that doesn't go well; it is not a failure but simply the next step.

参考译文
领导艺术的真谛

[1] 我卸任大学校长一职之后，用了差不多五年时间撰写一部论述领导艺术的书。我走遍美国各地，与这个国家最得力、最成功的九十位领导者会面，其中六十位是企业领导，三十位担任公职。我的目的是找出这些领导人的共同特质，这任务之艰难超出了我的料想。我曾一度觉得他们不同之处多于相同之处。他们有的善于理性思维，有的善于直觉判断；有的为事业成功而讲究穿着，有的则穿得普普通通；有的谈吐优雅、善于辞令，有的说话简简单单、不善辞令；有的咄咄逼人，有的温文尔雅。

[2] 最后我得出一些结论，其中最重要的一点可能就是领导者与管理者之间的区别：领导者知道该做什么，管理者则知道怎样去做。这两类角色同样举足轻重，但却有很大区别。我经常看到身居要职的人把某项不该做的事也处理得井井有条。

[3] 经过几年的观察和交往，我发觉这群领导人在某种程度上都具备四种能力：引起注意、善于表达、赢得信赖与驾驭自我的能力。这些领导人明显具备的第一种特质是吸引他人的能力，这不光是因为他们有远见，而且还因为他们表现出极强的献身精神。领导人以其远见卓识启迪别人，将别人吸引到自己周围。

[4] 我最想采访的人是利昂·弗莱彻。他是个神童，长大后成了著名的钢琴家、乐队指挥和音乐研究专家。有一年夏天我在科罗拉多，碰巧弗莱彻担任阿斯彭音乐节的指挥。我驾车穿过阿斯彭闹市区时，看到两个携带乐器、汗流浃背的年轻大提琴手，于是我把他们送到音乐练习场去。途中，我问他们关于弗莱彻的事。其中一人说："我告诉你他为什么这么出色——他从不浪费我们的时间。"

[5] 弗莱彻不仅同意跟我见面，而且还让我观摩他的排练和指挥课。我把他的工作方式与那句朴质的话"他从不浪费我们的时间"联系起来。每当弗莱彻站在乐队前面，便能准确地知道自己想要的乐调。他不浪费时间，因为他的意图永远明确。

[6] 总之，第一种领导能力是通过一系列的意旨或远见来引起众人的注意，这类意旨或远见没有神秘的或宗教的含义，而是具有结果、目标或方向的意义。

[7] 第二种领导能力是表达能力。为了让别人清楚他们的理想和把众人团结在自己的周围，领导人必须善于表达自己的见解，沟通和团结是相辅相成的。

[8] 第三种领导能力是赢得信赖的能力。信赖对所有机构都是至关重要的。信赖

的主要决定因素是可靠性，我称作恒久性。当我跟这些领导人的董事会成员或职员谈话时，我不止一次听到这样一些话："她始终如一""不管你喜欢不喜欢，你知道他的论据及主张是什么"。最近的一项研究表明，人们宁愿追随那些彼此观点也许并不一致但是可以信赖的人，而不是那些虽与自己意见相同但不断改变立场的人。

[9]　第四种领导能力是驾驭自我、了解及有效地运用自己技能的能力。驾驭自我是至关重要的：如果没有这方面的能力，领导人和管理人员就可能会成事不足，败事有余。

[10]　领导人通常有自知之明：他们了解自己的长处并加以发挥。我所调查的领导人似乎没有失败的概念。你我称作失败的事他们都叫作失误。在交谈时，他们用别的同义词代替"失败"，这些同义词有二十多个，如出错、差错、出师不利、当众出丑、栽了、失利、亏了、一团糟、弄错、差劲、砸锅……但都不是失败。一位最高行政主管告诉我，如果说她有领导诀窍的话，那就是尽早尽多地把要犯的错误都犯了，以免日后再出错。另一位说，犯错误无非是"另一种办事方法"。这些领导人吃一堑长一智，事情办得不好并不等于失败；相反，它使人们知道下一步该怎样走。

注释

1. 此处未译为"……这任务比我预计的需要更多的探索"或"……这任务所需要进行的调查工作比我预料的还要多"之类。请对照参考译文进行思考。
2. 请注意以上几句的汉译中四字词语的运用。
3. 此处的 wrong 并不是 correct 的反义词，而是 not suitable or appropriate 的意思。
4. define 的意思是 to describe the basic qualities of something，此处的汉译做了变通处理。
5 和 6. 注意这两处译文中四字词语的灵活运用，特别是本自然段最后一句，试想译成下面呆板译文，效果会怎样：领导人以其远见卓识吸引别人，他们的远见把人们带到从未到过的境地。
7. 此句译文中重复了"意旨和远见"几个字，将原句译成两个分句。这样表达层次清楚，意义明确。
8. 此处用两个四字词语组成的成语来翻译 do more harm than good 这一比较结构，准确、简洁。
9. 此处用了十一个同 / 近义词，给汉译选词带来一定困难，请对照参考译文推敲。

讲解

一、四字词语的运用及"词组堆叠句"

现代汉语里有十分丰富的四字词语。四字词语在结构上常分为两段，两段结构的意思相互对称或平行，如铜墙铁壁、欢天喜地、山清水秀等。也有前后两段并不对称的（如轻松愉快），或前后并不分段的（如锦上添花）。四字词语的句法功能也十分灵活，比如，（1）作谓语：这个古迹已名存实亡；（2）作宾语：这件事一定要弄个水落石出；（3）作后置状语：何必为这点小事闹得天翻地覆。有些四字词语，本身虽是名词性的，却可灵活地在句中充当相当于动词和形容词的功能，如：你们不要七嘴八舌，听他一个人说（像动词）。这个人长得浓眉大眼（像形容词）。在汉语中恰当地运用四字词语，可使句子结构紧凑、明晰，平添不少文采。译文中恰当使用四字词语，也能起到同样的作用。请比较下列各句的两种译文：

1. Ribentrop is a second-rate man with second-hand ideas.

   [a] 里宾特洛甫是个次等人物，思想是捡别人的。
   [b] 里宾特洛甫是个拾人牙慧的二流角色。

2. To see his likeness perpetuated in marble is to me today a sad but pleasing sensation.

   [a] 看到他的大理石塑像永存，今天对于我来说，有悲哀的，但也有高兴的感觉。
   [b] 今天看到他的这座永垂不朽的大理石塑像，我悲喜交加。

3. I repair to the enchanted house, where there are lights, chattering, music, flowers, officers (I am sorry to see) and the eldest Miss Larkins, a blaze of beauty.

   [a] 我来到那迷人的住宅，那里有灯光、谈话、音乐、鲜花、军官们（看见使我难过），还有最大的拉京士小姐，一个美的火焰。
   [b] 现在我朝着那家仙宫神宇走去，那儿灯光辉煌、人语嘈杂、乐音悠扬、花草缤纷、军官纷来（这是我看着极为痛心的），还有拉钦大小姐，简直是仪态万方，丰姿千状。

有时还可将汉语四字成语拆开使用，用得巧妙，可达到言简意赅的效果。

4. And I talked to him with brutal frankness.

   [a] 我同他谈话时，使用了令人不快的真诚的语言。
   [b] 我对他讲的话，虽然逆耳，却是忠言。

再观察下面几个译例:

5. He must make us feel that they are twins indeed, one dying if the other dies, one flourishing if the other flourishes.

   他必须使得我们觉得,他们实际上是一对孪生子,一枯俱枯,一荣俱荣。

6. For the first time Nora saw her husband for what he was...a selfish, pretentious hypocrite with no regard for her position in the matter.

   这是娜拉有生以来第一次认清了丈夫的庐山真面目:原来他是一个道貌岸然、自私自利的伪君子,在这个问题上根本不把她的处境放在心上。

7. Where he faced us again, he was huge and handsome and conceited and cruel.

   再次面对我们时,他已变得身材魁梧、相貌英俊、心高气傲、冷酷无情。

8. He slowed down, but still without any intention of stopping, until, as we came nearer, the hushed, intent faces of the people at the garage door made him automatically put on the brakes.

   他把车速放慢,但没打算停车,直到我们开近了,车行门口那群人屏息敛容的面孔才使他不由自主地把车刹住。

9. She remembered how in Nascosta even the most beautiful fell quickly under the darkness of time, like flowers without care; how even the beautiful became bent and toothless, their dark clothes smelling, as the mamma's did, of smoke and manure.

   她想起,在那斯科斯塔,最美丽的娇娃,因为不堪时艰,很快便姿容消退,就像无人护理的花朵一般;绝美佳人很快也就弯腰驼背,皓齿尽落,一身皂衣,就像老妈妈一样,散发着火烟和粪肥的臭味。

10. ...and all the farmers from around came, and they found against the wall of the farm a nest of eight great serpents, fat with milk, who were so poisonous that even their breath was mortal...

    四邻的农夫都来了,他们在农庄的围墙下找到一窝毒蛇,总共八条,让(人)奶喂得肥肥的,毒气喷人,当之者死。

11. And for once the world where she had lived and been so happy seemed to her truly to be an old world where the customs and the walls were older than the people...

一下子，这个她曾经生长于兹、怡然自乐的世界似乎真的变得老朽了，那些习俗，那些围墙比人还要老。

从对上述含有四字词语的译文的观察中不难发现，汉语行文，特别是记述、描写类文字中，有一种明显的以词组（特别是主谓词组和动词性词组——动宾、连动、兼语词组等，当然也包括上面译例中的四字词语）为句段构建句子的倾向。汉语中的词组在汉语的四级语法单位（词素、词、词组、句子）中占有特别重要的地位。朱德熙先生在《语法问答》中曾经说道："由于汉语的句子的构造跟词组的构造原则基本一致，我们就有可能在词组的基础上来描写语法，建立一种以词组为基点的语法体系。"语法学家郭绍虞先生在讨论词组时举了这样一个例子：

在帝国主义压迫下的善良人民所普遍遭受的命运就是家破人亡。

他认为这句话虽然通顺达意，但音韵感差，如拆成几个词组就简劲有力了：

善良的人民，在帝国主义压迫之下，家破人亡，是普遍的命运。

郭绍虞先生在《汉语语法修辞新探》中称这种句子为"词组堆叠句"。在我们的翻译实践（尤其是记叙、描写文字体）中也完全可以，而且应该顺应汉语的这种构句特点。试比较下面几对例句，体味词组堆叠在提高译文质量上的重要作用。

12. She was a tall silent woman with a long nose and grey troubled eyes.

    [a] 她是一个沉默的高个子女人，有着长长的鼻子和忧郁的神情。
    [b] 她个子挺高，沉默寡言，长长的鼻子，一双灰眼睛，流露出忧郁的神情。

13. This proposal of his, this plan of marrying and continuing at Hartfield—the more she contemplated it, the more pleasing it became. His evils seemed to lessen, her own advantages to increase, their mutual good to outweigh every drawback.

    [a] 他的这种提议，这种结婚与继续停在哈特菲尔德的计划——她越想越高兴。他的不幸似乎在减少，她自己的利益似乎在增加，他们共同的好处似乎超越了任何障碍。
    [b] 他提出的既能结婚又能留在哈特菲尔德的主意，她越思量越觉得妙。既对他无害，也对她有益，两全其美，尽可为之。

14. The emphasis was helped by the speaker's mouth, which was wide, thin and hard set.

    [a] 说话人那又阔又薄又紧绷绷的嘴巴，帮助他加强了语气。
    [b] 说话人的嘴巴，又阔又薄，绷得紧紧的，更加强了他的语气。

15. A few of the pictures are worth mentioning both for their technical excellence and interesting content.

[a] 其中有些照片既由于其技术高超又由于其内容有趣而值得一提。
[b] 有些照片技术高超，内容有趣，值得一提。

很明显，每一对译例的第二句都要优于第一句，因为这些句子顺应了汉语的构句方式。下面再看几个选自描述语篇的译例，请体味并总结所谓"词组堆叠句"的特点。

16. He was at this time in his late fifties, a tall, elegant man with good features and thick waving dark hair only sufficiently greying to add to the distinction of his appearance.

他这时已是年近六旬的人，一表人才，高个儿，眉清目秀，卷发又多又乌，略带花白，恰好衬出他那堂堂的仪表。

17. Her manner was gentle, and while she was pretty in a freckle-faced, red-haired little girl sort of way, she would turn few heads in the street.

她举止文雅，面有雀斑，满头红发，像个小女孩那么可爱，但走在大街上引不起多少人注意。

18. The morning of June 27th was clear and sunny, with the fresh warmth of a full-summer day; the flowers were blossoming profusely and the grass was richly green.

6月27日上午，天气晴朗，阳光明媚，鲜花盛开，绿草如茵，充满了盛夏之日的清新和温暖。

19. On one of those sober and rather melancholy days in the latter part of autumn, when the shadows of morning and evening almost mingle together, and throw a gloom over the decline of the year, I passed several hours in rambling about Westminster Abbey.

时方晚秋，气象肃穆，略带忧郁，早晨的阴影和黄昏的阴影，几乎连接在了一起，不可分别。岁云将暮，终日昏暗，我就在这么一天，到西敏寺去散了几个小时的步。

20. One night when the Bruhls had friends in for bridge—old Mr. Creegan and his wife—Bruhl suddenly appeared from upstairs with a pair of scarlet pyjamas on, smoking a cigarette, and gripping his revolver. After a few loud and incoherent remarks of a boastful nature, he let fly at a clock on the mantel, and hit it squarely in the middle.

一天晚上，家里来了客人，是老朋友柯利庚夫妇，准备玩桥牌。卜卢先生突然从楼上出现，身穿猩红睡衣，口衔香烟，手执左轮，粗声大气，语无伦次，自夸了几句之后，朝着壁炉台上的时钟放了一枪，打个正着。

21. It was a long road going into darkness and hills and he held to the wheel, now and again reaching into his lunch bucket and taking out a piece of candy. He had been driving steadily for an hour, with no other car on the road, no light, just the road going under, the hum, the roar, and Mars out there, so quiet. Mars was always quiet, but quieter tonight than any other. The deserts and empty seas swung by him, and the mountains against the stars.

此去路漫漫，伸向黑暗，深入群山。他掌握着方向盘，不时伸手从小提桶里拿糖果吃。沉着向前，走了一个小时，不见别的车辆，不见灯光，只见古道从车下滑过。发电机如吟如啸。汽车外，火星一片静寂。火星就是这么静的，不过今夜比往常更静。荒漠沧海，沧海荒漠，悠悠然飘过他身旁。还有那衬着星空的群山。

22. It was a day as fresh as grass growing up and clouds going over and butterflies coming down can make it. It was a day compounded from silences of bee and flower and ocean and land, which were not silences at all, but motions, stirs, flutters, risings, fallings, each in its own time and matchless rhythm. The land did not move, but moved. The sea was not still, yet was still. Paradox flowed into paradox, stillness mixed with stillness, sound with sound. The flowers vibrated and the bees fell in separate and small showers of golden rain on the clover. The seas of hill and the seas of ocean were divided, each from the other's motion, by a railroad track, empty, compounded of rust and iron marrow, a track on which, quite obviously, no train had run in many years. Thirty miles north it swirled on away to further mists of distance, thirty miles south it tunneled islands of cloud-shadow that changed their continental positions on the sides of far mountains as you watched.

绿草萋萋，白云冉冉，彩蝶翩翩，这日子是如此清新可爱。蜜蜂无言，春花不语，海波声咽，大地音沉，这日子是如此安静。然而并非安静，因为万物各以其特有的节奏在运动，或疾或徐，或起或伏。大地止而亦行，大海动而亦静。万寂交而万籁和，若真若假，若是若非。繁花在微微颤动。蜜蜂一群群地落在三叶草上，有如阵阵黄金雨。山涛海浪之间，隔着一条铁路，空空荡荡，铁轨生了锈，显然多年

没有通车了。这条铁路，往北三十英里，蜿蜒伸入远方的溟蒙；往南三十英里，盘旋于山阴之外，穿插于飘飘云影之中。

综观以上的词组堆叠句，可以看出它们的共同特点：(1) 都是由简短的词组（包括四字词语）排列而成，它们或整齐排列，或长短相间，达到一种韵律简劲、起伏有致的效果；(2) 词组间（即一个个语段间）多呈意合连接，很少使用连接词语。

二、比较结构的翻译

英语中比较结构的使用频率比汉语高，对比较结构一要准确理解，二要根据汉语表达需要灵活变通，不要一概呆板地译为"比……更……"之类的字眼（参阅注释1和8）。

1. I had gone away to college by now, and resettled in California. I kept in touch through my sister, but I was too busy working and eagerly seeking out all the magic things Hazel's books had told me about to give <u>much more than</u> a fleeting thought to Milltown.

   那时我已去上大学，在加州定居。我通过姐姐和家乡保持联系，但我学习太忙，在急切地探索黑兹尔那些书告诉过我的所有奇妙的事情，只是有时才想起米尔镇。

2. When he (son of Rawdon) was gone, he (Rawdon) felt more sad and downcast than he cared to own…<u>far sadder than</u> the boy himself, who was happy enough to enter a new career, and find companions of his own age.

   他走了以后，罗登闷闷不乐，然而心里的烦恼又不愿对人说。小罗登不比父亲，他到了一个新的环境，还有年龄相仿的同伴，倒很快乐。

3. Americans carry with them an appearance which is <u>more a result of attitude than of clothing</u>.

   美国人所呈现出的外表，与其说是衣着所致，还不如说是观念所致。

4. Hitler's mistakes gave Roosevelt the victory; just as at Waterloo it was <u>less</u> Wellington who won <u>than</u> Napoleon who lost.

   希特勒犯下的错误使罗斯福取得了胜利；正如在滑铁卢战场上，与其说惠灵顿打胜了，不如说是拿破仑战败了。

5. I hadn't the faintest idea what "this matter" was, but I was <u>more annoyed than interested</u>.

我一点儿也不知道"这件事"是指什么，但我兴趣不大，倒觉得厌烦。

6. The first object observed by Galileo, naturally enough, was the Moon. He was the first to see <u>more than</u> the shadows that people's imaginations had made into shapes.

   伽利略观察的第一个天体自然是月球。他所看到的已不再仅仅是被人们想象成各种形态的阴影。

7. My upbringing had been <u>more</u> that of a wild boy <u>than</u> that of a young lady.

   我早年所受的教育，使我不大像一个娇小姐，倒很像一个野孩子。

8. Goering, who had been looking forward, to put it mildly, to the day when he might succeed Hitler, <u>was more circumspect than</u> might have been expected.

   这位正在等待（说得客气一点）继承希特勒的位置的帝国元帅，竟出人意料地小心谨慎起来。

9. A dog will bark <u>more loudly</u> and bite <u>more readily</u> when people are afraid of him than when they treat him with contempt, and the human herd has something of this same characteristic.

   狗对于怕它的人要大吠并随时准备去咬，而对轻蔑它的人就不会这样，人类多少也具有同样的特质。

10. Fitness is <u>more than</u> a fad. It's a way of life, shown to slow and even reverse much of the deterioration associated with aging. It is being pursued by millions who realize that their medical fate lies <u>more</u> in their own <u>than</u> in their physicians' hands.

    保持健康并不仅仅是一种时尚，而是一种生活方式。事实证明，有了健康的体魄，就可以在很大程度上减缓甚至逆转随着年龄增长而造成的器官衰老现象。成千上万的人主动追求健康，因为他们认识到，自己的健康状况与其说是掌握在医生手里，倒不如说是由自己掌握的。

下面再观察一些含有否定比较结构的译例，注意译文一定要符合汉语的表达习惯，比如 It is not much more than noon. 可译为"刚过晌午"。You are no better than a coward. 可译为"你简直是个没胆量的小子"，等等。

11. The doctor had never seen him in better spirits.
    医生从未见他精神这么好过。

12. He could no more be a valet than he could be a stockbroker or a wire-walker.
    仆人的活他干不了，就像他当不了证券经纪人，也走不了钢丝一样。

13. The greatness of a people is no more determined by their number than the greatness of a man is determined by his height.
    一个民族的伟大不取决于其人口多少，正如一个人的伟大不取决于他的身高。

14. Everyone acknowledges that Newton was a great man; yet few have more than the vaguest acquaintance with his living personality.
    大家承认牛顿是一位伟大的人物，但对于他生前的为人，一般只有一个大概的了解。

15. China insists always on the need for self-reliance, no less in economic policies than in making revolution.
    中国始终坚持自力更生，不但干革命是这样，而且经济政策也是如此。

16. No more critical activity stands to be profoundly affected by global warming than agriculture, but scientists also consider it one of the most adaptable.
    在人类的重大活动中，受全球气候变暖影响最大的莫过于农业了，但科学家们认为农业仍是适应性最强的领域之一。

17. Extemporaneous speaking should be practiced and cultivated. It is the lawyer's avenue to the public. However able and faithful he may be in other respects, people are slow to bring him business, if he cannot make a speech. And yet there is not a more fatal error to young lawyers, than relying too much on speechmaking.
    即席讲演是律师联系公众的一条广阔途径，必须加以锻炼和培养。一个律师无论在其他方面怎样能干、可靠，如果他不善演说，人们不会轻易将诉讼事务委托给他。然而，过分地依赖演说才能，也往往是青年律师的一大致命缺点。

For Some Victims of Crimes, the Fear Never Leaves

[1] Blossom Jackson will never forget that November night when—at 10 minutes to 9—her sister-in-law[1] pounded on the door of her small Brooklyn house screaming, "They've killed Jackson."

[2] "I remember thinking, 'No. No. It's not Jackson, it's not my husband, it's not my Jackson,'" she said. "But it was.[2] He was lying in the street, right across from our house. The police said a man shot him over a parking space."

[3] Thousands of New Yorkers have had their lives shaken by violent crime, according to police statistics. And whether they have suffered through the murder of a husband or they themselves have survived an attack by knife-wielding robber or a purse snatcher, the victims say in interviews that they have found their lives changed.

[4] Some say fear and caution are now a part of their daily routine.[3] For others, there is anger at a criminal justice system which they believe has failed them. Still others say there is disappointment in their own cherished beliefs about people and a city they once loved.[4]

Aftermath of the Crime

[5] Then there are the New Yorkers who have been victimized so often that they have lost their fear and anger. Instead, they say, they have learned to live with threats and blows and thievery, as if these things were as natural as air and sun and rain.

[6] For most, the crime itself is just the beginning.

[7] It has been more than a year since Alfred Jackson, a 38-year-old Brooklyn plumber, was shot and killed by a neighbor because Mr. Jackson wanted to park in the spot where the man was walking his dog.[5]

[8] Mrs. Jackson can still remember her sister-in-law's screams, the cold night air and the swarm of neighbors and policemen.[6]

[9] In the weeks that followed her husband's killing, Mrs. Jackson said, she was numbed by shock. But gradually, the shock wore away, replaced by fear.

[10] "I know now that anything can happen in this city," she said. "My husband was a good, hard-working man. He never carried a gun; he was never in trouble. But that didn't matter.[7]"

[11] Mrs. Jackson said fear is now a part of her most ordinary days and her quietest nights.[8] "I'm scared," Mrs. Jackson, the mother of five children, said. "I'm scared when I go to work, or go out shopping, or take the kids to school. I can't wait to get back home and lock the door."[9]

[12] "It's very hard," she said, sitting in the living room of her home. "Sometimes I feel like I'm falling apart."

[13] "I have no social life." The young woman said. "Nothing. I'm just here."

Children Ask Questions

[14] The man who shot Alfred Jackson pleaded guilty to first-degree manslaughter, and last month he was sentenced to 5 to 15 years in prison. With good behavior, he will serve 10 years at the most.

[15] Mrs. Jackson now works six days a week at two jobs to make ends meet. She lives in fear, and she worries about her children, who she said "spend too much time just staring at the walls and asking questions about Jackson's death".

[16] Three months ago, Jan Chytillo, who works for the city, was mugged on a quiet street in a residential section of Queens. She said she and a friend had gone out to dinner that night, and were walking home together at about 10 o'clock, when a "very big, very tall man", accosted them and demanded their purses. When her friend resisted, he shoved her in the bushes, grabbed both purses, and then ran to a waiting car. He was never captured.

参考译文

一朝受害,永远心惊

[1] 布劳森·杰克逊永远不会忘记那天晚上的情景。那是十一月的一天晚上,差十分钟到九点,孩子他姑在纽约布鲁克林区他们这所小小的住宅前使劲敲门,一面喊道:"他们把杰克逊打死了。"

[2] "记得我当时就想:'不,不。不是杰克逊,不是我丈夫,不是我的杰克逊。'"布劳森·杰克逊说。"可是,那不是别人,正是他。他躺在大街上,就在我们的房子对面。警察说,为了争一块停车的地方,人家把他打死了。"

[3] 据警方统计,暴力犯罪活动对成千上万纽约人的生活造成危害。无论是丈夫被害,还是本人遇上了持刀抢劫或抢钱包的歹徒,受害者在接受采访时都说感到自己的生活变了样。

[4] 有人说,现在总是提心吊胆地过日子。有人感到愤怒,因为他们觉得刑事审判制度使他们失望。还有人说,过去他们认为人们是可以信赖的,自己喜爱的城市是可以信赖的,现在这种信念已经破灭了。

犯罪造成的后果

[5] 还有一些纽约人,他们屡次受害,已经不觉得害怕,也不感到气愤了。他们说,不但不害怕,不生气,反而对威胁、伤害、偷盗习以为常,觉得就像空气、太阳和雨水一样司空见惯了。

[6] 然而,对大多数受害者来说,犯罪活动本身只不过是事情的开始。

[7] 阿尔弗莱德·杰克逊,三十八岁,原先是布鲁克林一个水暖工人。他想在邻居遛狗的地方停放汽车,被邻居开枪打死。这件事发生已经有一年多了。

[8] 在那寒冷的夜晚,孩子他姑怎样喊叫,左邻右舍和警察怎样蜂拥而至,杰克逊太太记忆犹新。

[9] 杰克逊太太说,丈夫刚刚被害的那几个星期,她由于受打击而神情麻木,后来这种受打击的感觉逐渐消逝,又变得惶恐不安起来。

[10] "现在我明白了,在这座城市里,什么事都可能发生,"她说。"我丈夫是个勤勤恳恳的好人。他从来不带枪,也从来不去惹麻烦。不过这都没有用。"

[11] 杰克逊太太说，现在就是在最平常的白天和最寂静的夜晚，她都感到害怕。这位五个孩子的母亲说："我害怕。无论是去上班，上街买东西，还是送孩子上学，我都感到非常害怕。我总是急着赶回家来，还要把门锁上。"

[12] "实在难以忍受，"她坐在自家的客厅里对我说。"有时候我感到几乎支撑不住了。"

[13] "我没有社交活动。"这位年轻妇女说道。"什么活动也没有，只能待在家里。"

孩子们提出疑问

[14] 枪杀阿尔弗莱德·杰克逊的凶手承认犯了头等杀人罪，上个月被判处五至十五年徒刑。如果表现好，最多关十年。

[15] 杰克逊太太现在干两份工作，每星期工作六天，勉强维持生活。她生活在恐惧之中，而且为孩子担心，因为据她说，孩子们"老是对着墙发愣，老要问起杰克逊死的事"。

[16] 三个月以前，在市政部门工作的珍·齐蒂洛在昆斯住宅区一条僻静的街上被人拦劫。她说，那天晚上，她和一个朋友出去吃饭。大约十点钟，两人步行回家，忽然一个"又高又大的男人"朝她们走来，要她们交出钱包。她的朋友不从，那个人就把她推到灌木丛里，把这两个妇女的钱包都抢走了，随后就朝一辆停着的小汽车跑去。那个人一直没有抓到。（庄绎传译）

注释

1. sister-in-law 一词语义覆盖面很大，汉语中找不到一个对等的词语。译者依据文中提供的 Jackson 夫妇有小孩的事实，从孩子的角度译出这一词语，很巧妙，可说部分地解决了这个难题。
2. 汉译加了"不是别人"四个字，准确译出了原文的语气。
3. 此句顺应汉语表达习惯，未机械地译为"有的说，害怕和谨慎已成了他们日常生活的一部分"。
4. 此段汉译用"有人……有人……还有人……"等词语，层次非常清楚。另外，最后一句将"是可以信赖的"重复使用，既有加强语气的作用，也使汉译更为流畅。
5. 这句话被译成三个汉语句子，先交代杰克逊是怎样一个人，再说原因及事件，最后说出事件发生的时间。这样顺应了汉语常用的叙述结构。再如：
Edward Tede, a retired postman who lives in the Bronx, was attacked a month ago at a subway entrance in his neighborhood. It was late afternoon, he said, and he was

returning home after visiting his wife in the hospital.

爱德华·泰德是一位退休邮递员，住在布朗克斯区。一个月以前，他在离家不远的地铁入口处被抢。他说，那天他到医院看望妻子，黄昏时分，在回家的路上，就发生了这件事。

这两句汉译的信息排列为：人物背景情况——事件——事件发生的自然时序。

6. 注意这句话的译文，信息的重心有所调整。
7. 不能译为"但这都没关系"。
8 和 9. 注意这两句话的汉译在表达方式上所做的调整。试对照下面逐字死译的译文：
杰克逊太太说，害怕成了她最普通、最安静的夜晚的一部分。
我等不及赶回家并把门关上。

讲解

一、表达角度及方式的转换

如注释 1 所示，译者如果不换一个角度来译 sister-in-law，那么这个词就没法翻译了。英汉翻译中，表达角度和方式的适当转换，一可以使一些难译的语句以不同的方式得以迻译；二可以使译文更合乎汉语表达习惯。

1. The wild garden behind the house contained a central apple-tree...
   屋后荒芜的花园中央有一棵苹果树……（比较：屋后荒芜的花园里有一棵在中间的苹果树……）

2. I took home a briefcase full of troubles.
   我带着满满一皮包伤脑筋的问题回到家里。（比较：……带着盛满问题的皮包……）

3. She is in search of a goal that has eluded many U.S. cities—a way to keep her own city's image as a clean, green place to live, yet make way for the growth that would mean more jobs and preserve prosperity.
   她在寻求解决许多美国城市都未能解决的一个问题（比较：……逃避了许多美国城市的一个问题）——既保持城市绿化的生活环境和清洁的面貌，同时又容许有所发展，使更多的人就业并保持繁荣。

4. I haven't talked to a single coastal state that isn't doing some hard thinking about this and where the government isn't starting to put together some plans.
   我跟沿海许多州的官员谈过话，他们全都对此作过认真考虑，而且都在对一些计划进行综合考虑。（比较：我没有跟沿海任何一个州的没对此作过认真考虑，而

且没在对一些计划进行综合考虑的官员谈过话。）

5. His anger often derived from nothing: the set of a pair of fat lips, the casual heavy thump of the serving spoon into his plate, or the resentful conviction that the cook was not serving him enough.

往往只是为了芝麻大一点小事就惹他一肚子火（比较：他的火气无缘无故）：炊事兵撅着两片厚嘴唇啦，舀菜的大勺不小心咣地一声碰了他的碟子啦，要不然就是愤愤不平地认为炊事兵没给他盛够。（比较：炊事兵的两片厚嘴唇，舀菜的大勺不小心碰了他的碟子的沉重声音，或是认为炊事兵没给他盛够的不满念头。）

6. Observe a child; any one will do. You will see that not a day passes in which he does not find something or other to make him happy, though he may be in tears the next moment. Then look at a man; any one of us will do. You will notice that weeks and months can pass in which every day is greeted with nothing more than resignation, and endured with polite indifference.

仔细观察一个小孩，随便哪个孩子都行。你会发现，他每天都会发现一两件令他快乐的事情，尽管过一会儿他可能会哭哭啼啼。再看看一个大人，我们中间任何人都行。你会发现，一周复一周，一月又一月，他总是以无可奈何的心情迎接新的一天的到来，又以悠然自得、满不在乎的心情挨过这一天的时光。（注意：原文是以 a day/weeks and months 的角度，而译文是从"他"的角度来阐述的。）

7. The dry riverbed was only a clatter of teetering stones now, ricocheting off my feet as I passed...

我走在干涸的河床上，只听见石头被我踩得咯噔咯噔地响（比较：干涸的河床上只是一片石头滑动的咯噔声……），有的从我脚边咕噜一声蹦开去……

8. I did not know what the future held of marvel or surprise for me. Anger and bitterness had preyed upon me continually for weeks and a deep languor had succeeded this passionate struggle.

但不知今后等待着我的是什么，会使我欣喜，还是惊骇。几个星期以来我又气又恨，感到非常苦恼。这种感情上的激烈斗争过去之后，我感到浑身无力。（注意后一句中是用人称主语"我"重新表达原文内容的。）

9. The most important day I remember in all my life is the one on which my teacher, Anne Mansfield Sullivan, came to me. I am filled with wonder when I consider the immeasurable contrast between the two lives which it connects.

在我的记忆里，安妮·曼斯菲尔德·沙利文老师来的那一天，是我一生中最重要的日子。从这一天开始，我的生活和以前截然不同（比较：这一天连接起来的两种截然不同的生活）。一想到这一点，我就感到非常高兴。

10. It would have been difficult to find a happier child than I was as I lay in my crib at the close of that eventful day and lived over the joys it had brought me, and for the first time longed for a new day to come.

当那感慨万千的一天就要结束时，我躺在自己的小床里，感受这一天带给我的那些快乐，我觉得没有人比我更幸福了（比较：很难找到比我更快乐的孩子了）。一生中第一次我期盼着新的一天的到来。

11. In 1959, I wrote my autobiography for an assignment in sixth grade. In twenty-nine pages, most half-filled with earnest scrawl, I described my parents, brothers, pets, house, hobbies, school, sports and plans for the future.

一九九五年我写过一个自传，那是六年级的一次作业。二十九页的自传中几乎每页上字数都不多，潦潦草草却又十分认真地写了我的父母、兄弟、宠物、房子、爱好、学校、体育活动和未来的计划。（比较：二十九页中，大部分都是半页的急切而潦草的字迹，我描写了……）

视角或表达方式的转换涉及句子结构，但绝不仅仅是句子结构问题。译者采用不同的视角，必然引领或启发读者也从不同的视角构建相应的情景。更有趣的是，视角的转换会给译者带来一定的重构情景的自由度，造成叙述焦点的变化。比如下面一个译例：

12. ...and before the carriage arrived in Russell Square, a great deal of conversation had taken place about the Drawing-room, and whether or not young ladies wore powder as well as hoops when presented, and whether she was to have that honour: to the Lord Mayor's ball she knew she was to go.

[a] 马车到达勒赛尔广场之前，她说了不少话，谈到进宫觐见的情形和年轻姑娘觐见时的服装，譬如说，裙子里是不是得撑个箍，头上要不要带洒过粉的假头发。她还不知道自己有没有机会进宫，不过市长开的跳舞会她是一定会有请帖的。（杨必 译）

[b] 马车还没到拉塞尔广场，她们已经开始大谈起客厅，以及年轻女子出席活动该戴裙箍，是不是也该擦粉才对，她不知道是不是有幸出席那类活动。她知道他会应邀出席市长老爷举行的舞会。（贾文浩等译）

两种译文都出现了叙述视角的转换，由 conversation 为叙述起始点转为用人称

代词"她/她们"做起始点。但两位译者所"见到"的情景有些不同:译文 [a] 的人称是"她",单数;而译文 [b] 先用"她们",复数,后又转为"她"。哪个对?都对。因为从上文看,Amelia 和 Rebecca 同在一辆马车上,而从谈话内容看,肯定是前者主导了她们之间的谈话,后者出身贫微,不可能知道所谈内容,恐怕只有发问和聆听的份儿。现在值得关注的是,译文 [a] 一直以"她"(Amelia)为主线叙述,而译文 [b] 则将 Rebecca 对谈话的参与也呈现出来。这两种译文对心理情景的诱发作用也会有所不同,阅读译文 [a] 时我们脑中只有"她"(Amelia),而阅读译文 [b] 我们"看到"的是两个人。叙述视角的变化意味着心理情景的切换,意味着意义传译的变化。

二、译文的增益

译文有时有必要增加一些文字(如注释2),一般是出于下列几种考虑:

(一)为汉语行文的连贯

1. The powder in place, he rammed a long iron rod to tamp down the charge. But the tamping-iron rubbed against the side of the shaft, and a spark ignited the powder.

   装上炸药之后,他把一根长长的铁棍伸进去,想把炸药捣实。不料,铁棍擦过洞壁时,迸出火星,点燃了炸药。

   加字之后,"擦过——迸出——点燃"形成了连贯的动词系列。

2. Her family of 13 was so poor that a brother once tried to mold a Thanksgiving turkey out of a couple of pounds hamburger.

   过去她家有13口人,曾经穷到感恩节买不起火鸡,她的弟弟只好用几磅汉堡包模拟做了一只。

3. Noontime came and went; Nixon, who rarely had lunch, and Kissinger, who rarely missed it, skipped the meal and went right on talking for almost four hours.

   正午到了,又谈到偏午,尼克松很少吃午饭,而基辛格是很少不吃午饭的,但这回两人都不曾想到这顿饭,接连谈了差不多四个钟头。

4. Indeed, the Teheran government's handpicked delegation to the Copenhagen Conference couldn't have been better chosen by Allah himself to defend the Islamic revolution.

   说真的,由德黑兰政府一手挑选出来在哥本哈根会议上为伊斯兰革命辩护的代表，堪称精挑细选，即使是真主本人，也未必能选出比这更好的代表团了。

5. ...Pat tiptoed into the house and sat in the living room quiet as a mouse, at least Pat thought he was. On hearing the racket, Molly hurried down from upstairs. She saw red as soon as she spotted what Pat was doing.

……派特到家后，就像只老鼠似的蹑手蹑脚地窜进客厅，一声不响地坐下来。他自认为做到了神不知鬼不觉。可天晓得摩利耳尖，闻声从楼上下来。她一看到派特那德行，不禁勃然大怒。

6. One couple, who just got married, was headed home in a colorfully decorated cart pulled by a good-looking horse. The horse, however, was not in a good mood. It neighed, kicked, and bucked high in the air, misbehaving miserably. That infuriated the groom and he said: "That's one!" The horse didn't pay any attention to the driver and kept on misbehaving. The groom said: "That's two!" That didn't stop the horse at all from being rambunctious. The groom said: "That's three!" He took out a pistol and shot the horse dead.

一对新婚夫妇驾着一辆装饰华丽的马车沿回家的路进发，拉车的是匹相当挺俊的马。可不知怎么搞的，那匹马闹起情绪来了，不停地长啸、乱踢、蹦得半天高，简直是不可驾驭。这下子可气坏了新郎，他叫道："这是第一次警告！"那匹马丝毫不在意，依旧在那儿乱踢。新郎再喊道："第二次警告！"马还是没安静下来。新郎又喊了："第三次警告！"说着便拿出一把枪，把马给杀了。

注意：however 未译为"然而"，而是多用了几个字，显然增强了上下句的连贯性。

（二）出于修辞上的考虑

7. It catered to large appetites and modest purses.

它迎合胃口大而钱包小的吃客。

原文运用了提喻修辞法，译文宜点明所涉及的人。

8. He must loiter about country churches, attend wakes and fairs and other rural festivals, and cope with the people in all their conditions, and all their habits and humours.

他一定要在教堂里消磨一下时光，参加纪念守护神节日的活动，逛逛集市，与村民们同庆他们的节日，和身世各异的人打交道，并了解他们的习惯和性情。

134

为迎合汉语动宾搭配的需要，译文增加了几个动词。

9. The thesis summed up the new achievements made in electronic computers, artificial satellites and rockets.
论文总结了电子计算机、人造卫星和火箭等三个领域中的新成就。

上例中加了概括词"等三个领域"，汉语中习惯使用这样一些概括词。再如：The Soviet Union, the United States, China, England, France and Japan are now enlarging cooperation in cultural and scientific fields. 译为：苏、美、中、英、法、日等六国正在扩大文化和科学领域的合作。

（三）为了将意思表达得更明确，易于读者理解

10. The blond boy quickly crossed himself.
那个金发小男孩立刻在胸前画十字，祈求上帝保佑。

11. As a result, a few token meetings were being set up through Foggy Bottom, the more-than-ever appropriate nickname for the Department of State. It describes Secretary Rogers' influence—foggy and at the bottom.
结果在"雾谷"开了几次象征性的会议。"雾谷"这个绰号今天对国务院来说是再贴切不过了。它描述了国务卿罗杰斯的影响——虚无缥缈如雾，地位低下如谷。

12. In April, there was the "ping" heard around the world. In July, the ping "ponged."
四月，全世界听到中国"乒"的一声把球打了出去，到了七月，美国"乓"的一声把球打了回来。

13. As often as I've read this speech, getting a lump in my throat every time, I've never detected one stylistic problem, much less 13.
尽管我常常阅读这篇讲演词，而且每次总是觉得喉头发哽，心情激动，可我却从未发现过有什么文体错误，更不用说有十三处之多了。

此句摘自"If Lincoln Had Used a Computer"一文，句中speech指林肯的Gettysburg Address。据说某个计算机程序可纠正文体错误，该文作者将林肯的这篇著名演说输入电脑，结果发现了13处文体方面的问题，于是就此发表评论。

14. Now, I had decided, I had to become a miser with words and stretch every sentence like a poor man spending his last dollar.

我决定对词汇要像守财奴对钱那样不轻易放过；也要像穷人过日子，把每个句子当作身边最后一块钱，尽量拖延，慢慢花掉。

15. And their conclusions are not just pie in the sky—they're based on an astonishing experiment in which a dog was frozen for 15 minutes, then revived in perfect health!

    他们的结论可不是天上掉馅饼，异想天开，那是有实验做依据的。在那次令人惊讶的实验中，一只狗冷冻了15分钟然后复活，而且十分健康。

16. Two groups, one of men and lads, the other of women, had come down the lane just at the hour when the shadows of the eastern hedge-top struck the west hedge midway, so that the heads of the groups were enjoying sunrise while their feet were still in the dawn.

    [a] 篱路上已经来了两班工人，一班是男人和孩子，一班是女人，他们来的时候，正好是东边树篱顶儿的影子落到西边树篱的中腰上，因此他们的头在朝阳里，他们的脚仍旧在黎明里。

    [b] 大路上走来两帮人，一帮是男的，一帮是女的，这时东面树篱的阴影正好落至西面树篱的中部，所以，这些男工女工的头部已在朝阳的照晒之下，而脚部却仍在黎明的阴影之中。

    译文 [b] 采用了增益的办法，请对照译文 [a] 加以考虑。

Think About It

Frank Conroy

[1] When I was sixteen I worked selling hot dogs at a stand in the Fourteenth Street subway station in New York City, one level above the trains and one below the street[1], where the crowds continually flowed back and forth. On my break I came out from behind the counter and passed the time with two old black men who ran a shoeshine stand in a dark corner of the corridor. It was a poor location, half hidden by columns and they didn't have much business. I would sit with my back against the wall while they

stood or moved around their ancient elevated stand, talking to each other or to me, but always staring into the distance as they did so.

[2]   As the weeks went by I realized that they never looked at anything in their immediate vicinity—not at me or their stand or anybody who might come within ten or fifteen feet. They did not look at approaching customers once they were inside the perimeter. Save for the instant it took to discern the color of the shoes, they did not even look at what they were doing while they worked, but rubbed in polish, brushed, and buffed by feel while looking over their shoulders, into the distance, as if awaiting the arrival of an important person. Of course there wasn't all that much distance in the underground station, but their behavior was so focused and consistent they seemed somehow to transcend the physical. A powerful mood was created, and I came almost to believe that these men could see through walls, through girders, and around corners to whatever hyperspace it was where whoever it was they were waiting and watching for would finally emerge. Their scattered talk was hip, elliptical, and hinted at mysteries beyond my white boy's ken,² but it was the staring off, the long, steady staring off, that had me hypnotized. I left for a better job, with handshakes from both of them, without understanding what I had seen³.

[3]   Perhaps ten years later, after playing jazz with black musicians in various Harlem clubs, hanging out uptown with a few young artists and intellectuals, I began to learn from them something of the extraordinarily varied and complex riffs and rituals embraced by different people to help themselves get through life in the ghetto.⁴ Fantasy of all kinds—from playful to dangerous—was in the very air of Harlem. It was the spice of uptown life.

[4]   Only then did I understand the two shoeshine men. They were trapped in a demeaning situation in a dark corner in an underground corridor in a filthy subway system. Their continuous staring off was a kind of statement, a kind of dance. Our bodies are here, went the statement, but our souls are receiving nourishment from distant sources only we can see. They were powerful magic dancers, sorcerers almost, and thirty-five years later I can still feel the pressure of their spell.⁵

[5]   The light bulb may appear over your head, is what I'm saying, but it may be a while before it actually goes on. Early in my attempts to learn jazz

piano, I used to listen to recordings of a fine player named Red Garland, whose music I admired. I couldn't quite figure out what he was doing with his left hand, however; the chords eluded me. I went uptown to an obscure club where he was playing with his trio, caught him on his break, and simply asked him. "Sixths," he said cheerfully. And then he went away.

[6]　I didn't know what to make of it. The basic jazz chord is the seventh, which comes in various configurations, but it is what it is. I was a self-taught pianist, pretty shaky on theory and harmony, and when he said sixths I kept trying to fit the information into what I already knew, and it didn't fit. But it stuck in my mind—a tantalizing mystery.

[7]　A couple of years later, when I began playing with a bass player, I discovered more or less by accident that if the bass played the root and I played a sixth based on the fifth note of the scale, a very interesting chord involving both instruments emerged.[6] Ordinarily, I suppose I would have skipped over the matter and not paid much attention, but I remembered Garland's remark and so I stopped and spent a week or two working out the voicings, and greatly strengthened my foundations as a player. I had remembered what I hadn't understood, you might say, until my life caught up with the information and the light bulb went on[7].

[8]　Education[8] doesn't end until life ends, because you never know when you're going to understand something you hadn't understood before. For me, the magic dance of the shoeshine men was the kind of experience in which understanding came with a kind of click, a resolving kind of click. The same with the experience at the piano. Indeed, in our intellectual lives, our creative lives, it is perhaps those problems that will never resolve that rightly claim the lion's share of our energies. The physical body exists in a constant state of tension as it maintains homeostasis, and so too does the active mind embrace the tension of never being certain, never being absolutely sure, never being done, as it engages the world. That is our special fate, our inexpressibly valuable condition.

参考译文

想想看：知识是如何得来的

弗兰克·康罗伊

[1]　十六岁那年，我在纽约十四大街地铁站里卖热狗。摊位在地下一层，再下面是轨道层，人们来来往往，川流不息。闲在的时候，我就走出柜台找两个擦皮鞋的黑人哥们聊天，他们在人行通道一个黑乎乎的角落里摆了个摊。那个位置可不怎么样，半掩在好几根柱子后面，少有人光顾。我常常是靠墙坐下，而他俩则是围着那古老的脚凳或站立或走动，或互相说话或跟我说话。不过，这时候他们的目光总是盯着远处的什么地方。

[2]　一周一周过去了，我注意到，他们从不看近处——不看我，不看他们的摊子，也不看任何走进十或十五英尺范围的人。除去瞥一眼皮鞋是什么颜色的，他们根本不看手中的活计，只管涂上鞋油，刷一刷，再凭感觉用布打亮，而眼睛却一直望着远方，就像在等待什么重要人物的出现。当然，地铁站里还能看多远，可他们就是这么专注、执着地望着，好像超越了空间阻隔。我产生了一种很强烈的感觉，我几乎相信这两个人的目光能穿越墙壁，透过梁柱，拐弯抹角，到达一个超级空间，那里某个他们等待和盼望的人最终将会出现。他们什么都谈，用的都是些时髦的词儿，简略隐晦，话里有话，我一个白人小孩是听不懂的。倒是他们注视远方的目光，那久久的、专注的目光，深深把我迷住了。后来我找了个更好的活儿，他们和我握别，但他们注视远方的目光我一直搞不明白。

[3]　在接下来的大约十年里，我和黑人乐手们在哈莱姆各个俱乐部里演奏爵士乐，和几个年轻的艺人和大学生在市郊混世界。这时候我才开始从他们身上了解到，要在贫民窟里谋生活，不同的人自有不同的生活习惯和方式，五花八门，错综复杂。哈莱姆贫民区连空气里都弥漫着从玩世不恭到充满危险的形形色色的各种幻想。这是市郊贫民生活的调味剂。

[4]　直到这时，我才算真正理解了那两个擦皮鞋的年轻人。他们囿于龌龊的地铁通道那黑漆漆的角落，哪有尊严。他们直视远方的眼神就是一种宣言：我们虽然委身于此，但我们的灵魂正汲取着只有我们才能看得到的遥远源泉的滋养。那直视远方的眼神也是一种舞姿：他们是精力充沛、魔力四射的舞者，近乎巫师之舞。三十五年后的今天，我仍能感到他们那种魔力的气势。

[5]　这事要是打个比方,就像人人头上都可能会出现的一盏灯,但要它真的亮起来,恐怕就得等一段时间了。我刚学爵士钢琴曲的那段时间,常听一个叫雷德·盖尔兰德的著名钢琴手的录音,他的曲子我喜欢极了。可我怎么也搞不懂他左手的指法是怎样的,和弦是怎么弹出来的。于是我去了市郊一家不知名的俱乐部,他正在那儿演三重奏,我抓住他演出的空档,直接问了他这个问题。"六和弦。"他兴冲冲地答道,然后就走了。

[6]　我不懂他的意思。基本爵士和弦是七和弦,有各种不同的配合,别的我就不懂了。我钢琴是自学的,在乐理和和声方面知之甚少。听到他说"六和弦",我就极力在我已有的知识里寻找契合点,可是怎么也找不到。他的话我一直耿耿在心,成了一个诱人的迷。

[7]　又过了几年,我开始和一个贝斯手搭档,我多少有些偶然地发现,如果贝斯奏出根音,而我弹出一个基于第五音的六和弦,就会产生这两种乐器的有趣和弦。要在以往,我一准不会怎么留意而把这事忽略过去,但现在我记得盖尔兰德的话,所以就专门花了一两周的时间把这个和弦配置弄了出来,这可大大加强了我作为一个乐手的底气。对过去没理解的事,可以说,我一直放在心上,直到有一天我顿然开窍,于是我头上那盏灯亮了。

[8]　生命不息,求知的过程就不会停止,因为你永远不知道,过去没弄明白的事情,说不定什么时候你就会顿然领悟。对我来说,理解那两个擦鞋匠的奇特眼神就是这样一种顿悟的实际体验,一种豁然开朗的体验。对和弦的理解也是如此。确实,在我们求知和立业的过程中,或许正是这些无法理解的问题耗去了我们大部分精力和能量。我们的身体为了适应外界因素而达成自身稳定,总是处在一种张力之中。同样,我们活跃的大脑在应对外部世界的时候也总是处于一种永远无法确知、无法确信和无法完成的张力之中。这就是我们特定的命运———一种具有无以言表的价值的处境。

注释

本文原是作者给爱荷华大学文学院毕业生所做的一次演讲,后以"Think About It—Ways We Know, and Don't" 为题在 *Harper's Magazine* 上发表,2001 年被 Robert Atwan 以现在的标题收入 *The Best American Essays Third College Edition*(Houghton Mifflin Co.),本单元对原文有所删减。题目参照 *Harper's Magazine* 所用标题,译为《想想看:知识是如何得来的》。

1. 试比较"夹在地面和轨道层之间"或"在轨道层上面,街面下面"之类的译文。考虑现在的译文是否更符合汉语的表达习惯?
2. 注意这句话的译文如何摆脱原文结构束缚,力求写出地道、达意的汉语。
3. what I had seen 即"我所看到的",说得很笼统,据上文应该指的就是 the staring off,译文宜具体化为好。
4. 这是个长句。对原句信息要适当拆解组合,重构符合汉语行文习惯的句子。
5. 以上三个句子,作者分别解释了 a kind of statement 和 a kind of dance 的具体含义。译文对 a kind of statement, a kind of dance 采取了分而述之的方法,先说"他们直视远方的眼神就是一种宣言:……",再说"那直视远方的眼神也是一种舞姿:……",这样读起来逻辑层次更清楚。
6. [5][6][7] 三个自然段都涉及和弦(chord)的知识。译者如没有这方面的知识,一定要请教有关人士或参阅有关资料。
7. 这句话的译文采取了点出主题(what I hadn't understood),再加主谓的句构。这更符合汉语表达习惯(参阅本章 Unit Four 的讲解部分)。
8. 此处的 education 不宜机械地译为"教育",结合全文立意,指的应该是不断求知的过程。

讲解

克服翻译体

如注释 2、3 所示,译者必须保证译文能被读者接受,力避翻译体(translationese)。所谓翻译体,即指不能摆脱原文语言结构形式束缚而生成的不自然、不符合译语表达习惯、不中不西的别扭话。造成这种现象的原因,一是拘泥于英文句法和表达方式,二是汉语写作意识不强。译文写作中,务必多想想已经读过的汉语文字,力求把英语信息用汉语所习惯的方式重新表达出来。如:

1. I was standing beside his bed and he was sitting up between the sheets, clad in his underwear, with a great portfolio in his hands.

我正站在麦基床边,而他坐在两层床单中间,身上只穿着内衣,手里捧着一大本相片簿。

译文中划线部分十分别扭,改译为:他只穿内衣,裹着被单坐着。

2. Its wings, as the photographs had indicated, were its most startling feature. Except that the photographs hadn't prepared us for the actuality. In proportion to the length of the fuselage, which was some forty feet, they

stretched out to more than eighty.

　　就像照片上所展示的那样，机翼是它最为触目的部分；<u>只是这张照片还没有为我们准备接触实际</u>。和长约四十英尺的机身相称，机翼伸展达八十多英尺。

　　译文的划线部分既别扭又不能达意，改译为：只是照片上无法看出实物的大小罢了。这样便通顺达意了。

3. They are not perfect ovals—like the egg in the Columbus story, they are both crushed flat on the contact end—but their physical resemblance must be a source of perpetual confusion to the gulls that fly overhead.

　　它们并不是正椭圆形——而是像哥伦布故事里的鸡蛋一样，在碰过的那头是压碎了的——<u>但它们外貌的相似一定是使头上飞过的海鸥惊异不已的源泉</u>。

　　译文划线部分可改为：但它们形状极为相似，凌空飞过的海鸥见了，永远也别想分辨清楚。

4. One day when Diana was 12 years old, one of her legs collapsed under her.

　　黛安娜 12 岁时，有一天她突然摔倒，一条腿压在身下。

　　改译：黛安娜 12 岁时，有一天，她一条腿一软，突然摔倒了。

5. I watched her walk through the door. She smiled as our eyes met, and I found myself stammering a hello.

　　我看着她从门外走进来。我们的目光相遇时，她朝我微微一笑，而我发现自己结结巴巴地说了声"你好"。

　　"发现自己说"应不是汉语中固有的说法，改译为：我也不禁结结巴巴地说了声"你好"。

6. I can no longer remember our conversations, but they were never as important as her mere presence.

　　我已记不起我们谈了些什么。不过，那些谈话永远不像她仅仅在我面前存在一样重要。

　　改译：当时的谈话已记不起了，不过，只要有她在我身边，谈什么并不重要。

7. She confusedly realized this reversal of her attitudes, but could not make out what it portended. Only, she felt a need of Bette, of the new sort of relationship which she had discovered with her.

她糊里糊涂地意识到自己这种相反的态度,但是不知道它会带来什么。她只感到需要贝蒂,需要像她才发现的这种新的关系。

改译:她觉得不知怎的,自己的态度全变了,但弄不清这会招致什么结果。只是,她感到需要贝蒂,需要她刚刚发现的她们之间的这种新的关系。

再阅读下面译例,看译者是如何顺应汉语表达方式的:

8. The sun was two hours higher now...
   又过了两个钟头,太阳升得更高了……

9. ...and his hand splayed over the cane's crook with a futile sort of clinging.
   他张开手掌放在拐棍的弯把上,想抓又抓不牢。

10. The discoloration of ages had been great.
    年深日久,房屋的颜色褪得很厉害。

11. "I don't understand it, such a dandy fellow. Now he's all bloated up..." He made a plump apple of his hands.
    "真不可思议,这个公子哥儿。现在他浑身浮肿……"说着他用手比划了个大苹果的样子。

12. He had sixty years or more and was bent with carrying milk bottles.
    他年过六旬,拿着牛奶瓶都直不起腰来。

13. Bill and David soon sailed into continuously overcast and foggy weather.
    比尔和大卫驾船航行了不久,天气就变得阴沉多雾起来。

以上译例说的是,译文要顺应汉语的表达习惯,不要说别扭话。另外还要注意英汉两种语言在句法结构上的一个明显差异:英语重形合,汉语重意合。形合结构不可死板地搬进汉语,要把形合的"形"变一变,将汉语句子组织得"散"一点,这才符合我们的行文习惯。关于形合、意合,第四章的 Unit One 和 Unit Two 还有专门讨论。下面是几个译例:

14. An indelible image of that politically and personally wrenching time is the picture of his son, the young John F. Kennedy, aged three, saluting the coffin of his famous father as it passes in the funeral procession.
    他的三岁的儿子,稚嫩的小约翰·F·肯尼迪,向经过出殡队伍中大名鼎鼎的父亲的灵柩行礼致敬的模样,成为那个国家和个人都黯然神伤的时刻留在人们心中难以忘怀的形象。

　　改译：那时，他的儿子小约翰·F·肯尼迪才三岁。孩子向着出殡队伍中声名显赫的父亲的灵柩行礼，那样子成了那个令政界和国民都黯然神伤的时刻的一个永不磨灭的形象。

15. Parenthood means never really being alone, until the day the kids leave home and you're left with no idea what to do with all the time and energy you used to spend chasing after them.

　　当了家长，就不得清净，直到孩子离开家而你却不知道如何打发从前用来紧追其后的所有时间和精力为止。

　　改译：做了父母，就别想清闲，除非有一天孩子长大离开了家，你不再忙前忙后，可那时你又不知该如何打发空出来的时间和精力了。

16. Any consideration of China's transformation since 1949 must recognize the dramatic improvement in China's global posture.

　　任何对中国1949年以来变化的思考一定会意识到中国国际地位的大幅提升。

　　改译：只要回顾一下中国1949年以来发生的变化，就一定能认识到中国国际地位的大幅提升。

17. Norman E. Borlaug, 95, an American plant pathologist who won the Nobel Peace Prize in 1970 for starting the "Green Revolution" that dramatically increased food production in developing nations and saved countless people from starvation, died Saturday at his home in Dallas.

　　95岁的美国植物病理学家诺曼·E·博洛格，曾以启动显著提高发展中国家粮食产量并将无数人从饥饿中拯救出来的"绿色革命"而获诺贝尔和平奖，周六在达拉斯家中辞世。

　　改译：95岁的美国植物病理学家诺曼·E·博洛格，周六在达拉斯家中辞世。他曾发起"绿色革命"，显著提高了发展中国家的粮食产量，并将无数人从饥饿中拯救出来，因而获得1970年诺贝尔和平奖。

18. During the past five years, print has been clobbered by television and has generally failed to respond by emphasizing the analytic and investigative stories that TV cannot do so well.

　　在过去五年内，报刊受到电视的打击而未能找出对策，它们大都没能做到强调电视做不好的分析性调查性报道。

改译：过去五年中，报刊一直受到电视的打击，而大都未能找出对策。它们应该强调自己的优势，那就是，报刊上的调查、分析性的报道，是电视所不能匹敌的。

最后一点，还要注意运用意译的方法，力求摆脱原文表层结构的束缚，忘其形而译其意，力戒死译。忘形不是不顾及形式，相反，译者必须对原文字斟句酌，条分缕析，弄清结构所表达的准确意义，然后才可发挥汉语表达能力，将理解到的意义忠实再现。如：

19. Whoever, in our circumstances, has made trial of pain, even with all the alleviations which, for us, usually attend it, must know the irritation that comes with it. Tom no longer wondered at the habitual surliness of his associates; nay, he found the placid, sunny temper, which had been the habitute of his life, broken in on, and sorely strained, by the inroads of the same thing.

[a] 无论什么人，在我们这里的环境下，经受了疼痛的折磨，即使有常常伴随着我们而来的慰藉，也一定知道，疼痛要带来烦恼愤怒的。托姆对于伙伴们经常脾气恶劣，再不觉得奇怪；而他要保持一生习惯的温和愉快，也很是勉强，他也被同样的坏脾气闯进来了。

[b] 凡是在我们这样的环境中经历过一番苦难的（即便这苦难中也会有一些慰藉）一定都知道：一个人在苦难中，脾气总是很暴躁。汤姆对伙伴们乖戾的脾气已不足为奇；何止如此，他发现连自己往常那平和、乐观的天性，在苦难的不断侵扰下，也难以保持下去了。

我们看到，译文 [a] 过于拘泥于原文结构和用词，似乎在力求忠实，而实际上却不顺不达，难以卒读。

[20] It is the statement of missionaries, that, of all races of the earth, none have received the Gospel with such eager docility as the African. The principle of reliance and unquestioning faith, which is its foundation, is more a native element in this race than any other; and it is often found among them, that a stray seed of truth, borne on some breeze of accident into hearts of the most ignorant, has sprung up into fruit, whose abundance has shamed that of higher and more skillful culture.

[a] 据传教士的报告，地球上的全体民族，没有一个民族能接受福音，像非洲民族那么热情而易教。信赖的真谛和赖以为基础的盲目信仰，在这个种族里，和其他种族比较起来，更是本地原有土生的成分；在他们中间往往发生这样的事情：真理的一粒

飘荡的种子，乘着某一事件的微风，吹进最愚蠢的心里就发芽、成长，其果实之丰盛，叫文化较高较精深的地方的收获，感到惭愧。

[b] 传教士们都说，在全世界所有民族中，没有一个民族接受福音像非洲人那样迫切和驯从。这种驯服心理的基础是信赖和笃诚，非洲人的这一天性，较之其他民族，更是一种与生俱来的特质。黑人中时常见到这种情况：一颗随风飘荡的真理的种子，借着某个偶然的机会落到一些最愚昧的心田中，后来开花结果，茂盛无比，往往让某个更高级、更成熟的文明种族感到羞愧无地。

将 eager docility 译为"热情而易教"显然不如"迫切和驯从"更精准达意；第二句中 reliance and unquestioning faith 共同修饰 the principle，而不能如译文 [a] 那样把 the principle of reliance 与 unquestioning faith 视为并列成分，进而将定语从句 which is its foundation 译得模糊不清；is more a native element in this race than any other 和 borne on some breeze of accident 的两种译文，译文 [b] 无论在理解和表达上都好于译文 [a]，因为译文 [b] 的理解更准确，表达也更符合汉语习惯；译文 [b] 将 higher and more skillful culture 中的 culture 具化为某个"种族"，宜于汉语行文，而译文 [a] 强用"收获"对译原文的 that（=abundance）反显佶屈聱牙。我们看到，理解不准或失误与表达上的过于刻板（"死译"）共同造成了翻译腔现象。

What's Right About Being Left-handed

[1] Imagine you are Alice, stepping through the looking glass. Suddenly everything is reversed. Doorknobs are on the wrong side of doors. The gearshift in your car is in the wrong place. Handles on can openers are on the wrong side and turn the wrong way.

[2] Millions of people wake up every day in just such a predicament. They are left-handed and must face the built-in bias of a world designed for the right-handed majority. In a society of rights (form Anglo-Saxon riht, for "direct, upright, correct") and righteousness, the southpaw is left (Anglo-Saxon lyft "weak") with leftovers and left-handed compliments.[1]

[3] Why we are left- or right-handed remains one of the great unsolved mysteries of science. We know that nearly two out of three lefties are male and that left-handedness runs in families. According to one study, almost half the offspring of two left-handed parents will be southpaws. The Scots-Irish family Kerr (from the Gaelic word for "left") produced so many left-handers that in 1470 the family built its castle's spiral stairways with a reverse twist to favor southpaw swordsmen.

[4] On the other hand, heredity alone cannot explain lefties. At least 84 percent of them are born of two right-handed parents. And in 12 percent of genetically identical twins, one will be right-handed, the other left.

[5] Perhaps the greatest puzzle of all is not why some people are left-handed, but rather why so few are. In virtually every other species, from chimpanzees to chinchillas, roughly equal numbers of individuals will favor either the right or the left. However, scientists are trying to set things right, and they are beginning to gain insight into the many ways southpaws differ from "northpaws", by considering how their brains work.

[6] Many of the circuits in the human central nervous system operate through crossed laterality—that is, the right hand is "wired" to the left side of the brain, and vice versa[2]. In at least 95 percent of right-handers, the speech-language center is in the brain's left hemisphere. Yet only about 15 percent of left-handers are similarly hooked up, with speech controlled by the opposite, or right, hemisphere. According to Jerre Levy, a biopsychologist at Illinois' University of Chicago, about 70 percent of left-handers have speech controlled by the left side of the brain, while the remaining 15 percent have their language-control centers in both hemispheres.

[7] Broadly speaking, the left side of the brain is thought by some scientists to process linear, logical information, while the right side tends more toward processing emotion and mood. This may be why lefties are at significantly higher risk of schizophrenia, phobias and manic-depression, and in one study were shown to be three times more likely to attempt suicide.

[8] Southpaws can be more sensitive to a variety of drugs too. Peter Irwin, a senior clinical research scientist at Sandoz Institute in East Hanover, New Jersey, found that, after taking such medications as aspirin, antidepressants,

sedatives and antihistamines, lefties had greater changes in electrical activity in the brain than righties did. As if this weren't enough, southpaws appear to be twice as prone to autoimmune diseases, including diabetes, ulcerative colitis, rheumatoid arthritis and myasthenia gravis.

[9] With such liabilities, how have left-handers managed to survive at all? The good news is that there is a very bright side to being a lefty. Camilla Benbow, associate professor of psychology at Iowa State University, surveyed students who scored in the top 100th of one percent in math on America's Scholastic Aptitude Test. She discovered that fully 20 percent of these math geniuses were left-handed—double the proportion of lefties in the population.³ Mensa, the high-I.Q. society, estimates that 20 percent of its members are left-handed.

[10] Indeed, the ability to integrate what some researchers call the more "logical" left side of the brain and the more "intuitive" or "artistic" right side may have helped lefties excel.

[11] Among history's most famous left-handed warriors were Alexander the Great, Julius Caesar, Charlermagne, Joan of Arc and Napoleon (as well as his consort, Josephine). Michelangelo sculpted David holding, in his left hand, the sling used to slay Goliath.

[12] For years, many lefties have felt they were targets of discrimination. But they have begun to assert their rights. In 1980, when part-time police officer Franklin W. "woody" Winborn was fired in Riverside, Missouri, activists rallied to his cause. A southpaw, Winborn had refused to wear his gun holster on his right side. In Seattle, a postal clerk and lefty named Robert B. Green was told to follow the usual procedure of holding mail in the left hand and sorting with the right.

[13] Winborn settled his case out of court, and Green was permitted to continue his left-handed sorting. Lefthanders International of Topeka, Kansas, took a keen interest in both protests. Its founder, Dean Campbell, asks, "Why must the left-handed live in a world designed to handicap us?" His group has issued a "Bill of Lefts", which asserts in part that "left-handers shall be entitled to offer their dominant hand in a handshake, salute or oath".

[14] Says Campbell, smiling impishly, "If the right side of the body is controlled by the left brain, and vice versa, then we left-handed people are the only ones in our right mind[4]."

参考译文

当个左撇子有什么不好

[1] 假设你是艾丽丝，一步跨入了镜子里面。突然一切都颠倒了。门把手装到门的那一边去了。车挡装错了地方。罐头起子的柄是反的，转向也是反的。

[2] 数以百万计的人们每天一睡醒就是处于这种尴尬的境况中的。他们是左撇子，因而必须面对这个为惯用右手的大多数人设计的世界的根深蒂固的偏见。在一个"rights"（右，源于盎格鲁撒克逊语中"riht"一词，意为"正面的、正直的、正确的"）和"righteousness"（正义）的社会里，左撇子的"left"（左，源于盎格鲁撒克逊语中"lyft"一词，意为"软弱"）就只能与"leftover"（剩余物）和"left-handed compliments"（挖苦的恭维话）联系在一起了。

[3] 我们为什么习惯用左手或是用右手，仍然是科学中的一个未解之谜。我们知道几乎三分之二的左撇子都是男性，而且左撇子具有遗传性。一项研究表明，父母双方都是左撇子，他们的后代中几乎有一半也是左撇子。苏格兰和爱尔兰混血的克尔家族（克尔，Kerr，源于盖尔语中"左"一词）繁衍出的左撇子太多了，以致这个家族在 1470 年把其城堡的螺旋梯修成反向的，以方便左撇子剑手。

[4] 但是，仅仅遗传一说还不能把问题解释清楚。至少百分之八十四的左撇子的父母都是惯用右手的。同卵双胞胎中有百分之十二是一个用右手，另一个则是左撇子。

[5] 也许最大的谜中之谜并不是为什么有些人是左撇子，而是为什么左撇子这么少。事实上，从黑猩猩到南美栗鼠的所有动物种群里，爱用左爪和爱用右爪的在数量上大体是相等的。无论如何，科学家们正在设法理出个头绪来，而且通过对人们的大脑功能的研究，正在开始对左撇子不同于"右撇子"的许多方面有所了解。

[6] 人的中枢神经系统的许多神经纤维是通过交叉传导起作用的，即右手与大脑左侧"相连"，而左手则与大脑右侧"相连"。至少百分之九十五的惯用右手的人的语

言中枢是位于大脑左半球的。然而仅有大约百分之十五的左撇子的情况符合这一规律,即其语言机能是由大脑的另一侧,即右侧大脑半球控制的。据伊利诺斯芝加哥大学的生物心理学家杰尔·利维说,大约百分之七十的左撇子的语言是由左脑控制的,而其余百分之十五的语言控制中枢则位于大脑的两个半球内。

[7] 总而言之,一些科学家认为左脑操纵条理性或逻辑思维,而右脑则更多地倾向于操纵感情和情绪。这也许就是为什么左撇子患精神分裂症、恐惧症和狂躁抑郁症的危险明显较高以及在一项研究中所表明的企图自杀的可能性比常人高三倍的原因。

[8] 左撇子对许多药物的过敏反应可能更为强烈。新泽西州东汉诺威桑多兹学院的高级临床医学研究员彼得·欧文发现,在服用阿司匹林、抗抑郁症药、镇静剂和抗组胺剂等药物之后,左撇子脑电图出现的波动比惯用右手的人要大。好像这还不够,左撇子患自体免疫性疾病的可能性似乎也要高出一倍,其中包括糖尿病、溃疡性结肠炎、风湿性关节炎和重症肌无力症。

[9] 有如此之多的不利因素,左撇子们怎么生存下来了呢?令人欣慰的是,作为一个左撇子还有极其有利的一面。爱荷华州立大学的心理学副教授卡米拉·本鲍调查了在美国学术能力测试中前万分之一的数学得分最高的学生。她发现在这些数学天才中足足有百分之二十是左撇子——比参试人员中左撇子所占百分比高出一倍。美国高智商团体门萨学会估计其成员的百分之二十是左撇子。

[10] 的确,或许正是这种被研究人员称为更具"逻辑性"的左脑与更具"直觉性"或"艺术性"的右脑结合起来的能力,使左撇子们成了佼佼者。

[11] 历史上最著名的左撇子军人有亚历山大大帝、尤利乌斯·恺撒、查理曼大帝、贞德和拿破仑(及其妻子约瑟芬)。米开朗基罗雕塑了左手握弹弓的大卫王,弹弓是用来射杀哥利亚的。

[12] 多年以来,许多左撇子觉得他们是人们歧视的对象。不过他们已经开始起来维护自己的权利了。1980年,当兼职警官弗兰克林·W·"伍迪"·温伯在密苏里州里弗赛德遭到开除的时候,维护左撇子权益的积极分子们纷纷表示站在他一边。温伯是个左撇子,他拒绝把枪套带在右侧。在西雅图,一个名叫罗伯特·B·格林的邮局职员被命令要遵循常规操作方法,即左手持信右手分拣。

[13] 温伯未经法庭便解决了问题,而格林也被允许继续用左手分拣信件。堪萨斯州托皮卡的使用左手者国际协会对这两起抗议事件都极感兴趣。这个组织的创始人安迪·坎贝尔质问:"为什么使用左手的人必须生活在一个旨在羁绊我们的社会里?"

他的组织发表了一份"使用左手者权利宣言",其中主张"使用左手者有权使用他们的主手握手、敬礼和宣誓"。

[14] 坎贝尔顽皮地笑着说:"如果身体的右侧受大脑的左侧支配而左侧受右脑支配,那么我们这些左撇子就是唯一使用右脑的,即头脑正常的人了。"(齐世和译)

注释

1. 在英语中 right 既有"右",也有"好的、公正的、合法的"等意义,left-handed 除了"用左手的"意思之外,还有"笨拙的、无诚意的、可疑的"等贬义。本句中,作者把 right 和 righteousness 联系起来,又把 left-handed 及其所含的词根 left 与 leftover 等词联系起来。另外,词组 be left with 本义为"被给予",而 left 又正好和 left(左)拼写相同。以上这些都是英语语义所特有的,译为汉语,这些语义特点很难表达出来。本句的译文似已竭尽全力,但恐仍未能将原文再现得十全十美。本文标题的翻译也有同样的困难。从全文内容看,文章标题有两重意义:一是左撇子也是有优势的;二是左撇子不应受到歧视,应得到与右撇子一样的生活、工作权利。而 right 一词的这种双关意义,在汉语中很难表达,如译为"左撇子好在哪里"似只译出了第一种含义。现将标题译为"当个左撇子有什么不好",可谓正说反译,旨在再现原标题的双层意义:当个左撇子有什么短处!又有什么不对的!

2. vice versa 不能简单地译为"反之亦然",那样会导致语义不清。又如:
For the bound man's fame rested on the fact that he was always bound, that whenever he washed himself he had to wash his clothes too and vice versa, and that his only way of doing so was to jump in the river just as he did every morning when the sun came out, and that he had to be careful not to go too far for fear of being carried away by the stream.

被捆缚的人的名声就在于他总是被捆着,他每次要洗澡,总得连衣服一起洗,每次要洗衣服,也得连带洗个澡。每天清晨,太阳刚露面,他就跳进河里去洗澡,但他总是非常小心,不敢离岸太远,以免被激流冲走。

3. 这句话中有两个数字,务必翻译准确。100th of one percent 即 1/100 × 1/100 = 万分之一。double 即增加到两倍,或增加了一倍。另外,population 一词应理解为:the total set of items, persons, etc. from which a sample is taken。

4. in our right mind 既有"头脑正常"的意思,又有"在右脑中"的意思。译文并未完全译出其双关意义,恐只能加注作为补救:英语中"右"(right)一词兼有"正确、正常"的意思。

讲解

原文的不可译性

注释1和4都涉及原文信息难以再现的情况，即原文的不可译性。总的来说，任何一种语言的语篇都是可以译为另一种语言的，其所含信息也是可以在很大程度上再现的。因为人类生活在同一个世界上，其共性的东西在跨文化交际中总是起主导作用的。当然，也应看到人们是生活在不同的社会、文化、历史环境中的，语言编码体系也各不相同，这就导致了跨文化交际中信息绝对保真的困难性。译者有时会遇到一些十分难译，甚至无法翻译的词语和句子。造成不可译性的因素有两类，一类是社会、文化上的，另一类是语言上的。

本文一开始所提到的 Alice，以及后文中提到的亚历山大、圣女贞德、大卫王等西方文化背景中普通读者都十分熟悉的名字，对一般的中文读者来说恐怕就会生疏得多了。针对此类文化背景上的差异，译者可用加注或在译文中简要提供有关信息的方法，提高原文的可译性及译文的可读性。本文译者采取了前一种方法，下面就是译者所加的附注，供参考：

1. Alice：英国作家 Lewis Carroll 所写的小说 *Alice's Adventures in Wonderland* 的续集 *Through the Looking Glass* 中的女主人公；2. Alexander the Great：亚力山大大帝（356B.C.—323B.C.），马其顿国王；3. Julius Caesar：尤利乌斯·恺撒（100B.C.—44 B.C.），古罗马将军、皇帝、政治家、历史学家；4. Charlemagne：查理曼大帝，法兰克王、西罗马帝国皇帝（742—814）；5. Joan of Arc：圣女贞德（1412—1431），法国民族英雄；6. Michelangelo：米开朗基罗（1475—1564），意大利雕刻家、画家、建筑家、诗人；7. David：大卫王，《圣经》中古以色列王；8. Goliath：哥利亚，《圣经》中非利士勇士，为大卫王所杀。

文化差异在语言上的体现是很值得研究的。比如爱斯基摩人对"雪"有五种叫法；我们如何能将它们译成英语或汉语呢？据说在汉语里，古文中用二十五个不同的字来称呼不同种类的马匹，而现代汉语中就只剩下三四个复合词来表达那二十五个词所涵盖的语义。一种文化尚有如此之变迁，异族文化之间就更不需说了。

由于语言差异所造成的不可译性，似乎更加棘手。本章 Unit Six 注释1中讨论的 sister-in-law 一词的译法，就是译者克服语言差异所造成的不可译性的一次尝试。不过，假使那篇文章中找不到任何有关 Jackson 夫妇是否有孩子的线索，那这个词可就真的完全不可译了。有一本书，题为 *Son-rise*，作者叙述了他们夫妇帮助身患残疾的儿子战胜困难，成为有用之才的感人故事。很明显，这一书名来自 sun-rise

一词。英语读者看到这个书名马上会联想到,作者的儿子历尽千辛万苦终于像太阳那样升起在希望的地平线上。这一书名中文怎么译呢?译成《儿子像太阳一样升起》,则臃肿拖沓,色彩全无。恐怕译者只能根据全书内容,另起炉灶了。还有一篇文章,讲的是两个搞出版发行的书商终成眷属的故事,标题很妙:"Book Lovers Became Booked Lovers",译成《爱书人成为登了记的夫妻》显然不行;译为《爱书人终相爱》也许好一些,但仍有言犹未尽之感。

对于语言差异所造成的不可译性,译者们总是千方百计地挖掘译语中各种可行的表达方式,以求把不可译性降到最低点。本章 Unit Six 中 sister-in-law 一词的翻译通过转换表达角度得以完成,本单元中 right 一词的翻译可通过加注的方法得以解决(见注释 1 及 4),再看下面几例:

1. As a Revenue worker explained to me, "Just about everyone who comes in here is antagonistic. Instead of taking offence, we've displayed boards with comic strips that poke fun at the IRS, which we jokingly call the Income Removal Service."

  正如一位税收人员所说的:"几乎每一个来到这的人都充满敌意,当然不能再火上添油,我们摆出开国内税务局(IRS)玩笑的漫画板报。我们把这个 IRS 戏称为'收入转移局'。"

  上述译文最后一句会让汉语读者感到不知所云,应加注说明。即:

  "……我们摆出一块展示牌,上面画了嘲弄国内税务局的漫画,把'国内收入署'戏称为'收入转移署'。"

  译注:英语中"国内收入署"的首字母缩略词是 IRS,也可视为 Income Removal Service(收入转移署)的首字母缩略词。

2. At a diplomatic cocktail party, an American lady asked the wife of the Chinese Ambassador: "What kind of 'nese' are you?" "What do you mean?" "I mean are you Japanese, Pakistanese or Chinese." "I'm Chinese," answered the Chinese lady respectfully. She also posed this question to the American lady: "What kind of key are you?" "What do you mean that?" "I mean, are you a Yankee, a monkey or a donkey?"

  在一个外交使节的鸡尾酒会上,有位美国女士问中国大使的夫人说:"你是何种'人'啊?""你是什么意思?""我的意思是说,你是日本人、巴基斯坦人还是中国人?""我是中国人。"这位中国女士很恭敬地回答,而她也向这位女士提出了同样的问题:"你是何种'仔'啊?""什么意思?""我是说,你是牛仔、猴仔还是驴仔？"

3. Writing in the British *Journal of Hygiene*, he suggested that the cholera came, literally, out of thin air—as contaminated discharges from high-flying commercial aircraft.

他在英国《卫生杂志》上发表文章，指出这一地区的霍乱病实属祸从天降——是民航飞机在高空排放的污染物所致。

英语成语 out of thin air 是"无中生有"的意思，用在此处也可照字面理解为"来自稀薄的空气"（高空飞行的民航飞机），用得很巧妙。译文用了成语"祸从天降"也算是一语双关，取得了和原文近似的修辞效果。

4. This paper is our passport to the gallows. But there's no backing out now. If we don't hang together, we shall most assuredly hang separately.

[a] 这个文件是我们走向绞架的通行证。但是现在已经没有回头路可走。如果我们不紧紧团结在一起，那就一定会被一个一个地绞死。
[b] 这张纸片就是咱们上绞架的通行证。今儿个谁都不准往后缩。咱们要是不摽到一块儿，就保准会被吊到一块儿。

原文中 hang 出现两次，hang together 意为 remain united，第二个 hang 取 be hanged on the gallows 之意。译文 [a] 意思传达准确，但未能再现原文同词异义的修辞特点。译文 [b] 力求用"摽"和"吊"达到与原文相近的效果。

5. Julia: ...Best sing it to the tune of "Light of Love".
Lucetra: It is too heavy for so light a tune.
朱丽娅：……可是你要唱就按《爱的清光》那个调子去唱吧。
露西塔：这个歌儿太沉重了，和轻狂的调子不配。

原文中 light 出现两次，是同音异义，译文用"清光"和"轻狂"谐音，与原文效果近似。不过，必须指出，不论译者如何绞尽脑汁总是有无法翻译的语句，如注释 4 所涉及的 right 一词的双关意义，便无法在译文中再现，只能通过加注的方法解决。

6. The other day I was at the airport attempting to buy a ticket to Washington and the attendant said, "I'm sorry, I can't sell you a ticket. Our computer is down."

"What do you mean your computer is down? Is it depressed?"

"No, it can't be depressed. That's why it's down."

前几天，我在机场打算买一张去华盛顿的机票，而售票员却说："很抱歉，我不能卖给你机票，我们的计算机失灵了。"

"你说你们的计算机'is down'是什么意思？它机能降低了吗？"

"不，它（的按钮）按不下去了，所以它就失灵了。"

这段文字实际上译犹未译。汉语中夹杂英文，中国读者怎么能看得懂呢？在这段对话中，作者运用双关语以达到幽默的效果。down 兼有"出故障"和"心情沮丧"之义，depressed 既有"心情沮丧"之义，又有"下压"之义。所以才造成了对话中的误会。将此段译成汉语，几乎不可能。有人提出了下述变通译文。请对比思考：

"……我们的计算机飞了。"

"飞了？它难道长了翅膀啦？"

"什么长翅膀？我是说它废啦！用不了啦。"

不过，这个译文有些另起炉灶的味道，也并非十分理想。像这样独具语言特性的文字，也许只能采取在译文中保留这两个英语单词，然后加注的办法了。至于下面一段文字，恐怕只能望文歔欷，承认它不可译了。

7. This typxwritxr is xxcxllxnt xxcxpt for onx kxy. Thx 25 othxr lxttxrs work finx; but just onx goof-off lousxs up thx wholx job. Amxrica has thx samx problxm.

打字机的一个键出了问题：e 都打成了 x，作者正是巧妙地运用了这一点，辛辣地指出了美国所存在的问题。这段英文读来颇有趣味，可要译成汉语，恐怕只能作罢了。

For Better or Worse but Not for Lunch!¹

[1] "For better or worse but not for lunch" is not a laughing matter for our friend Sue. "When Elliot retired, he spent the first week reorganizing my kitchen and putting all my canned goods and spices in alphabetical order," Sue said. "This wasn't the kind of togetherness I wanted!"

[2]　One challenge of retirement is managing all that extra time together. If you have just retired—or are contemplating retirement—here are some tips to start out right².

[3]　Make a plan. Realize that change is coming and greet it with a spirit of adventure. Be willing to try new things.

[4]　Talk it out. Share your expectations with each other. Let go of unrealistic expectations and accept each other as a packaged deal³. If you keep the communication lines open and positive, you can foster a loving spirit of cooperation.

[5]　Balance times together and times apart. Too much togetherness can be too much. You need some personal space. But you also need to reconnect.

[6]　Learn to work together and share responsibility. Divide up the work so you are both contributing.⁴ For instance, at the Arps, Dave does the dishes and is affectionately called the kitchen elf. In the morning, Claudia gets up and has a hot pot of coffee ready for Dave, who isn't the morning person.

[7]　Serve others. Retirement offers you the opportunity to make a difference⁵ in your world by serving others. Consider volunteering at your church or local ministry, or becoming marriage mentors for younger couples.

[8]　Celebrate. It's time to celebrate! Anything goes, from dinner at your favorite restaurant to climbing a mountain together or taking a cruise.

[9]　Never retire your marriage. When you face all those lunches together, accept the challenge. Retirement offers you an opportunity to reinvent your marriage, and you can find new fulfillment together. We're convinced that Robert Browning was right when he said, "Grow old along with me! The best is yet to be." Maybe he was even talking about retirement!⁶

参考译文

同甘共苦，莫共午餐！

[1]　对我们的朋友苏尔来说，"同甘共苦，莫共午餐！"这句话可不是说着玩的。"埃利奥特退休后的头一周，就来拾掇我的厨房，把罐装的食品调料都按字母顺序排整齐。"她抱怨说，"这哪是我想要的朝夕相处啊！"

[2] 退休后面临的挑战之一，就是共同安排好那些多余的时间。如果你刚刚退休——或正在考虑退休——请参考下面这几项建议，开始美好的退休生活。

[3] 制订计划。认识到生活即将发生变化，并以进取的精神去迎接它。要乐于尝试新事物。

[4] 通过讨论，消除分歧。交流彼此的期望。放弃那些不切实际的期望，并把对方作为一个整体来接受。只要保持沟通渠道畅通有效，就可以培养出一种亲密合作的精神。

[5] 聚散有度。聚在一起的时间太多，易生厌烦。双方都需要私人空间。当然，有分还必须有合。

[6] 分工合作，共担责任。把要做的事情分分工，这样双方都能做出各自的贡献。比如在阿尔普家，戴夫负责洗盘子，被亲切地称为"厨房小精灵"；而克劳迪娅起床后便为丈夫准备好一壶热咖啡，因为戴夫爱睡懒觉。

[7] 服务他人。退休后便有了为他人服务的好机会，这也使自己的生活世界更丰富多彩。可考虑在教堂或当地政府部门的志愿活动，也可为年轻夫妇当婚姻顾问。

[8] 庆祝庆祝。是庆祝一下的时候了！到喜爱的餐厅吃一顿，或一起爬山，或乘游轮观光，怎么都行。

[9] 莫让婚姻也退休。当天天都要一起共进午餐的时候，请接受这个挑战吧。退休给了你们再创婚姻生活的机会，可以共享新的成就。我们深信罗伯特·勃朗宁的话是对的："和我一道慢慢变老！最美好的日子还在前头。"或许，他也在谈论退休生活呢！

注释

1. For better or worse but not for lunch 是美国当前很流行的一句俏皮话。说的是一辈子共甘苦的老夫老妻，一旦退休整日待在一起，反而造成很多家庭问题。2001 年心理学家 Sara Yogev 写过一本书 *For Better or for Worse...but Not for Lunch: Making Marriage Work in Retirement*，专门探讨退休后的家庭生活问题。而这句话是在模仿常出现在婚礼誓言中的一个词语 for better or worse 的基础上构成的。
2. start out right 意为"有个正确的开端"。
3. a packaged deal 意为"一揽子交易"，此处指接受对方的全部，即接受其优点也包容其缺点。

4. 注意结构分析，不要译成"分工合作对你们都有好处"。
5. to make a difference 意为 to have an important effect on something, especially a good effect (*Macmillan English Dictionary for Advanced Learners*)。
6. 这是 Robert Browning 一首广为传颂的爱情诗的头两句。

 讲解

互文性

本单元注释 1 提到，for better or worse but not for lunch 来自一本书的标题 "For Better or for Worse...but Not for Lunch: Making Marriage Work in Retirement"，而这个书名又是在模仿常出现在婚礼誓言中的一个词语 for better or worse。也就是说，由婚礼誓词而生出那本书的标题，又由那本书的标题产生了本篇文章的标题。注释 6 提到本文引用了 Robert Browning 的两行诗句。不同语篇的语句间存在的这种关联就被称为互文性。

据 Robert de Beaugrande 和 W. Dressler 在 1981 年出版的 *Introduction to Text Linguistics* 中的论述，互文性指"某一语篇的生产和接收取决于交际参与者对其他语篇的了解的种种依赖现象"。(...the ways in which the production and reception of a given text depends upon the participants' knowledge of other texts.) Basil Hatim 和 Ian Mason 在 1997 出版的 *The Translator as Communicator* 中则将其定义为"语篇理解的先决条件，包括一个语篇作为符号实体对另一先前见到过的语篇的依赖"。(...a precondition for the intelligibility of texts, involving the dependence of one text as a semiotic entity upon another, previously encountered, text.)

这两个定义都强调了语篇世界中一个语篇对其他语篇的依存性，在这个意义上讲，没有哪个语篇是自足的，一个语篇的功能和意义只有在和其他语篇产生联系和互动之后才会显现和趋于完整。笼统地说，语篇的依存性体现在两个层面上：一是语篇个体间的依存；二是某一语篇与某一类语篇间的个体与群体间的依赖和联系。语篇个体间的依存关系常见的形式有：引语、典故、模仿和参照（quotation, allusion, parody, reference）等。每个语篇都可能包含先于它存在的语篇的某些成分，形成一种历时的或共时的功能/意义网。语篇个体与群体间的联系指的是某个语篇与同类体裁语篇（比如小说、散文、科学论文、新闻等）间的关系。一般来说，构建中的译文要依从于同类体裁语篇的行文规范，才能为自己在已存的互文关系网中找到可被接受的适当位置。语篇的作者和读者必须在相当程度上共享一套用语篇作为信息载体进行交际的常识和规范，共享程度越高，则实现交际意图的效率也就越高。

在英译汉实践中，最常见的是原文和其他源语语篇间存在的互文关系。译者首先必须具有识别的能力，然后才可能在译文中做适当处理。下面我们进一步分析一下本单元原文中出现的两个互文现象。

刚才我们提到，Sara Yogev 的专著标题中的 *For Better or for Worse...but Not for Lunch* 是在常用婚礼誓言中的一个词语 for better or worse 的基础上构成的。这个婚礼誓言一般是这样的：

I, (Name),
Take you, (Name),
To be my (wife/husband);
To have and to hold,
From this day forward,
For better, for worse,
For richer, for poorer,
In sickness and in health,
To love and to cherish,
"Till death do us part." (or, "As long as we both shall live.")

誓言由司仪牧师念出，新郎和新娘分别重复。这表达了一对新人同甘苦共患难、白头偕老的爱情承诺。Sara Yogev 别出心裁在 for better or for worse 后面加上 but not for lunch，诙谐而形象地点出老夫妻一生甘苦与共，退休后却难以适应三餐共进、终日厮守的生活窘境。不论是 for better, for worse 还是 for better or for worse, but not for lunch，在美国文化中已经充分地语境化，形成一个互文链条，成为英美社会人们知识结构的一部分。将这样的语句译为汉语，译者必须考虑译语读者的社会、文化背景以及相关知识和经验。很明显，英语文化中这种互文关系汉语中基本不存在。

注解 6 所涉及的是一首诗。该诗第一节是：

Grow old along with me!
The best is yet to be,
The last of life, for which the first was made:
Our times are in His hand
Who saith "A whole I planned,
Youth shows but half; trust God: see all, nor be afraid!"

面对原文中这样的互文现象，译者要做两件事情。一是在自己头脑中建立和源语读者相同或相似的互文关系链。译者头脑中如果没有相关的知识储存，就必须立即从各种渠道获取。绝不可不甚了了，马虎应付。二是思考自己是否要在译文中重建这个互文关系，在何种程度上重建，以及如何重建。一般来说，译文完全重现原文中的互文关系，或者说让译语读者完全领会源语读者所领会到的互文关系，是很难的。但总是可以想方设法为译语读者提供某些行文线索和背景资料的。行文线索指在遣词造句上尽可能引发译语语境中读者的连贯思考。比如一种汉译本将这篇文章的标题译为"同甘共苦，不为午餐！"，就未能给读者提供思考线索，一个"为"字，提示的是"目的"。而本单元的译文虽然只改了一个字，却为读者提示了"虽然可以共甘苦，却不能一起吃午餐"这样合乎原文逻辑的思路。再加上译者注释，简要提供我们已提到的某些背景信息，重建相关语境，便可保证译语读者的理解路径基本合乎原文的互文逻辑了。

至于文章结尾那首诗，译者首先要能够识别其和勃朗宁原诗的互文关系，二是要查找有无汉语译文，如有广为接受的汉译便可拿来引用。勃朗宁的这一首诗我们没发现现成译文，译者可自行翻译，但也要顾及整个原诗以及诗歌的翻译方法。比如译成"和我一道慢慢变老！前面的日子才是最好"，也许读来更像两行诗句。

关于引用，我们再看一个译例：

1. Life, as every biography and obit I have ever read confirms, is what happens when you are making other plans.

叶子南谈到这句话的翻译时就谈到互文性问题［见《中国翻译》2004（2）：92］，他说本句涉及当年甲壳虫乐队歌手列农（John Lennon）的一句歌词 Life is just what happens to you while you're busy making other plans。所以翻译时，不宜意译成：所有的自传和讣告都说明了人一生的起伏荣枯都是出于意料之外的，而应尽量照字面翻译成：每一本传记，每一则讣告都毫无例外地印证，人生就是在你制订计划时意外发生的事情。

除了源语语篇间的互文关系，还有一个构建中的译文和已存在的译语语篇间的互文关系问题。译文一旦形成，就成为译语语篇世界中的一员，它必须在和业已存在的语篇的互动中生存，已存在语篇对它的交际功能既能促成，也会制约。译语读者对译文的解读和释义，互文关系起着重要作用。曹明伦在评论"Scotland"一文的汉译时［《中国翻译》2007（2）：86］指出，将 Bob Roy 译为"洛布洛伊"，将 Walter Scott 译为"斯科特"，而不是已有的多种汉语译本中的"罗布·罗伊"和"司各特"，就等于放弃了已在汉语语言或文化中积累起来的一笔文化财富。在我们看来，这也是一种巨大的互文性损失。译文和译语语篇世界其他语篇的互文关系的建立，首先有赖于译者的自觉操作，然后还取决于读者对相应互文关系的认可，两个环节缺失一个,互文关系便无法在实际交际过程中发挥作用。

有时候,源语语篇中会涉及与某译语语篇的互文关系。也就是说,原文中涉及与译语有关的某些引语或内容。比如下面一段选自 *Guardian* 网站(www.guardian.co.uk)对我国国庆 60 周年庆典的报道:

2. Events began with a 60-gun salute. Hu Jintao—chairman of the Central Military Commission, general-secretary of the Communist Central Committee and Chinese president—stood in an open-topped limousine to review the troops along Chang'an Avenue. He wore a black Mao suit, while other leaders wore Western suits.

"Hello comrades!" he shouted at intervals. In perfect unison, the troops replied: "Hello commander!" and "Serve the people!"

Later, standing on the Tian'an men rostrum—the spot where Mao proclaimed the creation of the new China—Hu declared: "[We] have triumphed over all sorts of difficulties and setbacks and risks to gain the great achievements evident to the world." "Today, a socialist China geared toward modernisation, the world and the future towers majestically in the East."

英语原文凡是引用汉语语篇的部分,原则上应找到引文相应出处忠实引录,凡涉及中文有关语篇的也要查实并根据中文语篇做适当处理。上述报道最后一段划线部分显然涉及胡锦涛主席的讲话,也就是说,它本来就是根据胡主席的讲话译成英语的。针对这种情况,译者必须找到汉语讲话稿,并参照英语中的行文回译成汉语。我们查到的相应语句是:

……勤劳智慧的我国各族人民同心同德、艰苦奋斗,战胜各种艰难曲折和风险考验,取得了举世瞩目的伟大成就,谱写了自强不息的壮丽凯歌。

今天,一个面向现代化、面向世界、面向未来的社会主义中国巍然屹立在世界东方。

第二段涉及胡主席阅兵时说的话和受阅士兵的回答。我们看到的相应汉语报道是这样的:

受阅总指挥房峰辉:"主席同志,受阅部队准备完毕,请您检阅!"

胡锦涛:"同志们好!"

受阅部队:"首长好!"

胡锦涛:"同志们辛苦了!"

受阅部队:"为人民服务!"

161

依据这种互文关系，汉译中我们可引用胡主席讲话中的相应部分，并对阅兵场面做适当处理：

庆祝大会在 60 响礼炮中开始。中央军委主席、中共中央主席、国家主席胡锦涛乘坐敞篷轿车检阅了长安街上的受阅部队。他身穿中山装，而其他领导人则身着西装。

"同志们好！""同志们辛苦了！"胡主席时而喊道。士兵们则齐声回答："首长好！""为人民服务！"

随后，站在毛主席当年宣布新中国诞生的天安门城楼上，胡主席说："[我们] 艰苦奋斗，战胜各种艰难曲折和风险考验，取得了举世瞩目的伟大成就"，并宣布"今天，一个面向现代化、面向世界、面向未来的社会主义中国巍然屹立在世界东方。"

由于人类社会、文化交际的日益频繁，由于不同文化间的互动和交流的加强，或者更具体地说，由于翻译活动的日趋频繁，互文关系不但在各种文化内部交织成密集而繁杂的网络，也在不同文化和语言之间形成了跨语言和跨文化的网络，从而为每一个语篇个体都注入了互文层次上的语篇意义潜势。因此，译者不仅需要调动涉及原文的互文关系，还要在构建译文时注意关照译语中业已存在的种种互文关系，以保证构建的译文能融入译语语篇世界中去。

交际参与者的头脑中都储存着一张语篇世界的关系网络，语篇作者、读者和译者在解读或构建译文的过程中，都会用各自认为关联性最强的某几个语篇作为参照。一个语篇的交际价值体现在它和外部世界的关联上，也体现在它和语篇世界中相关语篇的关联上。失去了这种关联，语篇只是一连串无意义的书写符号。

另外，还有一种情况也应提一下。原文中时常会引用他人的只言片语，如一个词、词组或半个句子。翻译时，这些直接引语一般要保留，但要注意引语要自然流畅地融入汉语行文之中。如下面两个译例：

3. It is rare in the North to finish high school, but something made Angutigiak keep going when others around her quit, although by her own account she is "a very lazy person" who "never had goals to get A" in school.

在加拿大北方，很少有人读完高中，可就是在周围的学生纷纷退学的时候，不知是什么力量促使安古缇吉亚克坚持下来，尽管她说自己是个"很懒的人"，上学时"从来没想过要得优秀"。

4. She has, as she puts it, "grown very far" from her old friends in Salluit.

用她自己的话说，她与萨卢伊特村的老朋友们"已经有了很大距离"。

A Few Earthy Words (Excerpts)[1]

Scott Russel Sanders

[1] In a speech delivered in 1952, Rachel Carson warned, "Mankind has gone very far into an artificial world of his own creation. He[2] has sought to insulate himself, in his cities of steel and concrete, from the realities of earth and water and the growing seed. Intoxicated with a sense of his own power, he seems to be going farther and farther into more experiments for the destruction of himself and his world."

[2] Carson voiced these worries before the triumph of television or shopping malls, before the advent of air-conditioning, personal computers, video games, the Internet, cell phones, cloning, genetic engineering, and a slew of other inventions that have made the artificial world ever more seductive. Unlike Earth[3], the artificial world is made for us. It feeds our bellies and minds with tasty pabulum; it shelters us from discomfort and sickness; it proclaims our ingenuity; it flatters our pride. Snug inside bubbles fashioned from concrete and steel, from silicon and plastic and words, we can pretend we are running the planet.

[3] By contrast, the natural world was not made for our comfort or convenience. It preceded us by some billions of years, and it will outlast us; it mocks our pride, because it surpasses our understanding and control; it can be dangerous and demanding; it will eventually kill us and reclaim our bodies. We should not be surprised that increasing numbers of people choose to live entirely indoors, leaving buildings only to ride in airplanes or cars, viewing the great outside, if they view it at all, through sealed windows, but more often gazing into screens, listening to human chatter, cut off from "the realities of earth and water and the growing seed".[4]

[4] The more time we spend inside human constructions, the more likely we are to forget that these bubbles float in the great ocean of nature. A decade before Carson issued her warning, Aldo Leopold, in *A Sand County Almanac*, recognized this danger as the central challenge facing the conservation

movement: How do we nurture a land ethic in people who have less and less contact with land? How do we inspire people to take care of their home places if they feel no sense of place?

[5]　If we aim to foster a culture of conservation, we'll have to work at changing a host of things, from ads to zoos, from how we put food on our plates to how we imagine our role in the universe. Out of all these necessary changes, I wish to speak about one that is close to my heart as a storyteller,[5] which is the need to root language once more in the earth. We need to recover the fertile meanings of words that arise out of our long evolutionary contact with dirt and wind, rivers and woods, animals and plants.

[6]　At the root of language,[6] we often find an earthy wisdom. Take the word "growth",[7] for example. When Donella Meadows and her colleagues published a report in 1972 on the prospects for the continued expansion of the human economy, they called their book *The Limits to Growth*. The very title provoked outrage in many circles, because a prime article in the technoindustrial creed[8] is that there are no limits to growth. According to this creed, any constraints imposed by nature will be overcome by technical ingenuity or the free market. Mining, drilling, pumping, clearing, plowing, manufacturing, and consuming—along with the human population that drives it all—will expand forever, the boosters claim. Politicians and business leaders speak of growth as unbounded and unambiguously good.

[7]　Our ancestors knew better. If we dig down to the root of "growth", we find a verb that means to turn green, as grass does in the spring. In fact, "grow", "grass", and "green" all rise from the same Indo-European stem. Grass turns green in the spring, shoots up vigorously during the summer, then dies back and lies fallow through the winter. Season after season, the wilted grass turns to humus, enriching the soil. Molded into this word, therefore, is a recognition that growth is bounded, that it obeys the cycles of sun and rain, that it restores to the earth more fertility than it takes out.[9]

[8]　If the phrase "sustainable growth" means perpetual expansion, then it is a delusion. Cancer shows that rampant growth soon becomes malignant. The sprawl of cities over the countryside and the spread of bellies over belts teach us that, beyond a certain point, expansion leads to misery, if not disaster. Nothing in nature expands forever. Certainly nothing on Earth

grows unchecked, neither bodies nor cities nor economies. Buried in the word "growth" is the wisdom of people blessed with outdoor understanding, people who watched the grass rise and fall each year like a green wave.[10]

参考译文

求源返璞见真义（节选）

司各特·罗素·桑德斯

[1]　雷切尔·卡森在1952年发表的一篇讲演中警告说："人类在自己创建的人造世界中已经走得太远了。人们试图将自己圈在钢铁和混凝土建造的城市里，而与由土地、水和生长的种子构成的现实世界隔绝开来。他们自觉力量无穷，自我陶醉，进行着越来越多的毁灭自身和整个世界的实验，似乎正越走越远。"

[2]　卡森在表达上述忧虑的时候，电视和购物中心还未风行，空调、个人电脑、视频游戏、因特网、手机、克隆技术、基因工程，以及其他一些使这个人造世界变得更具诱惑力的发明也还未问世。和自然世界不同，人造世界是为我们建造的。它既提供美味佳肴也提供精神食粮；它庇护我们不受疾病和不适环境的侵扰；它昭示着人类的智慧；它满足着我们的自尊。舒舒服服地待在由钢铁和混凝土、由硅和塑料、由单词和短语构成的泡沫里，我们自以为在主宰着这个星球。

[3]　与之形成鲜明对照的是，自然世界并非为人类的舒适或方便而存在。它先于我们数十亿年，而且会比人类存在得更为久远。它嘲弄我们的自尊，因为它超越了我们的理解和控制能力；它可能百般刁难，带来危害；它最终将毁灭我们并收回我们的尸体。难怪，越来越多的人选择了完全足不出户的生活，即便偶尔离开人造建筑也还是待在汽车或飞机里，就算看到了外面的大千世界（真不知他们看到了没有），也只是隔着密闭的窗户而已；而更多的时候，他们只是凝视着屏幕，听人们胡聊，与"土地、水和正在生长的种子构成的现实世界"全然隔绝开来。

[4]　我们在人造建筑中待得越久，就越容易忘记这些人造建筑泡沫是漂浮在大自然的浩瀚海洋上的。在卡森发出警告的十年前，奥尔多·利奥波德在《沙县年鉴》中就把这一危险看作环境保护运动所面临的主要挑战：既然人们和大地的接触越来越少，还怎么培养他们的土地伦理？如果人们丧失了家园的感觉，还怎么激励他们呵护好自己的家园呢？

[5] 如果我们要培养一种环境保护文化,就必须致力于改变一系列的事情,从广告到动物园,从我们怎样把食物放进盘子里到如何设想我们在宇宙中的作用。在所有这些必要的改变之中,我只想谈一点。那就是,再一次把语言植于大地之中——作为一个讲故事的人,这也最贴近我的心田。我们需要重新发现那些产生于我们与土、与风、与河流和树林、与动物和植物的长期进化接触中的词语的丰富含义。

[6] 对语言追根溯源,我们常常会发现某种返璞归真的智慧。就拿 growth(生长、增长)这个词来说吧。唐奈勒·梅多斯和她的同事 1972 年发表了一份报告,讨论人类经济持续扩张的前景,书名叫《增长的局限》。不料这个书名竟激起了方方面面的极大愤怒,因为科技工业信条中最重要的一点就是增长无止境。根据这种信念,所有来自大自然的制约都可通过技术革新或自由市场机制加以克服。这种信念的支持者认为,采矿、钻探、采油、开荒、耕种、制造以及消费——再加上促使这一切发生的人类,都会不停地增长下去。政治家和企业家们认为增长是无限制的,是绝对有益的。

[7] 我们的祖先则很明智。如果我们深挖 growth 一词的词源,就会发现一个意为"变绿"的动词,比如小草在春天变绿。实际上,grow(growth 的动词形式)、grass(草)和 green(绿色)都出自同一个印欧语词根。小草春天变绿,夏天茁壮生长,而冬天便枯萎休眠了。季节更迭,枯萎的小草变成腐殖质,使土壤更加肥沃。因此,融进这个词语中的是这样一种认识:增长是有限度的,要顺应太阳和雨水的变化周期,而且它给予大地的养分要多于它向大地的汲取。

[8] 如果"可持续增长"是永恒扩张的意思,那它只是一个幻想。癌变已表明,无节制的增长很快就会变为恶性的。城市向乡村的蔓延,肚皮向腰带的膨胀,这些都告诉我们,超越了某个界点,扩张带来的即便不是灾难,也是痛苦。自然界里没什么东西是可以无限度扩展的。当然,地球上也没有可以无限增长的东西,不论是身体、城市还是经济。深深蕴含在 growth 这个词里面的,是那些深谙自然界真谛的人的智慧,那些人目睹了小草年复一年的枯荣,就像一阵阵绿浪。

注释

1. 本文发表于土地和人类中心(Center for Land and People)2002 年出版的 *The Story Handbook: Language and Storytelling for Land Conservationists* 上。作者桑德斯是印第安纳大

学英语和文学创作系教授，兼该中心顾问委员会成员。所谓 earthy words 系指在词源上与大地和自然界有关的词语。除了节选部分以外，文章还讨论了 resource、wealth、community、health、patriotism 等词语，分析了这些词语所体现的人与自然界的关系，揭示了人类祖先的智慧。作者认为，这些词语的原始意义揭示出人类的福祉有赖于他们所共享的大地的福祉，耗尽自然资源，人类无异于自毁。译文根据全文的主旨，将题目译为《求源返璞见真义》。

2. 文中用 he 复指 mankind，汉语用"他"复指"人类"似不大合适。故用"人类……人们……他们"构成新的照应链。
3. 这里的 Earth 指作为太阳系行星之一的地球，和 the artificial world（人造世界）相对，故译为"自然世界"。
4. 注意分析这个长句的结构和意向。作者在批评人类与自然隔绝的现象，一句 only to ride... 表达的是失望和无奈。
5. 作者自称 storyteller，因为他是 *The Story Handbook* 的撰稿人。这本书的介绍中这样说：In *The Story Handbook*, contributors Tim Ahern, William Cronon, John Elder, Peter Forbes, Barry Lopez, and Scott Russell Sanders help us think about the power of stories of people and place, and how those stories can advance the work of land conservation toward creating meaningful change in our culture.
6. the root of language 当指语言之源，词语之根。
7. 作者分析的是英语单词 growth 的词源，译文应给出英语，并注明汉语意思。
8. a prime article 中的 article 并非"文章"之意，a prime article in the technoindustrial creed 也不能译为"有关……信条的重要文章"。这里的 article 应取"条款""项目"之意，可译为"……信条中的重要一条"，如 article of faith 就是"信条"之意。technoindustrial creed 指一种认为技术在推动社会进步中具有无限力量和潜力的信念，可译为"科技工业信条"。
9. 这句话的主句是倒装结构，正常词序应该是：A recognition...is molded into this word.（一种认识被融进了这个词语）。而 recognition 带有三个由 that 引导的同位语从句，分别陈述了这个认识的内容。
10. 这同样是一个倒装句。be blessed with... 意为 to have something very good or special。

讲解

翻译伦理

Unit Three 讨论了翻译的标准，现在我们顺着这个思路向前推进，从更宏观也更深刻的角度探讨一下怎样做一个好的译者。

讨论翻译标准的时候，我们特别指出翻译不仅仅发生在语言层面，涉及不同类型的语篇的交际功能、结构特点以及相应的翻译策略，而且发生在社会－文化层面，思想意识、翻译目的等非语言因素也都会对译者的行为产生很大影响，甚至起着决定性作用。归根结底，翻译是沟通不同文化和人群的交际活动。正因如此，德国功能派翻译理论家 Christiane Nord 提出了"功能＋忠信"（function ＋ loyalty）的翻译准则。她在 Translating as a Purposeful Activity 一书中给这两个概念下了如下定义：Function refers to the factors that make a target text work in the intended way in the target situation. Loyalty refers to the interpersonal relationship between the translator, the source-text sender, the target-text addressees and the initiator. 也就是说，功能指的是保证译文在目标情境中实现预期交际功能的种种因素；忠信指的是人际关系，译者和跨语言、文化交际的其他参与者，特别是和源语作者以及译语读者间的关系。译者不能随意篡改原文，也不能欺骗自己的读者。这用 Nord 在一篇名为"Loyalty Revisited"的文章（发表在 Target 2002 年第 2 期上）中的话说，"忠信"是一种"伦理限定"（ethical limitation）。这个准则告诉译者，他们对与翻译活动有关的人负有不可推卸的社会责任。

关于译者的社会责任，或者叫翻译伦理，近年来译界多有讨论。Andrew Chesterman 在 Target 2002 年第 2 期上也有一篇文章，在分析了理论家们的各种主张之后，他指出翻译伦理可以是一种承诺（commitment），就像医生的职业誓言《希波克拉底誓言》（Hippocrati Oath）一样，译者也应该有自己的职业操守。他还提出了一份译者的职业誓言，共有九条。以下是第 3、4、7、9 条：

- I will use my expertise to maximize communication and minimize misunderstan ding across language barriers.
- I swear that my translations will not represent their source texts in unfair ways.
- I will be honest about my own qualifications and limitations; I will not accept work that is outside my competence.
- I will do all I can to maintain and improve my competence, including all relevant linguistic, technical and other knowledge and skills.

我们看到，第 3 条说的是跨语言交际的实效：最大程度的沟通，最小程度的误解。第 4 条是对源语作者的承诺：对原文的任何变动都应该是有理由的，绝不肆意篡改。第 7 条是对翻译的发起人或赞助人说的：任何译者都不是万能的，能胜任的接受，否则应陈明自己的局限性。第 9 条是对自己的要求：精益求精，艺无止境，语言和相关知识水平都要不断提高。

总的来看,我们作为翻译的学习者和实践者,应特别重视对源语作者和译语读者所应担负的道德责任:不能肆意篡改(不管是无意还是有意的)原文的基本意义和作者的交际意图;不能欺骗(哪怕是无意的)我们的读者,对我们的译文所传达的信息,一定要认真谨慎地多次审核,尽量减少错译、误译。而要做到这一点,必须在语言和知识两个层面不断地提高。

本单元这篇文章 A Few Earthy Words(节选)的汉译已有人正式发表。下面我们引用其中一些语句,以便进一步讨论翻译的标准和伦理问题。

下面是第3自然段最后一个长句的汉译:

越来越多的人选择完全足不出户的生活,<u>离开楼群也只是为了开汽车或坐飞机,透过密封的窗户去看一看外面的大千世界,假设他们去看的话,也不过如此。</u>但是,在更多的时候,他们凝视着屏幕,倾听人们的闲聊,与"土地、水和正在生长的种子的现实世界"隔绝开来——这一切我们都不必大惊小怪。

试想译语读者看到这一段译文会得到怎样的信息,会如何理解作者的意思呢?划线部分传达的信息似乎是"人们为了看看大千世界还是会离开楼群的,不过,即使去看了,也和不看差不多"。作者是这个意思吗?作者的意思是"即便离开人造的建筑也只是又钻进一个人造空间;即便看了也还是隔着车窗或舷窗,也还是和自然界隔绝开来的"。其实这句话,结合整个段落及全文,指向十分明确:抨击与自然隔绝的人类生活方式。负责任的译者必须设法把这种意图传达给自己的读者。

下面是第6自然段头几句的汉译:

在语言的基点,我们经常发现乡土的智慧。就拿"生长"这个词来说吧。1972年,唐奈勒·梅多斯与其同事发表了一篇关于人类经济继续发展前景的报告,书名是《增长的极限》。就是这个书名引起了许多方面的愤怒,因为一篇有关专家管理型工业信条的重要文章讲发展没有限度。

这段译文所显示的是由关键词语的误解所导致的误译。这对作者不公平,对读者也是误导。

首先,earthy 一词应怎样理解?是双语词典中表明的诸如"泥土的""现实的""朴实的""粗俗的"意思吗?我们在第二章 Unit One 就讲过,对词义的准确理解在于对其所在语境的分析和认识。单独一个词可能有许多意思,从词典上找一个"对等词",没人会说你错。但一个词语一旦进入特定的语境,它的释义范围就缩小了,它的意义就不由词典决定了。译者必须依据具体语境确定它的意义。这篇文章所论几个词语,其词源均与自然界有不解的渊源,让现今的人们体味到,先人在创造这些词语时是深深懂得人与自然的关系的。也就是说,这是几个揭示了人与自然关系的词语,几个植根于支撑人类繁衍发展的大地的词语。本文的意图就是溯根求源,由词的发源谈到人类的进化,唤起人们重归大自然的愿望,所以才有了本译文的标题《求源返璞见真义》。其次,作者分析的是英语词语的词源,而上面译文只给出 growth 一词的一个对等词"生长",这样一来,当读者读到《增长的极限》这个书名时,就很难把"生长"和"增长"联系起来,实现连贯的解读。这无形中给读者设置了一个语言障碍。最后,如注解 8 所分析的那样,article 一词理解错了,造成对读者的误导。

分析了本单元的一些实例之后,我们必须再一次指出,把翻译标准、策略或质量的讨论提升到伦理层面是十分必要的。面对不同的翻译任务,面对不同的读者群,译者采取的翻译策略和方法可以是不一样的,但有一点万变不离其宗,那就是对翻译这个职业的高度责任感。

为了成为一个合格的译者,除了上面提出的承诺,尤其是第 9 条(不断自我完善),以及勤于实践以外,还要培养以批评的眼光阅读他人,特别是较为成熟的译者的译作的习惯。一方面学习他人的敬业精神(如金隄用 15 年时间悉心研究考证才译成乔伊斯花 7 年写成的巨著《尤利西斯》),悉心揣摩,领会其翻译原则,学习其翻译技巧;另一方面也要学会以严肃的学术态度审视译文,发现其不足甚至错误之处,仔细分析以资借鉴。能识别错误,自己就不会犯类似错误;能看出问题,自己对翻译的理解就又加深了一点。这也是提高自我的有效途径。

小结

译文的构建是一种特殊形式的写作。说它特殊,一是因为译者表达的内容并不是他自己的原创,而是他与原文沟通过程中所获取的信息;二是因为他不能随意按自己的方式写作,译文写作的遣词造句、修辞方法、文理脉络等都要参照原文定夺。说白了,译者是用自己的笔传别人的话。不过,别人的话我们无法左右,笔却是在我们手中,译文怎样写,我们是有一定的自主权的。

译文的优劣,除了理解,就看译者的写作水平如何了。汉语记叙文写不好的人,很难相信他会把英语小说翻译得多么好;汉语论说文写得颠三倒四的人,也很难将英语的论文译得文从字顺。要做一个好的译者,必须孜孜不倦地提高源语和译语的阅读和写作水平。源语(及其文化)和译语(及其文化)是译者的两条腿,不论哪一条弱了,都是蹩脚。

要提高译文的写作水平，必须用心将所译语言对组在句法、修辞、文体、语用等方面的特征时时处处加以对照，尤其留意其不同之处，以及相互间的影响和渗透之处。这样，你才能在动笔翻译时，把握好内容和形式这一对矛盾：原文的哪些形式可以保留，哪些要变通，哪些又可引进。本章已经讨论了一些焦点问题，大家在学习中可自己发现问题，自己积累语料，进而总结出自己的翻译心得。

练习

1. 翻译下列段落。

(1)

Sept. 11 delivered both a shock and a surprise—the attack, and our response to it and we can argue forever over which mattered more. There has been so much talk of the goodness that erupted that day that we forget how unprepared we were for it. We did not expect much from a generation that had spent its middle age examining all the ways it failed to measure up to the one that had come before—all fat, no muscle, less a beacon to the world than a bully, drunk on blessings taken for granted.

⚠ 提示

运用增益法、话题转换，注意代词的翻译。

(2)

Easy Ways to Avoid an Argument (Excerpts)

It's natural to take offence if someone is rude. You may think, what a jerk! But blurting out how you feel sets an adversarial tone and will only make matters worse. Dealing with difficult people is a part of everyday life. And there are non-combative ways you can stand up for yourself without stepping on anyone's toes and starting an argument. I call these techniques "Tongue Fu!"

Handle hassles with humour. At an airport, I saw a tall young man walking towards me. People were pointing at him, giggling. As the towering fellow approached, I could say why. His T-shirt announced "No, I Am Not a Basketball Player". As he passed, I turned and saw the back of his shirt, which said "Are You a Jockey?"

I chased after him to ask where he had bought his terrific shirt. "This is nothing," he said, grinning. "I have a whole drawer full at home. My favourite says 'I'm 6'13" and the Weather Up Here Is Fine.'"

He went on to explain, "I grew almost 30 centimetres between the ages of 16 and 18. People were always making smart aleck remarks. My mom finally said, 'If you can't beat them, join them.' She was the one who thought I should wear these shirts." Clever young man, clever mom.

When people complain, don't explain. The phone rings at work. You answer it and the caller launches into a complaint: "I asked for a catalogue three weeks ago and I still don't have it! What kind of business are you running anyway?"

Don't bother explaining that half the staff is off with fly. Although they may be well-intentioned, such explanations usually add to the complainer's irritation because they come across as excuses. If the complainer had a legitimate gripe, avoid belabouring what went wrong. Instead, agree, apologize and then move on to what can be done about it. Simply say: "You're right. I'm sorry you haven't received it yet. If I can have your name and address again. I'll personally put it in the post to you today."

One effective way to sidestep stalemates is to say, "We're both right!" and move on to a safer topic. Say you and your mate disagree about how to discipline your teenager, and your discussion is escalating into an argument. Just because you aren't seeing eye to eye doesn't mean you're enemies. Saying "Hey, we both want the same thing" can get you out of the adversarial mode and working together again.

Or you can gracefully bow out before you even bow in. I was talking to several colleagues, and the conversation turned to an election campaign. It had become ugly, with each party charging the other with dirty deeds. My companions were on opposite sides of the political fence, and their discussion became heated. One turned to me and asked, "Who do you think should be elected?" I wasn't about to get involved in their no-win debate. I put my hands up and said with a smile, "Leave me out of this one."

No matter what the situation is, arguments are a waste or, at best, a misuse of time. By avoiding fruitless arguments, everyone wins.

⚠️ **提示**

注意词语表达。

(3)
Today it is out of vogue to speak in terms of character. But there is no more essential aspect of any person.

Character is made up of those principles and values that give your life direction, meaning and depth. These constitute your inner sense of what's right and wrong based not on laws or rules of conduct but on who you are. They include such traits as integrity, honesty, courage, fairness and generosity—which arise from the hard choices we have to make in life. So wrong is simply in doing wrong, not in getting caught.

Yet some people wonder if our inner values matter anymore. After all, hasn't our noted bank executive succeeded in every visible way, despite his transgressions?

This question demonstrates a quandary of our modern life. Many have come to believe that the only things we need for success are talents, energy and personality. But history has taught us that over the long haul, who we are is more important than who we appear to be.

During the nation's first century and a half, almost everything in the literature of success and self-help focused on what could be called the character ethic. Such eminent figures as Benjamin Franklin and Thomas Jefferson made clear their belief that we can only experience true success and happiness by making character the bedrock of our lives.

⚠️ **提示**

注意英语和汉语在表达方式上的不同，译文要通顺、达意。

2. 改进下列段落的译文。

(1)
The ability to do several things at once has become one of the great measures of self-worth for 21st century Americans. It's called multitasking, and it takes many forms.

As one example, why go out to lunch when you can eat at your desk, talk (or at least half-listen) to a client on the phone, scroll through your e-mail, and scan a memo simultaneously?

And why simply work out on treadmill when you could be watching television and talking on a portable phone at the same time? What a feeling of satisfaction and accomplishment—three activities for the time commitment of one! Ah, such efficiency.

同时做几件事的能力已经成为21世纪美国人衡量自我价值的重要尺度之一。这叫作多任务处理，它的表现形式五花八门。

举个例子，当你可以一边在办公桌前吃饭，一边和客户通电话（或至少是半听半说）、查阅电子邮件、浏览备忘录时，为什么还要出去吃午饭呢？

还有，既然你可以在看电视的同时用移动电话通话，为什么还要费时费力去处理那些单调的工作呢？用做一件事的时间去完成三项工作——那是一种什么样的满足感和成就感！啊，了不起的效率呀。

(2)

Road ecology should be especially useful to countries like China and India, which are on what Sperling calls "a roadbuilding frenzy". To Europeans it's mostly old news. For decades they have used ecopassages to help cram roads, people, and wildlife ever more tightly together. In the 1990s the Dutch rescued their badgers from the brink of threatened status by constructing 200 badger pipes. Barcelona recently embarked on an effort to integrate its urban sprawl with wildlife. The city's chief planner? Richard Forman. "Europe, they're way ahead of us." he says, and sighs. "Our highway system has just gotten ahead of society."

像中国和印度这样的国家，更应该关注公路生态学，因为这些国家正在掀起斯珀林所说的"建路狂潮"。公路生态对欧洲人来说，已经是老新闻，因为他们使用生态通道解决公路拥挤已经有几十年了。荷兰人为拯救濒于灭绝的獾，为它们修建了200条通道。最近，西班牙的巴塞罗那已经行动起来，要把郊区的野生动物通道连成网络。这个城市的总设计师正是理查德·福曼。他感叹道："欧洲人已经走在我们前面，而我们的公路系统却已经走在了社会的前面。"

(3)

Eight years ago, Richard Forman, a landscape ecologist at Harvard University, had what he describes as "a little epiphany". Forman had gained renown with his book *Land Mosaics: The Ecology of Landscapes and Regions* and was subsequently invited to join a national council on the impact of

the U.S. transportation network on ecology. The council focused largely on climate, but Forman realized that he and his colleagues were missing the point. "It occurred to me that the most conspicuous feature of the landscape was the least known—roads."

八年前,哈佛大学地貌生态学家理查德·福曼"心灵顿悟",写出了《陆地马赛克:地貌与地方生态学》一书。这本书为他赢得了声望,后来,他还应邀参加了一个探讨美国交通网对生态影响的会议。会议讨论的焦点主要是气候,但福曼认识到,他和他的同行正在走入歧途:"猛然间,我意识到,最显著的地貌我们却了解得最少,那就是公路。"

(4)
"There will be a skill shortage in many countries in the next century," says Kean. The people with the skill that companies need are looking to an enjoyable working environment that recognizes the whole person, she says. They do not want a corner office; they want freedom. They want to turn up in jeans and open-necked shirts, have plenty of holidays (even if they are unpaid) to do their own thing, spend time with the family. Nothing will keep them away from their children's sports day or school prize-giving. They don't want to be on the road too much. Overseas postings and trips have lost a lot of their attraction for this new breed of executives.

The implications for management styles is profound. Clock watching companies who like their staff to be in for fixed hours need not apply (remember, it's a seller's market). Tomorrow's executives will be hot on productivity, cold on arbitrary work patterns. They want to work at home and come in after the traffic's gone. And they might leave before 5 p.m., but who cares as long as they've done the job? Herculean hours are out. For the new breed, a 70-hour working week isn't something to boast about, it's an admission of lousy time management. Is all this just another manifestation of undisciplined staff who don't know how to work and can't organize themselves to get to the office on time? Far from it, argues Kean: "The new workplace isn't a soft environment. It's highly productive." The underlying presumption is that you can love your work and get a lot done. In fact, the new breed know they have to deliver or they won't survive. Theory aside, the new workplace is rapidly becoming a reality. In the United States, a booming executive job market makes it easier for employees with the required skills to write their own workstyle.

基恩说:"在下个世纪,很多国家将出现技术匮乏现象。"她说,拥有公司所需要的技术的人正在寻找一个舒心的、能承认一个完全的人的工作环境。他们不希望有一个办公角落,他们希望有自由。他们希望穿着牛仔裤和开领衬衫出现,享受充足的休假日(即使在休假期间不付工资)来料理私事,和家人团聚。什么也不能把他们阻挡在孩子的运动日或学校颁奖日的门外。他们不希望离家远行的日子太多。到海外任职和出差对这类新雇员的诱惑程度已锐减。

这些管理风格含义深邃,对于希望自己的职员必须受固定时间的约束、老是看着钟上下班的公司并不适用(记住,这是卖方市场)。明天的管理人员将对生产能力表现热衷,对专横的工作方式无动于衷。他们希望在家里工作,等交通高峰期过后再来上班。他们或许在下午五点钟前就离开,但是只要他们完成了自己的工作,谁还会干涉呢?艰苦的工作时间结束了。对于新型的雇员,70小时工作周不是什么值得夸耀的东西,只不过是对糟糕的、以时间来计算的管理方式的承认。所有这些难道是那些不知道如何工作和无法组织自己准时上班的未受过训练的职员的又一个表现形式吗?根本不是。基恩认为:"新的工作地点不是一个软环境,它是一个产量很高的地方。"潜在的假设是,你会爱你的工作,并且能完成很多工作。实际上,这种人知道,他们必须实践诺言,否则他们就待不下去。撇开理论不说,这一新的工作地点正在迅速地成为现实。在美国,一个蓬勃兴起的管理人员工作市场使得具有需要的技术的雇员较为容易地显露他们自己的工作风格。

3. 翻译下列短文。

On the Pleasure of No Longer Being Very Young[1]

G. K. Chesterton

[1] There are advantages in the advance through middle age into later life which are very seldom stated in a sensible way. Generally, they are stated in a sentimental way; in a general suggestion that all old men are equipped with beautiful snowy beards like Father Christmas and rejoice in unfathomable wisdom like Nestor[2]. All this has caused the young people to be skeptical about the real advantages of the old people, and the true statement of those advantages sounds like a paradox. I would not say that old men grow wise; and many old men retain a very attractive childishness and cheerful innocence. Elderly people are often much more romantic than younger people, and sometimes even more adventurous, having begun to realize how

many things they do not know. It is a true proverb, no doubt, which says, "There is no fool like an old fool." Perhaps there is no fool who is half so happy in his own fool's paradise. But, however this may be, it is true that the advantages of maturity are not those which are generally urged even in praise of it, and when they are truly urged they sound like an almost comic contradiction.

[2]　For instance, one pleasure attached to growing older is that many things seem to be growing younger; growing fresher and more lively than we once supposed them to be. We begin to see significance, or (in other words) to see life, in a large number of traditions, institutions, maxims, and codes of manners that seem in our first days to be dead. A young man grows up in a world that often seems to him intolerably old. He grows up among proverbs and precepts that appear to be quite stiff and senseless. He seems to be stuffed with stale things; to be given the stones of death instead of the bread of life; to be fed on the dust of the dead past; to live in a town to tombs. It is a very natural mistake, but it is a mistake. The advantage of advancing years lies in discovering that traditions are true, and therefore alive; indeed, a tradition is not even traditional except when it is alive. It is great fun to find out that the world has not repeated proverbs because they are proverbial, but because they are practical.³ Until I owned a dog, I never knew what is meant by the proverb about letting a sleeping dog lie, or the fable about the dog in the manger. Now those dead phrases are quite alive to me, for they are parts of a perfectly practical psychology. Until I went to live in the country, I had no notion of the meaning of the maxim. It's an ill wind that blows nobody good. Now it seems to me as pertinent and even pungent as if it were a new remark just made to me by a neighbour at the garden gate. It is something to come to live in a world of living and significant things instead of dead and unmeaning things. And it is youth in revolt, which sees its surroundings as dead and unmeaning. It is old age, and even second childhood, that has come to see that everything means something and that life itself has never died.

[3]　For instance, we have just seen a staggering turn of the wheel of fortune which has brought all the modern material pride and prosperity to a standstill. America, which a year or two ago seemed to have become one vast Eldorado⁴ studded with cities of gold, is almost as much embarrassed as England, and really much more embarrassed than Ireland. The industrial

countries are actually finding it difficult to be industrial, while the old agricultural countries still find it possible to be industrious. Now, I do not pretend to have prophesied or expected this, for a man may cheerfully call a thing rotten without really expecting it to rot. But neither, certainly, did the young, the progressive, the prosperous, or the adventurous expect it. Yet all history and culture is stiff with proverbs and prophecies telling them to expect it. The trouble is that they thought the proverbs and history a great deal too stiff. Again and again, with monotonous reiteration, both my young friends and myself had been told from childhood that fortune is fickle, that riches take to themselves wings and fly, that power can depart suddenly from the powerful, that pride goes before a fall, and insolence attracts the thunderbolt of the gods. But it was all unmeaning to us, and all the proverbs seemed stiff and stale, like dusty labels on neglected antiquities. We had heard of the fall of Wolsey[5], which was like the crash of a huge palace, still faintly rumbling through the ages; we had read of it in the words of Shakespeare, which possibly were not written by Shakespeare; we had learned them and learned nothing from them. We had read ten thousand times, to the point of tedium, of the difference between the Napoleon of Marengo and the Napoleon of Moscow[6]; but we should never have expected Moscow if we had been looking at Marengo. We knew that Charles the Fifth resigned his crown, or that Charles the First lost his head; and we should have duly remarked "Sic transit gloria mundi", after the incident, but not before it. We had been told that the Roman Empire declined, or that the Spanish Empire disintegrated; but no German ever really applied it to the German Empire, and no Briton to the British Empire. The very repetition of these truths will sound like the old interminable repetition of the truisms. And yet they are to me, at this moment, like amazing and startling discoveries, for I have lived to see the dead proverbs come alive.

[4]   This, like so many of the realizations of later life, is quite impossible to convey in words to anybody who has not reached it in this way. It is like a difference of dimension or plane, in which something which the young have long liked at, rather wearily, as a diagram has suddenly become a solid. It is like the indescribable transition from the inorganic to the organic; as if the stone snakes and birds of some ancient Egyptian inscription began to leap about like living things. The thing was a dead maxim when we were alive

with youth. It becomes a living maxim when we are nearer to death. Even as we are dying, the whole world is coming to life.

[5]　Another paradox is this: that it is not the young people who realize the new world. The moderns do not realize modernity. They have never known anything else. They have stepped on to a moving platform which they hardly know to be moving, as a man cannot feel the daily movement of the earth. But he would feel it sharp enough if the earth suddenly moved the other way. The older generation consists of those who do remember a time when the world moved the other way. They do feel sharply and clearly the epoch which is beginning, for they were there before it began. It is one of the artistic advantages of the aged that they do see the new things relieved sharply against a background, their shape definite and distinct. To the young these new things are often themselves the background, and are hardly seen at all. Hence, even the most intelligent of innovation is often strangely mistaken about the nature of innovation and the things that are really new. And the Oldest Inhabitant will often indulge in a senile chuckle, as he listens to the Village Orator proclaiming that the village church will soon be swept away and replaced by a factory for chemicals. For the Oldest Inhabitant knows very well that nobody went to church in the days of his childhood except out of snobbishness, and that it is in his old age that the church has begun once more to be thronged with believers. In my capacity of Oldest Inhabitant (with senile chuckle), I will give one instance of a kindred kind. A man must be at least as old as I am in order to remember how utterly idiotic, inconceivable, and crazily incredible it once seemed that any educated or even reasonably shrewd person should confess that he believed in ghosts. You must be nearly the Oldest Inhabitant to know with what solid scorn and certainty the squire and the parson denied the possibility of the village ghost; the parson even more emphatically than the squire. The village ghost was instantly traced to the village drunkard or the village liar. Educated people knew that the dead do not return in the world of sense. Those who remember those times, and have lived to see a man of science like Sir Oliver Lodge[7] founding quite a fashionable religion, are amused to hear a young man say the world is moving away from the supernatural. They know in what direction it has really moved.

> ⚠ **提示**

1. 此文是英国作家 G·K·切斯特顿（1874—1936）的名篇，用词精练，句式严谨。译文应再现这种清晰、流畅的笔锋。
2. 4、5、6、7 这几处都涉及相关背景知识，查一查看怎样处理好。
3. 注意此句否定结构的理解。

4. 改进下列文章的译文。

I'm Sick of the F Word

Anya Bateman

[1] Recently some friends who hadn't been to a movie for years treated themselves to a picture that had received rave reviews and several Academy Awards. I asked how they had enjoyed their night out. "It was a good movie," Judy said. "An excellent story-line and great acting, but..." When she hesitated, I had a good idea what she would say next. "But the language was foul! The foulest I've ever heard, and I've been around. Things sure have changed."

[2] Yes, they have. Words once reserved for rest-room walls are now common stuff in films, plays, books and even on television.

[3] The "F word", long taboo, is now high fashion. As columnist John Leo noted recently in *U.S. News and World Report*, stand-up comedian Eddie Murphy tossed out hundreds of four-letter words in a single performance; New York Mets baseball star Lenny Dykstra, in a book snatched up by many a young fan, uses the F word the way others use punctuation; and David Mamet's Pulitzer Prize-winning play, *Glengarry Glen Ross*, is littered with the you-know-what word.

[4] Movie-makers are in the thick of the expletive explosion. But, whatever the medium, the massage seems to be that foul language is in, so get used to it.

[5] I realize there are those who contend that entertainment merely depicts life as it is. "It's the real world," they say. "It's how people talk!" Indeed, my friend noticed that others in the theater hadn't appeared offended by the on-screen obscenities. In fact, the people behind her were using much the same

language. "Is it us?" she asked. " Are we the different ones?"

[6] I admit that sometimes it seems to be the case. Not long ago, I was sitting on a bus behind two women who apparently believe that no noun is complete without an obscene adjective attached. And many of us have worked in offices that can best be described as a locker room after a big loss. But regardless of this "evidence", I think most people are uncomfortable with the assault on our language. Even the young can recognize what should be said and what should not.

[7] A friend told me about a commuter who grew so tired of the stream of obscenities coming from members of his car pool that he planned to quit the group. He tried to think up excuses, but they all sounded phony. Finally, he decided that the others should know his real reason. He leveled with them. To his surprise, the two worst offenders immediately promised to clean up their act, and insisted he continue with the car pool.

[8] Some people, of course, don't take so kindly to criticism. However, if we attack the problem and not the person, we can turn criticism into a compliment. A secretary managed this when she told her boss: "I think so highly of you that it always surprises me when I hear you use bad language. I can't help feeling concerned about the impressions you may be making on others who don't know you as well as I do." Talk about impact. Her boss later admitted that no amount of blunt criticism could have had as purging an effect as his secretary's caring, convincing words.

[9] Even gentle and artful criticism takes courage—a courage I, for one, haven't always had. I still regret that a number of years ago I failed to speak out as language pollution became the norm in a writing class I was taking. It began when one of the students asked our instructor if it was permissible to use a certain word in his story. "By all means," he said. "It's real life; it's how people talk." Soon others began lacing their prose with "real life". Of course, it wasn't real life at all, but what the students thought was expected.

[10] I copped out by not objecting. I was afraid of what the others would think of me, fearful that if I spoke up I would appear unsophisticated.

[11] What happened in that classroom probably reflects what is happening in society at large. Isn't language pollution increasing because we are too eager

to follow what others tell us is fashionable? Because we are not exercising our right—and obligation—to speak out against it?

[12] When a filmmaker I know put together a short documentary about his young son's soccer heroics, his mother was appalled to find the script riddled with profanity. "But Craig," she objected, "my grandson just doesn't talk this way. He never has."

[13] "Oh, Mom, I know that," Craig replied. "But you've got to put that kind of thing in nowadays. People expect it. It's the trend."

[14] I rest my case.

我讨厌脏话

安娜·贝特曼

[1] 最近，多年不看电影的一些朋友看了一部电影。这部电影曾获得过热烈的好评，并且获得了几种学院奖。我问他们那个晚上过得怎么样。"这原是一部好电影，"朱迪说，"极好的故事情节，杰出的表演，但……"，当她犹豫时，我就知道她下边要说些什么了。"但语言太脏了！我所见所闻不少，这可是我听到的最下流的脏话。事情确实是变了。"

[2] 的确，事情变了。曾经是不登大雅之堂的言语，如今充斥于电影、戏剧、书籍之中，甚至充斥在电视上。

[3] 长期以来禁忌的"脏话"，如今却十分时髦。专栏作家约翰·利奥最近在美国《新闻与世界报道》中指出，独白喜剧演员埃迪·墨菲仅在一场演出中就一连串地说出了数百个下流黄色的字眼；纽约梅茨垒球明星莱尼·戴克斯屈拉在一本许多球迷争相购阅的书中，用脏字就像用标点符号一样；戴维·梅墨特获得普利策奖的剧本《苏格兰船形帽》也塞满了你知道的那种字眼。

[4] 电影制作人员正处于咒骂词的爆炸中心。无论何种媒介传播的信息似乎都染上了脏话，那也就习以为常了。

[5] 我发现有些人认为娱乐仅仅是按生活本身来描写生活，他们说："这是真实的世界。人们就是这样交谈的！"的确，我的朋友注意到电影院里的其他人也并未因银幕上的猥亵的语言而显得生气。事实上，在她座位后面的人们都在使用着差不多

相同的语言。"是不是我们?"她问道,"是我们与众不同吗?"

[6] 我承认有时候情况似乎确实如此。不久前,我在公共汽车上,坐在两位妇女的后面,显而易见,她们认为名词若不加上一个下流的形容词就不完整。我们多数人是坐办公室的,可以说是锁在远远听不到这些脏话的更衣室里。但是不管这种迹象怎么样,我认为大多数人对糟蹋我们的语言总会感到不舒服。甚至年轻人也能辨别什么该说,什么不该说。

[7] 一位朋友告诉我,有个长期合伙用车上下班的人,他十分厌烦用车的伙伴们滔滔不绝的下流话,打算从这伙人中退出去。他想编造一些理由,但它们听上去都不真实。最终他下决心让大伙知道他的真正原因,便坦率地对他们说了。出乎他的意料,两个最恶劣的家伙马上保证不再说脏话,并坚持要他继续合伙用车。

[8] 当然,有些人并不是这样和善地来对待批评的。然而,如果我们对事而不对人,我们能把批评变成一种恭维话。一位秘书在批评她的上司时掌握了这一点:"我认为我非常尊敬你,但每当你说粗话的时候常常使我感到吃惊,我不能不关心你可能会给那些并不像我这样了解你的人留下的印象。"谈到效果,她的上司后来承认,没有任何直截了当的批评能达到他的秘书关心而令人信服的言辞所达到的那种净化的效果。

[9] 即使是温和而巧妙的批评也需要勇气—— 一种对一个人包括我在内不总是具备的勇气。几年前,在我所参加的一个写作班上语言污染成风,对此我却未能指出,我至今还感到遗憾。事情是这样开始的。一位学生问我们的教师是否允许在他的故事里使用某个词。"完全可以,"教师说。"那是现实生活;人们就是那样交谈的。"很快,其他人就用"现实生活"来修饰他们的文章。当然,那根本不是现实生活,然而学生们所想的倒是人们所预料到的。

[10] 我没有提出反对而是回避。我不知别人会怎样看待我,也怕如果我说出来的话,我会显得幼稚可笑。

[11] 教室里发生的事情或许反映出整个社会发生的事情。语言污染的日益加剧,难道不是因为我们没有履行我们的权利——和义务——去响亮地反对它吗?

[12] 当我认识的一位电影制作人将有关他儿子的足球业绩辑录在一起成为一部纪录短片时,他母亲发现剧本里充满了污言秽语,十分震惊。"克雷格,"她反对道,"我

孙子就不是这样说话，他从来也没这样说过。"

[13] "妈妈，我知道，"克雷格回答道。"但如今你必须把这种东西塞进去，人们向往这种东西。这是一种潮流。"

[14] 我不再讲下去了。

第四章 叙事、描写文体的翻译

前两章分别讨论了理解和表达方面的问题。从第四章起我们将关注不同语篇类型，即不同文体的语篇的翻译。

第三章 Unit One 的讲解和 Unit Three 的讲解部分已经提到过语篇的文体。不同文体的语篇在遣词造句、谋篇布局上存在差异，其翻译策略和方法也不尽相同。上一章的小结中还提出"译文构建实际上就是一种特殊类型的写作"的观点，强调了译者译语写作能力的能动作用。基于这样的认识，翻译教学中将文体与写作结合起来未尝不是一个贴近实际的有效途径。第四章和第五章将分别聚焦叙事、描写文体和说明、论说文体——这也正是写作教学中经常使用的分类方法。

本章讨论的叙事、描写文体包括小说、散文、传记等文学性较强的一类语篇。讨论要点包括：一、汉语在此类语篇中特别显示出的有别于英语的一个重大区别，即多用短句、短语，少用关联词语的重意合的特点；二、在描写和叙事时译者必须发挥自己的形象思维能力；三、动词和形容词的翻译技巧；四、归化和异化问题。这些要点不只涉及叙事、描写文体的翻译，但在此类语篇的翻译中体现得更突出些。

# Lambing Time

[1]   My first experience of bottling a lamb came towards the end of the season, when one ewe lambed a double out in the field one afternoon.¹ After having the first one she wandered some distance away, and when Charlie found her she was busy with the second, already an hour or two old. He brought them all down to the pen, and shut them up. Whether she had forgotten about the first lamb when the second was born, I don't know, but she would not feed it, or in fact have anything to do with it. All that night she neglected it, refusing to allow it to suckle. Charlie, who never believed in interfering if it could be avoided, left her alone, hoping that she would eventually come round. Next morning she was as determined as ever not to acknowledge it, and during the day she bunted the poor mite away from her with such energy that by tea-time its head was bleeding and it was very weak.² Charlie shook his head about it.

[2]   "No good," he muttered, "er'll never take to it now."

[3]   "Bring it down to the house," I said. "We'll give it a bottle."

[4]   Charlie carried it tenderly into the kitchen; it was astonishing how tender his rough hands could be with an ailing creature and how dexterously he handled the mite. It was now too cold and weak to lift up its head, let alone stand. Together we warmed it by the fire, while the cook stood by, pityingly.

[5]   "Poor little thing, you'll never rear it!" she said, with the typical lugubriousness of a domestic. She warmed a little milk while I fetched some brandy, and we gave it sips from a spoon. It revived with astonishing rapidity. Within an hour it struggled to its feet and could stand. Charlie had a bottle and teat laid by in readiness for any emergencies, which he brought down after tea, and by then the lamb was ready and eager to suck.³ He showed me the proper way to warm milk for bottle-feeding lambs. It appeared that milk warmed over the fire was liable to give them collywobbles, and⁴ the correct method was to heat a poker red-hot in the fire and stir the milk with it,

repeating the process until the milk was warm—a lengthy and tedious job, I found.

[6]　A few days later one of the ewes lambed with a dead lamb, and Charlie took the semi-orphan[5] (now thriving splendidly) away from us to give to the bereaved mother. I, in my ignorance, expected him to introduce the stranger into the pen and the ewe to be overjoyed to see him and adopt him immediately.

[7]　But it was not so at all. The introduction[6] was not nearly so simple. First the dead lamb was skinned, and the skin draped across the back of our pet, who was, of course, too large for it, so that it had to be firmly bound on with string.[7] I had always wondered how the ewes knew their own lambs; now I learned that it was partly by voice, but chiefly by smell, looks not entering into it at all.[8] This is why, when a lamb runs up to feed, the mother always turns her head round and touches it. I had imagined it to be merely a gesture of affection, but it seems it is to smell the lamb and make sure that it is her own. If a lamb makes a mistake about its mother—and for feeding purposes one ewe is as good as another to a hungry lamb![9]—then it is sent about its business[10] with a hearty bunt from the outraged ewe.

[8]　When the pet lamb was ready, looking the funniest little object imaginable, Charlie took him into the pen and set him down. Then he called up the sheep dog, Rusty, and we all stood outside and watched.

[9]　The ewe stamped her foreleg a time or two, then walked slowly over and smelt the lamb suspiciously. I held my breath expecting to see her drive it away after all Charlie had said,[11] but after a prolonged sniff she gave a pleased "baa" and nuzzled it gently. The smell being that of her own dead lamb, she was ready to take to him, despite his queer appearance. The lamb having become accustomed to a bottle, made no attempt to suckle, and after a few moments, Charlie penned the ewe up in its corner with his knee and gently introduced the lamb to its new means of livelihood. At first he was rather stupid about it, but once he got a taste of milk he sucked away greedily, and Charlie stood up with satisfaction, "There, they'll do now."

参考译文

产羔季节

[1] 我第一次用奶瓶喂羊羔,是在产羔季节临近结束的时候。有一天下午,一只母羊在野地里下了一对羊羔。下完了头一只,她就溜达到别处去了。等查理找到她的时候,她正忙着照料第二只,这第二只生下来已经有一两个钟头了。查理把它们全都带回羊圈,关了起来。是不是她生了第二只就把第一只忘了,我不知道,反正她不肯喂它,实际上她根本就不理睬它。整整一夜她都不管它,不让它吃奶。查理一向认为,只要能避免,就不要插手,所以就没有管,希望她终究会改变主意。第二天早晨,她还是照旧坚决不认它。而且就在这一天,她使劲把可怜的小家伙从身旁顶开,结果到下午喝茶的时候,小家伙头破血流,浑身无力。查理看到这种情况,摇了摇头。

[2] "不妙,"他自言自语地说道。"她不会认它了。"

[3] "把它弄到屋里来吧,"我说。"咱们用奶瓶喂它。"

[4] 查理小心地把它抱到厨房里。令人惊奇的是,在照料一只生病的小动物的时候,查理的一双粗手有多么温柔,他伺候小家伙,有多么熟练。小家伙这时又冷又弱,连头也抬不起来,更不要说站着了。我们两个人一起让它在灶旁暖和起来,厨师站在一旁,显出怜悯的样子。

[5] "这可怜的小东西,你们是没法把它养活的!"她带着仆人特有的忧郁表情说道。她热了一点儿奶,我拿来了一点儿白兰地,我们用调羹一小口一小口地喂它。小羊羔很快缓了过来。没出一个小时,它就挣扎着站起来,而且能站住了。查理喝过茶以后,拿来了一个带橡皮奶头的瓶子,放在手边,以备不时之需,这时羊羔已经在急切地等着吸奶了。查理教我用奶瓶喂羊羔应该怎样热奶。好像在火上热奶,羊羔喝了会肚子痛,所以正确的做法是把捅火棍烧红,放到奶里搅动,这样反复数次,直到把奶搅热——我觉得这个活儿既费工夫又没意思。

[6] 过了几天,一只母羊产了一只死羔。于是查理就把我们这里那个孤儿似的小家伙(这时长得好极了)拿去送给那位失去孩子的母亲。我出于无知,以为查理会把这位生客送到圈里,母羊见了也一定会很高兴,马上就会收养它。

[7] 但情况完全不是这样。往圈里送可不那么简单。要先把死羔的皮剥下来,披在我们的小宝贝身上,小宝贝当然太大,盖不过来,所以要用绳子牢牢地捆在它身

上。过去我一直不明白母羊是怎样认出自己的羊羔的；这时我才知道，一方面是靠听声音，但主要是靠闻味儿，根本不用看长相。这就是为什么每当一只羊羔跑上前去吃奶的时候，母亲总要扭过头来，碰它一碰。原来我以为这不过是一种亲热的表示，但是现在看来，这是为了闻一闻羊羔的味道，来断定是不是自己生的。要是一只羊羔认错了母亲——因为对于一只饿了的羊羔来说，找任何一只母羊吃奶都是一样的——生气的母羊就会使劲一拱，把它拱到一边去。

[8]　我们心爱的羊羔打扮好了以后，样子甭说有多滑稽了。查理把他送进羊圈，放了下来，接着他又把护羊狗罗斯蒂招呼到身旁，我们都站在外面注意观察。

[9]　母羊蹬了蹬前蹄，慢慢走上前去，带着怀疑的神态闻了闻小羊羔。尽管查理说没问题，我还是屏住呼吸，担心母羊会把羊羔赶走。可是母羊闻了半天，只愉快地"咩"了一声，便轻轻地用鼻子在羊羔身上蹭了起来。她闻到了自己那只死羔的味道，所以就愿意认它了，虽然它样子很怪。羊羔因为已经习惯于用瓶子吃奶，所以不去吃母羊的奶。过了一会儿，查理用膝盖把母羊堵在一个角落里，然后慢慢地让羊羔适应这新的生活方式。起初它不知如何是好，可是一尝到奶的味道，便大口大口地吸起来。查理满意地站起身来，说道："现在行了。"（庄绎传译）

注释

1. 这一句被拆开，译成两个句子。这样安排有利于语篇的连贯：第一句点出主题，第二句开始叙述，与下文的叙述连在一起。另外，bottle 作动词一般为 put into bottles，此处据上下文意为 feed the lamb with a bottle。
2. 注意比较上面这两句话的原文和其译文在结构上的差别。英语主从分明，形式构架突出；汉语小句串接，层层推进，不重形式，而重意义上的连贯。
3. 此句中的定语从句在译文中移到句首译出，这是因为汉语比起英语来对自然时间顺序的遵守更为严格。
4. 连词 and 译为"所以"，因为前半句说的是"在火上热奶不行"，后半句说的是"正确做法"，译为"所以"使逻辑关系顺畅、自然。
5. semi-orphan 不能机械地译为"半孤儿"。小羊羔的母亲并没死，只是不认它，所以它不是真正意义上的 orphan，故加前缀 semi。译者根据上下文采取了变通的译法。
6. 此处 introduction 译为"往圈里送"也是根据上下文定的，可再参阅第二章 Unit One 的讲解部分。
7. 与注释 2 所涉及的句子相似，此句汉译也体现了汉语小句意合串接的句式特点。原句中的 who was, of course, too large for it 译为"小宝贝当然太大，盖不过来"，将介词的含义用动词译出，也体现了汉语多用小句的特点。
8. 句中 by voice、by smell 等介词短语的意义在汉语中也是用"听""闻"这样的动词译出的。另外，注意本句中时态所表达的语法意义：had wondered; learned。译文中用词汇手段加以再现："过去我一直不明白；现在我知道"。
9. 注意此句的汉语表达，避免翻译腔。
10. send sb. about his business 是一习语，意思是 to tell sb. to mind his own affairs and stop annoying one。
11. after all = in spite of, 如：After all we had done, he was still ungrateful.

 讲解

英译汉中的意合趋势（总论）

英语句子以主句的主干（主＋谓＋宾）为中心，可以叠加多种形式的从属成分——从句、分词短语、介词短语，等等——形成一个明显的形式结构。汉语的形式结构不像英语那么明显，主要靠小句的串接、意义的连贯来组建句子。这在叙述、描写文体中尤为突出。因此，英译汉时就会经历一种从形合结构向意合结构转化的趋势。这种趋势常体现在两个方面：一是把英语句子拆开，成为两个、三个句子（参阅注释1）；二是把英语从属成分译为汉语小句，成为小句串接的意合结构（参阅注释2、7和8）。

下面一个长句选自 Edgar Allan Poe 的 *The Fall of the House of Usher*，是个典型的形合结构，请对照汉语译文阅读。

It had so worked upon my imagination as really to believe that about the whole mansion and domain there hung an atmosphere peculiar to themselves and their immediate vicinity: an atmosphere which had no affinity with the air of heaven, but which had reeked up from the decayed trees, and the gray wall, and the silent tarn: a pestilent and mystic vapor, dull, sluggish, faintly discernible, and leaden-hued.

在我的想象中，我好像真的看到，从朽木灰墙里，从静悄悄的小湖上，散发出一种神秘的、令人讨厌的雾气。这种雾气呈铅灰色，阴沉呆滞、隐隐约约，笼罩着整幢房子及其四周。这种特别的雾气同天空的大气没有任何关系，只有这幢房子及附近才有。

可以看出，译者把 an atmosphere 所带的两个定语从句分别与宾语从句（...that...there hung）的内容进行了重新组合，将原句译成了三个句子，层次清楚，与原文异曲同工。翻译实践中，这样的长句、这样的调整并不十分多，更常见的是将英语中的某个成分译为汉语小句，以顺应汉语叙事、描写的行文习惯，下面分几种情况加以考察。

一、将从句和 -ing/-ed 分词短语译为小句

1. He had to win his way into the heart of a laughing girl who had no serious thought of loving any man...least of all, Ichabod Crane.
   他必须排除障碍去获得一个愉快的村姑的欢心，而这个村姑从没有认真地考虑过要爱任何男人，尤其是去爱波德·克莱恩。

2. In September what the skeptical German generals called a "miracle" occurred.
   九月间发生了一件事情，将信将疑的德国将军们称之为"奇迹"。

3. I spent the next hour chasing, squawking chickens all over the yard.
   我赶了一个小时的鸡，那些鸡满院子乱飞乱叫。

4. However, the entertainment industry had hardly finished celebrating the apparent blocking of that loophole when another major problem appeared—software (designed by a Norwegian teenager) that allows the contents of digital video disks to be shared over the web.
   这个漏洞显然是堵上了，然而，娱乐界的欢乐劲还未过去，就又出现了一个大问题。挪威一个十几岁的少年设计了一个软件，用这个软件就能在网上分享数字视频磁盘的内容。

5. British playwright Alan Bennett, who enjoyed a peaceful childhood—the only stress came when his father was learning the double bass—spent some time studying the life and works of Kenneth Grahame before adapting *The Wind in the Willows* for the stage.
   英国剧作家艾伦·贝内特曾享有祥和的童年生活。家中出现过的仅有的一次危机是由于父亲学习演奏低音提琴而引起的。贝内特将《杨柳风》改编为舞台剧之前，曾花了一些时间研究肯尼恩·格雷厄姆的生平及其作品。

关于从句和 -ing/-ed 分词短语的拆译，还可参看第四章 Unit Two 及第五章 Unit One、Unit Two 的讲解部分。

二、将某些名词结构译成小句

6. He was pale, and there were dark signs of sleeplessness beneath his eyes.

   他脸色煞白，眼圈黑黑的，看得出他一夜没睡好。

7. The walk up Fifth Avenue through the slush of the sidewalks and the dankness of the air had tired him.

   纽约第五大街人行道上污雪成浆，空气阴冷潮湿，走这一段够累的。

8. Yet for all the wonders in the future, Michael Smith still will suffer from headaches, hangnails, indigestion, crime, taxation, mother-in-law and new products that don't work.

   尽管将来会有这一切奇迹，史密斯仍将不免有个头痛脑热，手指上长个倒刺，患点消化不良症，等等；也难免由于社会上的犯罪行为、众多的捐税、难办的岳母、不管用的产品而吃点苦头。

9. He was a clever man; a pleasant companion; a careless student; with a great propensity for running into debt, and a partiality for the tavern.

   他是个聪明人，谈吐非常风趣，可是不肯用苦功。他老是东借西挪，又喜欢上酒店喝酒。

10. Again the writing space is small, but your thoughtfulness will be appreciated.（源语作者在谈论如何用简短的书信与远离自己的亲朋保持联系，沟通感情。）

    这样也就没有多大篇幅好写，但你惦记人家，人家还是感激的。

11. Twenty-five years after its creation our organization has still not succeeded in attaining those two objectives.

    我们这个组织已建立了二十五年，依然未能达到这两个目标。

12. The pompous vanity of the old schoolmistress, the foolish good-humour of her sister, the silly chat and scandal of the elder girls, and the frigid correctness of the governess equally annoyed her.

    女校长最爱空架子和虚面子；她妹妹脾气好得痴呆混沌；年纪大的学生喜欢说些无聊的闲话，讲讲人家的隐私；女教师们又全是一丝不苟的老古板。这一切都同样叫她气闷。

从上述译例可看出，译成小句的英语结构很多都是 Noun 1 + of + Noun 2（例 4、5、8、10），还有 one's + Noun（例 9），adj. + Noun 及 Noun + of...（例 7）等。例 8 的谓语 suffer from 带有七个宾语，照英语结构译显然行不通，译者将七个名词分为两组，译成两个句子，行文地道。

三、将介词短语译为小句

13. Marion looked up at him with hard eyes.
    马里恩抬起头望望他，目光冷酷。

14. Martin limped across the yard and into the sheltering darkness.
    马丁一瘸一拐地穿过庭院，躲到阴影里。

15. ...away she skimmed, over the lawn, up the path, up the steps, across the veranda and into the porch.
    她一蹦一跳地跑开了。越过草坪，走过小径，登上台阶，穿过游廊，然后进了门。

16. Up in his room he sat for a few minutes at the window looking down into the familiar street below.
    他上楼进屋，在窗前坐了几分钟，眺望窗下那熟稔的街景。

17. ...he pulled his ankles away, but the dog humped forward in patient pursuit.
    他把脚挣开，可那条狗不厌其烦，弓着身子又凑了上来。

18. When they had been married a year, they had a fine son with dark curls and a golden skin.
    夫妻俩结婚一载，生下一个漂亮的儿子。他一头乌黑卷曲的美发，皮肤金光透亮。

19. Punctually at five minutes to five Lampe, his servant, waked Professor Kant and by five, in his slippers, dressing-gown and night-cap, over which he wore his three-cornered hat, he seated himself in his study ready for breakfast.
    早晨5点差5分，仆人兰普准时叫醒康德教授；5点，教授趿着拖鞋，披着晨衣，戴着睡帽，睡帽上罩顶三角帽，坐在书房准备用餐。

20. On the wings of hope, of love, of joy, Miss Meadows sped back to the music hall, up the aisle, up the steps, over to the piano.

美多斯小姐仿佛插上了希望的翅膀、爱情的翅膀、欢乐的翅膀，一路飞奔到音乐厅，她穿过通道，跑上台阶，三步并两步走到钢琴前。

21. With hair a little thin on his head, and legs that could not possibly do more than three and a half miles an hour on the road, there he was, with three families behind him.

他头发有点稀疏，两条腿一小时走不了十里半路，就这样一个人，一生居然有过三拨家小。

22. Unemployment has soared as the hulks of fishing boats rust away on the salt-encrusted seabed.

裸露的海床布满白花花的海盐渍，一艘艘锈迹斑斑的渔船搁浅其中，从而导致失业率急剧上升。

下面请再观察三个段落汉译的意合化趋势，看译者是如何使用拆译方法的。

23. Albert Speer and a remarkable lady witness whose dramatic appearance in the last act of the drama in Berlin will shortly be noted have described Hiltler's reaction to Goering's telegram. Speer had flown into the besieged capital on the night of April 23, landing in a cub plane on the eastern end of the East-West Axis—the broad avenue which led through the Tiergarten—at the Brandenburg Gate, a block from the Chancellery.

阿尔伯特·斯佩尔和另外一位了不起的目击者后来详细记述了希特勒收到戈林电报时的反应。这位目击者是一个妇女，她在柏林那场戏中最后一幕忽然登场的经过，下文就要述及。斯佩尔是在4月23日晚上坐了一架小飞机到被围的首都来的，飞机降落在离总理府只有一条街的勃兰登堡门附近，那是在横贯动物园的东西轴心大街的东头。

请特别注意第一句中 whose... 定语从句及第二句中有关降落地点部分汉译的重新组织。

24. Shanghai, which means "above the sea", is on the Whangpoo River, the lowest tributary at the mouth of the Yangtze River. Whereas the territorial limits of Greater Shanghai, 320 square miles by government grant, reach up to the confluence of the two waters, the main city itself sits astride the

Whangpoo, ten miles to the interior. Cosmopolitan Shanghai was born to the world in 1842 when the British man-of-war *Nemesis*, slipping unnoticed into the mouth of the Yangtze River, reduced the Woosung Fort and took the city without a fight.

上海的含义是"位于海之上",它位于长江流入大海之前最后一条支流黄浦江之畔。城市的主要部分离海岸有十英里,横跨黄浦江两岸,而政府划为大上海的面积共有 320 平方英里,直达黄浦江和长江汇合的地方。1842 年英国战舰"尼米悉斯号"潜入长江口,击毁吴淞炮台,不战而占据了上海,从此上海就变成了一座国际城市。

特别注意从句及分词短语是如何汉译的,注意线性顺序的重新安排。

25. By the middle of August 1944, the Russian offensives, beginning June 10 and unrolling one after another, had brought the Red Army to the border of East Prussia, bottled up fifty German divisions in the Baltic region, penetrated to Vyborg in Finland, destroyed Army Group Center and brought an advance on this front of four hundred miles in six weeks to the Vistula opposite Warsaw, while in the south a new attack which began on August 20 resulted in the conquest of Rumania by the end of the month and with it the Ploesti oil fields, the only major source of natural oil for the German armies.

俄国从 1944 年 6 月 10 日开始发动夏季攻势,节节胜利,到 8 月中旬,红军已打到了东普鲁士边境,在波罗的海地区包围了德军五十个师,深入到芬兰的维堡,消灭了中央集团军群,在 6 个星期内在这条战线上推进了 400 英里,到达维斯杜拉河,与华沙隔河相望。同时,在南线,俄国也从 8 月 20 日起发动新攻势,到月底就占领了罗马尼亚,这样也就占领了德军天然石油的唯一重要来源——普洛耶什蒂油田。

原句的主句及由 while 引导的状语从句被拆成两个句子;其次,名词短语、分词短语及从句都有译成汉语小句的意合转换。

Vanity Fair (Excerpt 1)

[1]   While the present century was in its teens, and on one sunshiny morning in June, there drove up to the great iron gate of Miss Pinkerton's academy for young ladies, on Chiswick Mall, a large family coach, with two fat horses in blazing harness, driven by a fat coachman in a three-cornered hat and wig, at the rate of four miles an hour.¹ A black servant, who reposed on the box beside the fat coachman, uncurled his bandy legs as soon as the equipage drew up opposite Miss Pinkerton's shining brass plate, and as he pulled the bell, at least a score of young heads were seen peering out of the narrow windows of the stately old brick house.² Nay, the acute observer might have recognized the little red nose of good-natured Miss Jemima Pinkerton herself, rising over some geranium-pots in the window of that lady's own drawing-room.

[2]   "It is Mrs. Sedley's coach, sister," said Miss Jemima. "Sambo, the black servant, has just rung the bell; and the coachman has a new red waistcoat."

[3]   "Have you completed all the necessary preparations incident to Miss Sedley's departure, Miss Jemima?" asked Miss Pinkerton herself, that majestic lady; the Semiramis of Hammersmith, the friend of Doctor Johnson, the correspondent of Mrs. Chapone herself.³

[4]   "The girls were up at four this morning, packing her trunks, sister," replied Miss Jemima; "we have made her a bow-pot."

[5]   "Say a bouquet, sister Gamma, 'tis more genteel."

[6]   "Well, a booky⁴ as big almost as a hay-stack; I have put up two bottles of the gillyflower-water for Mrs. Sedley, and the receipt for making it, in Amelia's box."

[7]   "And I trust, Miss Jemima, you have made a copy of Miss Sedley's account. This is it, is it? Very good—ninety-three pounds, four shillings. Be kind enough to address it to John Sedley, Esquire, and to seal this billet which I have written to his lady."

[8] In Miss Jemima's eyes an autograph letter of her sister, Miss Pinkerton, was an object of as deep veneration as would have been a letter from a sovereign. Only when her pupils quitted the establishment, or when they were about to be married, and once, when poor Miss Birch died of the scarlet fever, was Miss Pinkerton known to write personally to the parents of her pupils,[5] and it was Jemima's opinion that if anything could console Mrs. Birch for her daughter's loss, it would be that pious and eloquent composition in which Miss Pinkerton announced the event.[6]

[9] In the present instance Miss Pinkerton's "billet" was to the following effect—"The Mall, Chiswick, June 15, 18—

[10] "Madam, —After her six years' residence at the Mall, I have the honour and happiness of presenting Miss Amelia Sedley to her parents, as a young lady not unworthy to occupy a fitting position in their polished and refined circle. Those virtues which characterize the young English gentlewoman, those accomplishments which become her birth and station, will not be found wanting in the amiable Miss Sedley, whose industry and obedience have endeared her to her instructors, and whose delightful sweetness of temper has charmed her aged and her youthful companions.[7]

[11] "In music, in dancing, in orthography, in every variety of embroidery and needle-work, she will be found to have realized her friends' fondest wishes. In geography there is still much to be desired; and a careful and undeviating use of the backboard, for four hours daily during the next three years, is recommended as necessary to the acquirement of that dignified deportment and carriage, so requisite for every young lady of fashion.

[12] "In the principles of religion and morality, Miss Sedley will be found worthy of an establishment which has been honoured by the presence of The Great Lexicographer, and the patronage of the admirable Mrs. Chapone.[8] In leaving the Mall, Miss Amelia carries with her the hearts of her companions, and the affectionate regards of her mistress, who has the honour to subscribe herself,

Madam,
Your most obliged humble servant,
Barbara Pinkerton

"P. S. —Miss Sharp accompanies Miss Sedley. It is particularly requested that Miss Sharp's stay in Russell Square may not exceed ten days. The family of distinction with whom she is engaged, desire to avail themselves of her services as soon as possible."

参考译文

名利场（节选一）

[1]　当时我们这个世纪刚开始了十几年。在六月里的一天早上，天气晴朗，契息克林荫道上平克顿女子学校的大铁门前面来了一辆宽敞的私人马车。拉车的两匹肥马套着雪亮的马具，肥胖的车夫戴了假头发和三角帽子，赶车子的速度不过一小时四英里。胖子车夫的旁边坐着一个当差的黑人，马车在女学堂发光的铜牌子前面停下来，他就伸开一双罗圈腿，走下来按铃。这所气象森严的旧房子是砖砌的，窗口很窄，黑人一按铃，就有二十来个小姑娘从窗口探出头来，连那好性子的吉米玛·平克顿小姐也给引出来了。眼睛尖点的人准能看见她在自己客厅的窗户前面，她的红鼻子恰好凑在那一盆盆的牵牛花儿上面。

[2]　吉米玛小姐说："姐姐，赛特笠太太的马车来了。那个叫三菩的黑佣人刚刚按过铃。马车夫还穿了新的红背心呢。"

[3]　"赛特笠小姐离校以前的必要手续办好没有，吉米玛小姐？"说话的是一位威风凛凛的女士，也就是平克顿小姐本人。她算得上海默斯密士这一带地方的赛米拉米斯，又是约翰生博士的朋友，并且经常和夏博恩太太通信。

[4]　吉米玛小姐答道："女孩子们清早四点钟起来帮她理箱子了，姐姐。我们还给她扎了一捆花。"

[5]　"妹妹，用字文雅点，说一束花。"

[6]　"好的。这一簇花儿大得像个草堆儿。我还包了两瓶子丁香花露送给赛特笠太太，连方子都在爱米丽亚箱子里。"

[7]　"吉米玛小姐，我想你已经把赛特笠小姐的费用单子抄出来了。这就是吗？很好，共是九十三镑四先令。请你在信封上写上约翰·赛特笠先生的名字，把我写给他太太的信也封进去。"

[8]　在吉米玛小姐看来，她姐姐亲笔签字的信和皇帝上谕一般神圣。平克顿小姐难

得写信给家长；只限于学生离校，或是结婚，或是像有一回那可怜的白却小姐害猩红热死掉的时候，她才亲自动手。吉米玛小姐觉得她姐姐那一回通知信里的句子又虔诚又动听。世界上如果还有能够使白却太太略抒悲怀的东西，那一定就是这封信了。

[9]　这一回，平克顿小姐的信是这样的：契息克林荫道一八一一年六月十五日。

[10]　夫人——爱米丽亚·赛特笠小姐在林荫道已经修毕六年，此后，尽堪在府上风雅高尚的环境中占一个与她身份相称的地位，我因此感到万分的荣幸和欣喜。英国大家闺秀所特有的品德，在她家世和地位上所应有的才学，温良的赛特笠小姐已经具备。她学习勤勉，性情和顺，博得师长们的赞扬，而且她为人温柔可亲，因此校内无论长幼，一致喜爱她。

[11]　在音乐、舞蹈、拼法以及刺绣缝纫方面，她的造诣一定能不负亲友的期望。可惜她对于地理的知识还多有欠缺。同时我希望您在今后三年之中，督促她每天使用背板四小时，不可间断。这样才能使她的举止风度端雅稳重，合乎上流女子的身份。

[12]　赛特笠小姐对于宗教道德的见解非常正确，不愧为本校的学生（本校曾承伟大的字汇学家光临参观，又承杰出的夏博恩夫人多方资助）。爱米丽亚小姐离开林荫道时，同窗的眷念，校长的关注，也将随她而去。

　　　　　　　　　　　　　　　　夫人，我十分荣幸，能自称为您的谦卑感恩的仆人。
　　　　　　　　　　　　　　　　　　　　　　　　　　　　　巴巴拉·平克顿

附言：
夏泼小姐准备和赛特笠小姐一同来府。夏泼小姐在勒塞尔广场盘桓的时间不宜超过十天。雇用她的是显要的世家，希望她在最短时间内开始工作。（杨必译）

注释

1. 这句话拆译成三个句子，大体按照"时间——事件（来了一辆马车）——细节描写（马、车夫）"的顺序排列，层次清楚，符合汉语的叙事习惯。参阅本章 Unit One 的讲解部分。
2. 这句话拆译成两个句子。第一个句子中的小句与英语的小句大体对应，只是排列顺序有所调整。英语的动词排列顺序是：...reposed...uncurled...drew up，汉语改为：……坐着……停下……伸腿……。显然，汉语更习惯于按自然发生顺序排列动作或事件。

第二个汉译句子中，名词短语 narrow windows 和 stately old brick house 被译成两个小句，整个句子的格局是先描写房子然后再陈述相关事件。这种将描写和叙述分列开来的构句方法，在英译汉中也是常常使用的。另外，为了行文的连贯，pulled the bell 实际上被译了两次，分别出现在两个句子中。

3. 此句中的名词词组均被译成了汉语小句，参阅本章 Unit One 的讲解部分。
4. bow-pot 是方言，意为"花束"。姐姐 Pinkerton 给她纠正，要她用正规字 bouquet，可她又听成了 booky。译文试图用"一捆花儿""一束花儿"和"一簇花儿"再现原文的含义。
5. 这是个倒装句，形式结构严谨：Only when...or when..., and once, when..., was Miss Pinkerton Known to...。为顺应汉语行文习惯，译者将原句拆为两句，先点出事实（"难得写信"），再说明条件（"只限于……她才……"）。
6. 这句话被拆为两句。第一句大致相当于原句中定语从句所含信息，第二句大致相当于原文中 if..., it would be... 两个小句的内容。这样就形成了先交代背景情况，再进行评述的行文格局，顺应了汉语的习惯。
7. 这一自然段由两个长句组成，请注意观察译文的意合趋势（参阅本章 Unit One 的讲解部分）。特别是 whose industry and obedience 及 whose delightful sweetness of temper 这两个名词短语被译为汉语小句"她学习勤勉，性情和顺"及"她为人温柔可亲"。另外，还有一点也应特别留意：这里译的是一封书信，其文体正规，句式缜密，用词讲究，这在汉译时也应体现出来（参阅第三章 Unit One 的讲解部分）。
8. 这个定语从句在译文中被拆出，放在括号中，显然是为了使译文更为连贯。

讲解

一、英译汉中的意合趋势——时间序列问题

在本章 Unit One 的讲解部分，我们从语法结构的角度讨论了英汉转换中的意合趋势。汉语形式结构较弱，所以汉语词语、小句的排列就特别依重于意义、逻辑上的连贯。而在叙述动作、事件时，汉语一般是按自然时间顺序将小句排列成句的。英译汉时，若能顺应这一规律，则非常有利于汉语语句的组织、建构，使译文层次清晰，叙述流畅。请先来观察一个译例：

1. She found herself minus the leg one week after consulting a doctor about a persistent swelling she attributed to hard work and play in New York City—it was an inoperable bone tumor. While it saved her life, an ensuing year of chemotherapy reduced the once stunning model to a bald shadow of her former self.

   在询问医生为什么发生持续肿胀一个星期之后，她失去了一条腿。她曾认为是

由于工作劳累和在纽约市游玩造成的。这是一个不宜手术的骨瘤。虽然手术挽救了她的生命,但接踵而来的长达一年的化疗使这位一度艳丽销魂的时装模特儿秀发脱落、枯瘦如柴,尽失昔日风采。

可以看出,译文划线部分有些不够连贯。其症结在于:译者未能遵循汉语行文时所依照的时序原则。试按时间顺序重新翻译,看整段文字的连贯性有无改善:

她腿上出现了一个持续不消的肿块。原以为是在纽约又工作又游玩累的,看医生之后才知道是个骨瘤,而且不能手术切除。一周后,她便截了那条腿。

再观察下面译例,体会这些译者是如何按照自然时序组织译文的:

2. Eisenhower's purpose now was to split Germany in two by joining up with the Russians on the Elbe between Magdeburg and Desden.

艾森豪威尔现在的目的是要在马格德堡与德累斯顿之间的易北河上与俄国人会师,把德国一分为二。

3. Upon my entrance, Usher rose from a sofa on which he had been lying at full length, and greeted me with a vivacious warmth.

厄谢尔直挺挺地躺在沙发上,我一进去,他就站起来,热情地向我打招呼。

4. We had been dismayed at home while reading of the natural calamities that followed one another for three years after we left China in 1959.

自从我们在1959年离开后,中国连续三年遭到自然灾害。当我们在国内读到这方面消息时,心情颇为沉重。

5. One of the gunman's first victims was an elderly man who was struck by the truck and shot in the head as he attempted to get up.

在最先受害的人中有一位老人。他被卡车撞倒在地,正要站起来,歹徒朝他头部开了一枪。

6. At other houses the doors were slammed in my face, cutting short my politely and humbly couched request for something to eat.

我到了另外一些人家,谦恭有礼地暗示我想讨点东西吃,话还没讲完,大门就冲着我的脸砰的一声关上了。

7. I always had an idea that you were at least seven feet high, and was quite astonished at your return from India to find you no taller than myself.

我一向以为你至少身高七英尺,后来你从印度回来,我发现你不过跟我一样高，真是意想不到。

8. There was a story that the present box had been made with some pieces of the box that had preceded it, the one that had been constructed when the first people settled down to make a village here.

据说以前那只箱子是首批村民来这里定居建村时做的，而目前这只箱子则是用它的一些木材制成的。

9. Last year France's attention was riveted on the plight of 48 families who camped out for five months on the Place de la Reunion after being evicted from apartments, many of which had no running water.

去年，有48户人家被从其中许多连自来水都没有的公寓中赶出来，在协和广场露宿了五个月，他们的境遇引起了法国全国的密切关注。

10. It was she who had recommended him to go to Mr. Aylmer's when, on the first morning of his residence in Putney, he had demanded, "Any decent tobacconist's in this happy region?"

在普特尼镇住下后的第一个早晨，他曾经问她"这可爱的地方有像样的烟草店吗？"当时就是她推荐自己去艾尔默烟草店的。

11. It shows what effect the times were having of me when I say that I saw myself confidently dubbed "Mr. Delirium Tremens Twain" in the next issue of that journal without a pang—notwithstanding I knew that with monotonous fidelity the paper would go on calling me so to the very end.

这家报纸第二天大胆地授予我"酗酒狂吐温先生"的称号，而且我明白它会一个劲地永远这样称呼下去，但是，我当时看了竟无动于衷，现在想来，足见这种时势对我起了多大的影响。

12. In the first months of school, Levine got 53 e-mail missives from Erin, who drops her mom a few chatty lines whenever she is near a terminal.

在埃林上学的头两个月，每当在计算机终端附近时，她就去打上几行字跟母亲聊天。这段时间莱文共收到埃林的53封电子邮件。

13. She (Florence) was determined to pluck out of Hardy's mind the things said in the derogatory diary that Emma had kept about her husband (Hardy), and which he (Hardy) destroyed after her (Emma's) death.

埃玛生前记过一本诋毁丈夫声誉的日记，她死后哈代已把日记毁掉。弗罗伦斯决心要把日记内容也从哈代头脑中清除掉。（埃玛和弗罗伦斯分别为哈代的第一任和第二任妻子。）

14. James Brindley of Staffordshire started his self-made career in 1733 by working at mill wheels, at the age of 17, having been born poor in a village.

斯塔福郡的詹姆斯·布林德雷出身于一个贫苦的农村家庭；1773年，他17岁，就着手改良磨坊的车轮，从而开始了他那自我奋斗的生涯。

从上述译例可以看出，在将英语的信息进行重新组织的过程中，自然时间顺序不失为一个可行的参照原则。汉语由于缺乏形式构句手段，一般是按照某些具体的概念原则把句法单位组织在一起的。叙事时的时间顺序原则只是其中之一。

二、英译汉中的意合趋势——叙事和描写的分立

除时间顺序原则之外，汉语叙事时还常常把叙事和背景描写的语句分开，而不像英语那样描写性词语或小句只是句中的从属成分。如注释2所涉及的句子就是这样的。再看几个译例：

1. Following him down the musty corridor of the gloomy French hotel where Ausable had a room, Fowler felt disappointed.

这个句子含有两个动作：following 和 felt，musty 和 gloomy French 等词语则是描写这家旅馆的。试比较下面两种译文：

[a] 福勒跟着奥萨布尔走过他租了一个房间的阴暗的法国旅馆的发霉的走廊，感到十分失望。
[b] 奥萨布尔住在一家阴暗的法国旅馆里，旅馆的通道中充满发霉气味。福勒跟着他走过通道，感到很失望。

译文 [b] 先交代背景情况，然后才叙述事件，显然比译文 [a] 更符合汉语的行文习惯。再看下面一些译例，注意描述部分（划线部分）被分立的情况：

2. With wife Michelle, daughters Sasha and Malia and his White House retinue in tow, Mr. Obama struck out into the wilderness on the third day of a four-day tour through western mountain states aimed at defending his health care reform bid.

奥巴马此次西部山区之旅为期四天，主要目的是为他的医疗改革方案进行辩护。在整个行程的第三天，奥巴马和妻子米歇尔，女儿萨莎和玛丽娅以及他的白宫随从人员忙里偷闲，游览了西部荒野。

原文的划线部分被译为译文的第一句，交代了奥巴马此行的背景情况，第二句

再说他有什么活动。

3. The boy and the woman were already seated by a spread table-cloth when the man came down to them, dressed in his business suit and vest and tie and hat as if he expected to meet someone along the way.

等到男人走过来时，女人和孩子早已挨着地上铺开的桌布边坐好了。男人身穿上班的套装和背心，系着领带，戴着帽子，似乎估计路上会遇到什么人似的。

4. Gerald Ford was walking through a group of several hundred admirers in a pleasant, sunlit park in front of the California State Capitol at Sacramento, shaking hands with people in his amiable, relaxed way.

萨克拉门托的州议会大厦前的公园里，阳光普照，景色宜人，几百位杰拉尔德·福特的支持者聚集在那里。福特穿过人群，像以往那样平易近人、轻松愉快地同人们握手。

5. There was a troubled frown on his weather-beaten face, which had been disfigured by scars from a highway accident in which Rosealie's parents had been killed.

他心事重重，双眉紧锁，饱经风霜的脸上疤痕累累，显得很难看。这伤疤是一次车祸留下的，罗莎莉小姐的双亲就死于那次事故。

6. The noise of an air-raid siren, lugubrious and seeming to spring from pain, as if all the misery and indecision in the city had been given voice, cut her off.

一阵空袭警报打断了她的话。凄凉的警报声像是由于疼痛而发出的悲号，似乎这个灾难重重、动乱不安的城市也长上了嗓门。

7. As Natalie turned from the window, her eyes caught a gleam from the topaz eyes of the tiger in the hallway.

纳塔莉从窗口转过身，一双眼睛正瞥见放在过道里的老虎，那一对透明晶亮的黄玉眼睛闪烁着光芒。

8. The desire to move about unknown in the well-clad world, the world of the frequenters of costly hotels, the world to which he was accustomed, had overtaken him. Moreover, he felt hungry. Hence he had descended to the famous restaurant.

这是个衣冠华丽的世界，是豪华饭店常客们的世界，也是他所熟悉的世界。他极想在这个世界里默默无闻地来往,再说,他也饿了,于是便下楼来到这家著名的餐厅。

9. During the whole of a dull, dark, and soundless day in the autumn of the year, when the clouds hung oppressively low in the heavens, I had been passing alone, on horseback, through a singularly dreary tract of country.

是年秋天某日,天气阴沉,昏暗而又寂静,云层低压,令人窒息。整整一天,我独自一人策马行进,穿过一条异常沉闷的乡间小路。

10. In the winter of 1897, James Lecky, exchequer clerk from Ireland, and privately interested in phonetics, keyboard temperament, and Gaelic, all of which subjects he imposed on me, dragged me to a meeting of a debating society called The Zetetical: a junior copy of the once well-known Dialectical Society founded to discuss John Stuart Mill's Essay on Liberty when that was new.

1879年的冬天,詹姆斯·莱基拉我去参加一次辩论会。莱基是爱尔兰人,在财政部门当职员,有空喜欢研究语音,练习弹琴,学习盖尔语,他还硬让我也学这些东西。这次他带我去参加的辩论会是一个名叫"探索学会"的团体举办的。当年约翰·斯图尔特·米尔的文章《论自由》刚刚发表的时候,成立过一个"辩证学会"来讨论这篇文章,这个学会曾名噪一时,探索学会就是仿照这个学会建立起来的,只是没有它那么有名罢了。

11. In a little red schoolhouse at Reims, where Eisenhower had made his headquarters, Germany surrendered unconditionally at 2:41 on the morning of May 7, 1945.

1945年5月7日凌晨两点四十一分,在艾森豪威尔司令部所在的莱姆斯的一所学校里,德国无条件投降了。这所学校不大,房子是红色的。

12. As I sat down on that hot and humid evening, there seemed to be no solutions to the problems thrashing around in my brain.

黄昏时分,既闷热,又潮湿,我坐下来,满脑子翻腾起伏的问题似乎找不到解决办法。

The Page Turner (Excerpts)

Lynne Sharon Schwartz

[1]　The page turner appears from the wings and walks onstage, into the light, a few seconds after the pianist and cellist, just as the welcoming applause begins to wane.[1] By her precise timing the page turner acknowledges, not so much humbly as serenely, lucidly, that the applause is not meant for her: She has no intention of appropriating any part of the welcome.[2] She is onstage merely to serve a purpose, a worthy purpose even if a bit absurd—a concession, amid the coming glories, to the limitations of matter and of spirit. Precision of timing, it goes without saying, is the most important attribute of a page turner. Also important is unobtrusiveness.

[2]　But strive though she may to be unobtrusive, to dim or diminish her radiance in ways known only to herself, the page turner cannot render herself invisible, and so her sudden appearance onstage is as exciting as the appearance of the musicians; it gives the audience an unanticipated stab of pleasure. The page turner is golden-tressed—yes, "tresses" is the word for the mass of hair rippling down her back, hair that emits light like a shower of fine sparkles diffusing into the glow of the stage lights.[3] She is young and tall, younger and taller than either of the musicians, who are squarish, unprepossessing middle-aged men. She wears black, a suitable choice for one who should be unobtrusive. Yet the arresting manner in which her black clothes shelter her flesh, flesh that seems molded like clay and yields to the fabric with a certain playful, even droll resistance, defies unobtrusiveness.[4] Her black long-sleeved knit shirt reaches just below her waist, and the fabric of her perfectly fitting black slacks stirs gently around her narrow hips and thighs. Beyond the hem of her slacks can be glimpsed her shiny, but not too conspicuously shiny, black boots with a thick two-inch heel.[5] Her face is heart-shaped, like the illustrations of princesses in fairy tales. The skin of her face and neck and hands, the only visible skin, is pale, an off-white like heavy cream or the best butter.[6] Her lips are painted magenta.[7]

[3]　In the waiting hush, the page turner lowers her body onto a chair to the left and slightly behind the pianist's seat, the fabric of her slacks adjusting around her recalcitrant hips, the hem rising a trifle to reveal more of her boots.[8] She folds her white hands patiently in her lap like lilies resting on the surface of a dark pond and fixes her eyes on the sheets of music on the rack, her body calm but alert for the moment when she must perform her task.

[4]　After the musicians' usual tics and fussing, the pianist's last-minute swipes at face and hair, the cellist's slow and fastidious tuning of his instrument, his nervous flicking of his jacket away from his body as if to let his torso breathe, the music begins.[9] The pager turner, utterly still, waits. Very soon, she rises soundlessly and leans forward—and at this instant, with the right side of her upper body leaning over the pianist,[10] the audience imagines him, feels him, inhaling the fragrance of her breast and arm, of her cascading hair; they imagine she exudes a delicate scent, lightly alluring but not so alluring as to distract the pianist, not more alluring than the music he plays.

[5]　She stays poised briefly in that leaning position until with a swift movement, almost a surprise yet unsurprising, she reaches her hand over to the right-hand page. The upper corner of the page is already turned down, suggesting that the page turner has prepared the music in advance, has in her patient, able manner (more like a lady in waiting, really, than an idle fairy-tale princess), folded down all the necessary corners so that she need not fumble when the moment arrives. At the pianist's barely perceptible nod, she propels the page in the blink of an eye through its small leftward arc and smooths it flat, then seats herself, her body drifting lightly yet firmly, purposefully, down to the chair. Once again the edge of her short shirt sinks into her waist and the folds of her slacks reassemble beguilingly over her hips; the hem of her slacks rises to reveal more of her shiny boots. With her back straight, her seated body making a slender black L shape, once again she waits with hands folded, and very soon rises, quite silently, to perform the same set of movements. Soon this becomes a ritual, expected and hypnotic, changeless and evocative.

参考译文

翻乐谱的女孩

琳恩·沙伦·施瓦茨

[1] 翻乐谱的女孩出现在舞台侧翼，走上台来，比钢琴手与大提琴手稍晚几秒，恰在欢迎的掌声开始减弱时，走进灯光。时间把握得正好，她想表明，掌声并非为她所起，她也无意沾光——这与其说是谦卑，倒不如说是一种沉静和清醒。她只为一项使命而来，一项很有价值却稍显荒唐的使命——在即将来临的辉煌之中，服从于物质和精神的双重限制。把时间掐捏到正好，不用说，是乐谱翻页员最重要的特质。同样重要的是：不能喧宾夺主。

[2] 尽管翻谱女孩竭力表现得低调，用她独有的方式淡化自身的光彩，却无法让观众对她视而不见。她的兀然登场，与两位音乐家的亮相一样令人兴奋，观众意想不到地一阵喜悦。金色长发，波浪般垂到肩头，闪闪烁烁，阵阵柔光，漫然融入舞台灯光的辉煌。比起两位身材魁梧、相貌平平的中年演奏家，她是那么年轻，身材又是那么修长。她一身黑衣，对一个无意张扬的人来说，黑色太合适了。然而，她的肌肤在黑衣下透出一种诱人的气质，想不去注目都不行：她的身体仿佛就是依服装线条而塑成，却又调皮地，甚至滑稽地对抗着织物的裹挟。黑色长袖针织衫刚到腰下，裁剪合体的黑色便裤，随着紧致的臀部和大腿的活动微微颤抖。裤脚下，可以瞥见一双闪闪发光但又不过分惹眼的黑色皮靴，粗粗的高跟，足有两英寸。她的心形脸庞，恰如童话插图中的公主。没被黑色裹住的只有脸、颈和双手，肤色白净，像纯奶油般细腻。双唇上轻涂两抹微微带紫的红色唇膏。

[3] 在等待的寂静中，翻谱女孩在钢琴家左侧稍后的一把椅子上坐下，长裤紧裹着她丰满坚实的腰胯，有的地方被拉紧，有的地方被挤皱。裤脚向上一提，靴子露出来的就更多了。她耐心地将双手重叠，放在腿间，真像睡莲小憩在暗色的池塘上。她双眼注视着谱架上的乐谱，身体平静而警觉，等待着必须完成自己使命的时刻。

[4] 像往常一样，演奏前乐手们总要这里动动，那里摸摸：钢琴手最后用手在脸上和头上一掠；提琴手细心稳重地调调音准，然后紧张地把外衣向外拽了一下，似乎这样身体呼吸就更顺畅了。之后，音乐开始了。翻乐谱的小姑娘一动不动，静静地等着。过了一小会，她无声地站起来，俯身向前，身体右侧靠向钢琴手。就在此时，观众开始了遐想：觉得乐师一定呼吸到了姑娘酥胸玉臂和如瀑长发散发的幽香。

他们想象着，姑娘的玉体香气习习，虽说诱人，却又不至于使演奏者分神，毕竟乐曲才是他的最大关注。

[5]　女孩俯身静候，不一会，只见她迅速地把手伸向乐谱的右面一页，动作有点蓦然，但绝不会惊到观众。页面上角已经打了折，这说明她事先做过准备，已经把该翻的页码都耐心而干练地折好了，省得临时再翻找。（看来，她更像是宫廷侍女，而不是无所事事的神话公主。）在钢琴手几乎不被人觉察的点头示意下，小姑娘眨眼间就将页面向左划过一个小小的弧形翻了过去，又用手抚平。然后身体一挪，轻轻地，却又是果断有力地坐回自己的椅子。短上衣的下摆又复归腰下，裤子上的褶皱又诱人地在臀胯部聚集起来；裤脚又是向上一提，露出了更长的一段鞋帮。她腰背直挺，坐姿宛如一个优雅的大写字母 L。又是双手叠起端坐等候，又是不失时机地起身，无声无息地，重复着同样的动作。很快，这便成了一套仪式，让人期待，让人陶醉，虽一成不变，却令人神往。

注释

1. 此句中的动词 appears、walks 和介词 into 分别译成了"出现""走上（台来）"和"走进（灯光）"，构成由三个动词组成的句子。这种句式在汉语叙事语篇中十分常见。此处不宜将前两个动词合二为一，囫囵译成"……从台侧走上舞台……"。
2. has no intention of appropriating any part of the welcome 可直译为"她绝不想分享哪怕一丝一毫不属于她的掌声"，但这样稍嫌死板，"分享"一词也再现不出 appropriating 的意义。不如当作一个整体的翻译单位译出。
3. 作者说姑娘是"金色长发（golden-tressed）"，紧接着对 tresses 进行了解释，说"这个词正好来形容女孩的一头披肩长发"。英语中 tress 是个文雅（literary）词，但译成汉语"金色长发"，似乎没有什么要进一步说明了。所以译文不如舍弃对这个词语的解释，集中着墨描写女孩的长发为好。更需要说明的是，emit 和 diffuse 两个动词要力求翻译妥切。后者译为"漫然融入"，加了个副词以求更为准确；前者没有以动词机械应对，而是将其意融入四字结构构成的短句中，整句形成一个意合的流水句，以短句形式铺排开来，更合散文行文特点。
4. 主语 the arresting manner in which her black clothes shelter her flesh 中的动词 shelter，孤立地看，可能会译为"裹住"之类，如："这身黑衣却以如此吸引人的气质裹住她的肌体"，这样翻译太呆板，也难以尽意。建议将其作为一个整体（一个翻译单位），诱发想象，然后再将所得画面用汉语重新表述出来。同位语部分（flesh that...）拆出译成一句，seems molded like clay and yields to the fabric with a certain... resistance 中的一个动词和两个有动态倾向的词语，同样宜先在脑中构想出画面，然后用汉语重述。句中的谓语部分，先于同位语部分译出，且译为汉语的无主句。

5. 介词短语 with a thick two-inch heel 被拆开译出，比"带着厚厚的两英寸高跟"自然达意。
6. 不能译为"唯一没有被黑色裹住的脸、颈和双手"，因为这已经是三个部位了，并非"唯一"。an off-white like heavy cream or the best butter 的译文省去了后面的喻体，并稍作调整以适应汉语描写习惯。
7. 这个短句的译文有意加长了一些，以避免行文突兀，戛然而止。试比较：双唇则抹成紫红。
8. 此句中 the fabric... 和 the hem... 是两个独立主格结构，英译时均拆译成小句（参阅本章 Unit One 的讲解部分）。注意，前者的表达要尽量顺应汉语描写习惯，如译为"裤子也随之适应着她那不驯服的臀部"，则显生硬，也不尽意。不如换角度表述（参阅第三章 Unit Six 的讲解部分），另外还要注意此处和 the folds of her slacks reassemble beguilingly over her hips 的呼应。
9. 句中 tics and fussing、swipes、tuning、flicking 都具有动态意义，翻译时均以动词应对，注意调动自己的形象思维能力，译出画面而不拘于原文文字表层。
10. 句中 rises 和 leans 都是动词，leaning 是动态词，这三者都译为动词，构成汉语常见的动词句。

 讲解

动词的翻译

本单元原文选自 *The Beat American Essays 1998*，文章以细腻的笔触描绘了翻乐谱的女孩，从出场到谢幕整个钢琴演奏过程中的举止、动作、神态，人物特点鲜明，惟妙惟肖。原文较长，本单元只摘选了开头的几个自然段，借以探讨动词的翻译问题。

动词是叙事的关键之关键，对英语中的动词要理解透彻，对译文中要使用的动词要运用准确、得体。"准确"即要再现原文的动态，"得体"则是要符合汉语叙事的习惯。

译词要将这个词放在句子中理解，译句子要将这个句子放在段落中理解，译段落要将这个段落放在全篇中去理解，译全篇则要将整个语篇放在文化大背景中去理解，这就是语篇意识。语篇和语境密不可分，相互给予、厘定和丰富各自的意义。

译一个动词，首先不要将它看成一个孤立的词，要看它的搭配、上下文和使用的语境。注释 2、4、8 都涉及动词的翻译单位问题，这个翻译单位往往不是一个词或词组，而至少是一个小句。

其次，不要以为只有动词才描述动作，分词、介词、独立主格结构都具有动态描述的功能（可称之为动态词），应捕捉其动态形象，汉译以动词应对（如注释 9、

10 所示)。

第三，理解原文所描述的一个动作，要运用自己的想象力，这时我们翻译的就不再是一个词语，而是完整的动态形象了（如注释 8 所示），译文的任务就是要把这个形象再现出来。

第四，要学会运用汉语中的动词语段。汉语语法学者在对汉语句型进行分类时提出动向句和名向句（申小龙，2004）。动向句就是以动词或动词短语为要素线性展开的句子。申小龙将其分为二段句、三段句，等等。如三段句：晚上带点饭菜回家，放在炉子上热一热，实在怕费时就吃点方便面。不妨看一看下面摘自《孔乙己》和莫言的《奇遇》中的两个段落：

我从十二岁起，便在镇口的咸亨酒店里当伙计，掌柜说，我样子太傻，怕侍候不了长衫主顾，就在外面做点事罢。外面的短衣主顾，虽然容易说话，但唠唠叨叨缠夹不清的也很不少。他们往往要亲眼看着黄酒从坛子里舀出，看过壶子底里有水没有，又亲看将壶子放在热水里，然后放心：在这严重监督下，羼水也很为难。所以过了几天，掌柜又说我干不了这事。幸亏荐头的情面大，辞退不得，便改为专管温酒的一种无聊职务了。（鲁迅：《孔乙己》）

自然是一路无事。临近村头时，天已黎明，红日将出未出时，东边天上一片红晕，村里的雄鸡喔喔地叫着，一派安宁景象。回头望来路，庄稼是庄稼道路是道路，想起这一路的惊惧，感到自己十分愚蠢可笑。（莫言：《奇遇》）

我们看到，汉语叙事是如何用动词语段的铺排来完成的：施事者不一定以主语形式出现，从语境中可理解就行；点出一个主题，接下来就可以一段一段进行评说，言尽句止。这些行文特色正是译文写作过程中需要发扬的地方。

下面选择一些典型的译例，综合讨论一下动词的翻译问题。

1. In the second day of the voyage they came to the highlands. It was the latter part of a calm, sultry day, that they floated gently with the tide between these stern mountains. There was that perfect quiet which prevails over nature in the languor of summer heat; the turning of a plank, or the accidental falling of an oar on deck was echoed from the mountain side and reverberated along the shores; and if by chance the captain gave a shout of command, there were airy tongues that mocked it from every cliff.

航行次日，他们到达了高原地区。时值一个平静闷热的下午，他们在一座座岿然不动的大山之间，随着潮水轻轻漂浮。在令人困倦的炎热夏季，大自然宁静无比。转动一块木板，或者浆意外落到甲板上，山边和岸边都会发出回响。假如船长偶尔大声发出指令，每座悬崖峭壁也会传来飘忽的回音。

原文划线的词语都需要进一步推敲，尤其是动（态）词。echoed 和 reverberated 表述的是两个不同的动态过程，不宜笼统地表达为"山边和岸边都会发出回响"，对 mocked 的词义也不应囫囵吞枣。下面改译试图将动词的意义再现得更准确一些：

　　航行次日，他们到达了高原地区。那是个平静闷热的下午，他们在一座座巍峨的山峰之间，随着潮水平稳地航行。在炎炎夏日的慵懒中，大自然一片宁静。翻动一块木板，或者船桨意外落到甲板上，都有回音从山坡上传下来，又沿着海岸震荡开去。如果偶尔船长大声发出什么指令，那每座悬崖峭壁都会传来飘忽的模仿声。

2. When the infant had taken its fill the young mother sat it upright in her lap, and looking into the far distance dandled it with a gloomy indifference that was almost dislike; then all of a sudden she fell to violently kissing it some dozens of times, as if she could never leave off, the child crying at the vehemence of an onset which strangely combined passionateness with contempt.

　　当婴孩吃足了奶之后，那位年轻的母亲让婴孩坐直在自己腿上，自己的眼睛瞧着远方，带着一种几乎算成憎恨的阴郁的冷漠，拨弄着婴孩；接着，她突然不顾轻重地把婴孩亲吻了几十遍，仿佛永远亲不够似的，孩子经不住由疼爱和鄙夷奇特结合起来的猛烈进攻，哇地哭了起来。

　　上面译文中，连词"当……之后"以及代词"自己"完全可以省去。动词"拨弄"欠妥，末尾"孩子经不住……猛烈进攻"翻译腔十足，可以改进。试比较下面改译，留心动词句段的运用。

　　婴儿吃饱了，那位年轻的母亲就把他放在大腿上，让他坐正了，用膝头颠着他玩，眼睛却望着远方，脸色既忧郁又冷淡，差不多是憎恶的样子；过了一会，她突然伏下脸，在婴儿的脸上没轻没重地亲了几十下，仿佛永远也亲不够。这阵猛烈的亲吻，疼爱里面奇怪地混合着鄙夷，孩子被弄得大声哭了起来。

3. "Stop thief! Stop thief!" There is a passion for hunting something deeply implanted in the human breast. One wretched breathless child, panting with exhaustion, terror in his looks, agony in his eye, large drops of perspiration streaming down his face, strains every nerve to make head upon his pursuers.

　　"抓扒手！抓扒手！"兜捕围攻某个目标，这种癖好在人类心中是根深蒂固的。一个可怜的孩子，累得上气不接下气，神情充满恐惧，目光溢出痛苦，大颗大颗的汗珠从脸上直往下淌，每一根神经都绷得紧紧的，为的是摆脱追捕的人群。（荣如德译）

注意译文如何将划线的四个从属成分都译为动词短语铺排开来的。

下面几例出自语言学家、翻译家吕叔湘之译笔：

4. Father got holes in his socks even oftener than we boys did in our stockings. He had long athletic toes, and when he lay stretched out on his sofa reading and smoking, or absorbed in talking to anyone, these toes would begin stretching and wiggling in a curious way by themselves, as though they were seizing on this chance to live a life of their own. I often stared in fascination at their leisurely twistings and turnings, when I should have been listening to Father's instructions about far different matters. Soon one and then the other slipper would fall off, always to Father's surprise, but without interrupting his talk, and a little later his busy great toe would peer out at me through a new hole in his sock.

父亲的袜子比我们孩子们的更容易长窟窿。父亲的脚指头长而好运动，每逢他靠在沙发上，看着书，抽着烟，或是专心和人说着话，这些脚指头就自动地开始欠伸和扭动，仿佛抓住了一个自由地生活一番的机会似的。我常常出神地看它们从容不迫地扭来转去，父亲对我说的是些什么全然没有听见。一会儿，父亲的拖鞋落了下来，一只，两只，常常叫他瞿然一下，但是不足以打断他的谈锋；再过这么一会儿，他的忙碌的大脚指头儿就会在他的袜子上钻了一个新的窟窿出来朝我偷看。

got holes 译为"长窟窿"，lay stretched out 译为"靠在沙发上"，以及 peer at me through a new hole 中的 through 译为动词"钻了一个新的窟窿出来朝我偷看"，用词十分精妙，正好符合原文诙谐、活泼的语调。还要特别注意译者对 ing 分词的翻译，使其所描述的动态跃然纸上。

5. Father's heavily starched shirts too, were a problem. When he put one on, he pulled it down over his head, and thrust his arms blindly out right and left in a hunt for the sleeves. A new shirt was strong enough to survive these strains without splitting, but life with Father rapidly weakened it, and the first thing he knew he would hear it beginning to tear. That disgusted him. He hated any evidence of weakness, either in people or things.

父亲的浆得挺硬的衬衫也是一个问题。父亲穿衬衫的时候，先往头上套，然后两只胳臂一左一右盲目地冲刺，寻找那两只袖子。一件新衬衫自然结结实实，经得起这一番冲杀，可是在父亲手里过日子，不久就衰弱了，开始裂缝。这叫父亲生气。他最恨软弱的行迹，无论是见之于人还是见之于物。

　　此例可突出显示汉语叙事中动词句的运用。原文划线部分第 1 句将动词和动态词（in a hunt for the sleeves）依次译为动词语段铺排开来，准确生动地再现了原文描述的一系列动作。试比较：父亲那浆洗过头的衬衫也是个麻烦。当他穿衬衫时，他要将衬衫从头上罩下来，然后伸出双手去四处摸索着寻找袖子。原文划线部分第 2 句注意译者如何将 life with Father 译出其动态"在父亲手里过日子"，还有对 the first thing he knew he would hear it beginning to tear 的简略化处理。试比较：一件新衬衫能禁得起这样的拉力，但是父亲的常年穿着已使这种抗拉能力变得非常差了。而且他知道的第一件事情是他听到了衬衫开始撕破的声音。哪种译文更符合汉语叙事模式呢？

6.　The contrariness of the needle and the limp obstinacy of the thread made him swear. He stuck the needle in the sofa while he wet his fingers and stiffened the thread again. When he came to take up his needle, it had disappeared. He felt around everywhere for it. He got up, holding fast to his thread, and turned around, facing the sofa to see where it was hiding. This jerked the spool off onto the floor, where it rolled away and unwound.

　　针的顽梗，线的消极抵抗，闹得父亲咒骂连声。他把针插在沙发上，重新在指头上蘸唾沫，捻线头。等他回过来取针的时候，针不见了。他的手到处摸索。他站起来，一只手捏紧了线头，转过身来对着沙发，看它躲到哪儿去了。这一来，把线轴扯得滚到地上，一路滚着一路把线放开。

　　看译者是如何翻译动词的：一个"闹"字比原文还要生动；stiffen the thread 译为"捻线头"，这正是地道的汉语说法；最后两个句子译为动词句，流畅自然，"把线……"和"一路滚着……"前面分别省去了"他"和"线轴"，正是汉语多省略的特征的体现。

Spring[1]

[1]   Springs are not always the same. In some years, April bursts upon our Virginia hills in one prodigious leap—and all the stage is filled at once, whole choruses of tulips, arabesques of forsythia, cadenzas of flowering plum. The trees grow leaves overnight.

[2]   In other years, spring tiptoes in. It pauses, overcome by shyness, like my grandchild at the door, peeping in, ducking out of sight, giggling in the hallway. "I know you're out there," I cry. "Come in!" and April slips into our arms.[2]

[3]   The dogwood bud, pale green, is inlaid with russet markings. Within the perfect cup a score of clustered seeds are nestled. One examines the bud in awe: Where were those seeds a month ago? The apples display their milliner's scraps of ivory silk, rose-tinged. All the sleeping things wake up—primrose, baby iris, blue phlox. The earth warms—you can smell it, feel it, crumble April in your hands[3].

[4]   The dark Blue Ridge Mountains in which I dwell, great-hipped, big-breasted, slumber on the western sky. And then they stretch and gradually awaken. A warm wind, soft as a girl's hair, moves sailboat clouds in gentle skies. The rains come—good rains to sleep by—and fields that were dun as oatmeal turn to pale green, then, to kelly green.

[5]   All this reminds me of a theme that runs through my head like a line of music. Its message is profoundly simple, and profoundly mysterious also: Life goes on. That is all there is to it. Everything that is, was; and everything that is, will be.

[6]   I am a newspaperman, not a preacher. I am embarrassed to write of "God's presence". God is off my beat. But one afternoon I was walking across the yard and stopped to pick up an acorn-one acorn, nut brown, glossy, cool to the touch; the crested top was milled and knurled like the knob on a safe. There was nothing unique about it. Thousands littered the grass.

[7]   I could not tell you what Paul of Tarsus encountered on that famous road to Damascus when the light shone suddenly around him, but I know what he felt. He was trembling, and filled with astonishment, and so was I that afternoon. The great chest-nut oak that towered above me had sprung from such an insignificant thing as this; and the oak contained within itself the generating power to seed whole forests. All was locked in this tiny, ingenious safe—the mystery, the glory, the grand design.

[8]   The overwhelming moment passed, but it returns. Once in February we were down on the hillside pulling up briars and honeysuckle roots. I dug with my hands through rotted leaves and crumbling moldy bark. And behold: at the bottom of the dead, decaying mass a wild rhizome was raising a green, impertinent shaft toward the unseen winter sun. I am not saying I found Divine Revelation. What I found, I think, was a wild iris.

[9]   The iris was doing something more than surviving. It was growing, exactly according to plan, responding to rhythms and forces that were old before man was young. And it was drawing its life from the dead leaves of long-gone winters. I covered this unquenchable rhizome, patted it with a spade, and told it to be patient: Spring would come.

[10] And that is part of this same, unremarkable theme: Spring does come. In the garden the rue anemones come marching out, bright as toy soldiers on their parapets of stone. The dogwoods float in casual clouds among the hills.

[11] This is the Resurrection time. That which was dead, or so it seemed, has come to life again—the stiff branch, supple; the brown earth, green. This is the miracle: There is no death; there is in truth eternal life.

[12] So, in the spring, we plunge shovels into the garden plot, turn under the dark compost, rake fine the crumbling clods, and press the inert seeds into orderly rows. These are the commonest routines. Who could find excitement here?

[13] But look! The rain falls, and the sun warms, and something happens. It is the germination process. Germ of what? Germ of life, germ inexplicable, germ of wonder. The dry seed ruptures and the green leaf uncurls. Here is a message that transcends the rites of any church or creed or organized religion. I would challenge any doubting Thomas[4] in my pea patch.

[14] Everywhere, spring brings the blessed reassurance that life goes on, that death is no more than a passing season. The plan never falters; the design never changes. It is all ordered. It has all been always ordered.

[15] Look to the rue anemone, if you will, or to the pea patch, or to the stubborn weed that thrusts its shoulders through a city street. This is how it was, is now, and ever shall be, the world without end. In the serene certainty of spring recurring, who can fear the distant fall?

参考译文

春

[1] 春天并非总是一模一样的。四月，有时不知怎地一跃，就来到了弗吉尼亚的山坡上——自然的大舞台上转眼到处生机勃勃。郁金香组成了大合唱，连翘展示出优美的舞姿，洋李奏起了华彩乐段。一夜之间，林木着装，绿叶瑟瑟。

[2] 四月有时又蹑手蹑脚，像我的小孙女一样，羞羞答答地倚在门外，向里探探头，一闪又不见了，只是在门厅里咯咯地笑。"我知道你在那儿藏着呢。"我喊道。"进来！"春天这才悄然跑进了我的怀抱。

[3] 山茱萸的蓓蕾，淡绿清雅，表面点缀着褐色斑痕，活像一只完美无缺的小杯，一撮撮种子，半隐半现地藏在里面。我敬畏地观察着这蓓蕾，暗自发问：一个月之前，这些种子在什么地方呢？苹果花开，展示出一片片染了玫瑰红的象牙色薄绸。一切冬眠的东西都在苏醒——美丽的樱草花，纤细的蝴蝶花，还有蓝色的草夹竹桃。大地开始变暖——这，你既可以嗅到，也可以触摸到——抓起一把泥土，四月便揉碎在你的手心里了。

[4] 黛色的兰岭山，那是我居住的地方，它像臀丰乳高的女郎，依然安睡在浩瀚的天幕之下。后来，她终于伸开懒腰，慢慢醒来了。一阵阵和煦的风，像少女的柔发，将帆船似的云朵吹送到温和的天空。下雨了——催人入睡的喜雨——像燕麦片粥一样微暗的原野，起初淡绿素雅，继而翠绿欲滴。

[5] 这使我想到一个话题，它像一首乐曲不断萦绕在我的脑际，平淡无奇，却又奥秘无穷：生命绵延不断。一切一切都在于此。任何事物，现在如此，以往如此，将来也必定仍然如此。

[6]　我是一个新闻工作者,并不是传道士。我决不会就"上帝的存在"而挥笔撰文,上帝不属于我工作的范围。一天下午,我在院里漫步,无意中停下来,拾起一颗橡子——那是一颗栗色的,光滑的,摸一摸凉凉爽爽的橡子。冠毛茸茸的顶部早已磨平,酷似保险箱的隆起球形旋钮。它没有丝毫出奇之处。成千上万颗这样的种子撒满了草地。

[7]　我不知道使徒保罗在通向大马士革的大道上,突然被圣光包围时看见了什么,但是我知道他的感觉如何。他大吃一惊,情不自禁地颤抖着;而那天下午,我也跟他一样。高耸入云的橡树拔地而起,它不正是从一颗如此这般微不足道的种子里迸发出来的吗?而橡树本身蕴藏着的生殖力足以孕育出一片又一片的橡树林。神秘的色彩,雄伟的气魄,壮观的形象,这一切一切,都封锁在这只微小而奇妙的保险箱内。

[8]　这种令人倾倒的时刻,逝去了还会再来。二月里的一天,我下山去拔石南和忍冬根。我把手伸进腐败的枯叶和碎树皮中去挖。看,在这层毫无生气的枯枝败叶底下,一棵根茎正朝着那看不见的冬日,伸出一个干劲十足的绿芽来。我不想把这说成是神的启示。我发现的大概不过是一株野生的蝴蝶花罢了。

[9]　这株蝴蝶花绝不仅仅是为了一己的生存而挣扎,它是在准确无误地按照自然发展进程而生长着,它是在响应那比人类启蒙时期还要古老的节奏与力量。它在从久久逝去的冬日的片片枯叶中奋力汲取生命。于是,我把这棵势不可当的幼芽重新埋好,再用铁锹拍了拍,让它稍安勿躁:春天一定会来的。

[10]　这个平凡主题又奏起了一章:春天来了。花园里芸香银莲,花团锦簇,像一列列光彩熠熠的小铅兵一样,整齐地排列在石墙头。山茱萸像无拘无束的云朵飘浮在山间。

[11]　这是万物复苏的时节。那些已经死去或貌似死去的东西都复活了——僵硬的枝条柔软起来,暗褐的大地泛起了绿色。这便是奇迹之所在。这里没有死亡,有的只是千真万确的永恒生命。

[12]　春天,我们用铁锹翻开园子里黑油油的沃土,打碎土块,把地面平整好了,再把那些毫无生气的豌豆种子成垅成行地播下去。这都是些平凡至极的劳作,这里有什么激情可言呢?

[13]　可是你瞧,雨下起来了,阳光也暖和起来了,接着,奇迹来了。这便是那萌芽的过程。什么样的萌芽?生命的萌芽,神秘的萌芽,奇迹的萌芽。干瘪的种子裂开

了，卷曲的绿叶伸展了。这里包含着一种信息，它胜过任何教会的仪式、任何教义、任何有组织的宗教。有谁不信，我的豌豆田可以打消他的怀疑。

[14]　春天处处带来赏心悦目的复苏景象，生命在继续，死亡不过是一个早已逝去的季节而已。大自然从不步履蹒跚，从不三心二意。一切都是有条不紊。一切一切，从来都是这么有条不紊。

[15]　如果愿意，你就去看一看吧！看一看芸香银莲，看一看无边的豌豆田，看一看顽强的小草——它们早已伸出叶尖，沿街铺展开去。这便是世界何以无止境的原因。过去如此，现在如此，将来也永远如此。春回大地，此时此刻，又有谁还惧怕那遥远的秋天呢？（宋德利译）

注释

1. 这是一篇散文，细腻的描写和真挚的情感交融在一起。译者不仅要译出基本信息——字面上的意思，还要译出原文的韵味。这就需要在选词、句式安排及形象化词语的运用上仔细琢磨，不仅要注意字、句上的局部效果，更要注意段落、篇章的整体效果。请将译文和原文仔细对照研读，加以品评和体味。
2. 文章前两段的主题是 Springs are not always the same。作者接着用两组形象生动地描绘出春天有时一跃而至，有时又悄然而来的情景。译者应充分发挥自己的形象思维能力，将原文的文字化为画面，再将这一幅幅画面用汉语加以表达。另外，第一段最后一句，译者用三个四字词组译出，节奏明快，符合该文的文体特点。
3. 在译 crumble April in your hands 时，译者显然运用形象思维，将原文含而未陈的一个细节在汉译中加以补充："抓起一把泥土……"。
4. doubting Thomas 语出《圣经》，意为：a person who habitually doubts，此处采取意译方法。

讲解

形象化语言及形象思维

　　形象化语言泛指明喻、暗喻、类比、拟人等修辞手段。它的作用是在读者头脑中引起鲜明的形象对比，将抽象化为具体，将无形变为有形，将遥远生疏的事物拉到读者眼前，变得显而易见，容易理解。它能增强文学描述的生动性和论说文的力度。

　　在形象化语言的翻译中，译者应该透过语义概念层，想象出原文所描述的形象,也就是要发挥自己的形象思维能力。形象化语言的翻译一般有两种对策。在译语读者可接受的情况下,可按原文形象译出;在读者接受有困难或很难接受的情况下,则可转换形象或译为非形象化语言。第一种对策如下列译例所示:

1. Habit is a cable: we weave a thread of it every day, and it becomes so strong that we cannot break it.

   习惯就像一条大绳索:每天只编上一小根细线,可一旦变粗了,我们便无法把它扯断。

2. Lazer light shines at a single wavelength, and all the light waves march together in step like soldiers on parade.

   激光以单一波长传播,而且所有光波齐步前进,宛如阅兵式上的士兵行列。

3. I sensed a wrongness around me, like an alarm clock that has gone off without being set.

   我觉得周围的气氛有些不对劲:就像一只闹钟,没上闹条就响了。

4. No man is an island, entire of itself; every man is a piece of the continent, a part of the main: if a clod be washed away by the sea, Europe is the less, as well as if a promontory were, as well as if a manor of thy friends or thine own were; any man's death diminishes me, because I am involved in mankind.

   谁也不是一座自成一体的岛屿;每一个人都是这片大陆的一块泥土,是大陆的一部分:这块土被海水冲走,就像一个岬角、或你友人的或你自己的庄园被冲走一样,都会使欧洲变小;无论谁死去都有损于我,因为我和整个人类息息相关。

5. Jos, a clumsy and timid horseman, did not look to advantage in the saddle. "Look at him, Amelia dear, driving into the parlour window. Such a bull in a china-shop I never saw."

   乔斯胆子小,骑术又拙,骑在鞍上老不大像样。"爱米丽亚,亲爱的,快看,他骑到人家客厅的窗子上去啦。我一辈子没见过这样儿,真正是大公牛到了瓷器店里去了。"

6. Old Marley was as dead as a door-nail. Mind! I don't mean to say that I know of my own knowledge what there is particularly dead about a doornail. I might have been inclined, myself, to regard a coffin-nail as the deadest piece of iron-mongery in the trade.

   老马莱是已死定,就像一根门钉钉死在门上那样了。注意我并不是说,钉死了的门钉有什么特别可说的。我自己倒认为棺材钉才是铁器行业中,钉得最死的东西。

以上各例均采取将原文形象直译的方法,不过有时候,源语读者所认可的形象在译语文化中却无法或很难被读者接受。这时就只能采取第二种对策,即转换形象或用非形象化语言意译。比如,同是 door-nail 这一形象,在下面译例中就采用了转换形象的方法。

7. "I should rather say not! In that connection hope is as dead as a doornail."

"我看没有希望!在这方面,希望已如石沉大海。"

8. In almost every case, all of the information they need to answer those questions is already available. But they have no idea how to find the needle in the haystack, how to distill it and how to make the judgements required to guide those corporations.

几乎在每一种情况下,回答这些问题所需的信息他们全有了,但是他们不知道怎样去大海捞针,怎样去提炼它,怎样做出指导公司所需的判断。

有时,转换形象很难做到,因为在译语中找不到相应的形象化词语。这种情况下则可采取意译的方法。如:

9. My opinion of you is that no man knows better than you when to speak and when others to speak for you; when to make scenes and threaten resignation; and when to be as cool as a cucumber.

我对你的看法是:没有人比你更懂得什么时候该开口,什么时候该由别人替你开口;什么时候该闹起来,以辞职相威胁;什么时候又该保持冷静。

10. You're always shoving it down my throat that you're the one with the job, but it's not so wonderful. I'm working far harder than you.

你总是强使我相信你工作干得顶出色,其实却没什么了不起。我干起活来比你勤快得多。

11. "I'll write," I promise solemnly. Alas, my good intentions produce only imagined letters never embraced by paper, never kissed by stamps.

"我一定写信。"我郑重地答应说。可是,哎呀!我的良好愿望只是停留在想象中,我的信从未写到纸上,也从未盖上过邮戳。

这样翻译,虽然转换了原文的形象,但基本信息未变。翻译实践中切忌只顾保留原文形象却造成译文接受障碍的做法。比如 A fine old gentleman with a face as red as a rose. 如译成"一位漂亮的老绅士，脸色红得像一朵玫瑰"，恐怕很容易使中国读者联想起少女的形象。A thought struck him like a silver dagger. 如译成"有个想法像银白色的匕首一样触动了他"，也会使译语读者觉得不好理解。形象化词语的翻译关键在于"形象化"。源语作者用形象来表达自己的思想，译者要调动自己的形象思维去理解原文的寓意，同时又要考虑译语读者对原文形象的接受程度，以决定采取何种翻译方法。

其实，译者形象思维的运用不仅限于对形象化词语的翻译。对某些动作、情景的描述文字，译者同样需要运用形象思维去构想出原文描述的形象，然后用译文再现于译语读者面前。请观察下面译例：

12. Keeping his body twisted so that his gun still covered the fat man and his guest, the man at the window grasped the frame with his free hand to support himself as he rested his weight on one thigh. Then he swung his other leg up over the window sill.

跨坐在窗台上的男子把全身重量都压在一条大腿上，一面用没拿枪的手抓住窗框保持身体平衡，一面扭着身子用枪继续逼着胖子和他的客人。接着他提起另一条腿，让它转过去并且跨过窗台。

这段文字中并没使用形象化词语，却给我们勾勒出了一个个动态画面。它描写的是一个入户行窃的歹徒用枪逼迫主人又夺窗而逃的一系列动作。很明显，最后一句译得很别扭。其症结恐怕不只是用词造句的问题，而是译者只从文字到文字，从概念到概念，忽视了形象思维的重要性。其实原文最后一句的动作形象很容易加以想象，甚至可以亲自模仿一下：接着他另一条腿向上一摆，便越过了窗台。

13. Tess, having quickly eaten her own meal, beckoned to her eldest sister to come and take away the baby, fastened her dress, put on the buff gloves again, and stooped anew to draw a bond from the last completed sheaf for the tying of the next.

[a] 苔丝已经急忙吃完了饭，把她大妹妹叫过来，接走了小孩，自己把衣服系紧了，又戴上了黄皮手套，重新弯下腰去，走到刚才一束好的那一抱麦子跟前，抽出做绳子用的麦穗，去捆另一抱麦子。

[b] 苔丝快速吃完自己的午饭，招呼大妹妹走到身边，抱走婴孩，接着她系紧裙子，又戴上浅黄色皮革手套，弯下腰，又从先前捆好的麦捆中抽出麦秸，做成草索，去捆另外一捆了。

译文 [b] 比译文 [a] 多了一个动作环节——"做成草索"，因此更容易在读者头脑中引发连贯的画面。这恐怕是译者运用形象思维构想出苔丝这一系列动作,然后再诉诸文字表达的结果。

翻译描述性文字的过程中适当地运用和发挥译者的想象能力,是非常有益的。著名翻译家杨苡曾撰文谈过她是如何译出 Wuthering Heights 一书的书名的:一夜疾风呼啸,雨点敲窗,宛如凯瑟琳在窗外哭泣。她住的房子外面本来就是片荒凉的花园。这时她把眼前的景物和小说中的描写融合在一起,想象着小说所描写的景象和氛围,感到自己仿佛置身于小说中约克郡旷野附近的那座古老房子里。突然,灵感从天而降——"呼啸山庄",书名译出来了。这时,对 Wuthering Heights 的翻译已不再是寻求相应的文字,而是寻求相应的形象,标题成了全书形象的凝缩。1982 年《译林》和《外国语》组织的全国首次文学翻译竞赛中名列榜首的姚远在谈成功经验时,几次提到运用形象思维解决难词难句翻译的问题。如在译 I gave him a back rub, marveling at the symmetrical knit of muscle, the organic tension. 一句时,译者感到不好用汉语表达,于是他便具体地想象出小伙子健美的倒三角形背部,将原句描写的形象再现为:我给他揉了会儿背,他那匀称的肌肉,紧绷绷的身板,真令人赞叹不已。

形象思维不仅有助于描述性文字的翻译,也可用于说明性文字的翻译。请对比下面译例中的两种译文:

14. Measuring lengths of a meter or so accurately has always been a problem to engineers. The conventional method is to take what are called length bars, that is, pieces of metal of fixed and accurate length—put them end-to-end and then make up the total length by adding slip gauges—slabs of metal of known thickness.

    [a] 精确测量一米左右的长度一直是工程师们面临的难题。传统的方法是使用量棒——一种有固定精确长度的金属棒。先把量棒首尾相接,然后加入量片(有固定厚度的金属片)补齐全部长度。

    [b] ……先把量棒沿着所要测量的长度首尾相接排列起来,在最后剩下的长度不到一个棒的情况下,用量片(有固定厚度的金属片)补齐。

译文 [b] 显然比译文 [a] 的描述效果好,原因很简单:译文 [a] 只是字面上的对译,而译文 [b] 的译者显然是先想象出测量的操作过程,再用汉语加以表述的。形象思维可展示一幅幅连续完整的画面,这就为译者视译文行文及表达的需要添加一些必要的细节提供了依据。这一点还可参阅注释 3。

Vanity Fair (Excerpt 2)

[1]   Although schoolmistresses' letters are to be trusted no more nor less than churchyard epitaphs; yet, as it sometimes happens that a person departs this life, who is really deserving of all the praises the stone-cutter carves over his bones; who is a good Christian, a good parent, child, wife, or husband;[1] who actually does leave a disconsolate family to mourn his loss; so in academies of the male and female sex it occurs every now and then, that the pupil is fully worthy of the praises bestowed by the disinterested instructor. Now, Miss Amelia Sedley was a young lady of this singular species; and deserved not only all that Miss Pinkerton said in her praise, but had many charming qualities which that pompous old Minerva of a woman[2] could not see, from the differences of rank and age between her pupil and herself.

[2]   For she could not only sing like a lark, or a Mrs. Billington, and dance like Hillisberg or Parisot, and embroider beautifully; and spell as well as a Dixonary itself; but she had such a kindly, smiling, tender, gentle, generous heart of her own,[3] as won the love of everybody who came near her, from Minerva herself down to the poor girl in the scullery, and the one-eyed tart-woman's daughter, who was permitted to vend her wares once a week to the young ladies in the Mall. She had twelve intimate and bosom friends out of the twenty-four young ladies. Even envious Miss Briggs never spoke ill of her: high and mighty Miss Saltre (Lord Dexter's granddaughter) allowed that her figure was genteel; and as for Miss Swartz, the rich woollyhaired mulatto from St. Kitt's,[4] on the day Amelia went away, she was in such a passion of tears, that they were obliged to send for Dr. Floss, and half tipsify her with salvolatile. Miss Pinkerton's attachment was, as may be supposed, from the high position and eminent virtues of that lady, calm and dignified; but Miss Jemima bad already whimpered several times at the idea of Amelia's departure; and, but for fear of her sister, would have gone off in downright hysterics, like the heiress (who paid double) of St. Kitt's. Such luxury of grief, however, is only allowed to parlour-boarders. Honest Jemima had all the bills, and the washing, and the mending, and the puddings, and the plate

and crockery, and the servants to superintend.[5] But why speak about her? It is probable that we shall not hear of her again from this moment to the end of time, and that when the great filigree iron gates are once closed on her, she and her awful sister will never issue therefrom into this little world of history.

[3]   But as we are to see a great deal of Amelia, there is no harm in saying, at the outset of our acquaintance, that she was a dear little creature, and a great mercy it is, both in life and in novels, which (and the latter especially) abound in villains of the most sombre sort, that we are to have for a constant companion, so guileless and goodnatured a person. As she is not a heroine, there is no need to describe her person; indeed I am afraid that her nose was rather short than otherwise, and her cheeks a great deal too round and red for a heroine; but her face blushed with rosy health, and her lips with the freshest of smiles, and she had a pair of eyes which sparkled with the brightest and honestest good-humour,[6] except indeed when they filled with tears, and that was a great deal too often; for the silly thing would cry over a dead canary-bird; or over a mouse, that the cat haply had seized upon, or over the end of a novel, were it ever so stupid; and as for saying an unkind word to her, were any persons hard-hearted enough to do so—why, so much the worse for them. Even Miss Pinkerton, that austere and god-like woman, ceased scolding her after the first time, and though she no more comprehended sensibility than she did Algebra, gave all masters and teachers particular orders to treat Miss Sedley with the utmost gentleness, as harsh treatment was injurious to her.

[4]   So that when the day of departure came, between her two customs of laughing and crying,[7] Miss Sedley was greatly puzzled how to act. She was glad to go home, and yet most woefully sad at leaving school. For three days before, little Laura Martin, the orphan, followed her about, like a little dog. She had to make and receive at least fourteen presents, —to make fourteen solemn promises of writing every week: "Send my letters under cover to my grandpapa, the Earl of Dexter," said Miss Saltire (who, by the way, was rather shabby): "Never mind the postage, but write every day, you dear darling," said the impetuous and woolly-headed, but generous and affectionate Miss Swartz[8] and the orphan little Laura Martin (who was just in round-hand), took her friend's hand and said, looking up in her face wistfully, "Amelia, when I write to you I shall call you Mamma." All which details, I

have no doubt, Jones, who reads this book at his Club, will pronounce to be excessively foolish, trivial, twaddling, and ultra-sentimental.[9] Yes; I can see Jones at this minute (rather flushed with his joint of mutton and half pint of wine), taking out his pencil and scoring under the words "foolish, twaddling", & c. and adding to them his own remark of "quite true". Well, he is a lofty man of genius, and admires the great and heroic in life and novels; and so had better take warning and go elsewhere.

参考译文

名利场（节选二）

[1] 　一般来说，校长的信和墓志铭一样靠不住。不过偶然也有几个死人当得起石匠刻在他们朽骨上的好话，真的是虔诚的教徒、慈爱的父母、孝顺的儿女、贤良的妻子、尽职的丈夫，他们家里的人也真的哀思绵绵地追悼他们。同样的，不论在男学校女学校，偶然也会有一两个学生当得起老师毫无私心的称赞。爱米丽亚·赛特笠小姐就是这种难能可贵的好人，平克顿小姐夸奖她的话，句句是真的。不但如此，她还有许多可爱的品质，不过这个自以为了不起的、像智慧女神一样的老婆子因为地位不同，年龄悬殊，看不出来罢了。

[2] 　她的歌喉比得上百灵鸟，或者可说比得上别灵顿太太，她的舞艺不亚于赫立斯白格或是巴利索脱。她花儿绣得好，拼法准确得和字典不相上下。除了这些不算，她心地厚道，性格温柔可人，器量又大，为人又乐观，所以上自智慧女神，下至可怜的洗碗小丫头，没一个人不爱她。那独眼的卖果子馅饼的女人有个女儿，每星期到学校里来卖一次果子馅饼，也爱她。二十四个同学里面，倒有十二个是她的心腹朋友。连妒忌心最重的白立格小姐都不说她的坏话；连自以为了不起的赛尔泰小姐（她是台克斯脱勋爵的孙女）也承认她的身段不错。还有位有钱的施瓦滋小姐，是从圣·葛脱来的半黑种，她那一头头发卷得就像羊毛；爱米丽亚离校那天她哭得死去活来，校里的人只好请了弗洛丝医生来，用嗅盐把她熏得半醉。平克顿小姐的感情是沉着而有节制的，我们从她崇高的地位和她过人的德行上可以推想出来，可是吉米玛小姐就不同，她想到要跟爱米丽亚分别，已经哼哼唧唧哭了好几回，若不是怕她姐姐生气，准会像圣·葛脱的女财主一样（她付双倍的学杂费），老是不客气地发起歇斯底里病来。可惜只有寄宿在校长家里的阔学生才有权利任性发泄哀痛，老实的吉米玛工作多着呢，她得管账，做布丁，指挥佣人，留心碗盏瓷器，还得负

责上上下下换洗缝补的事情。我们不必多提她了。从现在到最后结束，我们也不见得再听得到她的消息。那镂花的大铁门一关上，她和她那可怕的姐姐永远不会再到我们这小天地里来了。

[3] 我们以后还有好些机会和爱米丽亚见面，所以应该先介绍一下，让大家知道她是个招人疼的小女孩儿。我们能够老是跟这么天真和气的人做伴，真是好运气，因为不管在现实生活里面还是在小说里面——尤其在小说里面——可恶的坏蛋实在太多。她反正不是主角，所以我不必过多形容她的外貌。不瞒你说，我觉得她的鼻子不够长，脸蛋儿太红太圆，不大配做女主角。她脸色红润，显得很健康，嘴角卷着甜眯眯的笑容，明亮的眼睛里闪闪发光，流露出最真诚的快活，可惜她的眼睛里也常常装满了眼泪。因为她最爱哭，金丝雀死了，老鼠偶尔给猫逮住了，或是小说里最无聊的结局，都能叫这小傻瓜伤心。假如有硬心肠的小人责骂了她，那就活该他们倒霉。连女神一般严厉的平克顿小姐，骂过她一回之后，也没再骂第二回。在她看来，这种容易受感触的性子，正和代数一样难以捉摸，不过她居然叮嘱所有的教师，叫他们对赛特笠小姐特别温和，因为粗暴的手段对她只有害处。

[4] 赛特笠小姐既爱哭又爱笑，所以到了动身的一天不知怎么才好。她喜欢回家，又舍不得离校。没爹娘的罗拉·马丁连着三天像小狗似的跟在她后面。她至少收了十四份礼物，当然也得照样回十四份，还得郑重其事答应十四个朋友每星期写信给她们。赛尔泰小姐（顺便告诉你一声，她穿得很寒酸）说道："你写给我的信，叫我祖父台克斯脱勋爵转给我得了。"施瓦滋小姐说："别计较邮费，天天写信约我吧，宝贝儿。"这位头发活像羊毛的小姐感情容易冲动，可是器量大，待人也亲热。小孤儿罗拉·马丁（她刚会写直体字）拉着朋友的手，呆柯柯地瞧着她说："爱米丽亚，我写信给你的时候，就叫你妈妈。"琼斯在他的俱乐部里看这本书看到这些细节，一定会骂她们无聊透顶，琐碎，全是废话，而且异乎寻常的肉麻。我想象得出琼斯的样子，他刚吃过羊肉，喝了半品脱酒，脸上红喷喷的，拿起笔来在"无聊""废话"等字样底下画了道儿，另外加上几句，说他的批评"很准确"。他本来是个一等的天才，不论在小说里还是在生活中，只赏识伟大人物、英雄好汉的事迹，所以我这里先警告他，请他走开。（杨必译）

注释

1. 这个小句用了两个 good，后一个同时修饰 parent、child、wife、husband 四个名词。译者根据 good 一词和不同名词的搭配关系，巧妙地将其译成"虔诚""慈爱""孝顺""贤良""尽职"等具体形容词,使译文流畅自然。试想,如将 good 笼统地译为"好",则会出现下面这样呆板、艰涩的句子:真的是好教徒、好父母、子女、妻子或丈夫。

2. Minerva 是罗马神话中司智慧、技艺及发明的女神。这里的"Noun 1 + of +Noun 2"结构是一种"喻体 + of + 本体"的语义关系,也就是说名词 2 被比作名词 1。再如,Two more interesting visitors meanwhile arrived in the madhouse of the Fuehrer's bunker. 又有两位有趣的客人来到疯人院般的元首地下避弹室。

3. 这句话中修饰 heart 的形容词一共有五个,如果机械地一个个译成定语,就难免变成这样:她有如此厚道、乐观、温柔、文雅、慷慨的心肠。译文对这些形容词采取了灵活的译法,把"……的心肠"的偏正结构变为"她……"的主谓结构,使行文更为自然;还将形容词进行了重新组合和变通,kindly、tender 和 gentle 译为"心地厚道,性格温柔可人",generous 译为"器量又大",smiling 译为"为人乐观"。

4. mulatto,黑白混血儿。注意,这里的 as for 短语在译文中被拆译成句子。

5. 这句话的谓语部分(had...to superintend)有六个宾语,译文处理得十分流畅自然。

6. 此句中的 rosy、brightest 和 honestest 均是移就格(transferred epithet),也称为转移修饰语。移就格指的是用形容词修饰和限定与其在逻辑上具有不同属性的名词的修辞方法。这种修辞格英汉双语均有,但用法不尽相同。rosy health 译为"玫瑰色的健康"显然行不通,brightest and honestest good-humour 译为"最明亮、最诚实的好心境",也会使汉语读者不知所云,所以译文并未直译。

7. 注意 between... 这一短语在汉译中是如何表达的。参阅第三章 Unit Six 的讲解部分。

8. 这里一共有四个形容词修饰 Miss Swartz,译文处理得很灵活。

9. 首先注意句末的四个形容词,译者译得很准确、自然。其次注意全句的语法结构,正常语序应为:Jones will pronounce all which details to be excessively foolish...。

 讲解

形容词的翻译

形容词在叙事、描写文体中出现频率颇高。它可作定语修饰名词,也可作表语。作定语时常常置于名词之前,但也可能出现在其后。如:At their edges rose the virgin forests, dark and cool even in the hottest noons, mysterious, a little sinister...(在这些田地的边缘上,是一片原始森林。即使在最热的中午时分,那里也是幽暗而阴凉的,显得神秘,并带几分阴森……)。翻译形容词时要注意两点:一是准确理解其在特定上下文及搭配中的含义;二是用汉语表达时要顺应汉语行文及修辞规范。下面主要谈谈两个或两个以上的形容词一起作定语或表语以及移就格的翻译问题。

两个或两个以上的形容词作定语或表语,翻译时一定要注意顺应汉语的表达习惯，既要译得准确，又要流畅自然。比如下面两例中的第一种译文因太拘泥于英语结构，不如第二种译文准确和流畅。

1. Then the man straightened himself; he was smiling and suddenly his face was bright and tremulous and old.

    [a] 然后，直起身来，微笑着，脸色忽然变得光亮、颤抖而又苍老。
    [b]……突然，他的脸有了光彩，脸上的肌肉抖动着，显得很苍老。

2. ...the boy carried the wooden box with the coiled, hard-braided brown lines, ...

    [a]……孩子抱着木头盒子，盒子里盛着盘在一起的、编得很硬的、褐色的钓丝，……
    [b]……盒子里盘着编得很结实的褐色的钓丝……

为了顺应汉语的行文及表达习惯和修饰特点，译者们常常运用下面一些译法，现用例句分别说明如下。

（一）运用连接词语

3. For Amelia it was quite a new, fresh, brilliant world, with all the bloom upon it.

    爱米丽亚觉得这世界五光十色，又新鲜，又有趣，又美丽。

4. "Ah, but to have parents, as you have...kind, rich, affectionate parents, who give you everything you ask for; ..."

    "唉，像你这样父母双全才好呢！他们又慈爱，又有钱，又疼你。你要什么就有什么……"

（二）将形容词拆散开来译，以免连成一串

5. Not very far from Naples, a strange city sleeps under the hot Italian sun.

    在意大利，距那不勒斯不远处，一座奇特的城市在骄阳下沉睡。

6. "And is your sister-in-law a nice pretty woman?"

    "你的嫂子大概很漂亮，为人一定也好，是不是？"

7. That altered, frightened, fat face, told his secret enough.

    他的胖脸蛋吓得走了样子，他心里的打算一看就知道了。

8. ..., yet she (Mrs. Sedley) could not bring herself to suppose that the little, humble, grateful, gentle governess, would dare to look up to such a

magnificent personage as the collector of Boggley Wollah.

可是赛特笠太太瞧着利蓓加不过是个温柔谦逊的家庭教师，对自己又感激，总不至于敢攀附像卜克雷·窝拉的收税官那么了不起的人物。

（三）将"形容词+名词"译为汉语的主谓结构

9. These are all-too-familiar reminders this summer that greater public attention needs to be given to resolving the persistent problems confronting America's outmoded, overcrowded, and violence-prone penal institutions.

这些事件提醒公众要更加注意解决美国监狱所面临的一些迁延已久的问题：设备陈旧过时，狱中拥挤不堪，因此很容易引起暴力事件。

10. "But we have a lot of small, very disruptive day-in-and-day-out problems on the factory floor," one industrialist said.

一位实业家说："在工厂办公楼里，我们面对着许多细小但破坏性却很大的问题，它们日复一日，无休无止地发生。"

11. I had known Elliott Temputon for fifteen years. He was at this time in his late fifties, a tall, elegant man with good features and thick waving dark hair only sufficiently greying to add to the distinction of his appearance.

我认识艾略特·坦波登已经有十五年。他这时已是将近六旬的人，一表人才，高个儿，眉目清秀，卷发又多又黑，微带花白，恰好衬出他那堂堂的仪表。

12. Somebody tapped me on the shoulder. I looked up from the exercise books of my young pupils, which I was just correcting, into the lined, kindly face of a little lay sister.

有人轻轻拍我的肩膀。我放下正在改的那些小学生作业簿，抬头一看，原来是个做杂役的修女，她个子矮小，满脸皱纹，和蔼可亲。

13. ...taking a glass of beer, I sat down at a little table by myself to meditate upon the necessary but tragic isolation of the human soul.

我买了一杯啤酒便独自在一张小桌旁坐下，默想孤独的灵魂虽属必然却也可悲。

（四）将形容词拆出译为一个小句

14. There were twenty-one of them in the dock: Goering eighty pounds lighter than when last I had seen him, in a faded Luftwaffe uniform without insignia and obviously pleased that he had been given the Number One

place in the dock—a sort of belated recognition of his place in the Nazi hierarchy now that Hitler was dead.

在被告席上共有二十一人。戈林比我上次看到他时体重减少了八十磅，他穿着一套褪了色的没有肩章的德国空军制服，由于坐在被告席的首位上显然很高兴，这是在希特勒死后对戈林在纳粹官阶中的地位的一种承认，不过时间太晚了。

15. Then and there he named the startled General lying wounded on his cot the new Commander in Chief of the Luftwaffe...

他就在当时当地任命这位躺在病榻上治伤的将军为空军总司令，使这位将军吃了一惊……

注释6已谈到形容词的移就格，这里再举些例子谈一谈。

移就格在英语、汉语中都有。英语中有 Gray peace pervaded the wilderness-ringed Argentia Bay in Newfoundland...（Herman Wouk, *The Winds of War*）汉语中也可以说："她们暂时压倒了我的听歌的盼望，这就成就了我的灰色的拒绝"（朱自清：《桨声灯影里的秦淮河》）。英语的移就格有时可以直译，如上面一句即可译为"一片灰色的宁静笼罩着阿根夏湾，四周一片荒凉"。但是，移就格在逻辑关系上是背离常规的，其修辞效果也恰恰就是利用了这一点。英语中可以接受的逻辑背离，在汉语中可能会不伦不类，让人不知所云。所以在较多的情况下，译者都须将这种有悖常理的逻辑关系重新理顺。请看下列译例：

16. We were at a particularly tipsy table.

我们这一桌人喝得酩酊大醉。(而不能译为：我们坐在一张特别醉的桌子周围。)

17. They walked together down the alley in six inches of powdery snow, the detective holding Michael's arm with affectionate firmness.

他们踩着六英寸厚的细细的积雪，沿着小巷走去，侦探紧紧抓着迈克尔的胳膊，倒像挺亲热似的。

18. Tom threw on both brakes impatiently, and we slid to an abrupt dusty stop under Wilson's sign.

汤姆不耐烦地把两个刹车都踩了，车子扬起一阵尘土，突然在威尔逊的招牌下面停了下来。

19. I had never spoken to her, except for a few casual words, and yet her name was like a summons to all my foolish blood.

除了偶然随便搭上一两句话以外，我从未跟她正式交谈过。然而，她的名字宛如战斗的号角，会使我这个愚蠢的家伙热血沸腾。

20. I began to have a feeling of defiance, of scornful solidarity between Gatsby and me against them all.

我开始感到傲视一切，感到盖茨比和我可以团结一致，横眉冷对他们所有的人。

21. Then out into spring fields, where a yellow trolley raced them for a minute with people in it who might once have seen the pale magic of her face along the casual street.

然后驶过春天的田野，一辆黄色电车和他们并排飞驶了一会儿。电车上说不定有人曾无意间在街头看见过她那张迷人的脸庞。

22. He perceived with the most painful clearness that he could never, never impart to her the terrific secret, the awful truth.

他很清楚因而也很痛苦，他永远也不能把这可怕的秘密和事实告诉她。

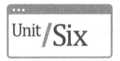

Impulse (Excerpts)[1]

Conrad Aiken

[1]　Michael Lowes hummed as he shaved, amused by the face he saw—the pallid, asymmetrical face, with the right eye so much higher than the left, and its eyebrow so peculiarly arched, like a "V" turned upside down.[2] Perhaps this day wouldn't be as bad as the last. In fact, he knew it wouldn't be, and that was why he hummed. This was the bi-weekly day of escape, when he would stay out for the evening, and play bridge with Hurwitz, Bryant, and Smith. Should he tell Dora at the breakfast table? No, better not. Particularly in view of last night's row about unpaid bills. And there would be more of them, probably, beside his plate. The rent. The coal. The doctor who had attended to the children. Jeez, what a life. Maybe it was time to do a new jump. And Dora was beginning to get restless again—

[2]　But he hummed, thinking of the bridge game. Not that he liked Hurwitz or Bryant or Smith—cheap fellows, really—mere pick-up acquaintances. But

what could you do about making friends, when you were always hopping about from one place to another, looking for a living, and fate always against you! They were all right enough. Good enough for a little escape, a little party—and Hurwitz always provided good alcohol. Dinner at the Greek's, and then to Smith's room—yes. He would wait till late in the afternoon, and then telephone Dora as if it had all come up suddenly. Hello, Dora—is that you, old girl? Yes, this is Michael—Smith has asked me to drop in for a hand of bridge—you know—so I'll just have a little snack in town. Home by the last car as usual. Yes. Gooo-bye!...

[3]　And it all went off perfectly, too. Dora was quiet, at breakfast, but not hostile. The pile of bills was there, to be sure, but nothing was said about them. And while Dora was busy getting the kids ready for school, he managed to slip out, pretending that he thought it was later than it really was.[3] Pretty neat, that! He hummed again, as he waited for the train. Telooralooraloo. Let the bills wait, damn them! A man couldn't do everything at once, could he, when bad luck hounded him everywhere? And if he could just get a little night off, now and then, a rest and change, a little diversion, what was the harm in that?

[4]　At half-past four he rang up Dora and broke the news to her. He wouldn't be home till late.

[5]　"Are you sure you'll be home at all?" she said coolly.

[6]　That was Dora's idea of a joke. But if he could have foreseen—!

[7]　He met the others at the Greek restaurant, began with a couple of araks, which warmed him, then went on to red wine, bad olives, pilaf, and other obscure foods; and considerably later they walked along Boylston Street to Smith's room. It was a cold night, the temperature below twenty[4], with a fine dry snow sifting the streets. But Smith's room was comfortably warm, he trotted out some gin and the Porto Rican cigars, showed them a new snapshot of Squiggles (his Revere Beach sweetheart), and then they settled down to a nice long cozy game of bridge.[5]

[8]　It was during an intermission, when they all got up to stretch their legs and renew their drinks, that the talk started—Michael never could remember which one of them it was who had put in the first oar—about impulse.[6] It

might have been Hurwitz, who was in many ways the only intellectual one of the three, though hardly what you might call a highbrow. He had his queer curiosities, however, and the idea was just such as might occur to him. At any rate, it was he who developed the idea, and with gusto.

[9] "Sure," he said, "anybody might do it. Have you got impulses? Of course, you got impulses. How many times you think—suppose I do that? And you don't do it, because you know damn well if you do it you'll get arrested. You meet a man you despise—you want to spit in his eye. You see a girl you'd like to kiss—you want to kiss her. Or maybe just to squeeze her arm when she stands beside you in the street car. You know what I mean."

[10] "Do I know what you mean!" sighed Smith. "I'll tell the world. I'll tell the cock-eyed world!..."

[11] "You would," said Bryant. "And so would I."

[12] "It would be easy," said Hurwitz, "to give in to it. You know what I mean? So simple. Temptation is too close. That girl you see is too damn good-looking—she stands too near you—you just put out your hand it touches her arm—maybe her leg—why worry? And you think, maybe it she don't like it I can make believe I didn't mean it..."

[13] "Like these fellows that slash fur coats with razor blades," said Michael. "Just impulse, in the beginning, and only later a habit."

[14] "Sure...And like these fellows that cut off braids of hair with scissors. They just feel like it and do it...Or stealing."

[15] "Stealing?" said Bryant.

[16] "Sure. Why, I often feel like it...I see a nice little thing right in front of me on a counter—you know, a nice little knife, or necktie, or a box of candy—quick, you put it in your pocket, and then go to the other counter, or the soda fountain for a drink. What would be more human? We all want things. Why not take them? Why not do them? And civilization is only skin-deep..."

[17] "That's right. Skin-deep," said Bryant.

[18] "But if you were caught, by God!" said Smith, opening his eyes wide.

[19] "Who's talking about getting caught?...Who's talking about doing it? It isn't that we do it, it's only that we want to do it. Why, Christ, there's been times when I thought to hell with everything. I'll kiss that woman if it's the last thing I do."

[20] "It might be," said Bryant.

[21] Michael was astonished at this turn of the talk. He had often felt both these impulses. To know that this was a kind of universal human inclination came over him with something like relief.

[22] "Of course, everybody has those feelings," he said smiling. "I have them myself...But suppose you did yield to them?"

[23] "Well, we don't," said Hurwtz.

[24] "I know—but suppose you did?"

[25] Hurwtz shrugged his fat shoulders, indifferently.

[26] "Oh, well," he said, "it would be bad business."

[27] "Jesus, yes," said Smith, shuffling the cards.

[28] "Oy," said Bryant.

[29] The game was resumed, the glasses were refilled, pipes were lit, watches were looked at.[7] Michael had to think of the last car from Sullivan Square, at eleven-fifty. But also he could not stop thinking of this strange idea. It was amusing. It was fascination. Here was everyone wanting to steal—toothbrushes, or books—or to caress some fascinating stranger of a female in a subway train—the impulse everywhere—why not be a Columbus of the moral world and really do it?...

参考译文

冲　动

康拉德·艾肯

[1] 迈克尔·洛斯一边刮脸，一边哼着歌儿。看着镜子里那张苍白而不对称的脸，觉得很好玩儿——右眼比左眼高出那么多，眼眉向上拱起，怪怪的，像个倒写的 V

字。今天也许不会像昨天那么糟。事实上，他知道不会，所以才这么哼哼呀呀的。今晚他可以到外面逛一逛，和赫维茨、布赖恩特、史密斯打打桥牌。他两周才有这么一次解脱的机会。吃早饭时要告诉多拉吗？不，最好别告诉她，尤其是考虑到昨晚刚为欠账的事吵了一架。一会吃饭时，他的盘子旁边可能又会放着一叠新账单：房租、煤钱、孩子们的医疗费。天哪，这是过的什么日子！也许该时来运转了。你看，多拉又开始见什么烦什么啦。

[2] 不过，他还是想着桥牌，嘴里哼着歌儿。这倒不是说他喜欢赫维茨、布赖恩特或者史密斯，那都是些小气鬼，萍水相逢而已。然而当你到处奔波谋生，命运潦倒时，又能指望交上什么样的朋友呢？这些人也蛮不错，一块儿玩玩，聚一聚。赫维茨还总能弄点好酒来。先是在希腊餐厅吃晚饭，然后去史密斯家——好，就这么办。等天快黑时再打电话给多拉，装得一切都像是偶然发生似的。你好哇，多拉，是你吗，亲爱的？我是迈克尔，史密斯邀我去打桥牌。所以，你看，我只能在城里凑合着吃一顿了。我坐末班车回家，和往常一样，对。再见！……

[3] 而且，一切也都十分如意。吃早饭时多拉虽然一声不吭，可并没有敌意。桌上倒是摆着一叠账单，可谁也没提还账的事。多拉正忙着打点孩子们上学，他装出以为要迟到的样子溜出家门。哈，干得真漂亮！等车的时候他又哼起歌来。"特鲁拉——鲁拉——鲁"。账单先别管它，让它见鬼去吧！一个人命运蹇蹩，四处碰壁，总不能一下子就把什么都干好吧？晚上偶尔出去玩玩，休息一下，散散心，又何害之有呢？

[4] 四点半钟他打电话给多拉，告诉她得很晚才能回家。

[5] "谁知你还能不能回来？"她冷冷地说。

[6] 这是句玩笑话。不过他要是能预见到……

[7] 他和那几个人在希腊餐厅见了面，先喝几杯烧酒暖暖身子，又喝了些葡萄酒，吃了不大新鲜的橄榄果和肉饭，还有几个不知名的菜。天色很晚了，他们才一起沿博伊尔斯顿大街朝史密斯家走去。夜很冷，气温在华氏20度以下，街上飘着干冷的小雪花。可史密斯家倒挺暖和、挺舒服。史密斯拿出杜松子酒和波多黎各雪茄，还把一位姑娘的近照给大家看。那是他在里维尔海滩结识的情人斯奎格尔斯。然后他们坐下来，没完没了地打起桥牌来。

[8] 打了几局，大家站起来伸伸腿脚，往杯子里添点酒。这时，有人扯起冲动这个话题来。迈克尔也记不清是谁开的头儿，多半是赫维茨。他虽说不上有学问，

但在那三个人当中,在很多方面也算是有知识的人了。不过,他对什么都好奇,这种话题也只有他才想得出来。不管怎么说,反正是他提出这个想法的,而且谈得津津有味。

[9] "当然啦,"他说,"谁都可能冲动。你就没有心血来潮的时候?当然有。多少次你想,假如我这么干会怎么样,可你没干。因为你清楚得很,一干就得给抓起来。你遇到一个你看不起的男人,想当面啐他。你看见一个可爱的小妞儿,想亲她一下。或是在电车上她靠你站着的时候,捏一下她的胳膊。你明白我的意思。"

[10] "我太明白了。"史密斯出了口长气。"我要对全世界说。要让这个荒唐的世界知道!……"

[11] "对,"布赖恩特说,"我也会这么做。"

[12] "你很容易就屈从于那些冲动的念头,"赫维茨说,"明白我的意思吗?很简单。诱惑近在眼前。你看到的那小妞儿太漂亮了,离你又那么近,一伸手就能碰到她的胳膊,也许是大腿。怕什么?你想,如果她不高兴,我也许能让她相信我这不是故意的……"

[13] "就像那些用刀片割皮大衣的家伙一样,"迈克尔说,"一开始只是心血来潮,可后来就成了恶习。"

[14] "没错……还有用剪子绞人家辫子的。他们想这么干,就干了……偷东西也是这样。"

[15] "偷东西?"布赖恩特说。

[16] "当然喽。怎么,我就常有这种念头……柜台上摆着个可爱的小东西,就在我眼皮底下——你知道,那是把可爱的小刀,或是一条领带、一盒奶糖——哧溜一下把它放进衣袋里,然后到别的柜台去,或者到冷饮柜前喝一杯。还有比这更自然的吗?谁不财迷?干吗放着不拿?文明只不过是摆摆样子罢了……"

[17] "可不是嘛,就是摆样子的。"布赖恩特说。

[18] "可要是给抓住了,天哪!"史密斯瞪大眼睛说。

[19] "谁说给抓住来着?……谁说去偷啦?我们不是真干,只是想干。啊,上帝,有时候我想我什么也不在乎了,我就是要亲亲那个小妞儿。"

[20] "那可真说不准。"布赖恩特说。

[21]　迈克尔听到这儿，心里一惊。这两种念头他就常常有。照他们这么说，这是人所共有的癖性，倒也觉得有点心安理得了。

[22]　"当然啦，人人都有一时冲动的念头，"他咧嘴笑笑。"我就有……不过假如你真的那么干了……"

[23]　"哟，我们可不干。"赫维茨说。

[24]　"我知道——假使你干了呢？"

[25]　赫维茨漫不经心地耸耸他的肥肩膀。

[26]　"哎呀，"他说，"那可就糟了。"

[27]　"啊，没错，"史密斯边说边洗牌。

[28]　"哎呀。"布赖恩特说。

[29]　桥牌又重新开始，大伙添酒，点烟，还不时看看表。迈克尔惦记着十一点五十从沙利文广场开来的末班车。但同时那个奇怪的念头也总是挥之不去。真有趣，真诱人。你看，这儿人人想偷——牙刷、书，还想在地铁车厢里摸摸哪个迷人的妞儿——冲动的欲望到处都有——干嘛不做个道德世界的哥伦布去亲自干一干呢？……

注释

1. 这篇短篇小说选自 Robert Penn Warren 和 Albert Erskine 编辑的 *Short Story Masterpieces*。这里节选的是小说的开头部分：迈克尔和朋友聚会，偶然谈起人的冲动欲望。后来，他借着几分酒劲儿，到商场里去实践了一下——偷了一个小小的保险刀架盒，被当场捉住后，送往警察局。他声称刚刚和几个朋友谈起冲动的话题，自己只是想尝试一下。但朋友拒绝为他作证，他被判管教三个月，妻子也离他而去。
2. amused by the face he saw 的译文中加了"镜子里"几个字，以保证译文叙述的连贯。like a "v" turned upside down 也可译为"像个倒写的'八'字"。正如"两块胛骨高高突出，印出一个阳文的'八'字"被译为 and his shoulder blades struck out so sharply, an inverted V seemed stamped there 那样。
3. 译文属意译。如直译为"装出以为时间比真正的时间要晚的样子"，恐很难为汉语读者理解。
4. 英美惯用华氏度，我国惯用摄氏度，所以须在译文中加字说明。
5. 此处的 nice long cozy 三个形容词可译得灵活一些。

6. 此处的形合结构的长句应顺应汉语叙事句的结构特点译得"松散"一些。如译为"那是在大家起身伸伸腿脚、添加饮料的间隙时间,有人提起了关于冲动这个话题——迈克尔也记不起是谁开的头儿",则和原文结构更一致。
7. 此处几个被动结构汉语宜用主动句译出。

 讲解

归化和异化

归化(domestication)和异化(foreignization)是两种翻译策略。

在翻译研究领域首先将这两个词语作为术语使用的是美国翻译学者 Lawrence Venuti。按照 Schuttleworth 和 Cowie 编写的 *Dictionary of Translation Studies*(《翻译研究词典》)中给出的定义,domestication 指译者采用透明、流畅的风格以尽可能减弱译语读者对外语语篇的生疏感的翻译策略(A term used by Venuti to describe the translation strategy in which a transparent, fluent style is adopted in order to minimize the strangeness of the foreign text for TL readers.);foreignization 则指刻意打破目的语的行文规范而保留原文的某些异域特色的翻译策略(A term used by Venuti to designate the type of translation in which a T T is produced which deliberately breaks target conventions by retaining something of the foreignness of the original.)。Venuti 十分强调翻译活动受特定社会文化价值驱动的特质。在他看来,翻译活动不是单纯的语言操作,而是跨文化的交际活动。在对英国和美国的文学翻译作品出版现状进行分析后,他得出结论,认为以英语为目的语、以英美读者为服务对象的翻译作品,归化翻译占绝对主导地位,以致造成翻译中的"种族中心主义",即使原文依从于目的语文化的价值观。因此他极力主张异化翻译原则,提倡所谓不通顺的译文,以突出原文的异域语言风格和文化特质,防止被目的语的规范所吞噬。

Venuti 的观点在翻译界颇受关注,也受到一些批评。Venuti 本人也意识到,异化翻译只是一个主观的、相对的概念。完全的和绝对的异化是不可能的。异化中总会有归化,因为译文总是要在译语文化氛围中被阅读和评判的。

Venuti 的翻译思想可追溯到 1813 年德国神学家和翻译家 Schleiermacher,他认为翻译有两种,一种是将源语作者拉向译语读者,另一种是将译语读者拉向源语作者。这前一种就相当于归化,后一种就是异化。

我国近代学界也有归化和异化的提法,鲁迅在 1935 年就使用过"归化"一词,而"异化"一词也包括在 1978 年出版的《现代汉语词典》中。我国翻译传统中,自周代出现翻译活动以来的意译和直译之争，粗略地说就是这种归化、异化翻译理念在翻译操作层面的表现。不同的是，Venuti 的 domestication 和 foreignization 强调对异域文化的态度，而我国译界谈论归化和异化主要是针对翻译操作的语言层面的，大体上是意译和直译之论的延伸和发展。但实际上语言层面和文化层面很难截然分开，所以将我国固有翻译传统中的意译／归化和直译／异化这两套术语放在当今国际翻译研究背景下审视，可以说，它们的含义和指向与 domestication 和 foreignization 是有很大程度上的重合的，这一点参较上文引用的 Schuttleworth 和 Cowie 编写的 Dictionary of Translation Studies 中的定义就可看出。

那么，在翻译实践中如何落实归化和异化这两个策略呢？一条最重要的原则是不能把它们对立起来，不能绝对化，不能非此即彼。在这方面，英国翻译学者 Peter Newmark 的翻译方法论颇具启示性。他提出了八种翻译方法，并把它们看成一个连续体，在两个极端的是 adaptation（改写）和 word-for-word translation（逐字翻译），位于中间的是 communicative translation（交际翻译）和 semantic translation（语义翻译）。communicative translation 是以读者为准的翻译方法，要保证译文的通达，顺应读者的阅读习惯，而 semantic translation 是以源语作者为准的翻译，要尽量保留原作的结构、修辞特点，以及文化内涵。把这些术语从各自的发端背景上剥离出来并从翻译实践的角度看，Newmark 关于 communicative translation 和 semantic translation 的阐述几乎就是对归化／异化原则的具体化。他对 communicative translation 和 semantic translation 两种翻译方法的关系的论述，也颇值得我们在学习翻译中借鉴。他认为不存在单一的 communicative translation 和 semantic translation，翻译实践中出现的往往是多种翻译方法的叠加。一种翻译可能 communicative translation 的倾向多一些，另一种翻译可能 semantic translation 的倾向明显一些。甚至对同一个句子的翻译你可以处理得 communicative 一些，也可以处理得 semantic 一些。另外，他认为，翻译实践基本是以 communicative translation 为主的。他还将翻译方法和语篇类型联系起来，非文学作品一般采用 communicative translation，而语言特点与其表达的内容同等重要的、以表达作者独特情感和思想以及特定文化内涵为主要功能的文学语篇应更倾向于使用 semantic translation 的方法。

对翻译初学者来说，应有意识地结合实践思考和把握好归化和异化这两个方法论原则。教学实践表明，归化是根本，是基础。不知道如何归化，便不会异化。译者必须了解目的语的行文规范。要知道，异化不等于翻译体，使用异化方法要考虑特定时代、特定读者群的接受能力。本单元的译文（以及本书其他单元和练习的译文）就是以归化为基础适当异化的译文。大家可结合注释 2、3、6、7 各条，考虑一下归化和异化翻译策略的实施问题。注释 2 中提到的 like a "V" turned upside down 的译文采用的是异化翻译，因为中国读者对英语字母十分熟悉，没必要非归化成 "倒写的'八'字"这样的译文。注释 3、6、7 涉及英汉句子结构的差异，译文都是归化译法。因为语言的结构是相对稳定的，即使要吸收外来表达方式，也是有选择的、渐进的。盲目异化只能导致译文怪异、艰涩，无益于读者接受和信息传达。当然，过分归化会造成读者的文化错觉，也是不可取的。本单元出现了英语中几个常用感叹词：Jesus (Jeez)、by God 和 Christ，我们如果把它们译为"老天爷"，恐怕就中国味太重了。可以说，任何译文都是归化和异化翻译策略相互结合的产物，而归化现在是主导策略，将来也还会是主导，因为对异域语言文化规范的接纳和吸收必须在本民族语言文化规范的根基上进行。

下面我们观察几个译例，借以体会一下不同译者的翻译策略取向，及其得失优劣。

1. The birch is softly rustling gold, which is now fluttering down like an unending stream of confetti.

   [a] 白桦树轻轻摇动金色的叶子，像无尽的五彩纸屑朝地面飘落。
   [b] 白桦婆娑轻摇，一片片金色的叶子飘飘落地，有如一溜绵绵不绝的庆典彩纸。
   [c] 白桦轻轻地摇落着金黄色的叶子，落叶飘啊飘，像不停飞舞的彩纸屑。

   以上三种译文，译文 [a] 最直，后两个显然趋于归化，而尤以译文 [c] 为甚。译文 [a] 最简洁，而从再现原文形象的角度看，后两个译文优于第一个。

2. That innate love of melody, which she had inherited from her balladsinging mother, gave the simplest music a power over her which could well-nigh drag her heart out of her bosom at times.

   [a] 她母亲很是爱唱民歌，她也由她母亲那儿继承了生来就好歌曲的天性，所以有的时候，最简单的音乐，对她都有一种力量，有时几乎能把她那颗心，从她的腔子里揪出来。
   [b] 这种对乐曲的天生的爱好，是她从爱唱民歌的母亲那儿继承的，就连最简单的音乐，有时也能对她产生一种回肠荡气、沁人肺腑的力量。

   译文 [a] 保留了原文的修辞特点，属异化翻译；译文 [b] 则将 drag her heart out of her bosom 加以归化，运用了两个四字成语，读来自然流畅。但原文的鲜明形象比喻丧失了。

3. But to live, —to wear on, day after day, of mean, bitter, low, harassing servitude, every nerve dampened and depressed, every power of feeling gradually smothered, —this long and wasting heart-martyrdom, this slow, daily bleeding away of the inward life, drop by drop, hour after hour, —this is the true searching test of what where may be in man or woman.

When Tom stood face to face with his persecutor, and heard his threats, and thought in his very soul that his hour was come, his heart swelled bravely in him, and he thought he could bear torture and fire, bear anything, with vision of Jesus and heaven but just a step beyond; but, when he was gone, and the present excitement passed off, came back the pain of his bruised and weary limbs, —came back the sense of his utterly degraded, hopeless, forlorn estate; and the day passed wearily enough.

> [a] 但是，活下去吧，——一天一天的时间挨过去，在卑贱、辛苦、低微、折磨的奴役之中，每一根神经都感到挫折与抑郁，每一种感觉的能力都被遏制，——这长期损耗在心上的痛苦牺牲，这缓慢的、一天天血在流去的内心生活，一滴复一滴，一小时又一小时——这是对男男女女的彻底考验，看他们到底是何等样人。
> 托姆和他的迫害者面对面站着，听着迫害者的威吓，自己心灵在思索，时候快到了。他的心勇敢地在里面胀大，他以为能够忍受拷打与火烧，怀着憧憬，耶稣和天堂只有跬步之远，任何痛苦都能忍受。但是，迫害者走了，当时的愤激过去以后，他伤痕累累的疲软四肢又痛起来了——极度受人贱视、被人遗弃、绝无希望的观念，又恢复了：这日子过得真是够厌倦的。
>
> [b] 可是要活下去，在卑微、痛苦、下贱、恼人的奴役下，一天一天消沉、颓唐、麻木不仁地挨下去，这种精神上的长期损耗和折磨，这种内在生命一点一滴、一个时辰一个时辰、一天一天的消蚀，这才是对人的本质最彻底的考验呢。
> 汤姆站在他的迫害者对面，听着他威吓的话，心想自己的时刻已经到来。这时，他反而觉得勇气百倍，觉得赴汤蹈火，在所不辞了，因为只要再跨一步，就可以见到耶稣和天堂了。然而等他一走开，当时那种慷慨激昂的气概一过去，肉体的创痛和疲惫又回来了，对自己处境的极端屈辱、绝望和走投无路的感觉又回来了，一天的时间就显得腻烦得不得了。

本译例包含两个自然段，先比较第一段的译文。译文 [a] 对原文句子结构几乎亦步亦趋，只有段末算是加上了译者自己的一种 paraphrase（"看他们到底是何等样人"）。译文 [b] 则是译者根据自己的理解，重新构建的语篇。通顺的同时让人觉得若有所失。再看第二个自然段。译文 [a] 将 his heart swelled bravely in him 直译为"他的心勇敢地在里面胀大"，可谓异化之典范，但紧接着出现了"跬步之远"这样古雅的词语。译文 [b] 舍弃了原文的修辞手法，用三个四字词语（勇气百倍、赴汤蹈火、在所不辞）意译出原文的含义。

[4] All noticed the change in his appearance. Cheerfulness and alertness seemed to return to him, and a quietness which no insult or injury could ruffle seemed to possess him.

"What the devil's got into Tom?" Legree said to Sambo. "A while ago he was all down in the mouth, and now he's peart as a cricket."

[a] 所有人都注意到了他外表的变化。欢快和机敏又回到他身上，一种任何侮辱和伤害都无法打乱的平静主宰了他。
"是鬼给他施了什么魔法吗？"雷格里问桑博，"刚才还满脸愁容，现在却<u>欢快得像只蟋蟀</u>。"

[b] 人们发现他变了，好像又恢复了以前那愉快而机灵的样子。他气定神闲，似乎什么凌辱、什么伤害也搅乱不了他的平静。
"真见鬼，汤姆是怎么了？"雷戈里问三宝，"前两天还垂头丧气的，<u>现在却这么神奇十足的</u>。"

我们看到，译文 [a] 在用词和句式上都力求贴近原文，是所谓语义翻译，其导致的结果就是读来有些异化感的译文；译文 [b] 则倾向于用汉语自如地重述原文，读来更接近汉语小说的语调，只是丢了原文的比喻形象：欢快得像蟋蟀。

小结

翻译叙事、描写语篇需要培养三个方面的能力。第一，此类语篇大都可以归在文学语篇的大范畴内，具有一定的文学性，这自然要求译者要有相当的文学修养。而培养文学品位的最有效途径恐怕就是多读文学作品。这不但包括英语文学作品，还必须包括汉语作品。通过阅读提高文学赏析水平，体味中西文学传统的异同。第二，必须提高审美能力——这是文学作品鉴赏中的第一要素。审美能力的培养涉及很多方面，本章只强调了对形象思维能力的培养。发挥形象思维的作用，学会解读形象化语言，运用形象化语言，这是译好此类语篇的关键之一。第三，要明确此类语篇中英汉两种语言在结构上的差异。把握好归化和异化的辩证关系，除非服务于强烈的学术目的（如将意识流的特点展示给文学研究人员），一般应遵从归化为本、适当异化的原则。

练习

1. 翻译下列段落。

(1)

He speaks in your voice, American, and there's a shine in his eye that's halfway hopeful.

It's a school day, sure, but he's nowhere near the classroom. He wants to be here instead, standing in the shadow of this old rust-hulk of a structure, and it's hard to blame him—this metropolis of steel and concrete and flaky paint and cropped grass and enormous Chesterfield packs aslant on the scoreboards, a couple of cigarettes jutting from each.

Longing on a large scale is what makes history. This is just a kid with a local yearning, but he is part of an assembling crowd, anonymous thousands off the buses and trains, people in narrow columns tramping over the swing bridge above the river, and even if they are not a migration or a revolution, some vast shaking of the soul, they bring with them the body heat of a great city and their own small reveries and desperations, the unseen something that haunts the day—men in Fedoras and sailors on shore leave, the stray tumble of their thoughts, going to a game.

> **提示**
>
> 这是当代美国作家 Don Delillo 的 Underworld 第一章的头几段，描写一个男孩想冲入体育场去看棒球比赛。注意相关的背景知识，如：Chesterfield 是一种香烟的牌子，Fedoras 是一种软呢帽。注意汉语的表达规范。

(2)

There was a woman who was beautiful, who started with all the advantages, yet she had no luck. She married for love, and the love turned to dust. She had bonny children, yet she felt they had been thrust upon her, and she could not love them. They looked at her coldly, as if they were finding fault with her. And hurriedly she felt she must cover up some fault in herself. Yet what it was that she must cover up she never knew. Nevertheless, when her children were present, she always felt the center of her heart go hard. This troubled her, and in her manner she was all the more gentle and anxious for her children, as if she loved them very much.

Only she herself knew that at the center of her heart was a hard little place that could not feel love, no, not for anybody. Everybody else said of her: "She is such a good mother. She adores her children." Only she herself, and her children themselves, knew it was not so. They read it in each other's eyes.

⚠ 提示

注意汉语表达的自然流畅。

2. 翻译下列短文。

(1)

The Scoop (Excerpts)

[1] A large *Chicago Questioner* delivery truck parted the traffic as it roared northward toward the Clark Street bridge. It shook the street, emitted carbon monoxide gas from its exhaust pipe, punctuated the atmosphere with the shrillness of an open cutout. And thundered onward.

[2] It was the first truck to be used for deliveries.[1] Dennis McDermott, a circulation slugger, stood on the tail gate and hung onto a stout rope. Husky and handsome, he expressed his pride in a characteristic leering frown.[2] He enjoyed the honor of having been assigned to this new truck while the other sluggers remained at work on horse-drawn vehicles.

[3] Bumping, the truck rattled over the Clark Street bridge. Dennis was tearing through the scenes of his boyhood.[3] He had grown up on the Near North Side, been educated on its streets, and he had served as an alter boy at the Holy Name Cathedral. Nuns had even looked at him with masked[4] wonderment, incapable of understanding why such an intelligent-looking boy, who seemed so holy and devout in his acolyte's cassock, should always be fighting the way he was. That had been before he had been ejected from school for the third and final time in his seventh grade. His father had been an Irish immigrant and an unskilled worker. A precinct Captain in Bart Gallivan's organization had gotten him a job as a street cleaner, and that had elevated Dennis' father to one of the most minor positions in the neighborhood political aristocracy. Dennis had always had before him

the example of the local hoodlums,[5] and in his small-boy manner he had emulated them, leading his gang in expeditions to roll[6] drunks, and in fights against neighborhood gangs of Jews and Wops. Reckless and possessed of volatile courage[7], he had grown to be a tough guy, hired as a slugger and strike-breaker, employed in the taxicab wars, and then by *The Questioner* in the newspaper circulation war. Twice, he had been arrested in hold-ups. Duke O'Connell, from Dennis' own neighborhood, had become State's Attorney, and he had sprung Dennis both times. He stood on the tail gate of the truck, delivering papers to the old corners, even to corners where he had sold newspapers himself. And just as earlier sluggers had gypped him by subtracting papers from his order and charging him for them, so he was now gypping newsboys who were acquiring an education similar to his own in the same kind of system.

[4] He clutched his supporting ropes more tightly as the truck curved about a corner. It drew up to a newsstand and Dennis flung down a bundle containing forty-five copies of the paper.

[5] "How many?" asked the newsboy, a tired-looking kid of twelve or thirteen with a hole in the knee of his left stocking.

[6] "What you ordered. Fifty!"[8] Dennis said in his habitually bullying voice.

[7] "Last night there was only forty-five. I counted 'em," the kid said with a nervous and uncertain air of defiance.

[8] "I said there was fifty!"

[9] "Well, I counted 'em!" the kid said, a whine creeping into his voice.

[10] Dennis squeezed the boy's left ear between two strong fingers, and asked him how many there had been.

[11] "I counted 'em!" the kid said, his voice cracking.

[12] Dennis gave him a back-handed slap in the mouth and said that there had been fifty copies. He collected for the papers and jumped on the truck as the sniffling newsboy opened the bundle.

[13] "How's it going, Wop?" Dennis asked Rocko Martini, at the next stop.

[14] "All right, Irish," Rocko replied, winking.

第四章 叙事、描写文体的翻译

⚠ 提示

1. 如照原句结构译为"这是第一辆用来分发报纸的卡车",是否会引起读者误解:一会儿还会出现第二辆、第三辆?如何处理呢?
2. characteristic leering frown 如何用通顺达意的汉语表达?
3. Dennis was tearing through the scenes of his boyhood 是说丹尼斯在回忆童年的生活,汉语表达是否需要加字?
4. masked 的意义如何理解?汉语怎样表达?
5. 此句可直译为"丹尼斯面前总有当地的流氓给他做榜样"。是否可将表达方式作一下变通?
6. 注意查字典,roll 意为 to rob a drunken or a sleeping person。
7. volatile courage 如何翻译?请多加推敲。
8. 注意:对话的翻译要符合口语体的要求,并注意每个人物应持的语气。

(2)

First Snow (Excerpt) [1]

John Boynton Priestley

[1] When I got up this morning the world was a chilled hollow of dead white and faint blues.[2] The light that came through the windows was very queer, and it contrived to make the familiar business of splashing and shaving and brushing and dressing very queer too. Then the sun came out, and by the time I had sat down to breakfast it was shining bravely[3] and flushing the snow with delicate pinks. The dining-room window had been transformed into a lovely Japanese print. The little plum-tree outside, with the faintly flushed snow lining its boughs and artfully disposed along its trunk[4], stood in full sunlight. An hour or two later everything was a cold glitter of white and blue. The world had completely changed again. The little Japanese prints had all vanished. I looked out of my study window, over the garden, the meadow, to the low hills beyond, and the ground was one long glare, the sky was steely, and all the trees so many black and sinister shapes. There was indeed something curiously sinister about the whole prospect. It was as if our kindly country-side, close to the very heart of England, had been turned into a cruel steppe. At any moment, it seemed, a body of horsemen might be seen breaking out from the black copse, so many

instruments of tyranny, and shots might be heard and some distant patch of snow be reddened. It was that kind of landscape.

[2]   Now it has changed again. The glare has gone and no touch of the sinister remains. But the snow is falling heavily, in great soft flakes, so that you can hardly see across the shallow valley, and the roofs are thick and the trees all bending, and the weathercock of the village church, still to be seen through the gray loaded air, has become some creature out of Hans Andersen.[5] From my study, which is apart from the house and faces it[6], I can see the children flattening their noses against the nursery window, and there is running through my head a jangle of rhyme I used to repeat when I was a child and flattened my nose against the cold window to watch the falling snow:[7]

>   Snow, snow faster:
>   White alabaster!
>   Killing geese in Scotland,
>   Sending feathers here![8]

[3]   This morning when I first caught sight of the unfamiliar whitened world, I could not help wishing that we had snow oftener, that English winters were more wintry. How delightful it would be, I thought, to have months of clean snow and a landscape sparkling with frost instead of innumerable gray featureless days of rain and raw winds.[9] I began to envy my friends in such places as the Eastern States of America and Canada, who can count upon a solid[10] winter every year and know that the snow will arrive by a certain date and will remain, without degenerating into black slush, until Spring is close at hand.[11] To have snow and frost and yet a clear sunny sky and air as crisp as a biscuit—this seemed to me happiness indeed. And then I saw that it would never do for us. We should be sick of it in a week. After the first day the magic would be gone and there would be nothing left but the unchanging glare of the day and the bitter cruel nights. It is not the snow itself, the sight of the blanketed world, that is so enchanting, but the first coming of the snow, the sudden and silent change.[12]

⚠ 提示

1. 本文作者普里斯特莱是英国近代著名小说家。这里是他的一篇散文的节选，文笔清新流畅，景物描写细致入微，立意颇为新颖。译笔要体现出汉语散文的文体特点，字里行间须仔细推敲，组句成文要流畅自然。
2. 句中的 "Noun 1+ of +Noun 2" 结构可否采用拆译方法？
3. bravely 何义？请查字典，仔细推敲。
4. 句中的介词短语 with the faintly flushed snow lining its boughs and artfully disposed along its trunk 是否可采用拆译的方法？
5. 这是一个长复合句，翻译时注意汉语行文的意合特点。
6. 这个定语从句如何处理为好？
7. 此状语从句如何译？除了译为"当……时"，还能怎么翻译？
8. 这首小诗是译成韵文还是散文？一般来说还是译为韵文为好。那么，汉译怎样押韵？
9. 这一感叹句的信息重心在汉译中是否要作适当调整？
10. solid 一词如何理解和翻译？请依照上下文定夺。
11. 注意这一长句的信息在汉译中的重新组织和安排。
12. 析清此句结构，避免误译。

第五章 说明、论说文体的翻译

　　如果说在叙事、描写语篇的翻译中形象思维很重要，那么在说明、论说语篇的翻译中逻辑思维就是关键了。说明文要把概念、过程、方法等表述清楚，议论文则是要支持和反驳某个观点，两者都要求表达准确、文理清晰。汉语和英语相比，信息的排列、逻辑关系的表达等方面都存在一些差异，这就要求译者在信息传译过程中准确理解原文的逻辑走向，在自己头脑中构建起明晰的逻辑模式，并运用恰当的转换方法写出同样逻辑连贯的译文。为此，我们将以翻译过程中逻辑关系的调整为主线，从词和句法的角度，也从信息线性顺序的角度，讨论译者应该熟悉和掌握的一些技巧。

The Energy Lesson

[1]   Ever since 1973, the energy policy pendulum has swung with depressing regularity from crisis to glut and back again.[1] A steady resting point somewhere between has not been reached. That would be a point at which transient fluctuations in oil prices were not jarring, and at which U.S. policy would accept the reality of a permanent shift from $3-a-barrel oil to $30-a-barrel oil.[2]

[2]   Now we are in the glut phase. Producers are being forced to drop prices sharply. And once again we hear that the energy crisis is over. It is not. Economic recovery alone would soak up much of the excess in the oil market.[3] Another war or revolution in the Gulf—which any prudent person must consider possible—could send the oil-importing nations back into crisis.[4]

[3]   In the United States, imports have dropped by half in the past couple of years. Domestic production is up, and consumption is down. The administration uses this improvement to buttress its case for dissolving the Energy Department.[5] But the appearance of less vulnerability to supply interruptions is deceptive and dangerous.[6]

[4]   Some important changes in U.S. energy use have occurred. The price of oil has been decontrolled, the strategic petroleum reserve is finally being filled, industry is using energy much more efficiently and the gas guzzler is an endangered species.[7] But the price of natural gas is still artificially low, consumers still have no reliable source of help for reducing energy use in their homes, mass transit compared with that of other advanced nations is terrible, and the lack of a substantial gasoline tax keep that unchanged.[8]

[5]   Nevertheless, the Reagan administration argues that higher energy prices have led to energy conservation and that there is therefore no reason for further federal support of research and other conservation programs. But the real issue is how much of what would be economically beneficial is not happening,[9] and will not happen, under current policies. Do most types of energy use—technologies for supply and distribution, consumer information,

manufacturing processes and the rest—reflect the reality of expensive energy or the history of cheap energy?[10] The answer varies by sector. Large businesses with access to expertise and capital have adjusted well. Most other sectors have not.[11] In residential and commercial buildings, which consume a quarter of all the energy used in America, only a tiny fraction of the economically desirable savings is being captured.[12]

[6] In short, a good beginning has been made, but it is only a beginning. To abandon conservation programs and dismantle research efforts now is to save small amounts of federal dollars at a very large longer-range cost to the economy.[13] And hopeful talk about the end of the energy crisis ignores the painful lessons of the past decade.[14]

参考译文

能源教训

[1] 自从1973年以来，我国能源政策就一直像钟摆一样经常摆来摆去，时而从危机向过剩摆动，时而又从过剩向危机摆动，令人忧心不已。至今，钟摆还没有在两个极端之间某一个安稳的地方停下来；而只有在这样一个安稳的地方停下来，石油价格变化无常的波动才不致引起震动，美国的政策也才会正视石油价格从每桶三美元长期不断地上升为每桶三十美元的现实。

[2] 现在，我们正处在过剩阶段。生产者纷纷被迫大幅度降价。我们又听到了能源危机已经过去的议论。其实不然。别的不说，只要经济回升，石油市场上的过剩现象大体上就会化为乌有。要是海湾地区再发生一场战争或革命（任何明智之士都不能不认为这是可能的），石油输入国家就可能再一次陷入危机之中。

[3] 过去两三年中，美石油进口已经减少了一半。国内产量上升，消费量下降。由于情况有了改善，政府就振振有词地主张撤销能源部。从表面上看，供应中断造成危害的可能性的确减少了，但是，这只是一种危险的假象。

[4] 美国在能源利用方面的确有了一些重大变化。石油价格管制取消了，战略石油储备最终趋于完成，工业中的能源利用率大大提高，耗油过多的汽车已濒于绝迹。但是，天然气价格仍然人为压低，消费者在住宅节能方面仍然得不到稳妥的帮助，公共交通同其他先进国家相比糟糕透顶，而且，由于汽油税不高，情况至今仍无改变。

[5]　尽管这样，里根政府仍然辩白说，能源价格的提高已经使能源有所节约，因此，联邦政府已经不需要再支持能源研究计划和其他节能计划了。但是，真正的问题是：究竟有多少事情从经济上来说本是有利的，可是在现行政策下，却没有得到实现，而且将来也不会得到实现？大多数利用能源的环节的现状又怎样呢，比如供应和分配技术、消费者信息、制造工艺等？究竟是反映了能源昂贵的现实呢，还是反映了能源低廉的历史呢？答案视不同部门而定。拥有技术人才和资本的大企业已经作了妥善的调整。大多数其他部门还没有适应这种现实。居民住宅和商业建筑所消耗的能源占美国全部能源消耗量的四分之一。这些地方实行节约，在经济上是可取的，可是现已实现的节约却微乎其微，还大有潜力可挖。

[6]　总之，我们已经有了一个良好的开端，但是，这也仅仅是开始而已。现在就放弃节能计划，停止能源研究工作，可以给联邦政府节省少量开支，但从比较长远的观点来看，只能使经济蒙受重大损失。那种能源危机已经过去的乐观论调，只能是对过去十年的痛苦教训的忽视。（张今译）

注释

1. 这句话的译文结构变化较大，话题由钟摆（pendulum）换成了能源政策（参阅第三章 Unit Four 的讲解部分），back again 实际上意为 from glut to crisis again，depressing 一词被拆出译成一个分句。所有这些变化都是为了顺应汉语的表达习惯。
2. 这句话是虚拟语气，表示一种假设的口吻，对这一语法意义，译者是用"而只有……才……"这样的汉语结构加以再现的。
3. 主语被译为表条件的小句，英语简单句被译成汉语复句。"只要……，……就会……"。另外，alone 一词被拆出，译成"别的不说"，放在句首。译得灵活自然。
4. 此句译法与上句相同。主语译为条件小句，整句译成复句："要是……，……就……"。
5. 译者将 this improvement 拆出译成原因小句。
6. 此句的译法与注释 1 所涉及的本文首句的译文相似，也是将原句拆开译成了多个小句。
7. gas guzzler 指耗油量大的汽车。endangered species，濒危物种，是比喻用法。
8. 此句中 the lack of a substantial gasoline tax 拆出译为分句"由于……"。
9. 此句译法参阅注释 1 及 6，注意从句的拆译方法。
10. 此问句很长，汉语中设问一般不会这么长，故译者将其拆成两个问句，读起来自然达意。另外，注意 type 一词根据下文译为"环节"，而未机械地译为"类型"之类的词语。
11. 此句中有省略，译文将省略部分补译进来，以顺应汉语的表达习惯。
12. 译者将原句中的定语从句单独译为一句，然后将主句译成几个小句，最后一个小句是译者加上去的，有利于将原句之意译尽。

13. 此句汉译由五个小句组成，大体分别对应原句作主语的两个不定式、系表部分及介词短语。介词短语被拆开译成两个小句，并在逻辑连接上做了调整（但从……看，只能……）。
14. 此句也是将主语和其余部分分开，译成了两个小句。

讲解

译文逻辑连接的调整（一）

本篇译文译得既灵活又准确。灵活，是指译文在句式安排和逻辑连接上不受原文羁绊；准确，是指无论句式怎么调整，原文信息并未丢失。本译文的翻译技巧主要体现在两个方面：一是将原文句子化整为零，拆成几个汉语小句（参阅注释1、6、9、12、13、14）；二是对逻辑关系的重新安排。后一种又可分为两类：对从句逻辑关系的调整（如注释12所示句子的翻译中，将定语从句单独译成一句）以及对其他结构间的逻辑关系的调整（如注释3、4、5、8所示句子的翻译）。下面主要谈一谈对非从句结构的逻辑关系的分析和调整问题。

在说明、论说类文章的翻译中要特别注意译文语篇的逻辑连贯。汉语语篇的逻辑推进层次和英语是有区别的，这就要求译者在构建汉语语篇时要在深入细致地理解和分析原文逻辑关系的基础上，进一步挖掘各句子成分间所存在的内在逻辑关系，并按汉语行文习惯及规范进行适当调整和变通。逻辑关系的调整是译者必须掌握的一种技巧，它有一定的规律可循，但不同译者间也会存在某些个体差异。让我们一起来观察下面一些译例：

1. With the fear of largely imaginary plots against his leadership, his self-confidence seemed totally to desert him.

   由于害怕有人阴谋推翻他的领导，他似乎完全丧失了自信。但所谓的阴谋在很大程度上是他自己假想出来的。

   介词短语（with...）被译为原因小句，其中的 largely imaginary 被拆出译成单独一句话，前面冠以转折连词"但"。

2. It is not only military secrets that they steal now. Today they are after trade and technical data, too. Growing contacts with other countries make their job easier.

   目前他们不光窃取军事秘密，也在猎取贸易和技术方面的情报资料。由于和其他国家的接触日益扩大，他们干这种勾当就容易多了。

   此译将原文前两句合在一起，成为递进关系复句（……不光……也……）。最

后一句的主语部分译为原因小句,这种逻辑调整常在英译汉译文中出现。再如:

3. And the taking of the Senate by the Republicans could make it easier for Reagan to implement an economic philosophy that is far different from the two major theologies—Keynesianism and monetarism—that between them have governed the management of the U.S. economy for the past generation.

由于共和党人控制了参议院,里根今后可能比较容易实施一种同凯恩斯学派和货币学派两大神学理论大不相同的经济理论。过去三十年来,美国经济一直是交替采用这两大理论来进行管理的。

下面一句则是将状语 by efficiently processing and dealing... 拆出,译成条件状语小句"如果……"。

4. The United States could benefit greatly—in research, in education, in economic development, and in scores of other areas—by efficiently processing and dealing with information that is available but unused.

美国如果能够有效地处理可用而未用的信息,就会在研究、教育、经济发展和其他几十个领域大大获益。

下面两句的主语是不定式,均被译为假设小句:

5. Not to train the child in the values his parents have found enduring is to neglect him. Not to educate him is to condemn him to repetitious ignorance.

如果我们不用家长们奉为圭臬的价值观念训练儿童的话,那就是对儿童疏于管教。如果我们不对儿童进行教育的话,那就要使儿童沦入世世代代的愚昧状态。

下面一例中第一句将主语和宾语译成了一种因果逻辑关系,后两句合在一起,译成递进关系复句。

6. Man's sudden concern for the environment has introduced a new dimension into international relations. It has heightened tensions between rich and poor nations; it has introduced a widened range of issues for potential conflict.

人们忽然关心起环境问题,因而我们必须从新的角度来看国际关系。对环境问题的关心不仅使富国和穷国之间的关系更紧张,而且还可能引起更大范围的种种矛盾问题。

下面一例第二个小句中的动词 resulted 在译文中被译成因果关系:"由于……结果……"。

7. Peter Bergen's *Holy War, Inc.* might have shown how bin Laden and al Qaeda put "netwar" doctrine into practice, but the rush to press resulted in its having few real revelations about the terrorists' actual modes of operation.

彼得·伯根的《圣战组织》一书也许揭露了本·拉登及"基地"组织如何把"网络战争"的教旨付诸实践。但由于此书出版仓促，结果对恐怖分子实际运作模式的内幕却没有进行多少真正的揭示。

与上句类似，下面一例也以动词 is complicated 为依据构建了其前后两部分信息（legal problem of enforcing patents 和 public relations problems caused by the rise of price）的逻辑关系：背景 + 推论。

8. For pharmaceutical companies, of course, the legal problem of enforcing patents is complicated by the public relations problems that flow from any action that tends to raise drug prices in the under-developed world.

在不发达国家中，任何企图提高药价的举动都会给药品公司带来公共关系问题，而这又必然使这些公司强化专利权的法律问题复杂化。

必须指出，逻辑关系的调整和变通绝不是译者随意而为的，它必须建立在对原文语篇（注意不是孤立的语句）逻辑层次的分析和译文语篇逻辑推进的需要之上。只见句子而不见语篇就难免会导致逻辑连接不当。请仔细观察下述译文，看有没有逻辑连贯上的问题。

9. According to the treaty of 1868 between the United States Government and the Sioux Indians, the land between the Missouri River and the Bughorn Mountains was granted to the Sioux forever. But within the territory lay the Black Hills, most sacred place of the Sioux, where braves went to speak to their gods. To many white men, however, the ponderosa-clad hills, which from a distance looked so strangely black, seemed a likely place to find gold. And in violation of the treaty, prospectors entered the Indians' holy mountains. By 1874 there were so many rumours about gold in the hills that the Army sent General Guster with one thousand men to reconnoiter the area. Geologists soon proved what everyone had so long suspected—the hills were indeed filled with gold.

So much for treaties. Within two years the whole of the Black Hills were being cut to build crude cabins. Sluice boxes, ditches, dams and hundreds of stamp mills cluttered the small creeks in Deadwood Gulch. When the Sioux exacted their fruitless revenge by massacring Guster and all his men at the battle of the little Bighorn in June 1876, the narrow main street of Deadwood was already lined with saloons, stores and hotels. These South Dakota hills had become the richest gold producing area of North America, and the stage for some of the most colorful sagas in the opening of the West.

根据美国政府同苏族印第安人于1868年签订的条约，密苏里河和比格霍恩山脉之间的这片土地永远划给了苏族印第安人。<u>但在这片土地上屹立着的黑山是苏族印第安人心目中最神圣的地方，勇士们到这里向他们的神灵祈祷。然而在许多白人眼里</u>，这片长满茂密的美国黄松、远望黑得出奇的山峦却像是一个很有可能找到金矿的地方。于是，探矿者们违反条约，闯入了印第安人的圣山。到了1874年，人们盛传山中有金矿，陆军部派卡斯特将军率领一千名士兵踏勘这一区域。地质学家们很快证实了大家猜测已久的事——山中确实遍布黄金。

条约成了一纸空文。不到两年，人们在黑山到处开凿，盖起了粗糙简陋的小屋。泄水槽、沟渠和水闸，还有数以百计的捣岩机杂乱无章地布满在戴德伍德干涸的条条小溪上。<u>在1876年的不比格霍恩山战斗中，苏族印第安人进行了徒劳无益的报复，尽管他们屠杀了卡斯特将军和他的全体部下。就在那个时候，戴德伍德狭窄的大街两旁就已经有很多酒楼、商店和旅馆。</u>这些南达科他州山峦已经成了美国北方最富饶的黄金产地，也成了西部开拓时期一幕幕有浓厚传奇色彩的演出舞台。

对照原文仔细阅读上面译文，并特别注意译文划线部分有无逻辑连贯不当之处。

先看第一段译文。第二句的"但"和第三句的"然而"显然逻辑不通。问题在于原文 But 的转折关系落在 within the territory lay the Black Hills 上，意即：条约虽把这片土地划归印第安人，但由于黑山的存在而出了问题。而译文中"但"字的转折关系则落在"黑山是苏族印第安人心目中最神圣的地方"，显然与原文有悖。再看整个语篇。原文语篇的逻辑推进可分为两个主要层次：虽然美国政府和印第安人有条约，但由于可能有金矿，白人违反条约大肆探矿，并派进军队。尽管印第安人进行反抗，但已徒劳，戴德伍德已成为白人开采黄金的宝地。依照这样的逻辑分析，不难看出，第二段译文划线部分的逻辑连贯也有些不当，可将原译相应部分改动如下：

……但屹立在这片土地上的黑山却引起了麻烦。在印第安人的心目中，它是最神圣的地方，勇士们常到这里来祈祷神灵。然而在许多白人眼里……

……苏族印第安人杀死了卡斯特将军和他的全体部下，但他们的报复是徒劳的，因为那时戴德伍德狭窄的大街两旁早已建起了许多酒馆、商店和旅馆。……

Politics and the English Language

[1]   In our time it is broadly true that political writing is bad writing. Where it is not true, it will generally be found that the writer is some kind of rebel, expressing his private opinions, and not a "party line".¹ Orthodoxy, of whatever colour, seems to demand a lifeless, imitative style. The political dialects to be found in pamphlets, leading articles, manifestos, White Papers and the speeches of Undersecretaries do, of course, vary from party to party, but they are all alike in that one almost never finds in them a fresh, vivid, home-made turn of speech. When one watches some tired hack on the platform mechanically repeating the familiar phrases—bestial atrocities, iron heel, bloodstained tyranny, free peoples of the world, stand shoulder to shoulder²—one often has a curious feeling that one is not watching a live human being but some kind of dummy: a feeling which suddenly becomes stronger at moments when the light catches the speaker's spectacles and turns them into blank discs which seem to have no eyes behind them. And this is not altogether fanciful. A speaker who uses that kind of phraseology has gone some distance towards turning himself into a machine. The appropriate noises are coming out of his larynx, but his brain is not involved as it would be if he were choosing words for himself.³ If the speech he is making is one that he is accustomed to make over and over again, he may be almost unconscious of what he is saying, as one is when one utters the responses in church. And this reduced state if not indispensable, is at any rate favourable to political conformity.

[2]   In our time, political speech and writing are largely the defence of the indefensible. Things like the continuance of British rule in India, the Russian purges and deportations, the dropping of the atom bombs on Japan, can indeed be defended, but only by arguments which are too brutal for most people to face, and which do not square with the professed aims of political parties.⁴ Thus political language has to consist largely of euphemism, question-begging and sheer cloudy vagueness. Defenseless villages are bombarded from the air, the inhabitants driven out into the countryside, the

cattle machine-gunned, the huts set on fire with incendiary bullets: This is called pacification[5]. Millions of peasants are robbed of their farms and sent trudging along the roads with no more than they can carry: This is called transfer of population or rectification of frontiers.[6] People are imprisoned for years without trial, or shot in the back of the neck or sent to die of scurvy in Arctic lumber camps: This is called elimination of unreliable elements.[7] Such phraseology is needed if one wants to name things without calling up mental pictures of them.[8]

[3] The inflated style is itself a kind of euphemism. A mass of Latin words falls upon the facts like soft snow,[9] blurring the outlines and covering up all the details. The great enemy of clear language is insincerity. When there is a gap between one's real and one's declared aims. One turns as it were instinctively to long words and exhausted idioms, like a cuttlefish squirting out ink.[10] In our age there is no such thing as "keeping out of politics". All issues are political issues, and politics itself is a mass of lies, evasions, folly, hatred, and schizophrenia. When the general atmosphere is bad, language must suffer.

[4] But if thought corrupts language, language can also corrupt thought. A bad usage can spread by tradition and imitation, even among people who should and do know better. The debased language that I have been discussing is in some ways very convenient. Phrases like "a not unjustifiable assumption", "leaves much to be desired", "would serve no good purpose", "a consideration which we should do well to bear in mind"[11], are a continuous temptation, a packet of aspirins[12] always at one's elbow. Look back through this essay, and for certain you will find that I have again and again committed the very faults I am protesting against.

[5] I said earlier that the decadence of our language is probably curable. Those who deny this would argue, if they produced an argument at all, that language merely reflects existing social conditions, and that we cannot influence its development by any direct tinkering with words and constructions. So far as the general tone or spirit of a language goes, this may be true, but it is not true in detail. Silly words and expressions have often disappeared, not through any evolutionary process but owing to the conscious action of a minority. Two recent examples were "explore every

avenue" and "leave no stone unturned"[13], which were killed by the jeers of a few journalists. There is a long list of fly-blown metaphors which could similarly be got rid of if enough people would interest themselves in the job; and it should also be possible to laugh the not un-formation[14] out of existence, to drive out foreign phrases and strayed scientific words, and, in general, to make pretentiousness unfashionable.

参考译文

政治与英语

[1]　在我们这个时代，说政治文章的写作是拙劣的写作，一般是正确的。若有不适用的地方，多半是因为那位作者是某种意义上的叛逆，发表的是他个人的意见，而不是"党派调门"。不论什么色彩，凡是正统的，似乎都要求你采用一种没有生气的、鹦鹉学舌的文风。当然，小册子、社论、宣言、政府白皮书、各部次官的讲话中可以找到的政治套话，在党与党之间或有差别，但是他们在一点上都是一样的，那就是你从里面几乎永远找不出一句新鲜的、生动的、自创的话。你看着一个神态疲惫的政客在讲台上机械地重复着听熟了的话——什么bestial atrocities、iron heel、bloodstained tyranny、free peoples of the world、stand shoulder to shoulder——你常常会有一种奇怪的感觉，你看到的不是一个活人，而是一个假人。这种感觉有时会突然变得强烈起来——特别是当你看到灯光反射在演讲者的眼镜片上，使眼镜片成了空白的圆片，它后面似乎没有眼睛存在的时候。这并不是纯属幻觉。使用这种词汇的演讲者已在某种程度上把自己变成了一台机器。他的喉部固然仍旧发出应有的声音，可是他的脑子却没动，而如果由他自己选词造句的话，他就会动动脑子。如果他发表的讲话是他一遍又一遍讲惯了的话，他很可能根本不知道自己在说些什么，就像我们在教堂里唱圣歌时口中念念有词一样。而这样意识降低的状态，对于政治上的驯服一致，如果不是不可或缺的话，说什么也是有利的。

[2]　在我们这个时代，政治讲话的写作多半是为不可辩解的事情进行辩解。像维持英国在印度的统治、俄国的清洗和流放、在日本投掷原子弹这样的事情，确实是可以辩解的，不过只能用大多数人所不能接受的蛮横的论据，而这又不合那些政党所标榜的宗旨。因此，政治语言就不免主要由委婉含蓄的隐语、偷换概念的诡辩和纯属掩饰的含糊其词所组成。没有设防的村庄遭到空中轰炸、村民给驱到荒野、牲畜

被机枪扫射、茅屋被燃烧焚毁：这叫作 pacificaton。千百万的农民被剥夺农田，身无长物，跋涉于途：这叫作 transfer of population 或 rectification of frontiers。未经审判即遭长期监禁，或者后脑崩上一枪，或者被遣送到北极圈伐木营中去患坏血病致死：这叫作 elimination of unreliable elements。如果你要称谓某种事物而又不愿在读者心目中引起它们的图像，这种用词是必要的。

[3]　这种虚饰的文风本身就是一种委婉其辞的隐语。一大堆拉丁字根的词汇像雪花一样落在事实上，模糊了界线轮廓，掩盖了一切细节。不诚实乃是语言明白的大敌。在一个人的真正意图和公开宣称的意图之间有距离时，他就会像出于本能一样求助于大话和空话，就像墨鱼放墨汁。在我们这个时代，"不问政治"这种事情是没有的。所有的问题都是政治问题，而政治本身又集谎话、遁词、蠢事、仇恨、精神分裂症之大成。总气候一坏，语言就受害。

[4]　但是，如果说思想可以腐蚀语言的话，语言亦可腐蚀思想。一种不良用法可以由于传统和模仿而传播，甚至在应该而且的确具有识别能力的人中间。我在上面谈到的低劣的语言在许多方面使用起来都是十分方便的。像 a not unjustifiable assumption、leaves much to be desired、would serve no good purpose、a consideration which we should do well to bear in mind 这样的短语，是一种不断的诱惑，是手边常备的一盒阿司匹林。回过头来看这篇文章，我敢说你一定会发现，我自己也一而再，再而三地犯了我所反对的毛病。

[5]　我在上面说过，我们语言的败坏也许是可以挽救的。反对此说的人可能会同你争辩——如果他们能提出论据的话。他们会说语言仅仅反映现在存在的社会情况，我们无法在词汇和结构方面直接修补来影响它的发展。就一种语言的总的调子和精神来说，这话可能不错，但是从细节上来说却不对。愚蠢的词和话之所以常常能够消失，不是由于什么演变的过程，而是由于少数人的有意识行动。比方说，最近 explore every avenue 和 leave no stone unturned 这两个词组就因为受到一些新闻工作者的嘲笑而被根除掉了。只要有足够的人愿意干这项工作，还有一大批用滥了的隐喻是可以用同样方式去除掉的。另外，也可以把 not un- 构词法嘲笑得无地自容，还应该在一般的句子中减少拉丁词和希腊词的数量，清除外来短语和用错地方的科学词汇。最后，总的来说，务必做到使虚饰的语言不再时髦流行。（董乐山译）

注释

1. 此句中 Where it is not true 这一地点状语从句译为汉语的条件分句,后面主句的逻辑关系也有所调整,译成了一个原因分句。参阅本章 Unit One 的讲解部分。
2. 这里的几个英语词组不能译成汉语,因为作者讲的是英语和政治的关系,译成汉语词组岂不成了汉语和政治的关系了。本篇译文是发表在一份双语杂志《英语世界》上的,读者都懂英语,故未加注汉译。当然,如果译文是给不懂英语的人看的,可以在英语词组后加括号注明汉语意义,如:bestial atrocities(兽行),iron heel(铁蹄),bloodstained tyranny(血腥专制),free peoples of the world(全世界的自由人民),stand shoulder to shoulder(肩并肩地站在一起)。对原文中其他词组,我们也提供了参考汉译,请见注释 5、6、7、11、13、14。
3. 该句中的 as... 状语从句译为由"而"引导的转折关系分句,这也是一种逻辑上的调整。
4. 此句中的两个定语从句,第一个译成前置定语,第二个译成一个分句,由表转换关系的连词"而"引导,这又是逻辑关系调整的一个例子。
5. pacification(绥靖)。
6. transfer of population or rectification of frontiers(人口迁移或边境整肃)。
7. elimination of unreliable elements(清除不可靠分子)。
8. 注意汉译信息焦点的变化:先条件后结论。参阅本章 Unit Five 的讲解部分。
9 和 10. 这两处比喻在译文中均照样译出,因为中国读者接受起来不仅毫无困难,而且会觉得新鲜、贴切。
11. a not unjustifiable assumption(一个并非无理的假设),leaves much to be desired(有待改进),would serve no good purpose(似无大用),a consideration which we should do well to bear in mind(一个极应记住的考虑)。
12. 此处的比喻也是直译的。
13. explore every avenue(探索各种途径),leave no stone unturned(不遗余力)。
14. not un-formation 为双重否定结构。

讲解

译文逻辑连接的调整(二)

本章 Unit One 的讲解部分着重谈了非从句结构的逻辑关系的分析和在译文中的调整问题。现在结合本单元注释 1、3、4 所涉及的几个句子的翻译,着重谈一下英语小句间逻辑关系在汉译中的调整。英汉两种语言在思维模式、行文方式及逻辑连贯上都是有差异的,汉译文不必(有时也不能)照搬英语小句间的语法逻辑关系。译者须根据对英语小句间潜在的逻辑关系的分析,对译文的逻辑连接进行适当调整，以保证译文的文通理顺。在诸多类型的英语从句中，对定语从句的逻辑调整最为多见。观察下面几个译例：

1. Experts say the latest Soviet target is Washington's Capitol Hill where vast amounts of classified information are held by congressional committees and members of their staffs.

   专家们说，苏联的最新目标是华盛顿的国会山，因为这里有大量属于秘密等级的情报放在国会的各种委员会和组成委员会的班子成员手里。

2. There could be problems if this Sunday's second round of the French election produces a president Mitterrand who does not want to offend the French Communist Party.

   如果本周日的法国第二轮选举选出密特朗担任总统的话，那就可能出现问题，因为密特朗不愿得罪共产党。

3. Now this is a schematic distinction which clearly does not apply in the practice.

   这两种学说的区分只有理论意义，在实践中显然并不适用。

4. Many things are safe underground which disappear in the wind and storms of the earth's surface.

   许多东西在地下是安全的，要是在地面上，一遇到大风和冰雪就会消失殆尽的。

5. Nature can produce children enough to make good any extremity of slaughter of which we are capable.

   不管我们的杀戮本领如何登峰造极，大自然都能降生足够的婴儿来补偿那些被残杀的生灵。

6. He conceived the idea of phrenology—a pseudo-science which had one thing to its credit: it prepared the way for the studies of some devoted neurologists in London and Paris.

   他提出了颅相学这一概念。颅相学并不科学，但有一点是可取的，它为伦敦和巴黎一些专心致志的神经病学家开展研究工作铺平了道路。

7. And both major parties usually try to give their new comers assignments that will help them win re-election, unless more senior members are competing for those seats or unless newcomers' states or regions are already appropriately represented on those committees.

两大政党通常力图给本党的新议员在委员会中分派职位，以帮助他们再次当选，除非资历更深的议员也在争取那些席位或新议员所在的州或地区在那些委员会中已有了适当的席位。

8. For though Adolf Hitler at first considered retiring to the Austro-Bavarian mountains near which he was born and in which he had spent most of the private hours of his life, and which he loved and where he had the only home he could call his own—on the Obersalzberg above Berchtesgaden—and there made a last stand, he had hesitated until it was too late.

阿道夫·希特勒最初诚然考虑过退到奥地利与巴伐利亚深山中去，进行最后的抵抗，因为他是在那附近出生的，一生中私下的大部分时间也是在那里度过的，他喜爱那个地方，在伯希特斯加登上面的上萨尔斯堡山上又有那唯一可说是属于他自己的家，但他迟疑不决，把事情耽误了。

译文先是将 there made a last stand 移到前面，与另一个谓语动词 considered retiring to the Austro-Bavarian mountains 一起翻译，然后将几个定语从句译为原因状语"因为……"。

9. On the other hand, the person who is really guilty and whose past experience has prepared him for such tests can distort the results by anticipating the crucial questions or deliberately giving exaggerated responses to neutral ones!

另一方面，一个真正犯了罪的人却可能因为曾经有过这方面的经验，而对关键问题有所防备，或对中性的问题故作夸大的反应，致使测试结果失真。

10 But it is not only big business that faces problems. Several writers have had to take court action to recover the use of their own names from websites that have registered them and then tried to sell the rights back or sought a cut of future sales revenue.

然而面临重重难题的不仅是大公司，还有作为个人的一些作者。有些网站注册了几位撰稿人的姓名，然后试图将注册的姓名使用权卖给这些作者，或在将来支付版税时打些折扣，结果作者们为了收回姓名使用权不得不采取诉讼行动。

例 10 中定语从句和主句的关系被调整为因果关系。

以上几例中的汉译文均对原文中定语从句逻辑关系进行了调整。本来定语从句与先行词之间只是一种语法上的限定关系，但其潜在的逻辑关系却是多种多样的，可能会表示原因（例1、2、8、9、10）、条件（例4）、让步（例5）、转折（例3、6）、目的（例7）等多种关系。

下面再观察几个状语从句与主句间逻辑关系调整的例子。

11. He seemed to exhibit courage and manliness when others chickened out.

    别人都害怕了，可他却显示出一副勇气十足的大丈夫气概。

12. Where others might have been overwhelmed by heartbreak, U Thant has persevered, undaunted, in his great work with rare faith, devotion and detachment.

    在别人可能已经悲痛欲绝了，而吴丹却勇敢无畏，以罕见的信念、献身精神和不偏不倚的态度，坚持他那伟大的工作。

13. Where a vessel has vertical sides, the pressure on the bottom is equal to the height of the liquid times its density.

    如果器壁垂直，则容器底的压力等于液体高度乘以液体的密度。

上一单元和本单元讲述了非从句及从句译成中文后逻辑关系的调整问题。这种调整一般要经历如下思维过程：对原文信息进行切分——确立逻辑层次——构建译文。保证译文语篇的逻辑明晰流畅是译者必须关注的一个问题。请参阅第三章 Unit Two 的讲解部分。

Congress at Work

[1] Someone once remarked that the British and the Americans are two peoples separated by the same language. Most epigrams exaggerate for effect, and this one is no exception. But it is nevertheless, undeniably true that some commonly used words mean different things in these two cultures.[1] Consider the seemingly single term—"the government".

[2] To parliamentarians trained in British terminology, "the government" means the cabinet: a group of the legislature's own members, chosen by it[2]

to devise public policies, to manage the legislature's major activities, and to exercise executive powers. In theory, at least, the government continues office only so long as it commands the support of a majority of the legislature.[3] Losing that support, it may be turned out of power at almost any moment.

[3] When Americans say "the government", they mean something quite different: It connotes the whole governmental structure—executive, legislative and judicial. Americans assume a situation in which the branches of government are deliberately separated and in which the powers of each check and balance those of the other.[4]

[4] The president, in whose hands the U.S. governmental system places the executive power, owes neither his election to that office nor his tenure in it to the legislature, the Congress. The president is elected by the people for a term fixed by the U.S. Constitution. It is not unusual for a U.S. president to be of one political party while another party holds majorities in one or both chambers, or houses, of Congress—the House of Representatives and the Senate.[5]

[5] Members of Congress are also elected by the people, but from individual districts and states rather than from the nation as a whole; votes cast for U.S. senators and representatives (known also as congressmen and congresswomen) are separate from those cast for the president. The tenure of the legislators does not depend upon the president; their terms are fixed by the Constitution.

[6] Through its basic control of legislation, especially over the purse, and its power to investigate, the Congress may intrude not only upon the way the executive branch makes policy but also upon the way in which it implements it[6].

[7] Another difference between the U.S. and parliamentary systems concerns the concept of "political party". In the British tradition, a political party connotes a group relatively cohesive in ideology and disciplined in action. Playwright William S. Gibert's satirical line that members of parliament "vote just as their leaders tell 'em to" is not as accurate as it once was, but it is still close enough to the mark.

[8] In contrast, the two major U.S. political parties are vast, sprawling, decentralized conglomerations of varied ideological positions whose

members do not feel obliged to vote the way the party leaders tell them to do. In fact, most members come to Congress as independent entrepreneurs, willing to go along with party policy only to the extent that it does not conflict with what they perceive to be the wishes and interests of their constituencies.

[9] What are the consequences for a legislature of a constitutional structure that deliberately pits the executive and legislative branches against each other and a party system whose individual members are unabashedly independent and indifferently constrained by party discipline[7]?

[10] Most legislatures—whether they are presidential or parliamentary—find it at least convenient and usually essential to establish some sort of committee system, if only for the division of work. What sets American congressional committees apart from those in parliamentary systems is the nature of their work.[8]

[11] The U.S. Congress views itself as at least an equal partner with the president in the development of policy. Consequently, congressional committees are not merely panels for technical review and minor perfection of legislation. They have been described as the "nerve ends of Congress—the gatherers of information, the sifters of alternatives, the refiners of legislation". They are the chief instrument for the critical review of executive branch proposals and of proposals form many other sources as well. On behalf of their parent bodies (the Senate or the House), committees winnow out what is and what is not acceptable, burying proposals that are not[9] and modifying, often quite extensively, whatever remains. Sometimes they identify public problems overlooked or ignored by the executive branch and develop proposals for dealing with them.

[12] In addition, U.S. congressional committees serve as the legislature's watchdog[10] over the executive branch. They are responsible for "oversight" of the organization and operation of the executive agencies: how efficiently and effectively those agencies perform their duties, and whether and how they are carrying out the intent of the laws enacted by the Congress.

[13] In the words of one U.S. president: "Congress in its committee rooms is Congress at work."

参考译文

国会的运转

[1] 有人曾说,英国人和美国人是被同一种语言分隔开的两个民族。警句为了求效果大多言过其实,这句也不例外。尽管如此,在这两种文化中,一些共用词汇表达了不同的事物,这一点却是千真万确的。让我们看看一个看似含义相同的词——"政府"。

[2] 对于那些受英国术语熏陶的议员们,"政府"指的是内阁,是立法机构本身的一批成员,由立法机构选出负责制定公共政策、处理议会的重大活动并行使行政权力。政府只有赢得议会多数成员的支持,才可以继续执政,至少在理论上是这样。失去了多数支持,政府几乎随时有可能下台。

[3] 美国人说到"政府",意思就完全不同了。它指的是整个政体,包括行政、立法和司法部门。按照美国人的做法,政府三大部门是有意识地分立的,每个部门与其他部门相互制衡。

[4] 美国政治制度将行政权力赋予总统,总统的当选和任期均不取决于国会这个立法部门。总统由人民选举,任期则由美国宪法规定。常常出现这样的情况,总统属某一政党,而另一政党却在国会的一院或两院(众议院和参议院)中拥有多数。

[5] 国会议员也由人民选举,但却是从各选区和州而不是在全国范围选举:选举美国参议员和众议员(也称国会议员)与选举总统分开进行。议员的任期不取决于总统,而是由宪法规定的。

[6] 国会凭借对立法的基本控制,特别是对国库的控制,以及调查的权力,不仅可以影响行政部门的决策方式,而且可以影响其施政方式。

[7] 美国的制度和英国议会制的另一个区别在于"政党"的概念。按照英国的传统,政党指的是一个在意识形态上相对统一、在行动上受党纪约束的群体。剧作家威廉·吉尔伯特有一句讽刺诗:"领袖怎样指教,他们就怎样投票。"此话虽已不像从前那样贴切,但仍然相当接近当前的现实。

[8] 相比之下,美国两大政党则庞大、散漫,各种意识形态汇聚一体而又各行其是,党员不认为有必要按照党领袖的要求去投票。事实上,多数议员作为独立的创业人进入国会,只有当他们认为有关政策没有违背其选民的意愿和利益时,他们才会遵循党的政策。

[9] 宪法机制有意使行政部门和立法部门对峙，而党员又各行其是，对党的纪律的约束满不在乎。有这样一种宪法，再加上这样一种政党制度，它们会对立法机构产生什么样的后果呢？

[10] 无论是由总统立法还是由议会立法，多数立法机构认为，即使出于分工目的，建立某种委员会制度，至少是方便的，而且通常又是很有必要的。美国国会委员会与英国议会制委员会的区别在于它们的工作性质。

[11] 美国国会认为自己在制订政策方面起码是总统的平等伙伴。因此，国会里的那些委员会不只是对法案作技术审查和少量修改的机构，它们被称为"国会的神经末梢——资料收集者、备选方案筛选者和法案条文推敲者"。它们是评审行政部门提案以及其他许多来历不同的提案的主要机构。委员会代表其母体（参议院或众议院），负责甄别哪些提案不可接受，哪些可以接受，驳回前者，对后者则往往会进行相当大量的修订。有时，它会提出行政部门无视或忽视的公共问题，并为解决这些问题制订提案。

[12] 此外，美国国会各委员会代表立法机构对行政部门实行监督。它们负责"监督"行政机构的组织和工作：这些机构是否有效履行其职责，是否和如何贯彻国会所颁布法律的意图。

[13] 用一位美国总统的话说："国会的运转就体现在委员会的会议室里。"

注释

1. "全心全意为人民服务，这是我们各项工作的宗旨。"——这句话中的划线部分叫作外位成分。它自成一个小句，后面小句中的"这"字复指前面的这个小句，然后继续进行阐述。它的信息结构可概括如下："外位成分 + 复指词 + 陈述"（有时复指词不在陈述之前，而在陈述结构的中间，如讲解部分的例3和例5）。这种外位结构在说明、论说文中应用很普遍，因为它能使文章条理清楚、重点突出。此处将原文的主语从句译为外位成分就达到了这种效果。
2. 注意，此处代词 it 指的是 legislature，而不是 cabinet。汉译时宜复原成名词，因为汉语多用名词复指的方法与上文衔接，而英语代词复指用得较多。汉语中代词用得不当或太多，会给读者造成理解上的困难。
3. 注意译文在信息顺序及信息重心上的调整。
4. 原文的主句及两个定语从句正好是三个信息单元，译成三个汉语分句。
5. 请继续注意观察本段中以英语小句为表现形式的信息单元与汉语分句间的对应关系。

6. 注意辨清两个 it 的所指。
7. 这是一个长问句。汉语的问句一般没有这么长，译者须对汉译结构进行适当调整。原问句以小句为基准可分出三个信息单元，可概略表述为：(1) 宪法使行政、司法对立；(2) 政党制度中党员相对独立，不守党纪；(3) 这些会对立法产生什么影响。汉语形式结构较弱，译者顺应这一特点，将原句拆为两句：第一句陈述事实，第二句先概括第一句内容，然后发问。

请进一步观察下面一段中两个长问句的译法：

Who were those warriors who had fought so long, so fiercely, so courageously, and—as admitted by observers of every color, and privately among Generalissimo Chiang Kai-shek's own followers—on the whole so invincibly? What made them fight like that? What held them up? What was the revolutionary basis of their movement? What were the hopes and aims and dreams that had made of them the incredibly stubborn warriors—incredible compared with the history of compromise that is China—who had endured hundreds of battles, blockade, salt shortage, famine, disease, epidemic, and finally the Long March of 6000 miles, in which they crossed twelve provinces of China, broke through thousands of Kuomintang troops, and triumphantly emerged at last into a new base in the Northwest?

这些战士战斗得那么长久，那么顽强，那么勇敢，而且正如各种政治色彩的观察家，就连蒋介石总司令自己的部下私下也承认的那样，从整体来说是那么所向披靡——他们到底是什么样的人呢？是什么使他们那样地战斗？是什么支持着他们？他们运动的革命基础是什么？是什么样的希望，什么样的目标，什么样的理想，使他们成为顽强到难以置信的战士呢？说令人难以置信，是同中国那部充满折中妥协的历史比较而言的；他们身经百战，经历过封锁、缺盐、饥饿、疾病、瘟疫，最后还有那六千英里的历史性长征，穿过中国的十二个省份，冲破千千万万国民党军队的阻拦，终于出现在西北的一个强大的新根据地上。

此段中的两个长问句之所以长，都是因为有较长的定语从句。第一个长问句先译出从句作为铺垫，而后发问。第二个则先提出问题，而后再译出从句。究竟怎样译为好，要依行文的具体需要而定。

8. 此句译文仍是以小句（包括不定式短语）为基准进行信息划分，在译为相应汉语分句时逻辑排列顺序有所调整。
9. 注意此处的省略现象。
10. watchdog 是一个比喻，此处采取意译方法。因为译成"看门狗""守望犬"都具有明显的贬义，而 watchdog 在英语中是没有这种贬义联想的。

讲解

一、外位成分的运用

注释 1 已对外位成分做了简单介绍，再看下面几例：

1. China's vast size and resources, her extraordinary economic progress over recent years, have made her an increasingly important player in the modern international economy.

   中国地大物博，近年来经济迅猛发展，这使得中国在现代国际经济中成为一支越来越重要的力量。

2. I'd never seen such a sensitivity to passions translated into metal and stone.

   金属和石头居然能如此细腻地表现感情，这我还是第一次见到。

3. It's a great advantage not to drink among hard-drinking people.

   在爱喝酒的人中间而自己不喝酒，那是很占便宜的。

4. The introduction of new varieties of rice and wheat in Asia and Latin America has been known as the "Green Revolution".

   亚洲和拉丁美洲引进了各式各样的稻麦新品种，人们称之为"绿色革命"。

5. It is no despicable feat to start a million brains running at nine o'clock in the morning, to give two million eyes something bright and brisk and amusing to look at.

   能在上午九点钟使得一百万人的头脑都活跃起来，使得两百万只眼睛都有一些鲜明、生动、有趣的东西看，这种本领可不能小瞧。

6. ...and it seemed marvelous to her that a machine could remember so much and was always there, ready and waiting to do its work.

   一台机器竟能记住这么多事情，而且有求必应，随时待命，她觉得这真是太妙了。

7. It is not a very pleasant thing to recognize that for the young you are no longer an equal.

   意识到你对青年人来说已经不是他们的同辈人，这种感觉不是很愉快的。

8. China's firm advocacy of the equality of all nations and respect for their independence and sovereignty touches a very responsive chord in our hearts.

   中国坚决主张世界各国一律平等，尊重各国的独立和主权，这一点引起我们强烈的共鸣。

对照下面译例的两种译文,体会一下应用外位成分的长处。

9. It is impossible to produce future shock in large numbers of individuals without affecting the rationality of the society as a whole.

   [a] 如果在许多人中间出现未来冲击,那么不影响整个社会的理性是不可能的。
   [b] 要在大批人中间造成未来冲击,而又不影响整个社会的理性,那是不可能的。

10. Another theory considers the source of psychic disturbance to be the dislocation of the individual's primary ties which comes with shift from the countryside to the city and from rural to urban occupations.

    [a] 另一种理论则认为,精神失调的根源是个人首属社会联系的解体。这是由农村进入城市,由农村职业转为城市职业造成的。
    [b] 另一种理论则认为,由于人们从农村迁入城市,由农业职业转为城市职业,造成了个人首属社会联系的解体,这才是精神失调的根源。

当然,必须提醒大家,译者不能只译句而不谋篇,即不能光顾应用外位成分,而影响语篇的整体连贯性。如下面这一语篇中,译者用了外位成分,却忽视了后两句译文的逻辑连贯。

11. Whatever the idealists may say, it is obvious that what matters to the public is success. Even the organizers of the Olympic Games admit this. Whoever comes first wins a gold medal but anyone who comes fourth gets nothing. What the administrators sometimes ignore is that anyone who wants to become an Olympic champion must do without spare time and possibly break off his studies. It is not surprising that athletes want some tangible reward.

   不管理想主义者怎么说,对公众来说,至关紧要的仍然是比赛成绩。就连奥运会的组织者们也承认这一点。得第一的获金牌,得第四的便什么也拿不到。任何想获奥运冠军的人都得牺牲掉自己的业余时间,还可能为之中断学业,这一点时常被运动会官员们所忽视。运动员想拿到一些实实在在的物质奖励,就不足为怪了。

可以看出,倒数第二句中外位成分表达的信息和最后一句是密切相关的,但却被复指代词"这"字引出的小句给隔断了。为了文气的流畅,此句还是不用外位成分为好。可改为:运动会官员们常常忽略这么一点,即任何想当奥运冠军的人都不得不放弃业余时间,甚至还可能中断学业。因此,运动员想拿到一些实实在在的物质奖励,就不足为怪了。

二、复合句的翻译

注释4、5、7、8均涉及以英语的小句（clause）为基准划分信息单元，然后将信息单元在汉语中重新组织的问题。在英汉翻译，尤其是政论文、说明文的翻译中，以英语小句为参照进行信息传译，是一条较为方便、稳妥的途径。我们这里说的英语小句不仅包括传统上所说的各类从句，也包括Quirk等在 *A Grammar of Contemporary English* 及 *A Comprehensive Grammar of the English Language* 中，章振邦等在《新编英语语法》中所提到的非限定性小句（non-finite clause）以及无动词小句（verbless clause）。非限定性小句指传统语法中所谓分词短语及不定式短语，无动词小句指下列句子中划线部分：

Unhappy with the result, she returned to work.
A case in both hands, Mabel stalked out of the house.

非限定性小句和无动词小句中虽然没有语法上的主谓成分，但在语义上是很容易确定其主题和述题的，如 a case in both hands 即相当于 he had/held a case in both hands。所以，无论是限定性小句（传统上的定语从句、状语从句、名词性从句等），还是非限定性小句，或无动词小句，都是可以提供主题和述题两部分信息的，这是译者在建构汉语译文时的重要参照。常常发生这样的情况：英语小句被译为与之相应的汉语小句或句段，只是排列的顺序可能有所调整，逻辑关系可能有所变通。因此，译者在翻译过程中，以英语小句作为基本信息单元考虑信息的传译和重新组织问题，是一个可行的思维途径。循着这样的思路反复实践，就能积累起自己翻译英语复合句的经验，摸索出得心应手的翻译方法。请观察下面译例，注意英语小句与汉语小句大体相对应的转换规律：

1. <u>Shaking off from my spirit</u> <u>what must have been a dream</u>, <u>I scanned more narrowly the real aspect of the building.</u>
            1   2   3

   那肯定是个幻觉，我从中挣脱出来，更加仔细地打量这座房子的真实面目。
        2   1   3

2. <u>Plugged into the intercommunication system</u>, <u>the man can now communicate with the rest of the crew</u> <u>no matter what noise is going on about him.</u>
           1   2   3

不管周围多么喧闹，插头一接上机内通话系统，他就能和同机其余的人通话。
　　　3　　　　　　　　1　　　　　　　　　2

3. There are many wonderful stories to tell about the places I visited and
　　　　　　　　1　　　　　　　　　　2　　　　　　　3
the people I met.
　　　4

我访问了一些地方，遇到了不少人，要谈起来，奇妙的事情可多着呢。
　　　3　　　　　　　　4　　　　　　2　　　　　　1

4. Jack had then nothing to live on, because whenever he had a good job,
　　　　　　　　1　　　　　　　　　　　　　2
the more he earned the more he spent, so that he never saved anything.
　　　3　　　　　　　　　4　　　　　　　　　　5

杰克当时无以为生，因为每逢找到好的工作时，总是挣得越多，花得也越多，
　　　　1　　　　　　　　　　2　　　　　　　　3　　　　　　4
结果毫无积蓄。
　　　5

5. He was irritated at Edwin taking what seemed to him like an unfair
　　　　　1　　　　　　2　　　　　　　　　　　3
advantage, though where the advantage lay he could not have said.
　　　　　　　　　4　　　　　　　　　　　　5

他觉得埃德温似乎占了便宜，十分恼火，可这便宜究竟是什么，他又说不出来。
　　　2+3　　　　　　　　　1　　　　　　　　4　　　　　　　5

请再观察下面几个译例。为简便，只用斜线大致切分出以小句为基准的信息单元，请仔细观察并体会译者对信息单元的组合及排列过程。

6. I cultivated it by creating distance,/slinking around like a lone wolf,/ feeding on my misanthropy with narrowed eyes/like a cat who removes herself to far corner of the yard/before devouring her victim, a mole or a blue jay,/lest someone take it away.

我和人们拉开距离以孤立自己，/像一只孤独的狼东游西荡，/眯起眼睛玩味自己的厌世思想，/就如同一只猫，在吞食猎物——一只鼹鼠或者坚鸟——之前，把它弄到院子的一角，/生怕被抢了去。

7. It is in this spirit/ that I extend to you most warmly an invitation to visit

Bangladesh/which will afford us an opportunity for further discussions on the world situation/and also to review bilateral relations.

本着这一精神，/我热情地邀请你访问孟加拉国，/以使我们有机会进一步讨论世界形势，/回顾双边关系的发展。

8. But while we cannot close the gulf between us,/we can try to bridge it/ so that we may be able to talk across it.

但是，虽然我们不能弥合双方之间的鸿沟，/我们却能够设法搭一座桥，/以便我们能够越过它进行会谈。

9. It is appropriate /that the children of Sri Lanka/who will be the beneficiaries of some of the development projects/now being carried out in Sri Lanka with the help of your great country/should show their appreciation and gratitude/by sending you a token gift in the form of "Mithura"/which will serve as a living symbol of the friendship between the children of our two countries.

斯里兰卡的儿童/将从你们伟大国家正在帮助建设的一些发展项目中获益，因此他们把"米杜拉"作为象征性的礼物送给你们，/以表示赞赏和谢意，/这是十分恰当的。/"米杜拉"将成为我们两国之间友谊的活的象征。

10. There is a saying in our country/that the elephant is an animal/which never forgets/and the choice of an elephant as a gift from the children of Sri Lanka is therefore of special significance/in that it symbolizes their appreciation and gratitude.

我国有句俗话说，/象从不忘事。因此，斯里兰卡儿童把象选作礼物是有特殊意义的，/它象征着儿童们的赞赏和谢意。

11. Pharmaceutical companies are also having severe problems/coping with copycat manufacturing by rivals in India and Egypt and elsewhere/that provides cheap medicines for local people,/but contributes little or nothing towards the research costs of the drugs.

制药企业也有一些棘手的问题，/那就是如何对付在印度、埃及和其他地方进行仿制的对手。/这些公司为当地人提供廉价药品，/但是在药品的研发费用方面却少有或没有贡献。

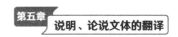

How Paper Shaped Civilization

Reid Mitenbuler

[1] In his impressive new book, *Paper: Paging Through History*, Mark Kurlansky picks up a seemingly mundane commodity to examine a wider phenomenon: historical attitudes toward disruptive technologies. His question: How do humans absorb and disseminate information? His answer helps reveal the evolution, both politically and economically[1], of how the world has come to be organized.

[2] Over centuries[2], writing moved across more than a dozen materials. Clay tablets dominated for three thousand years—"a considerably longer period than the reign of paper up until now," Kurlansky writes—because they had the advantage of being inexpensive, readily available, and easy to use. But the tablets' lack of portability was a problem. People turned to papyrus, the reedy plant found in marshy areas, but that disintegrated easily, and much of the world's supply was too spindly for making high-quality writing sheets. Wax was one alternative, but it was best for disposable writing,[3] so parchment was next in line, made by scraping and processing animal skins. As many as two hundred animals were needed to make a single book.

[3] "As with all new inventions, some saw parchment as the way of the future and others disdained it," Kurlansky writes. The concerns were political as much as economic. Parchment was more durable than papyrus and immune to Egyptian papyrus monopolies, but it was still relatively expensive and labor-intensive to produce. Rulers also fretted how rising literacy and access to new ideas might affect their populations. "A new way of thinking was emerging," Kurlansky writes, and it needed to be recorded in a new way. "Something as disposable as wax, as light as leaves, as cheap as clay, and as durable as parchment was needed."[4]

[4] Nobody knows the exact origins of paper. "It seems highly improbable that some lone genius stumbled upon the idea by him- or herself," Kurlansky

writes. Contemporary scholars suspect the Chinese invented the general papermaking process of breaking down cellulose fibers and randomly weaving them together, but the finer points of this story are murky. Perhaps because great stories work better with a central hero, Chinese schoolchildren are told that paper was invented in 105 C.E. by a eunuch in the Han court named Cai Lun. Demand for writing material surged during the Han era, which is when China's first comprehensive national histories were produced, when classic works that had been destroyed by previous dynasties were reissued, and when the first official version of Confucius's teachings were recorded.[5]

[5]   Over time, various Chinese innovations helped paper become stronger, thinner, and cheaper to produce. These innovations spread, particularly to an Islamic world enjoying its own great cultural ferment by the ninth century. "The Qur'an says that good Muslims should seek knowledge," Kurlansky writes, "and they did so passionately and with a great deal of ink and paper." (Arab words for paper, such as *kaghid* and *qirtas*—a word used in the Qur'an—are thought to be of Chinese origin.) Paper-loving Muslims helped spread mathematics, astronomy, medicine, engineering, agriculture, and literature to other parts of the world, including the West.

[6]   But Europe lagged behind. It's unclear why the continent used parchment for so long, but like all areas that were slower to adopt paper, this hindered its advancement.[6] Up until the thirteenth century, many kings and princes were still illiterate. The greatest argument for why Europeans eventually switched to paper is because it was cheap. They first used it to make better Bibles, then quickly learned to rely on it for other obsessions, like money and banking. Their various empires expanded as a result, and around the thirteenth century, Europeans began learning more about the advancements of other cultures. Europe "had become a different place", Kurlansky writes. "One discovery rolled in on the heels of another, which rolled in on the heels of yet another."[7]

[7]   There were limits to this spread of knowledge. Creating books was labor-intensive; they were hand-printed and dictated to scribes. This made them expensive, a problem that was compounded by a tendency to dress them up with heavy jeweled covers. The fourteenth-century Italian scholar

Petrarch almost had his leg amputated after dropping one of these books on it.

[8] Still, the demand for books only grew. By the fourteenth century, papermaking was a common industrial activity in Europe, which gave rise to printing, another great innovation that fueled the engines of human civilization—religion, business, art, and empire—for centuries to come.[8] As Kurlansky notes, the greatest single change in Europe during the centuries leading into the Renaissance were "the bustling of intellectual life coming out of the monasteries and into the universities and other places accessible to the general population".

参考译文

纸是如何塑造文明的？

里德·米腾布勒

[1] 在他令人瞩目的新作《纸的变迁：翻阅历史》中，马克·库兰斯基从一种看似普通的物品入手，来探究一个更为宽泛的课题：对待颠覆性技术更新的历史态度。他提出的问题是：人类如何接受和传播信息？他的答案从政治和经济两个方面揭示出社会组织形式的变革历程。

[2] 几十个世纪以来，书写材料变化了十几次。库兰斯基写道，泥板主导了三千年的历史，"比延续至今的纸张还更长"。原因是泥板具有价格便宜、随处可取、易于使用等优势。但泥板书不便携带是个大问题。于是人们转而取用纸莎草造纸，就是沼泽地带那种芦苇似的植物。但那种纸容易破碎折损，而且世界上大部分纸莎草都太纤细，不能制作高质量的书写纸。另一个选择是涂上蜡的木板——蜡板，但那最适合用于需要涂改的书写。于是又出现了羊皮纸，由动物皮打磨加工制成，做一本书要两百多动物的皮。

[3] 库兰斯基写道："如同对待历来所有新发明一样，有些人将羊皮纸视为未来的方向，而其他一些人则嗤之以鼻。"人们的关切来自政治和经济两个方面。羊皮纸比纸莎草纸更耐久，还可打破埃及人对纸莎草纸的垄断，但还是价格高了些，而且制作起来需要大量劳力。统治者还担心识字率的提高和新思想的传播会影响他们的臣民。库兰斯基写道，"一种新思想产生了"，就需要以一种新的方式加以记载。"一

种像蜡板一样好涂改,像纸莎草纸一样轻,像泥板一样廉价,又像羊皮纸一样耐久的材料于是呼之欲出。"

[4] 没人知道纸究竟是如何起源的。库兰斯基写道:"说某个天才突发奇想发明了造纸术,那是极不可信的。"当代学者认为,是中国人发明了将植物纤维打成纸浆再使之随意铺平的造纸术,然而更具体的细节就模糊不清了。或许是因为伟大的事件总要有一个中心人物才显得真实,中国的学童们被告知,造纸术是公元105年汉朝一个名叫蔡伦的太监发明的。两汉时期中国第一部通史编纂完毕,前朝毁坏的经典文献得以重新发行,孔子《论语》的官方注本也已刊行,因此当时对书写材料的需求大增。

[5] 随着时间的推移,中国发明了几项新技术,增加了纸张的强度,减少了厚度,造价也更低廉。这些新发明传播到了世界各地,尤其是九世纪时正在经历文化大繁荣的伊斯兰世界。"《古兰经》说,优秀的穆斯林要追求知识。"库兰斯基写道,"于是信徒们热心践行,耗用了大量的墨水和纸张。"(阿拉伯语中做"纸"讲的词语,比如《古兰经》里用的 kaghid 和 qirtas 等词语,据信就是源自汉语的。)喜欢用纸书写的穆斯林们把数学、天文学、医学、工程学、农学以及文学知识传播到世界各地,其中也包括西方诸国。

[6] 然而欧洲落后了。羊皮纸在欧洲使用了那么长时间,其原因尚不清楚,但正像较晚才使用纸张的所有其他地区的情况一样,这阻碍了欧洲的发展。直到十三世纪,许多国王和王子还目不识丁。欧洲人转而使用纸张的最大理由是它便宜。他们用纸来印刷更精美的《圣经》,后来又很快学会了做其他重要事情,如印钞票和开展银行业务。结果,欧洲诸王国开始扩张,到了大约十三世纪,欧洲开始向其他文化学习更多的新东西。欧洲"变成了一个不一样的地方",库兰斯基写道,"新发明一个接一个传来,首尾相接,源源不断。"

[7] 这种知识传播方法也有种种不足之处。书籍制作需要花费大量劳力;书稿要手写,然后口述给抄写员。这样书的价格就很高,更有甚者,封面还要用重重的珠宝加以装潢。十四世纪意大利学者彼特拉克不小心把一本这样的书掉在腿上,大腿被砸得险些截肢。

[8] 尽管如此,人们对书籍的需求还是只增不减。到了十四世纪,造纸已成为欧洲普遍的工业活动,而这又催生了另一项伟大发明——印刷术。在随后的几个世纪中,印刷术的发展为宗教、商业、艺术和帝国体制这些人类文明的引擎注入了新的动力。正如库兰斯基所指出的,在文艺复兴前的几个世纪中,欧洲最伟大的变革就

是"学术生活走出修道院,并走进大学及其他普通民众可以接触到的地方,从而带来了学术的繁荣"。

注释

1. 这两个副词修饰动词 reveal,不可译为"他给出的答案有助于揭示世界是如何在政治上和经济上进行组织的演化的"。
2. 据下文,此处 centuries 应指几千年以来,不可译为"几个世纪以来"。
3. 此句不宜译为"但蜡更适合一次性使用",disposable writing 直译成"一次性书写"也语焉不详,应该指蜡板上写字可以马上抹平修改。上句的 wax 也应译为"蜡板",而不应仅仅用一个字,译为"另外一种选择是蜡"。
4. 此句中的 wax、leaves 和 clay 都不宜直译为三种物质的名称,应指明是三种书写载体。
5. 定语从句 which is... 中含有三个由 when 引导的表语从句。译文将整个定语从句先译出,然后再译出主句,这两者间的逻辑关系是因果关系,故后一句前面加上"因此"一词。
6. 译文将 the continent used parchment for so long 抽出译为话题,其后的信息就很容易依次铺排,层层展开。
7. 这句话包含一个定语从句,如按句法直译为"一项发明紧跟着另一项发明传进来,而这后一项发明也是紧跟另一项发明传进来的。"这在汉语中显然难以接受,所以此处将整个句子看作一个翻译单位,按汉语表达习惯再现其意。
8. 此句包含两个定语从句。第一个 which gave rise to... 译成了递进的关系(而这又……);第二个 that fueled the engines... 拆出译成单独一句话。

 讲解

定语从句的拆译

本单元译文涉及不少定语从句的翻译问题。本章 Unit Two 的讲解部分曾讨论过定语从句的逻辑关系调整。现在着重说一说定语从句是否要拆译的问题,一般来说,即译成前置定语还是拆译成小句的问题。拆与不拆主要考虑如下因素:定语从句所表达的逻辑关系是严谨的限定关系,还是较松散的对先行词的阐发、说明的关系。如系前一种情况,不要拆译,包括为了行文的需要未译为前置定语,而是做了某种结构变通的情况,见译例 8 和 23;而后一种情况,则可根据行文需要在保证译文整体连贯的前提下拆译为小句。先观察下面几个不拆译的例子:

1. Britain was, of course, the birthplace of the industrial revolution, "the workshop of the world" and an imperial power whose colonies stretched around the globe.

的确，英国曾经是"产业革命"的诞生地，号称"世界的制造车间"，是一个殖民地遍布全球的雄伟帝国。

此句采取将定语从句译为前置定语的办法，这样"……制造车间"和"……雄伟帝国"形成并列结构，句子连贯、清晰。

2. Thus I see two differences between the spirit which now animates this country and that which animated it in 1914.

因此，我觉得目前激励这个国家的精神与1914年曾经激励过这个国家的精神之间有两个不同点。

句中两个定语从句限定关系密切，不可拆译。

3. During the 25 years which have intervened between the First and the Second German Wars—that is, between the night of 4 August 1914 and the morning of Sunday, 3 September 1939—I have often asked my friends to tell me in what way, and in what manner, they first became aware that Great Britain was at war. There had, on each occasion, been a preliminary stage during which war seemed to become every hour more inevitable; on each occasion, there had been announcements in the newspapers and speeches in the House of Commons; but what interested me particularly was to hear stories of the actual moment at which any given individual became conscious that we had passed from the sunlight of peace into the night of war.

在第一次世界大战和第二次世界大战间的25年中，即1914年8月4日夜到1939年9月3日星期天早晨之间，我常常问我的朋友们，他们是以何种途径，以何种方式第一次觉察到英国已进入战争状态的。每一次都有战争似乎正步步逼近、无法避免的预示阶段；每次报纸上都登有通告，下议院里也要发表讲演。但使我特别感兴趣的，是了解作为单个的人意识到我们已从和平阳光进入战争黑夜的那个真实时刻的故事。

上面一段中的三个定语从句都没有拆译，因为拆译会破坏汉语译文的连贯性。

下面是更多不拆译（即译成前置定语）的例子：

4. The magic tree—which colours the Canadian landscape in the autumn and sweetens the Canadian palate in the spring—is the maple tree.

这种在秋天为加拿大的风景添色、在春天使加拿大人的口中甜蜜的神奇的树，就是枫树。

5. He must distinguish infallibly between the little clod of manure, which sticks to the crocus of necessity, and that which is plastered to it out of bravado.

他必须准确无误地分辨出哪些是出于必要而黏在报春花上面的小小粪土块，哪些是为了虚张声势而有意涂抹在报春花上面的污泥。

6. However, even the prescient Tocqueville, who predicted 150 years ago that the United States and Russia Would emerge as two great contending powers, could not have foreseen that the nation that potentially could decide the world balance of power in the last decade of the twentieth century, and that could become the most powerful nation on earth during the twenty-first century, would be China.

然而，即使是150年前曾预言过美国和俄国将成为两个相互竞争的世界大国的颇有远见的托克维尔，也未能预见到在二十世纪最后几十年具有决定世界均势潜力并能成为二十一世纪地球上最强大的国家的，将是中国。

7. For men and women are not themselves; they are also the region they are born, the city apartment or the farm in which they are born, the city apartment or the farm in which they learnt to walk, the games they played as children, the old wives' tales they overheard, the food they ate, the schools they attended, the sports they followed, the poets they read, and the God they believed in.

因为不论男男女女，都不仅仅是他们自身，他们也是自己出生的乡土，学步的农场或城市公寓，儿时玩的游戏，私下听来的《山海经》，吃的食物，上的学校，关心的运动，吟奏的诗章，和信仰的上帝。

8. I shall not often refer to foreign novels in these lectures, still less would I pose as an expert on them who is debarred from discussing them by his terms of reference.

在这些讲演里，我不会经常提到外国小说，我更不会以外国小说专家自居，装出一副只是碍于这次讲座的委托书规定所限，不便对外国小说多加讨论的样子。

这个译例比较特殊。表面上看句子被拆译，但实际上没有。因为这个译文只是下面译文的变通：更不会摆出一副只是碍于此次讲座委托书规定而无法对外国小说加以讨论的外国小说专家的架子。如果加以拆译，即将定语从句 who is debarred from discussing them by his terms of reference 拆出并对逻辑关系加以调整，就可能出现下面扭曲原文意义的译法：我更不会摆出外国小说专家的架子，因为根据这次规定的讲课范围，是不得讨论外国小说的。

下面再看拆译的例子：

9. I thought, too, of the folly of those statesmen throughout history who have lacked the courage and the resourcefulness to face these basic challenges; who have employed their energies instead in repudiating the promise of human dignity.

我还想到历史上那些政治家的愚蠢，他们缺乏勇气和智慧去接受这些根本性的挑战；相反，他们却竭尽全力背弃人类的尊严。

10. We have brought all the way from Sri Lanka a baby elephant which the children of Sri Lanka wish me to present on their behalf to you the children of the People's Republic of China. We have named the baby elephant "Mithura" which means "friend" in the Sinhala language.

我们从斯里兰卡远道带来一只小象，斯里兰卡的儿童要我代表他们把这只小象赠送给你们——中华人民共和国的儿童。我们给这只小象取名为"米杜拉"，在僧伽罗文里就是"朋友"的意思。

11. In the spirit of frankness which I hope will characterize our talks this week, let us recognize at the outset these points:...

我希望我们这个星期的会谈将是坦率的。本着这种坦率的精神，让我们在一开始就认识到这样几点：……

12. A spirited discussion springs up between a young girl who insists that women have outgrown the jumping-on-the-chair-at-the-sight-of-a-mouse era and a colonel who says that they haven't.

席间，一位年轻的女士同一位上校展开了热烈的讨论。女士坚持认为，妇女如今已有进步，不再是过去那种一见老鼠就吓得跳起来的妇女。上校则认为妇女并没有多大改变。

13. Montgomery, the victor over Rommel in North Africa, who on September 1 was made a field marshal, drove his Canadian First Army and British Second Army two hundred miles in four days—from the lower Seine past the storied battle sites of 1914-1918 and 1940 into Belgium.

蒙哥马利在北非战胜了隆美尔后，已于9月1日晋升为元帅，如今率领加拿大第一集团军和英国第二集团军在四天之内挺进二百英里，从塞纳河下游，经过历史上有名的1914—1918年战场和1940年战场，进入比利时。

14. Another technique is dropping, in which partial bands are directly dropped from the line-frequency band, and where replenishment is also often possible.

 另一种技术是分路连接，部分通路从线路频带上直接分出来，而补给也往往是可能的。

15. He felt that books and the knowledge in them were part of a world that was against him, a world to which he did not belong and which he did not want to enter, the world of which the hateful teachers were representatives and symbols.

 他觉得书本知识是和他敌对的那个世界的一部分。他不属于，也不想进入那个世界，而那些可恨的老师都是那个世界的象征和代表。

16. Five score years ago, a great American, in whose symbolic shadow we stand today, signed the Emancipation Proclamation.

 一百年前，一位伟大的美国人签署了《黑人解放宣言》。今天，我们正是在象征着他的身影下，在此集会。

17. Only New York, it seems, attracts this peculiar populace of lone and homeless women who live in an isolated, mistrustful world of their own.

 看来只有纽约例外，它吸引了一群奇特的无家可归的孤独女人。这些女人生活在一个互不信任的、与世隔绝的自己的小天地里。

18. I spent some of the quietest Sundays of my life in Uncle Amos's yard, lying under apple trees and listening to bees and not listening to Uncle Amos who was bumbling away at something he did not expect me to listen to at all.

 我躺在苹果树下，耳边响着蜜蜂的嗡嗡声，无须用心去听艾默大叔永无休止的唠叨。他也完全没有要我听的意思。

19. The two economists, who have written papers and legal filings supporting Microsoft's position in it's antitrust case, said that government should act to keep companies from abusing their monopoly power to undercut competitors, but that "the application of antitrust principles should take account of the important ways new-economy industries differ from traditional ones".

 这两位经济学家曾写过多篇论文和法律材料，支持微软在这场反垄断案中的立场。他们说，虽然政府应该采取措施，制止公司利用其垄断地位来削弱竞争对手，但是"反垄断法的实施应考虑到新经济产业与传统经济产业的差异"。

20. What troubles some observers of the world of Internet-enabled software and services—which marches to slogans like "get big fast" and "winner take all"—is that a number of factors may make it a breeding ground for monopolies.

依存于因特网的软件业和服务业是喊着"迅速做大"和"赢者通吃"的口号发展的。一些观察家感到担心的是，正是这一发展过程中的一些因素使这些产业成了滋生垄断的土壤。

21. I have been doing chores, being for a brief spell alone in a house that recently was astir with bustle and echoed with the voices of a gathered family.

最近，一家人聚在一起，屋里忙忙乱乱，闹闹嚷嚷。这几天，家里就我一人，便一直在做家务。

上例中定语从句被拆出译为一句，交代背景信息。

22. He almost couldn't believe that he, Ken Lauder of Oakland, California, who had first arrived in Africa with the Peace corps, who had studied paleoanthropology at the University of Kenya while supporting himself as a bush tracker, a safari guide, a bartender at Nairobi's Naivasha Hotel, who had joined expeditions as truck driver, and had earned his degree on merciless digs that had taken down other students with heatstroke and dysentery—in a word, the old he, whom he knew only too well, had made two discoveries in one day.

他出生于加利福尼亚的奥克兰。最初是随和平队来非洲的，后来在肯尼亚大学攻读古生物学。他打工自助，干过狩猎巡视员，为科学考察队当过向导，在内罗毕的内瓦莎饭店当过酒吧侍者，还在探险队当过卡车司机。最后在近乎残酷的考古考察中，其他学生因患头痛和痢疾被一个个拖垮，而他却最终获得了学位。这就是他——凯恩·劳德，他太了解自己了。而现在正是这个凯恩，一天之内竟获得两项重大发现。对这他自己都不敢相信。

在这个长句的翻译中，译者也是先把从句所表达的背景信息译出，然后再译主句。译文流畅、自然。

拆译与否，不只取决于当前的句子，还要将句子放在上下文中从文脉整体走向考虑。看下面一个译例：

23. [It is generally agreed some adults who experience sexual abuse may recall memories of the abuse after forgetting it. There is no research to indicate recalled memories are more or less accurate than memories available all along.

The paper says it is impossible to distinguish a true from a false memory and it is dangerous to use confidence, vividness and detail as indicating truth.

False memories can be induced under hypnosis, and experiments have indicated it is possible, although difficult, to implant false memories of entire events by suggestion.]

The paper says further research is required into interview techniques and conditions under which false memories and reports of abuse are most likely to arise.

[人们普遍认为某些受性虐待的成年人在遗忘该经历后可以重新回忆起来。但研究无法表明，唤起的记忆和长期的记忆相比哪个更准确。

论文认为，要区分记忆真实与否是不可能的。而且，用（叙述者）是否自信、（叙述）是否生动、详细作为判断真实性的条件是很危险的。

在催眠状态下可以诱发虚假的记忆，而且实验表明，通过暗示法植入对整个事件的虚假记忆尽管十分困难，但还是有可能的。]

论文认为，需要进一步研究询问的技巧和条件——在这些技巧和条件下，不真实的记忆和有关受虐待的陈述最有可能产生。

要确定最后一句译文的拆译是否得当，就句论句，很难回答，必须结合上文考虑（括号中的段落）。上文在引述一篇论文的内容：用询问的方法获取他人记忆陈述时有许多不确定因素。因此才有了当前这一句的观点：须进一步研究如何避免失真的记忆陈述。显然，从文脉走向看，这一句还是不拆译的好。可直译为：论文认为，需要进一步研究最容易诱发不真实的遭受虐待的记忆和陈述的询问技巧和条件。再做变通（参阅译例 8），即：论文认为，需要进一步研究何种询问技巧和条件最容易诱发对所受虐待的不真实的记忆和陈述。顺便提一下，原译还将 false memories and reports of abuse 的语法关系搞错了，of abuse 应同时修饰 memories 和 reports。可参阅第二章 Unit Three 的讲解部分中有关识别定语修饰关系的例句分析。

Beauty (Excerpts)

Scott Russell Sander

[1] Judging from the scientists I know, including Eva and Ruth, and those whom I've read about, you can't pursue the laws of nature very long without bumping into beauty. "I don't know if it's the same beauty you see in the sunset," a friend tells me, "but it feels the same." This friend is a physicist, who has spent a long career deciphering what must be happening in the interior of stars. He recalls for me this thrill on grasping for the first time Dirac's equations describing quantum mechanics, or those of Einstein describing relativity. "They're so beautiful," he says, "you can see immediately they have to be true. Or at least on the way toward truth." I ask him what makes a theory beautiful, and he replies, "Simplicity, symmetry, elegance, and power."

[2] Why nature should conform to theories we find beautiful is far from obvious. The most incomprehensible thing about the universe, as Einstein said, is that it's comprehensible. How unlikely, that a short-lived biped on a two-bit planet should be able to gauge the speed of light, lay bare the structure of an atom, or calculate the gravitational tug of a black hole.[1] We're a long way from understanding everything, but we do understand a great deal about how nature behaves. Generation after generation, we puzzle out formulas, test them, and find, to an astonishing degree, that nature agrees. An architect draws designs on flimsy paper, and her buildings stand up through earthquakes.

[3] We launch a satellite into orbit and use it to bounce messages from continent to continent. The machine on which I write these words embodies hundreds of insights into the workings of the material world, insights that are confirmed by every burst of letters on the screen, and I stare at that screen through lenses that obey the laws of optics first worked out in detail by Isaac Newton.

[4] By discerning patterns in the universe, Newton believed, he was tracing the hand of God. Scientists in our day have largely abandoned the notion

of a Creator as an unnecessary hypothesis, or at least an untestable one.[2] While they share Newton's faith that the universe is ruled everywhere by a coherent set of rules, they cannot say, as scientists, how these particular rules came to govern things. You can do science without believing in a divine Legislator, but not without believing in laws.

[5]　I spent my teenage years scrambling up the mountain of mathematics. Midway up the slope, however, I staggered to a halt, gasping in the rarefied air, well before I reached the heights where the equations of Einstein and Dirac would have made sense. Nowadays I add, subtract, multiply, and do long division when no calculator is handy, and I can do algebra and geometry and even trigonometry in a pinch, but that is about all that I've kept from the language of numbers. Still, I remember glimpsing patterns in mathematics that seemed as bold and beautiful as a skyful of stars.[3]

[6]　I'm never more aware of the limitations of language than when I try to describe beauty. Language can create its own loveliness, of course, but it cannot deliver to us the radiance we apprehend in the world, any more than a photograph can capture the stunning swiftness of a hawk or the withering power of a supernova. Eva's wedding album holds only a faint glimmer of the wedding itself. All that pictures or words can do is gesture beyond themselves toward the fleeting glory that stirs our hearts. So I keep gesturing.

[7]　"All nature is meant to make us think of paradise," Thomas Merton observed. Because the Creation puts on a nonstop show,[4] beauty is free and inexhaustible, but we need training in order to perceive more than the most obvious kinds. Even 15 billion years or so after the Big Bang, echoes of that event still linger in the form of background radiation, only a few degrees above absolute zero. Just so, I believe, the experience of beauty is an echo of the order and power that permeate the universe. To measure background radiation, we need subtle instruments; to measure beauty, we need alert intelligence and our five keen senses.

[8]　Anyone with eyes can take delight in a face or a flower. You need training, however, to perceive the beauty in mathematics or physics or chess, in the architecture of a tree, the design of a bird's wing, or the shiver of breath through a flute.[5] For most of human history, the training has come from elders who taught the young how to pay attention. By paying

attention, we learn to savor all sorts of patterns, from quantum mechanics to patchwork quilts. This predilection brings with it a clear evolutionary advantage, for the ability to recognize patterns helped our ancestors to select mates, find food, avoid predators. But the same advantage would apply to all species, and yet we alone compose symphonies and crossword puzzles, carve stone into statues, map time and space.

[9] Have we merely carried our animal need for shrewd perceptions to an absurd extreme? Or have we stumbled onto a deep congruence between the structure of our minds and the structure of the universe?

[10] I am persuaded the latter is true. I am convinced there's more to beauty than biology, more than cultural convention. It flows around and through us in such abundance, and in such myriad forms, as to exceed by a wide margin any mere evolutionary need. Which is not to say that beauty has nothing to do with survival: I think it has everything to do with survival. Beauty feeds us from the same source that created us.

[11] It reminds us of the shaping power that reaches through the flower stem and through our own hands. It restores our faith in the generosity of nature. By giving us a taste of the kinship between our own small minds and the great Mind of the Cosmos, beauty reassures us that we are exactly and wonderfully made for life on this glorious planet, in this magnificent universe. I find in that affinity a profound source of meaning and hope. A universe so prodigal of beauty may actually need us to notice and respond, may need our sharp eyes and brimming hearts and teeming minds, in order to close the circuit of Creation.

 参考译文

美（节选）

斯科特·拉塞尔·桑德

[1] 从我认识的一些科学家（包括我的妻女伊娃和露丝），和通过阅读了解到的一些科学家那里，我得出了一个判断：人们在探求自然法则的旅途中，用不了多久必会与美不期而遇。一位朋友对我说："我不知道这种美是否与你看到的落日之美相同，但二者带给我的感受是一样的。"我这位朋友是物理学家，多年来致力于破解

星体内部的秘密。他向我讲述了当年第一次顿悟狄拉克的量子力学方程式,或是爱因斯坦相对论的方程式时的那种欣喜若狂的感觉。"那些方程式是如此美丽动人,"他说道,"你立刻就看出,它们一定是正确的,或者至少它们的指向是正确的。"我问他构成一个"美丽动人的"理论的要素是什么,他说是"简约、和谐、典雅和有力"。

[2]　为什么大自然会和那些我们认为很美的理论相吻合,其原因尚不明了。如爱因斯坦所言:这个世界最让人无法理解之处就在于,它是能够被理解的。在一个不起眼的星球上,生存着一种短命的两足生物,然而,正是这些微不足道的小生物,不但测量出了光速,而且揭示出原子的结构,还计算出了黑洞的引力,这一切是多么不可思议。要理解自然界所有事物,我们还要走很长一段路。但是,关于大自然的运作,我们委实已经知道的不少。一代又一代,人们设想出各种定理公式,并在实践中检验它们,然后发现,大自然竟然在令人吃惊的程度上与我们的设想相吻合。建筑师在薄薄的图纸上绘制出设计方案,依此建造的大楼就能够经受住一次次地震,屹然不倒。

[3]　我们发射一颗人造卫星,用它把讯息从一个大洲传到另一个大洲。我正在用来打字的这台机器体现着我们对物质世界运作机制的成百上千的认知成果,每敲出一串字母,就又一次印证了这些认知的正确性。我通过眼镜的镜片注视着屏幕,而镜片则遵守着由艾萨克·牛顿首先详细阐明的光学原理。

[4]　牛顿认为,探索宇宙的规律就是在追循上帝之手造就的痕迹。如今的科学家大都摒弃了"造物主"一说,认为那是个不必要的假说,或最多只是个无法验证的假设。他们相信牛顿的看法,即宇宙由无处不在的一整套法则所支配,但却说不出这些具体的法则究竟是如何支配世间万物的?从事科学研究,可以拒绝相信上帝的存在,但不能否认法则的存在。

[5]　少年时,我曾攀登数学之峰。可惜才到半山腰,便踉跄止步,在稀薄的空气中喘息着,远未达到足以理解爱因斯坦和狄拉克的方程式的高度。现在,我即使手边没有计算器,也照样可以进行加减法、乘法和长除法运算;必要时,还能应付代数、几何,甚至三角运算。但数学语言留给我的恐怕就只有这些了。不过,当初曾有幸窥见那些璀璨美丽如满天星辰的数学法则,我至今记忆犹新。

[6]　直到试图用语言描写美的时候,我才最为强烈地意识到语言的局限性。当然,语言可自创其自身之美,但它却无法传达我们所领悟到的世界之华美,正如相片拍不出鹰的迅捷,也拍不出超新星的震撼一样。伊娃的婚礼相册仅仅记录了婚礼场面

的星星点点。相片和文字能够做到的只是将人们导向外界那些触动我们心灵的稍纵即逝的辉煌。于是，我一直都在做这种导向工作。

[7] 托马斯·梅尔顿说，"自然万物无不令人联想到天堂"。上帝造物，生生不息，犹如演戏，幕幕相接。其间华美之景可随意择取，观之不尽。但要想捕捉那些不那么显而易见的美，就需要专门训练了。一百五十亿年前的宇宙大爆炸，其回声至今仍以只高于绝对零度数度的背景辐射的形式存在着。我想，与此同理，对美的体验也同样是弥漫于宇宙间的秩序和力量的一种回应。要测量背景辐射，我们需要精密的仪器；而要衡量美，则需要警觉的才智和敏锐的感官。

[8] 任何人都能用自己的一双眼睛从一张脸或一朵花上发现美带来的快乐。但是，要发现数学之美、物理之趣，或对弈之妙，要欣赏树木之婆娑、鸟翼之精巧，或是笛声之悠扬，就需要专门训练了。纵观历史，这种训练往往来自长者，他们教年轻人如何集中精力注意观察。通过观察，我们学会了鉴赏从量子力学到拼花被面等各种事物所显示出的种种模式。这种能力给人类带来一种进化优势，因为模式识辨力能帮助我们的祖先选择伴侣，寻找食物，并躲避猛兽。这种能力在其他物种身上也会有同样的体现，但只有人类能谱写出交响曲，创造出字谜游戏，把顽石化为雕像，还为时空划出坐标。

[9] 我们只是把对敏锐识别能力的本能需求推向了荒唐的极致，还是我们不经意间摸索到了人类大脑结构和宇宙结构之间深刻的一致性？

[10] 我相信后者是正确的。我坚信美不仅仅是生物学问题，也不只是文化传承问题。美就在我们周围，就在我们心中，那么充盈，那么多姿多彩，已远远超出了物种进化本身的需要。这样说当然并不意味着美和生存毫无关系；恰恰相反，我相信美和生存之间有着密不可分的联系。美对我们的滋养和上帝对人类的创造是同源的。

[11] 这让我们认识到，通过花的枝茎和人类的双手所传递的塑造力是多么神奇。这也让我们重新树立起对大自然的慷慨胸怀的信念。通过让我们体味人类的小小心灵和宇宙的博大智慧之间存在的相近之处，美让我们确信，人类之所以被如此完美而奇妙地创造出来，正是为了能在这恢宏的宇宙中，在这辉煌的地球上生活繁衍。在宇宙和人类的这种密切关系中，我找到了意义和希望的不尽源泉。宇宙之美，无处不在，正需要我们练就一双慧眼、一颗诚心和一个睿智的大脑，去发现美，去回应美，且由此而成就创世的圆满。

第五章 说明、论说文体的翻译

注释

1. 原句信息焦点在句首（How unlikely...），译文按汉语习惯将之调到句末（这一切是多么不可思议）。
2. 此句说当今的科学家们对"造物主"的概念有两种看法，或认为那种假设根本就没必要（unnecessary），或说得轻一点，至少也是无法验证的（untestable）。这里的至少（at least）也就是"说得温和些""说得好听些"的意思，译文采取了反说的方式译出，变成了"最多只能算是"的意思。
3. 原句的主谓信息在译文中置于句末，也是属于信息焦点调整的译例。句中 bold 取 bright and vivid 之意。
4. 此句采取了意译法，用汉语四字词语重表原句含义。
5. 句首的 you need training 在译文中置于句末，又是一个信息焦点调整的例子。句中 beauty 一词根据汉语词语搭配需要分别译成了"美""趣""妙""婆娑""精巧"和"悠扬"。

讲解

信息焦点的调整

注释 1、3、5 都涉及信息焦点的调整。

一个句子中的各个信息，其显要程度总是有区别的。汉语由于多采用意合方式组词成句，所以比起英语来更倾向于把最重要的信息（信息焦点）置于句末。这样，英译汉时便时常会发生将原句信息焦点移至汉译句子末尾的情况。观察下列各句：

1. It is not a free labour market, but a stagnating economy that threatens employment.

    影响就业的不是自由的劳动市场，而是停滞不前的经济。

2. You can get a good deal of fun out of observing the course of events in which you are no longer intimately concerned.

    你可以冷眼观察一些和你不再密切相关的事态发展，从中得到乐趣。

3. The question of whether or not you could go home again was a very real part of the sentimental and largely literary baggage with which we left home in the fifties.

    五十年代我们离家时，背负着一个装着伤感、多半是书籍的行囊。还能回家吗？——这个问题是行囊中实实在在的一部分。

4. Generally, there are two distinct philosophies on how to bring up the child so that in maturity he does not make a nuisance of himself.

怎样教养儿童才能使他长大成人后不致惹是生非、令人讨厌？关于这个问题，概括起来有两种截然不同的理论。

5. It is a measure of the once mighty German Army whose vaunted panzer corps had raced through Europe in the earlier years that at this moment of crisis the Supreme Commander should be concerned with scraping up five broken-down tank destroyers which could only be "put into battle in the next few days" to stem the advance of a powerful enemy armored army.

当年一度强大的德国军队曾以其不可一世的装甲部队在欧洲横冲直撞，而在目前这个紧急关头，最高统帅所考虑的不过是拼凑五门"再过几天才能投入战斗"的破烂的反坦克炮，去抵挡敌人强大的装甲部队的进攻，由此可见其狼狈处境。

6. The result, reflected in Ronald Reagan's effort to bolster America's nuclear arsenal, is the acceptance of the theory of limited war: that the only credible deterrent to a nuclear war is the willingness to fight one.

其结果就是接受有限核战争的理论，即对核战争唯一可信的遏制方法就是自己也愿意打一场这样的战争；罗纳德·里根竭力加强美国的核武库正是这种思想的表现。

7. As a consequence, U.S. nuclear doctrine was based on the threat of "massive retaliation" to punish Russian adventurism in areas deemed vital to the West.

因此，如果俄国在西方看作至关紧要的地区进行冒险，美国就要用"大规模报复"对它进行惩罚——这就是美国核方针的基石。

8. He will behave thereafter as he has been trained or indoctrinated to behave.

人们训练或教导他怎样待人接物，他以后也就会怎样待人接物。

9. Unemployment has climbed to 3 million as traditional industries such as steel, ship building and textiles have gone under to foreign competition and replacement have not been forthcoming in the newer technologies.

由于传统工业，如钢铁、造船和纺织业，挫于外国竞争，又未能用新技术去更新换代，致使失业人数已达 300 万。

10. People out here seem frankly puzzled and sometimes angered over Western reaction to what they are told by their own government is only

friendly Soviet military assistance to an ally.

这里的人只听到本国政府说，苏联仅仅是向一个盟国提供了友好的军事援助。因此，对西方的反应，他们坦率地表示不解，有时甚至表示愤怒。

11. And the worst of it is that it does not matter two straws to Nature, the mother of us all, how dreadfully we misbehave ourselves in this way, or in what agonies we die.

最糟糕的是，不管我们人类的这种丑行多么可怕，不管我们怎样痛苦地死去，大自然——我们大家的母亲——都将毫不介意。

12. We work ourselves into ecstasy over the two superpowers' treaty limiting the number of anti-ballistic missile systems that they may retain and their agreement on limitations on strategic offensive weapons.

两个超级大国签订了限制它们可保留的反弹道导弹系统的数目的条约并达成了限制进攻性战略武器的协议，为此，我们感到欣喜若狂。

13. The solution to the problem of Southern Africa cannot remain forever hostage to the political manoeuvres and tactical delays by South Africa nor to its transparent proposals aimed at procrastination and the postponement of the solution.

不管南非耍政治花招和策略上的拖延手段，还是提出显然旨在拖延问题解决的建议，都不能永远阻挡南部非洲问题的解决。

14. The German people had not been destroyed, as Hitler, who had tried to destroy so many other peoples and, in the end, when the war was lost, themselves, had wished.

曾经企图毁灭其他许多民族的希特勒，在战争最后失败的时候也想要毁灭德国人民，但与他的愿望相反，德国人民并没有被毁灭。

总的来说，汉语中的信息更多的是按事物的自然逻辑顺序排列，信息的焦点常常放在句末。如先陈述背景情况后总括或评论（例2至7），先因后果（例8至13），如此等等。

一个句子中信息排列的顺序，不仅仅取决于本句，还要考虑上下文的语义连贯和逻辑贯通。试分析下面的译例：

15. In a kindergarten, a group of small children are learning Beatles songs. The children are French; and so is the teacher. For half an hour in this nursery in the suburbs of Paris, she addresses them exclusively in English.

Their middle-class parents are digging into household budgets to prepare these children for the world to come.

在一所幼儿园里，一群孩子正在学唱披头士歌曲。孩子们是法国儿童，教师也是法国人。她在巴黎郊区的这所幼儿园的半小时里，全部用英语授课。孩子们的中产阶级父母为了使这些孩子为走进未来的世界做好准备，正努力节省他们的家庭开支。

这是一篇文章的第二段。文章的主题是：法语在世界上的地位正逐渐被英语所代替，法国人不得不力求适应这一趋势。这一段说：孩子们在学英语，老师们在教英语，家长们也在努力支持孩子们学英语。译文划线部分将原句信息焦点由前半句移至后半句，就句论句，无可厚非。但从全段的逻辑走向看，便有失连贯了。可见，此句不宜做信息焦点调整，仍可依原句译为：孩子们的中产阶级父母也正在节衣缩食，让孩子为进入将来的世界做好准备。

16. Wisdom in the modern world has been displaced by learning. Our eyes mirror the outside world without leaving an imprint on our souls. We prattle about scientific discoveries, but we have made scant use of them for our benefit.

    The day is not far off when we shall have to plunge back in search of the wisdom of the people. That day we shall have to seek out the illiterates of the world, the ones whose brains have not been addled by learning, to renew ourselves. We shall have to forget much in order to learn. And it is only after we have acquired that wisdom that we will know how to make use of what information we have acquired.

    现代世界的智慧已经被学问取代了。我们的眼睛只是映现出外面的世界，却没在我们的心灵深处留下什么印记。我们空谈科学发现，却很少利用它们为我们谋福利。

    我们将不得不回过头来认真探寻人们的智慧的一天离我们不会遥远。到那时我们将不得不请出世界上尚未受过教育的人，即那些大脑还没被所谓学问弄糊涂的人，来更新我们的思维。要得到智慧，先要舍弃不少学问。而且，只有在我们获得那种智慧之后，才会知道怎样去利用我们所学的知识。

    原句选自 Konrad Bercovici 的散文 The "Wisdom of the Illiterate"。上面是开头的两个自然段。作者主张：Let's go to the wisdom of the illiterates to find justice, beauty, tolerance and an understanding of the eternal occurrence of things。如果就句论句，上面划线部分译文并无不可。但从全文主旨和这两个自然段的衔接来看，信息焦点做如下调整似更有利：总有一天我们将不得不回过头来认真探寻人们的智慧，而这一天离我们不会太远。

About Electricity

[1] While the exact nature of electricity is unknown, a great deal is known about what it can do.¹ By the mere closing of a switch, buildings are lighted, wheels are turned, ice is made, food is cooked, distant voices are heard, and countless other tasks—ordinary and extraordinary—are performed.² Although a great number of uses for electricity have been discovered and applied,³ the field is by no means exhausted. Electric machines and devices that have been in use for many years are being improved and are now finding wider fields of application. Extensive research is constantly bringing forth and developing new devices. Much is still to be learned about electricity.

[2] Electricity is a convenient form of energy. It is well known that when fuels such as coal, oil, and gas are burned, energy is released.⁴ A waterfall, whether it is man-made or natural, also possesses energy. Yet, to be of value, this energy must be made available at points where it can be used conveniently. Electricity furnishes the most practicable and convenient means yet devised for doing this. The energy of burning fuel or of falling water is changed to a more convenient form—electricity—by electric machines.⁵ It is transmitted to distant points over electric circuits. It is controlled by other electric machines. At points where it is to be used, it is converted into useful work by still other electric machines and devices.

[3] Since electricity is a form of energy, the study of electricity is the study of energy, its conversions from one form to another, and its transmission from one point to another.⁶ Electric machines are energy-transmission devices and electric circuits are energy-transmission devices.

[4] Although no one knows precisely what electricity is, it has been possible to develop theories about electricity through experiment and by observation of its behavior. As a result, it is now believed that all matter is essentially electrical in nature.⁷

[5] In this introductory chapter, important ideas concerning electricity are presented⁸ together with a discussion of the basic units of measurement used in the study of electric circuits and machines.

Electric Current

[6]　In a conductor material, some of the free electrons are freely moving at random or "migrating" from atom to atom. When, in addition to this random motion, there is a drift or general movement of electrons along the conductor, this is called an electric current.

[7]　When a strip of zinc and a strip of copper are immersed in a solution of sulfuric acid to form a simple electric cell, the resulting chemical action causes the zinc strip to gain electrons from the solution, thereby causing it to become negatively charged. At the same time the copper strip has a tendency to lose some of its electrons, causing it to become positively charged. When the two plates are connected by a copper wire, which is a good conductor, the electrons on the zinc strip flow through the wire to the copper strip. This movement of the electrons from the zinc strip through the copper wire to the copper strip and back through the solution constitutes an electric current, and the entire path through which it flows is called a circuit. Thus, an electric current is merely the movement of electrons or negative charges through a conductor.[9]

[8]　Early experimenters recognized the fact that an electric current was a movement of charges along a conductor. Since the direction of the flow of current was not known, unfortunately it was arbitrarily chosen to be from a positively charged body to a negatively charged body (positive to negative), and this convention has been so firmly established that it is still in use. Thus, the conventional direction or positive direction of current flow is taken to be from positive to negative even though it is now known that the direction of electron flow, which actually constitutes an electric current, is from negative to positive.

参考译文

关 于 电

[1]　尽管对电的确切性质人们还不清楚，但对电能做些什么却已了解得很多了。只需合上电闸，房屋便可照亮，轮子便可旋转，冰就可以制出，饭就可以做熟，远处的声音便可听见，还有无数其他工作——平常的和不平常的——都能进行。虽然已经发现了电的大量用途并已付诸实践，但这绝不是尽头。已经应用了许多年的电机

第五章 说明、论说文体的翻译

和设备还在不断改进，开辟更为广阔的应用领域。通过广泛的研究，人们正在不断创造和改进各种新的电器设备。对于电，还有许多问题有待探明。

[2]　电是一种方便的能量形式。众所周知，煤、油和天然气之类的燃料燃烧时，会释放出能量。瀑布，无论是人工的还是天然的，也具有能量。但是，要想使能量有价值，就必须使它在使用方便的地方能被用上。电为此提供了到目前为止所发现的最方便可行的手段。借助于电机，燃料燃烧或水流下落所产生的能量可转换成更为方便的形式——电。电再通过电路传输到远处，它由另外一些电机来控制。在使用场所，还有另外一些电机和设备把电转化成有用的功。

[3]　因为电是能量的一种形式，研究电就是研究能量，研究能量从一种形式到另一种形式的转换，研究能量从一个地点到另一个地点的传输。电机是能量转化的设备，电路是能量转输的设备。

[4]　尽管没有人精确地知道电是什么，但人们却能够通过实验和对电的表现的观察建立起各种理论。结果，人们现在已认识到，一切物质从本质上讲都是带电的。

[5]　本章作为导言，介绍有关电的一些重要概念和研究电路及电机时所采用的一些基本测量单位。

电流

[6]　导电物体内有些自由电子在无规则地自由运动，即从一个原子"迁移"到另一个原子。当在这种无规则运动之外还存在电子沿导体的漂移或总的运动时，这种运动就叫作电流。

[7]　将一锌片和一铜片浸在硫酸溶液中形成一个简单电池，化学反应的结果使锌片从溶液中获得电子，从而带上负电。同时，铜片会失去部分电子而带正电。将这两个金属片用一根铜线（系良导体）连接起来，锌片上的电子就通过导线流往铜片。电子从锌片经铜线流往铜片，然后经溶液流回去的这一流动就构成电流，它所经过的整个途径称作电路。这样，电流只不过是电子即负电荷经过导体的一种运动。

[8]　早期的实验人员认识到一个事实，即电流是电荷沿导体的一种运动。由于那时尚不知道电流的流动方向，不巧把电流方向随意定成了是从带正电体到带负电体（从正到负）。这一惯例根深蒂固，至今仍然采用。于是，电流的规定方向即正向就被定为从正到负，尽管现在已经知道电子流（它实际上构成电流）的方向是从负到正的。

299

注释

1. 这里的被动语态汉译时加了"人们"二字作主语。
2. 这句中用了一连串的被动语态，汉译时都呈主动形式，即未用"被、受、为"等表示被动意义的词语。
3. 这里的被动语态译作无主句。
4. It is well known that... 之类的句型在说明、论说文章中用得很多，其译法一般也较固定。如：It is said that... 据说，有人说；It is usually considered that... 通常认为；It is found that... 已发现；It is reported that... 据报导，等等。另外，请注意本句中另外两处被动语态的译法。
5. 译文将原文中的 by electric machines 移到句首，译为状语。此句亦可译为："电机可将燃料燃烧或水流下落所产生的能量转换为一种更为方便可用的形式——电"。也就是将原文恢复成了主动形式。
6. 注意这句话的译文的指代衔接问题。原文中两个 its 都是指代 energy。一般来说，英语使用代词的频率比汉语高，汉语更习惯于重复同一名词以保证行文所指明白无误。再如，The patient shook her head and stretched out her hands towards the baby. The doctor put it in her arms. She kissed it on the forehead. (病人摇了摇头，把手向婴儿伸去。医生把孩子放到她怀里。她吻了吻孩子的前额。)
7. 注意 it is now believed that... 的译法，请参照注释 4。
8. 此处被动结构译为主动句，主语（"本章"）是根据上下文另立的。
9. 本段从句（包括非限定性从句）较集中，英语中从句结构的使用可使文章逻辑清晰、层次分明。汉译时务必保证同样的行文效果。试比较下面一种译文：
当一锌片和一铜片浸在硫酸溶液中形成一个简单电池时，化学反应结果使得这锌片从溶液中获得电子，从而<u>使它</u>变成带负电的。同时，铜片有失去其部分电子的倾向，从而<u>使它</u>带正电。<u>当</u>这两个金属片用一根铜钱（它是一种良导体）联系起来时，锌片的电子就通过这导线流往铜片……
上述译文的缺点在于：囿于原文句子结构，行文拖沓不畅。请将其与参考译文对照，特别注意划线词语。

讲解

一、被动语态的翻译

英语句子以"主语 + 谓语动词"为形式框架，当主语是受事时，一般要将谓语动词变为被动语态，于是就出现了被动句。英语用被动句的频率是相当高的。据统计，奥斯汀的小说《傲慢与偏见》头 30 页中有 135 个被动句，莫恩姆的《人性的枷锁》前 40 页中有 115 个被动句，议论、说明文中被动句用得就更为频繁，本单元文章所在的原文"Electric Circuits and Machines"中,平均每页就有十几个被动结构。汉语与英语不同,没有英语那样的"主语+谓语"的形式构架,汉语的"主语"和"谓语"其实是一种语义上的"话题"和"陈述"的关系。汉语的被动概念常常是语义上的,而不是语法上的。汉语中和英语被动句最接近的恐怕只有"被"字句,但"被"字句在现代汉语中用得很少。据统计,老舍的《骆驼祥子》共 211 页,"被"字句近 100 句,平均 2~3 页才一句。比如,下面这段英语中共 4 个被动语态,而其汉译中一个"被"字也未出现:

Great progress has been made. Not only is the sun now used for cooking, but it also supplies power for such things as beacon lights for ships and airplanes; it operates telephone lines, movie cameras, portable radios, electric clocks, and hearing aids. It is also being used to operate communications satellites. Some homes and office buildings in the United States are now being heated with solar energy.

人们在使用太阳能方面取得了很大进展。太阳能现在不仅用来做饭,而且用来为轮船和飞机导航的信标灯提供电能,它为电话线路、电影摄影机、袖珍收音机、电钟和助听器提供工作电源。目前它还用于操纵通信卫星。现在,美国的一些家庭和办公室也靠太阳能供热。

那么汉语是如何表达被动概念的呢?大致有如下几种方式:用"被、叫、让、给、由"等词语;用"是……的"结构,如"这本书是去年写的";语义上被动,形式上毫无体现,如"这套书卖光了"。基于英汉两种语言在被动概念表达上的种种差异,英语被动句汉译时常采取下面一些对策:

(一)译为带有"被、受、由、把、予以、遭、挨"等被动意义词语的句子

1. The process is similar to that performed at the transmit end, and the carriers are suppressed within the balanced modulators.

此项过程和在发送端所进行的相类似,载波被抑制在平衡调节器内。

2. Though the initial patents for low-pressure casting were issued as early as in 1910, it was not noted until recently.

虽然低压铸造的专利早在 1910 年就颁发了,但直到最近才受到重视。

3. Illness must be correctly diagnosed before they can be treated with medicine.

疾病必须先有正确的诊断,才能用药物加以治疗。

4. Besides voltage, resistance and capacitance, an alternating current is also influenced by inductance.
除了电压、电阻和电容以外，交流电还受电感的影响。

（二）原主语不变，在用词和结构上进行某些调整，译文是主动结构形式（参阅注释2）

5. Little of this vast body of law is, however, implemented in the Member States.
可是这一大套法律在会员国中很少执行。

6. Electricity can be transmitted over a long distance.
电能够远距离输送。

上述两句译文中的动词"执行""输送"前，依汉语习惯不必加"被"字，正如我们一般不会说"衣服被洗完了""书被装订好了"一样。有时还可以变换一个动词，以主动意义的角度来译被动语态，如：

7. Two P.L.A. battalions were ordered to join the local people in their fight against the rampaging flood.
两营解放军战士奉命与当地人民一起抗御肆虐的洪水。

8. The operation was designed to make the public believe that Concorde was a danger to the environment in terms of noise and air pollution.
这个行动计划旨在使公众相信，协和飞机就噪声和空气污染而言是危害环境的。

下面译例中，原文的主语也被保留，但句子结构有所调整，常用的结构有"是……的"或"……的是……""动词+宾语""为……所……"，等等。

9. This pyrometer is designed and produced by a Sino-American joint venture.
这种高温计是一家中美合资企业设计制造的。（或：设计制造这种高温计的是一家中美合资企业。可根据上下文而定。）

10. This innovation is highly estimated among the machine tool builders.
此项创新在机床制造商中得到了高度评价。

11. As soon as all the facts have been found out we can begin to formulate a theory.
一旦所有的事实都为人们所发现，便可着手构建理论了。

（三）译文中另立主语，主语来自原句或原句上下文（参阅注释 1、8）

12. In many instances definite impressions can be seen on dried bones, including the areas of attachment of particular muscles.
    在许多情况下，枯骨可显示出明显的压痕，包括特定肌肉群附着的部位。

13. Communications satellites are used for international living transmission throughout the world.
    全世界都将通信卫星用于国际间的实况转播。

14. This type of combination of protons and neutrons with planetary electrons is found to be existing in all substances.
    人们发现，质子、中子与绕一定轨道旋转的电子所构成的这种组合存在于所有物质之中。

（四）译成无主句（参阅注释 3）

15. Care should be taken to see that the machine is safely grounded.
    要精心检查，确保机器已安全接地。

16. The racist regimes in Southern Africa must be warned that they are up against an irreversible historical process.
    必须警告南部非洲的种族主义政权，他们是在对抗不可改变的历史进程。

17. When a motion picture is made, the visible action is photographed and, at the same time, the words the actors speak are "photographed" on the same film.
    拍摄影片时，既拍摄有形的动作，同时在同一软片上也"拍摄"了演员所说的话。

二、指代衔接与行文流畅

译文行文流畅达意是对译者的基本要求之一。而要达到这一要求，译文语句间的衔接是关键。所谓衔接，即用语法和词汇手段所达到的行文连贯。这里我们主要谈代词使用对行文连贯的影响。英语中代词使用频率比汉语高，连接词语用得也比汉语多，翻译时应注意英汉的这一区别，顺应汉语的行文习惯（参阅注释 6、9）。

1. If the ends of a conductor are connected to a low-reading voltmeter and the conductor is moved into the field of a magnet as shown in Fig. 5-1, a momentary reading will be noted on the voltmeter. As the conductor is

withdrawn from the field, the meter will deflect momentarily in the opposite direction. If the conductor is held stationary and the magnet moved so that the field cuts the conductor, the same results are obtained. The voltage developed across the terminals of the voltmeter when the conductor is moved through the magnetic field (or when the field is moved across the conductor) is known as an induced electromotive force. The current caused to flow in the conductor by the induced emf is sometimes called an induced current. The phenomenon whereby an emf is induced in a conductor when the conductor cuts or is cut by a magnetic field is called electromagnetic induction.

如果把一根导线的两端接到一个低数伏特计上，并使这导线往一个磁铁场里移动（如图 5-1），在伏特计上会看出一个瞬间的读数。当这导线移出磁场时，这测量仪表的指针又会瞬时地向相反的方向偏转。如果让这导线固定不动，而移动磁铁使磁场切割这导线，也会得到同样的结果。导线移过磁场（或磁场移过导线）时在伏特计的两个端柱间出现的电压称作感应电动势。受这电动势的驱使而在这导线中流动的电流有时称作感应电流。当导线切割磁场或被磁场所切割时，在这导线中会感应出电动势，这个现象叫电磁感应。

在上面这段正式发表过的译文中，原文中的许多 the 均被译成指示代词"这"。"这"多次出现似乎是为防止所指不清。从字面上看，是对 the 这一冠词的译法不当，而从语篇的角度看则说明译者对译语语篇的衔接特点还不大清楚。其实汉语中不用这么多指示代词，只要上文已有所交代，省去指示代词，不但所指不会混淆，反而会使行文更为流畅。试看一本中文教材中是如何叙述类似的内容的：

把一根直导线放在一个蹄形磁铁的磁场里，使导线跟磁场方向垂直（图 3-16）。当给导线通电时，导线就运动起来。这说明通电导线在磁场里要受到力的作用。

可以看出，在第一个分句中提到"一根导线""一个蹄形磁铁的磁场"之后，下文再提到"导线""磁场"时便不必说"这个导线"了。上下文这种同词复指衔接关系，中文读者已一目了然。过多地使用指示代词反而累赘。

另外，如注释 6 所示，英语的代词有时要译成其所代替的名词。如：

2. Wrought iron is almost pure iron. It is not frequently found in the school shop because of its high cost. It forges well, can easily be bent hot or cold, and can be welded.

熟铁几乎就是纯铁。熟铁在校办工厂里不太常见，因为价格很高。熟铁好锻，很容易热弯和冷弯，还能够焊接。

3. Seamless tubes without joints are made in various ways. A steel tube, for example, can be made by putting a hot "billet" or bar of steel into a vertical round container into which it will just slide, and forcing a round punch bar almost through it, pressing the steel against the side of the container, and producing a "bloom", shaped like a bottle, with a closed end. Then a "mandrel" bar is pushed into the hot bloom, which is then squeezed through a series of dies of gradually decreasing diameter until the tube is the required thickness. It may also be pushed through a series of rolls which roll the metal thinner and thinner.

没有接缝的无缝管可以用各种不同的方法制造。例如，把一块炽热的"钢坯"或钢料放进一个刚能滑进去的直立圆形容器中，再用强力将一根冲杆几乎穿透钢坯或钢料，从而把钢料挤压到容器的内壁上，制造出一个一端封闭的瓶形"粗坯"。然后，将一根"芯棒"推进到炽热的钢坯里，再把钢坯挤进一系列直径逐渐减小的凹模，直到管壁达到要求的厚度。还可以将钢坯推过一系列焊辊，把金属压得越来越薄。

上面这段原文中有三个 it，均指 a hot "billet" or bar of steel，后两个 it 都译成相应名词，而第一个 it 则省略掉了。不论是哪种译法都是为了达到所指明确、行文流畅的目的。

The Jeaning of America

Carin Quinn

[1] This is the story of a sturdy American symbol which has now spread throughout most of the world. The symbol is not the dollar. It is not even Coca-Cola. It is a simple pair of pants called blue jeans, and what the pants symbolize is what Alexis de Tocqueville called "a manly and legitimate passion for equality..." Blue jeans are favored equally by bureaucrats and cowboys; bankers and deadbeats; fashion designers and beer drinkers[1]. They draw no distinctions and recognize no classes; they are merely American[2]. Yet they are sought after almost everywhere in the world—including Russia,

where authorities recently broke up a teen-aged gang that was selling them on the black market for two hundred dollars a pair. They have been around for a long time, and it seems likely that they will outlive even the necktie.

[2]　This ubiquitous American symbol was the invention of a Bavarian-born Jew. His name was Levi Strauss.

[3]　He was born in Bad Ocheim, Germany, in 1829, and during the European political turmoil of 1848 decided to take his chances in New York, to which his two brothers already had emigrated. Upon arrival, Levi soon found that his two brothers had exaggerated their tales of an easy life in the land of the main chance. They were landowners, they had told him; instead, he found them pushing needles, thread, pots, pans, ribbons, yarn, scissors and buttons to housewives³. For two years he was a lowly peddler, hauling some 180 pounds of sundries door-to-door to eke out a marginal living. When a married sister in San Francisco offered to pay his way West in 1850, he jumped at the opportunity, taking with him bolts of canvas he hoped to sell for tenting.

[4]　It was the wrong kind of canvas for that purpose, but while talking with a miner down from the mother lode, he learned that pants—sturdy pants that would stand up to the rigors of the digging—were almost impossible to find. Opportunity beckoned. On the spot, Strauss measured the man's girth and inseam with a piece of string and, for six dollars in gold dust,⁴ had [the canvas] tailored into a pair of stiff but rugged pants. The miner was delighted with the result, word got around about "those pants of Levi's" and Strauss was in business. The company has been in business ever since.

[5]　When Strauss ran out of canvas, he wrote his two brothers to send more. He received instead a tough, brown cotton cloth made in Nimes, France—called "serge de Nimes" and swiftly shortened to "denim" (the word "jeans" derives from "Gênes", the French word for "Genoa", where a similar cloth was produced). Almost from the first, Strauss had his cloth dyed the distinctive indigo that gave blue jeans their name⁵, but it was not until the 1870s that he added the copper rivets which have long since become a company trademark. The rivets were the idea of a Virginia City, Nevada, tailor, Jacob W. Dacis, who added them to pacify a mean-tempered miner called Alkali Ike. Alkali, the story goes, complained that the pockets of his

jeans always tore when he stuffed them with ore samples and demanded that Davis do something about it. As a kind of joke, Davis took the pants to a blacksmith and had the packets riveted; once again, the idea worked so well that word got around; in 1873 Strauss appropriated[6] and patented the gimmick—and hired Davis as a regional manager.

[6] By this time, Strauss had taken both his brothers and two brothers-in-law into the company and was ready for his third San Francisco store. Over the ensuing years the company prospered locally, and by the time of his death in 1902, Strauss has become a man of prominence in California. For three decades thereafter the business remained profitable though small, with sales largely confined to the working people of the West—cowboys, lumberjacks, railroad workers, and the like. Levi's jeans were first introduced to the East, apparently, during the dude-ranch craze of the 1930s, when vacationing Easters returned and spread the word about the wonderful pants with rivets. Another boost came in World War II, when blue jeans were declared an essential commodity and were sold only to people engaged in defense work[7]. From a company with fifteen salespeople, two plants, and almost no business east of the Mississippi in 1946, the organization grew in thirty years to include a sales force of more than twenty-two thousand, with fifty plants and offices in thirty-five countries. Each year, more than 250,000,000 items of Levi's clothing are sold—including more than 83,000,000 pairs of riveted blue jeans. They have become, through marketing, word of mouth, and demonstrable reliability, the common pants of America. They can be purchased pre-washed, pre-faded, and pre-shrunk for the suitably proletarian look. They adapt themselves to any sort of idiosyncratic use; women slit them at the inseams and convert them into long skirts, men chop them off above the knees and turn them into something to be worn while challenging the surf. Decorations and ornamentations abound.

[7] The pants have become a tradition, and along the way have acquired a history of their own—so much so that the company has opened a museum in San Francisco. There was, for example,[8] the turn-of-the-century trainman who replaced a faulty coupling with a pair of jeans; the Wyoming man who used his jeans as a towrope to haul his car out of a ditch; the Californian who found several pairs in an abandoned mine, wore them, then discovered they were sixty-three years old and still as good as new and turned them

over to the Smithsonian as a tribute to their toughness. And then there is the particularly terrifying story of the careless construction worker who dangled fifty-two stories above the street until rescued, his sole support the Levi's belt loop through which his rope was hooked.

参考译文

美国牛仔裤史话

卡琳·奎因

[1]　本文讲述的是美国的一个坚实的象征物，如今已经遍及世界大部分地区。此物不是美元，甚至也不是可口可乐，而只是一条称作蓝色牛仔裤的普通裤子。这条裤子所象征的，如亚历克西·德·托克维尔所言，是"对平等的果敢而正当的渴求……"无论是官员还是牛仔，银行家还是赖账徒，时装设计师还是嗜酒成性者，都同样青睐蓝色牛仔裤。这种裤子对人不分高低贵贱，只要是美国人都可以穿。不过，牛仔裤几乎在世界各地都广受欢迎——其中包括苏联，其当局最近破获了一个在黑市上倒卖牛仔裤的青少年团伙，他们的牛仔裤卖到200美元一条。牛仔裤已经流行了很长时间，看来其生命力甚至可能超过领带。

[2]　这个无所不在的美国象征是一个出生于巴伐利亚的犹太人发明的，他的名字叫李维·施特劳斯。

[3]　他于1829年出生于德国的巴德奥切姆，1848年欧洲政治动荡期间，决定去纽约碰碰运气，他的两个哥哥已经移民去了那里。到了纽约，李维很快就发现，两个哥哥关于在这片充满机遇的土地上生活比较安逸的说法实在有些言过其实。他们说自己拥有土地，可他发现他们在向家庭主妇推销针线、锅罐、缎带、剪刀和纽扣。李维做了两年寒酸的小贩，拉着180来磅的杂货挨门挨户地叫卖，勉强维持生计。1850年，他的一个嫁到旧金山的姐姐愿意为他提供西行的路费，他急忙抓住这一机会，带着几卷帆布走了，打算卖给人家做帐篷用。

[4]　岂料这种帆布不适于做帐篷。不过，李维跟一个来自主矿脉的矿工交谈时了解到，人们很难买到能经得起采矿磨损的结实耐穿的裤子。机会向他招手了。施特劳斯当场用一根带子量了那人的腰围和裤长，请人用帆布做成一条粗硬而耐磨的裤子，卖得了6美元的砂金。矿工感到很满意，于是有关"李维的那些裤子"的消息不胫而走，施特劳斯从此做起了生意。自那以后，他的公司一直在经营。

第五章 说明、论说文体的翻译

[5] 施特劳斯用完了帆布，便写信叫哥哥再发一些过来，不想收到的却是法国尼姆产的一种坚韧的棕色棉布——称作"尼姆哗叽"（serge de Nimes），不久就简称为"劳动布"[英语单词 jeans（牛仔裤）源自法语地名 Gênes（英语称 Genoa），此地生产一种类似的棉布]。几乎从一开始，施特劳斯就把他的布料染成别具一格的靛蓝色，因此便有了蓝色牛仔裤之称。不过，直到 19 世纪 70 年代，他才往裤子上加了铜铆钉；长期以来，这铜铆钉也就成了公司的标志。给裤子加上铆钉是内华达州弗吉尼亚市的裁缝雅各布·W·戴维斯想出的主意，他这样做是为了抚慰一个名叫阿尔卡利·艾克的脾气暴躁的矿工。据说他抱怨他往口袋里装矿石标本时，口袋总是被撑破，要求戴维斯想想办法。戴维斯开了个玩笑，把裤子拿到铁匠铺，给口袋上了铆钉。这一招果然奏效，消息再一次不胫而走。1873 年，施特劳斯采纳了这一小发明，出资为之申请了专利——并雇用戴维斯做地区经理。

[6] 这时候，施特劳斯已把他的两个哥哥和两个姐夫招进了公司，并准备在旧金山开办他的第三个分店。此后的几十年间，公司在当地生意兴隆。1902 年施特劳斯去世时，他已成为加利福尼亚的知名人士。在以后的 30 年中，生意虽然不大，但一直在盈利，主要的销售对象是西部的劳工阶层——诸如牛仔、伐木工、铁路工之类的人。李维的牛仔裤最初被引进到东部，显然是在 20 世纪 30 年代的农场度假热潮中，西去度假的东部人回家后，便到处宣扬这种带铜铆钉的奇妙裤子。第二次世界大战期间，蓝色牛仔裤又一次走俏，被宣布为紧要商品，只卖给从事防务工作的人。该公司在 1946 年时还只有 15 名销售员，两个加工厂，密西西比河以东几乎没有什么业务，而 30 年后则发展成拥有 2.2 万多人的销售队伍，并在 35 个国家设有 50 家加工厂和办事处。每年，李维服装的销售量超过 2.5 亿多件——其中包括 8300 多万条钉有铜铆钉的蓝色牛仔裤。通过市场营销，口口相传，以及显而易见的可靠性，牛仔裤已成为美国的寻常裤装。人们还可以买到进行过水洗、褪色和缩水处理的牛仔裤，以符合无产者的形象。牛仔裤经过改造还可以供各种癖好的人使用。妇女们将裤管内缝拆开，将裤子改制成长裙；男人们将其从膝盖上方截下，变成冲浪时穿的短裤。人们还给牛仔裤缀上各式各样的装饰物。

[7] 牛仔裤已成为一种传统，在其发展过程中谱写了自己的历史——这历史如此丰富多彩，以至于公司在旧金山建立了一座博物馆。例如：19 世纪和 20 世纪之交的时候，一位列车员用一条牛仔裤代替失灵的列车挂钩；怀俄明州的一个男子用牛仔裤把汽车从沟里拖出来；加利福尼亚的一个人在一个废弃的矿井里捡到几条牛仔裤，穿上后发现这裤子已有 63 年的历史，还依然像新的一样，便将其捐给史密斯

学会，以表彰它的结实耐用。还有一个特别惊心动魄的故事：一个粗心的建筑工人悬挂在 52 层楼上，直至获救，他的唯一支撑点就是李维牛仔裤的裤带扣，他的安全绳就扣着这裤带扣。（孙致礼译）

注释

1. 如考虑到作者意在强调形形色色的人，则可译为"无论是官员还是牛仔，银行家还是穷光蛋，时装设计师还是啤酒肚们……"
2. American 是与 (draw) no distinctions 和 (recognize) no classes 相呼应的，其意义需放在上下文中体会，如照字面译为"它们只是美国的"，则在意义上与上文失去了连贯。
3. 此处或采取归化译法，用汉语常用词语概述所买物品：可他发现他们只是向家庭主妇们推销些针头线脑、锅碗瓢盆之类的小商品。
4. for six dollars in gold dust 意为"付给价值 6 美元的砂金"。
5. 注意 that 引导的定语从句在译文中逻辑关系的调整："因此……"。
6. 对 appropriated 一词的翻译，译者查阅了有关史实："经查阅，戴维斯因为无钱申请专利，便要求李维出资申请，李维慨然答应。实际上，那专利权归他们俩所有。所以，这里译作'采纳'较好"［见《中国翻译》2000（2）：75］。译者的注释给我们的启示是：词义的定夺，倚重于上下文。但这有时仍然不够充分。词汇使用的具体场景，历史、文化背景都对词义有一定的限定作用。
7. 以上两句中各有一个状语从句（when...），这体现了英语多用连接词语的形合特征。汉译时常化为形散意合的结构。
8. 此处的 for example 不宜直译为"例如"或"馆中的展品例如"。如何措辞应考虑上下文的连贯，即如何使用恰当的词语将第一句和下文列举的事件联系起来。用"例如"似与历史的丰富多彩相连，但是中间隔了一句；用"馆中的展品例如"又和下文不合，因为接下来说的是事例而并非展品。如译为"展览的内容包括"，连贯性可能更好些。

讲解

译文的连贯

本单元注释 2 和 8 讨论了词语翻译（译文的措辞）所造成的连贯问题，注释 5 和 7 涉及从句翻译，显示出英汉在语篇连贯方面的不同句法手段。连贯是合格的语篇必须具备的条件，不然就无法称为语篇，无法完成交际使命。要保证语篇的连贯须注意以下三个层次：一是运用语法和词汇手段使上下文相互衔接（第二章 Unit Six 讲解部分的"指代关系的理解"和第五章 Unit Six 讲解部分的"指代衔接与行文流畅"其实都属于这一范畴）；二是信息的排列合乎逻辑（第四章 Unit One 和

Unit Two 的讲解部分，第五章 Unit One、Unit Two、Unit Four 和 Unit Five 的讲解部分也都涉及信息的线性排列问题）；三是使语篇提供的信息与读者头脑中的知识能相互呼应。这里主要就前两个方面，结合译例进行进一步的讨论。

一、所用词语应相互衔接、呼应

1. "How could you tell Margaret what we talked about?" she cried. "What we say in the privacy of our own home is no one else's business! Don't you know that?"

   I stared down at my purple-pink skate laces.

   Apparently, moments after I left, Margaret telephoned Joseph at work. He called his brother Peter, who, in turn, called Mom and Helen and let them have it. He also called my mom's mom. The whole family was up in arms.

   "Don't you have any sense?" Mom demanded.

   I peeked up at her face, which had turned the color of my laces...

   "你怎么能把我们谈的事告诉玛格丽特？"妈妈大声嚷着。"我们在家里私下谈的，关别人屁事！你难道不明白这个道理吗？"

   我的眼睛盯着我紫色和粉色相间的旱冰鞋鞋带。

   很显然，我刚一离开，玛格丽特（舅妈）就给正在上班的约瑟夫（舅舅）打了电话。接着约瑟夫给哥哥彼得打了电话，彼得又打电话给妈妈和海伦，训了她们一顿。他还给外婆打了电话。于是，整个家庭都给折腾起来了。

   "你还懂点人事儿吗？"妈妈厉声责问。

   我偷偷看了我妈一眼，她的脸色已变得和我的旱冰鞋鞋带的颜色一样。

   译文的最后一句说妈妈的脸色气得像鞋带的颜色，而上文将鞋带的颜色说成是"紫色和粉色相间"。这就造成了一幅荒唐的画面：脸上一块紫一块粉。显然，是 purple-pink 的翻译出了问题。purple-pink 即 lavender，按中文表达习惯可译为"紫红色的"。这样和最后一句话就可相互呼应，在读者头脑中形成连贯的形象。

2. To me they were books only in the sense that matchbooks were, or phone books or home-appliance manuals by under-paid translators—not the kind of multi-coloured books that lit up the world's dark corners, that arrived like a new romance with no hint that acid-pulp would one day self-deconstruct. All at once, books from what was quaintly called the humanities

were purged, irrelevant to the discussion. The message was clear: Real books were something you put away like toys in order to grow up, to get over it, to get with the programme.

对我而言，这些书之所以称为书，只是因为纸夹火柴、电话号码簿，或由廉价译者翻译过来的家用器具指南等亦被称为书；它们决非那种绚丽斑斓、能将人世间的黑暗角落照亮的书，亦非那种读来如新奇的浪漫故事，就连那酸性的纸张似乎也会永世不灭的书。于是乎，被莫名其妙地称为人文领域的书籍被扫地出门，不予讨论。这其中的意思可谓明明白白：真正的书如同玩具一般，你可以将它们扔到一边，好让自己长大，摆脱它们，并随波逐流。

作者畅谈对真正的书籍的钟爱。他虽爱好文学，却学了法律。他发现法学书籍枯燥呆板，后又转而读起文学、历史、随笔、哲学等人文类书籍。这一段说的就是他对法律书籍与人文类书籍区别的感受。译文第一句中的划线词语造成了明显的连贯问题，因为在汉语中"纸夹火柴"这一词语根本就不会使人联想到"书"这个概念。可译为"火柴书夹"，以引起"书"的联想，对其含义则可加注予以说明。

我们在写作时会注意词语的配合、衔接，但在翻译时往往把对等词语的确定看成是词汇层次，至多是句子层次上的事，极易造成语篇层次上的连贯失调。

二、信息的排列顺序和逻辑关系

汉语重信息的意合，与英语相比使用形合手段要少，因此信息的排列顺序的重要性就更加突出。小句和小句须环环相扣，形成一条信息流，一步步向前推进。译文构建过程中稍有马虎就会造成连贯问题。如：

3. Furthermore, says Mr. Evans, it would increase costs significantly for small to medium-sized businesses, which would have to conduct regular searches to protect their own registered rights, hitherto done by the Patent Office.

埃文斯先生进而指出，这么一来，中小企业为了保护自己已经注册的专利权，不得不自己进行定期检索，而这种检索一向是由专利局负责的，从而大大增加了中小企业的成本。

译文划线部分有碍连贯。可将这一小句的信息嵌入前一个小句中，以保证信息的流畅：埃文斯先生进而指出，这么一来，中小企业为了保护自己已经注册的专利权，不得不自己进行本来由专利局负责的定期检索，从而使企业成本大大增加。

4. [Surely we ought to hold fast to life, for it is wondrous, and full of a beauty that breaks through every pore of Gold's own earth. We know that this is so, but all too often we recognize this truth only in our backward glance when we remember what it was and then suddenly realize that it is no more.]

We remember a beauty that faded, a love that waned. But we remember with far greater pain that we did not see that beauty when it flowered, that we failed to respond with love when it was tendered.

[a] 我们忆起已凋谢之美、消逝之爱，不禁怅然。但更令人痛苦的是：当初，美像鲜花一样绽放，我们却视而不见；别人将爱给予我们，我们也未能以爱相报。

[b] 我们能怅然忆起已凋谢之美、消逝之爱。但是，更令我们痛苦的回忆是，我们没有看见鲜花怒放时之美，没有在别人以爱对我们之时也以爱回报。

译文 [a] 的信息排列是：美像鲜花→我们不见；别人给予爱→我们未能回报。这样就形成了两对鲜明对照的信息。而译文 [b] 的信息排列是：我们不见（鲜花）美→未能（得到爱时）以爱相报。括号中的两个信息被嵌入更大的结构中，未形成译文 [a] 那样鲜明的逻辑关系。与上一段（在方括号中）联系起来看，译文 [a] 的连贯性更强些。

5. Can what remains of the Aral Sea be saved? People living around what were once its northern shores in Kazakhstan think they can salvage something from one of the world's biggest environmental disasters.

残留的咸海还能得救吗？位于哈萨克斯坦境内昔日的咸海北部海滨现已濒临干涸，但世代生活在那里的居民认为他们还有办法从这一全球空前的环境灾难中挽回损失。

译文将背景信息抽出译为一个小句，然后再进行陈述，保证了译文的连贯。下面几例也都是"背景信息 + 陈述的信息"这样的排列格局：

6. The home of bibimbap—a popular rice and vegetable dish favoured by ancient Korean kings and by pop star Michael Jackson when he toured South Korea—hopes its cuisine and culture will also be a hit with soccer fans.

全州当地有一种叫作"拌饭"的食品，是用大米和蔬菜做的大众美食，古代朝鲜的国王们都喜欢，流行歌星迈克尔·杰克逊当年到韩国巡回演出时也大加赞扬。全州希望本地的美食和文化也能博得球迷们的青睐。

7. If the battleground of this business war is the rights that people and companies have to exploit their own work, the weapons are patents, trademarks, design registrations and copyright.

个人和企业拥有多项权利来利用自己的成果。如果这些权利就是商战的论争主题，那么他们的武器就是拥有的专利、商标、设计登记和版权。

8. Mr. Dubacher has grown wise to his feathered charges in the 26 years since he turned his parents' 20-acre farm, nestled on the edge of the Berkshires, into a sanctuary for injured and unwanted birds.

杜巴切先生的父母在伯克希尔市郊有一座20英亩的农场，杜巴切先生把它变成了一处鸟类保护区，专门接纳受伤或无人想要的鸟。26年来，杜巴切先生已经学会如何对待这些长羽毛的受保护对象。

9. Viruses often cause massive failure in staple crops in developing countries. Two years ago, Africa lost more than half its cassava crop, a key source of calories, to the mosaic virus. Genetically modified, virus-resistant crops can reduce that damage, as can drought-tolerant seeds in regions where water shortages limit the amount of land under cultivation. Biotech can also help solve the problem of soil that contains excess aluminum, which can damage roots and cause many staple-crop failures. A gene that helps neutralize aluminum toxicity in rice has been identified.

病毒常常在发展中国家造成主要粮食作物大面积歉收。两年前，斑纹病使非洲损失了超过一半的木薯：这种作物是当地人的主要食物。经过遗传改性的抗病毒作物可以减少这种损失；同样，在可耕地面积因缺水而受到限制的地区，抗干旱种子也能起到这种作用。生物技术还能帮助解决土壤含铝过高的问题——这种土壤会损伤作物的根系并使许多主要作物歉收。目前，研究人员已经识别出一种有助于中和水稻里的毒性的基因。

这一段原文讲的是基因技术能解决的两个问题。译文条理不够清楚，症结在于信息的顺序排列不当。尤其划线的句子，给人一种要切换话题的感觉。试将信息线性顺序调整如下，看是否可增强译文的连贯性：

病毒常给发展中国家的主要粮食作物带来严重灾害。在非洲，人们的主要食品是木薯，但两年前，斑纹病毒使该地区的木薯损失大半。种植基因改良型抗病毒作物可以减少类似损失，就像在可耕地面积因缺水而受到限制的地区抗旱良种能减少损失一样。另外，铝含量超标的土壤会对农作物的根部造成损害，并导致主要作物歉收。基因技术也可以帮助解决这一难题。目前，研究人员已经在水稻中识别出一种有助于中和铝的毒性的基因。

最后，还应注意段与段之间的连贯。尤其是段落的首句，一定要与上一段的信息紧密衔接起来。

10. The authorities might have taken stronger steps against Wild had he not been so useful as a thief taker. He knew every criminal, as he employed most of them himself. Whenever it suited his purpose, he would hand a man over to the authorities for hanging. This brought him even more money, for a reward was generally offered for wanted criminals. It also provided Wild with a very effective means of controlling his men. Every man knew that if he disobey the boss he would be betrayed and would quickly find himself on the gallows.

Jack Sheppard, who had robbed for Wild and killed honest men so that Wild might grow rich, was one of those who fell out with the boss and was duly betrayed to the authorities.

要不是怀尔德在抓贼方面还有不小的作用，当局早就对他采取更强有力的措施了。他认识每一个罪犯，因为他亲自雇佣过其中大多数人。有时出于他自己的需要，他会向当局交出一个，处以绞刑。这使他捞到了更多的油水，因为缉拿罪犯往往是有赏金的。这也为怀尔德控制他的手下人提供了有效手段。每一个窃贼都清楚，如果自己违抗老板，就会被他出卖，很快走上绞刑架。

杰克·谢波德曾为怀尔德出力和杀害良民，结果使怀尔德得以富有。他就是和老板翻脸的爪牙之一，于是当然被出卖给了当局。

译文第二段的信息排列顺序（杰克·谢波德为怀尔德做坏事→违抗老板而被老板出卖）与上一段连贯性差，可改为：杰克·谢波德就是因与老板闹翻，被出卖给了当局。尽管他曾为怀尔德杀人越货，抢金掠银，让怀尔德大发横财。这样，信息排列（杰克·谢波德就是一例→尽管曾为老板卖命）就与上文（尤其注意上段最后一句）呼应了。

Leafing Through Maple Lore

Bill Casselman

[1]   The maple smoke of autumn bonfires is incense to Canadians. Bestowing aroma for the nose, chroma for the eye, sweetness for the spring tongue, the sugar maple prompts this sharing of a favourite myth and an original etymology of the word *maple*.[1]

[2]   The maple looms large in Ojibwa folk tales. The time of year for sugaring-off is "in the Maple Moon[2]". Among Ojibwa, the primordial female figure is Nokomis, a wise grandmother. In one tale about seasonal change, cannibal wendigos—creatures of evil—chased old Nokomis through the autumn countryside. Wendigos throve in icy cold. When they entered the bodies of humans, the human heart froze solid. Here wendigos represent oncoming winter. They were hunting to kill and eat poor Nokomis, the warm embodiment of female fecundity who, like the summer, has grown old.

[3]   Knowing this was a pursuit to the death[3], Nokomis outsmarted the cold devils. She hid in a stand of maple trees, all red and orange and deep yellow. This maple grove grew beside a waterfall whose mist blurred the trees' outline. As they peered through the mist, slavering wendigos thought they saw a raging fire in which their prey was burning. But it was only old Nokomis being hidden by the bright red leaves of her friends, the maples. And so, drooling ice and huffing frost[4], the wendigos left her and sought easier prey. For their service in saving the earth mother's life, these maples were given a special gift: Their water of life would be forever sweet, and humans would tap it for nourishment.

[4]   Maple and its syrup flow sweetly into Canadian humour. Quebeckers have the standard *sirop d'erable* for maple syrup, but add a feisty insult to label imitation syrups that are thick with glucose glop. They call this sugary impostor *sirop de poteau* "telephone-pole syrup" or "dead tree syrup".[5]

[5]   The contention that maple syrup is unique to North America is suspect,[6] I believe. China has close to 100 species of maple, more than any country

in the world. Canada has 10 native species. North America does happen to be home to the sugar maple, the species that produces the sweetest sap and the most abundant flow. But are we to believe that in thousands of years of Chinese history, these inventive people never tapped a maple to taste its sap? I speculate that they did. Could Proto-Amerinds who crossed the Bering land bridge to populate the Americas have brought with them a knowledge of maple syrup? Is there a very old Chinese phrase for maple syrup? Is maple syrup mentioned in Chinese literature? For a non-reader of Chinese, such questions are daunting but not impossible to answer. More to come on this in a future column.

[6] What is certain is the maple's holdfast on our national imagination. Its leaf was adopted as an emblem in New France as early as 1700, and in English Canada by the mid-19th century. In the fall of 1867, a Toronto schoolteacher named Alexander Muir was traipsing a street in the city, all squelchy underfoot from the soft felt of falling leaves, when a maple leaf alighted on his coat sleeve and stuck there. After it resisted several brushings-off, Muir joked to his walking companion that this would be "the maple leaf for ever!" At home that evening, he wrote a poem and set it to music, in celebration of Canada's Confederation. Muir's song, "The Maple Leaf Forever", was wildly popular and helped fasten the symbol firmly to Canada.

[7] The word *maple* is from *mapeltreow*, the Old English term for maple tree, with *mapl-* as its Proto-Germanic root, a compound in which the first *m-* is, I believe, the nearly worldwide *ma*, one of the first human sounds, the pursing of a baby's lips as it prepares to suck milk from mother's breast. The *ma* root gives rise in many world languages to thousands of words like mama, mammary, maia, and Amazon. Here it would make *mapl-* mean "nourishing mother tree", that is, tree whose maple sap is nourishing. The second part of the compound, *apl-*, is a variant of Indo-European *abel* "fruit of any tree" and the origin of another English fruit word, *apple*. So the primitive analogy compares the liquid sap with another nourishing liquid, mother's milk.

[8] That's my maple key. Take it or leaf it.[7]

参考译文

关于枫树的传说

比尔·卡斯尔曼

[1] 对加拿大人来说,秋天篝火中燃烧的枫树枝冒出的烟气就是熏香。糖枫树给人带来扑鼻的香气、耀眼的色彩和令人咂舌回味的甘甜,它促使我写下这篇文章,告诉大家我最喜爱的一个神话以及"maple"(枫树)一词的独特词源。

[2] 在奥吉布瓦族印第安人的民间传说里,枫树总会赫然显现出来,占有重要地位。每年熬制枫糖的时节就在"枫树月"里。在奥吉布瓦人的心目中,最原始的女性形象是一个聪明的老奶奶,名叫诺科米丝。有一个关于四季轮回的传说讲道,一群叫温迪格的食人恶魔在秋天的乡野追赶诺科米丝。温迪格们是在滴水成冰的严寒里生长起来的。它们侵入人体时,人的心脏就冻成冰块。在这个故事里,温迪格们代表将要来临的冬天。它们正在追逐可怜的诺科米丝,要把她杀死吃掉,因为她是女性旺盛生殖力的温暖的象征,而且像夏天一样已经衰老。

[3] 诺科米丝知道,她若是被抓必死无疑,于是她运用智谋蒙蔽那群冷酷的恶鬼。她躲进一片红色、橙色、深黄色的枫树林里。树林长在一挂瀑布旁边,瀑布的水雾使树木的轮廓变得模糊。当那些口滴馋涎的温迪格们透过水雾费力地窥探时,以为看见了一堆熊熊的烈火,以为自己追逐的猎物正在烈火中燃烧。其实诺科米丝老奶奶只不过是被她的枫树朋友们用红得发亮的叶子掩蔽起来了。于是温迪格们不追了。它们流着口水,喘着粗气,口水顷刻结成了冰,呵气顷刻凝成了霜;它们就这样走了,去寻找更容易捕获的猎物。那些枫树由于救了大地母亲诺科米丝的命,得到了上天的特别恩赐:它们的生命之液将永远甘甜,人类将汲取这汁液来获得营养。

[4] 枫树和枫糖浆甜蜜地进入了加拿大式的幽默之中。魁北克省人一般把枫糖浆叫作"sirop d'erable"(枫糖浆),但是对各种含有黏乎乎葡萄糖液的仿制枫糖浆,总要加上一个带强烈贬义的词。他们把这种糖浆的冒牌货叫作"sirop de poteau",意为"电线杆糖浆"或"枯树糖浆"。

[5] 有人说,枫糖浆只是北美洲才有,我认为这种说法不可信。中国有近百种枫树,比世界上任何国家都多。加拿大只有十个原生的品种。诚然,北美洲有幸成为汁液最甜、流量最多的糖枫树故乡。可是,要是说在中国几千年的历史上,善于创新的中国人从来没有采过枫树的汁液,没有尝过它的味道,我们能相信吗?我想他们是尝过的。那些最早跨过白令海峡的路桥来北美洲和南美洲繁衍生息的

原始印第安人，有没有可能带来关于枫糖浆的知识呢？中文里有没有表述枫糖浆的古老词语呢？中国文学里有没有提到枫糖浆呢？我这个不懂中文的人对这些问题有些望而却步，但也不是找不到答案。更多的情况有待于将来的专栏文章披露。

[6] 有一点是可以肯定的，枫树总是牵动着我们民族的想象力。早在 1700 年，枫叶就被用作新法兰西殖民地的徽记。到了 19 世纪中期，枫叶已成为英属加拿大省份的徽记了。1867 年秋季，多伦多市一个名叫亚历山大·缪尔的小学教师疲惫地走在市区的一条大街上，整个路面覆盖着一层松软的落叶，踩在脚下发出扑哧扑哧的声响。他走着走着，突然间一片枫叶落到他的外衣袖子上，粘住了。他掸了几次，叶片都没有掉，于是他对同伴开玩笑说：这叶子快成"永远的枫叶"了！当天晚上，他在家里写了一首诗，并谱了曲，以庆祝加拿大自治领成立。缪尔创作的这首名为《永远的枫叶》的歌曲，受到公众的热烈欢迎，也使人们把枫叶这个象征物与加拿大紧密地联系在了一起。

[7] "maple"（枫树）来自古英语表述枫树的词"mapeltreow"。"maple"的原始词根是 mapl-。这是一个复合词根，我相信它的第一部分 m- 就是那个几乎遍及全世界的 ma，即人类最早发出的声音之一，也就是婴儿撅起嘴唇要吸吮母乳时发出的声音。ma 这个词根在世界上许多语言里都有，构成了几千个词，如"mama"（妈妈）、"mammary"（乳房的）、"maia"（母亲[源于希腊神话]）、"Amazon"（亚马孙族女武士）等。在这里，它可以使 mapl- 指"有营养的母亲树"，也就是说，一棵有着营养丰富的枫液的树。这个复合词根的第二部分 apl- 是印欧语系的 abel 的变体，意为"任何树产的水果"，它也是英语中另一个表示水果的词"apple"（苹果）的词源。因此，这种原始的类比就使枫树的汁液可与另一种有营养的汁液——母乳——相媲美了。

[8] 这就是我的枫树指南，把它带走，或在此浏览吧。（谷启楠译）

注释

1. 这一段的汉译有一个显著的特点：不是照字面对译，而是按照原句的意思换一种说法写出来。比如第一句照字面应该是"秋天篝火的枫烟就是加拿大人的熏香"。这倒是挺简练，但汉语读者会觉得像电报文字，感觉没说全，少了些什么。第二句以 ...prompts this sharing... 为谓语加宾语的结构，照字面译就是"……促成了对……的分享"。而译文为"……（促使）我写下这篇文章，告诉大家……"。效果如何？读者会觉得很顺畅，因为它把事件的进程表述得更清楚。

2. Maple Moon 是奥吉布瓦人对每年枫树流出汁液的时段（大约三月中旬到四月中旬）的称呼，类似于美国人的 Harvest Moon。
3. a pursuit to the death 未译成"通向死亡的追逐"之类，而是用了一种解释性的行文方式，把对事态发展的预知展开来说：要是被抓住了，就会被弄死。请参阅注释 1 进一步思考。
4. 与注释 1 和 3 所分析的一样，drooling ice and huffing frost 未译成"嘴里滴着冰，呼着霜"，而是把事件的过程更完整地呈现出来：先是流口水、喘粗气，而后口水结冰，呵气成霜。
5. poteau 在法语中是 pole 的意思，sirop 就是 syrup 的意思。pole syrup 是个"死"的形象，而 maple syrup 是"活"的，这种对比就形成了一种嘲讽式的幽默。
6. 试比较："我认为，枫糖浆只是北美洲才有的观点值得怀疑"。而现译文说："有人说……我认为……"，似乎场景更宽了，说的是不同人的观点，而不只是一个物化的 contention。
7. key 可能有两个意思：a winged seed 或 something that helps you to understand。Take it or leaf it 显然是仿照 take it or leave it（要不要由你）而来。作者意欲增加一点诙谐幽默的成分，但汉译很难将其再现。

讲解

解释性翻译

注释 1、3 和 4 谈的都是一个问题——解释性翻译（Exegetic Translation）。什么叫解释性翻译呢？我们再来回顾一下注释中提到的句子。译者在处理这些句子时，加上了字面上并没有的东西，比如注释 1 中提到的 sharing 在译文中表述为"写（文章）"和"告诉"两个连贯的动作过程，而 sharing 照字面只是"分享"的意思。那么译者所加的信息是从哪里来的呢？译者凭什么加上这些信息呢？这涉及语言和翻译的以下三个特点。

其一，语言表达都是提喻性的。法国译界释义派学者 Marianne Lederer 认为，"所有情况下，就表达的概念而言，语篇的物质形式与其说是面面俱到的描写还不如说只是一种提示"（in all circumstances, with regard to the ideas expressed, the material form of a text is always more an indication than a description.）。这也就是说，语言的表层形式不是对某个情景、某个概念或某个事件、行为过程的所有细节的呈现，而只是点到而已。这种语言现象被 Lederer 借用修辞学中的一个词 synecdoche（提喻法），称为语言的提喻性。我们说话时只是点到某些细节，并相信其余的细节，我们要表达的思想或事物的整体就会被理解了。她还指出，不同语言的提喻结构会有所不同。两种语言说的是一回事，但点到的细节却有可能会不一样。比如，注释 3 中的 a pursuit to the death 点到了 a pursuit 和 to the death，就是个浓缩了的过程，因为事件的发展过程其实是先"被抓住"，然后才会"被弄死"。

其二，翻译是跨语境的。在源语语境中不必明说的信息，在译语语境中却可能必须明示，才能达到近似的交际效果。比如，第 [2] 自然段的 Ojibwa 译成"奥吉布瓦族印第安人"，加了"印第安"几个字，因为中文读者大都不知道作为印第安人一个分支的"奥吉布瓦人"，而熟悉"印第安人"，这样一加读者就有一个清楚的概念。

其三，按照法国翻译教学和理论研究的释义派观点，理解原文是译者的语言能力和相关知识以及个人情感与原文语篇相作用的结果。译者所掌握的各种相关知识和经验，甚至他的个人情感都会参与到对原文的解读和译文的构建过程中来。他从原文中所"看到"的不仅仅是那些"提喻点"，那些"只言片语"，而是完整的画面、过程或概念。他可以根据翻译的目的和读者的需求决定哪些地方要进行添加或解释。

正是由于上述特点，译文常常会比原文"长"些。这是"一种在目的语语篇中把源语语篇中未能明确传达出的额外细节加以表述、解释的翻译方法"（a style of translation in which the TT expresses and explains additional details that are not explicitly conveyed in the ST），也就是说，"译语语篇同时也是对源语语篇的扩充和解释"（the TT is, at the same time, an expansion and explanation of the contents of the ST）。这就是 Sandor Hervey 和 Ian Higgins 在 1992 年出版的 *Thinking Translation. A Course in Translation Method: French to English* 一书中对解释性翻译的定义。

这种翻译方法尤其适用于以信息功能为主的说明性文字的翻译。译者往往可以：增加事件或动作的过程细节；增加或调整情景细节；对概念或观点进行简单解释；对背景知识加以必要补充。再看下面翻译实例：

With speed increasingly seen as the key to competitive advantage, the dream is to marry the control of an established company with the responsiveness of a start-up. As Linda Applegate reports, advances in IT now mean that the "big small" company is finally feasible.

句中的 the "big small" company 如何翻译？"大规模的小公司"？显然不合汉语行文逻辑和表达习惯。于是译者根据上文提供的背景信息，采取了解释的方法，译为：

如今，速度越来越被认为是获得竞争优势的关键。人们向往着能将老牌知名企业的管理能力和新兴公司的快速反应能力结合起来。如同琳达·阿普里盖特在报道中所述，信息技术的进步意味着"健全高效的"公司体制终于成为可行的现实。

译者陈小慰就"big small" company 的翻译评论道，"不宜只看字面意义，而应根据上下文"进行理解和翻译。她建议还可译为"规模健全而又反应快速的公司""大而精干的公司""反应快速的大公司"等。

又如：

This year's report says a typical family will spend about $221,000 raising a child through age 17; that's 21% more than families spent the year I was born. Food and clothing are cheaper now, but housing and health care cost more. Turns out parents get a bulk discount; people with one child spend 25% more per child than families with two, and by the time you have three or more, you are spending 22% less on each one.

本年度报告表明，每个普通家庭把一个孩子供养到 17 岁需花费约 22.1 万美元；这比我出生那年的家庭开销要多 21%。食物和衣服现在要便宜些，但住房和医疗贵了。结果是孩子越多反而越省钱：就花在每一个孩子身上的费用而言，独生子女家庭比两个孩子的家庭要多 25%，3 个或更多孩子的家庭，能省 22%。

译文中"孩子越多反而越省钱"便是对 get a bulk discounted 的解释。这一段选自一篇题为"Kid Math"的文章，谈抚养子女的费用和心血，标题也可解释性地译为《生儿育女一本账》，而不是"儿童数学"之类。

The Origins of Modern Science (Excerpts)

A. N. Whitehead

[1]　The progress of civilization is not wholly a uniform drift towards better things. It may perhaps wear this aspect if we map it on a scale which is large enough.[1] But such broad views obscure the details on which rests our whole understanding of the process. New epochs emerge with

comparative suddenness, if we have regard to the scores of thousands of years throughout which the complete history extends. Secluded races suddenly take their places in the main stream of events; technological discoveries transform the mechanism of human life; a primitive art quickly flowers into full satisfaction of some aesthetic craving; great religions in their crusading youth spread through the nations the peace of Heaven and the sword of the Lord.[2]

[2] The sixteenth century of our era saw the disruption of Western Christianity and the rise of modern science. It was an age of ferment. Nothing was settled, though much was opened—new worlds and new ideas. In science, Copernicus and Vesalius may be chosen as representative figures: They typify the new cosmology and the scientific emphasis on direct observation. Giordano Bruno was the martyr: Though the cause for which he suffered was not that of science, but that of free imaginative speculation. His death in the year 1600 ushered in the first century of modern science in the strict sense of the term. In his execution there was an unconscious symbolism: For the subsequent tone of scientific thought has contained distrust of his type of general speculativeness. The Reformation, for all its importance, may be considered as a domestic affair of the European races. Even the Christianity of the East viewed it with profound disengagement. Furthermore, such disruptions are no new phenomena in the history of Christianity or of other religions. When we project this great revolution upon the whole history of Christian Church, we cannot look upon it as introducing a new principle into human life.[3] For good or for evil, it was a great transformation of religion; but it was not the coming of religion. It did not itself claim to be so. Reformers maintained that they were only restoring what had been forgotten.

[3] It is quite otherwise with the rise of modern science. In every way it contrasts with the contemporary religious movement. The Reformation was a popular uprising, and for a century and a half drenched Europe in blood. The beginnings of the scientific movement were confined to a minority among the intellectual elite. In a generation which saw the Thirty Years' War and remembered Alva in the Netherlands,[4] the worst that happened to men of science was that Galileo suffered an honourable detention and a mild reproof, before dying peaceful in his bed.[5] The way in which the persecution

of Galileo has been remembered is a tribute to the quiet commencement of the most intimate change in outlook which the human race had yet encountered. Since a babe was born in a manger, it may be doubted whether so great a thing has happened with so little stir.

[4]　The thesis which these lectures will illustrate is that this quiet growth of science has practically recoloured our mentality so that modes of thought which in former times were exceptional are now broadly spread through the educated world. This new colouring of ways of thought had been proceeding slowly for many ages in the European peoples. At last it issued in the rapid development of science; and has thereby strengthened itself by its most obvious application. The new mentality is more important even than the new science and the new technology. It has altered the metaphysical presuppositions and the imaginative contents of our minds; so that now the old stimuli provoke a new response. Perhaps my metaphor of a new colour is too strong. What I mean is just that slightest change of tone which yet makes all the difference. This is exactly illustrated by a sentence from a published letter of that adorable genius[6], William James. When he was finishing his great treatise on the *Principles of Psychology*, he wrote to his brother Henry James[7], "I have to forge every sentence in the teeth of irreducible and stubborn facts."

[5]　This new tinge[8] to modern minds is a vehement and passionate interest in the relation of general principles to irreducible and stubborn facts. All the world over and at all times there have been practical men, absorbed in "irreducible and stubborn facts"; all the world over and at all times there have been men of philosophic temperament who have been absorbed in the weaving of general principles. It is this union of passionate interest in the detailed facts with equal devotion to abstract generalization which forms the novelty in our present society. Previously it had appeared sporadically and as if by chance. This balance of mind has now become part of the tradition which infects cultivated thought. It is the salt which keeps life sweet. The main business of universities is to transmit this tradition as a widespread inheritance from generation to generation.

第五章 说明、论说文体的翻译

参考译文

现代科学的起源（节选）

A. N. 怀特黑德

[1] 文明的进展并不完全是一股步调一致、日趋完美的洪流。从足够宏观的角度看，或许是这样的，但宏观视角往往会模糊了细节，而这些细节恰恰就是我们理解文明进程的依据所在。假使我们从整个人类历史所穿越的几千几万年的角度来看，新时代的出现常常是相当突然的。与世隔绝的民族突然在主流历史事件中占有了一席之地；技术发明改变了人类的生存机制；一种原始的艺术形式迅速发展，充分满足了某种审美渴求；处于全力发展初期的伟大宗教，就在各民族中传播了天国的和平和上帝的威严。

[2] 公元16世纪目睹了西方基督教的分裂和现代科学的兴起。那是一个激荡变革的时代。新范畴和新观点层出不穷，但没有哪一个可以确定下来。在科学领域，可推哥白尼和维萨里为典型：他们代表着新的宇宙观和直接观察的科学理念。布鲁诺是殉道者：尽管他的殉难不是为了科学事业，而是为了想象和思辨的自由。他1600年的殉难迎来了严格意义上的现代科学的第一个新世纪。他的献身只具有一种未被觉察到的象征意义：因为随后的科学思想并不认可他那种笼统的玄想。宗教改革尽管重要，也只被视为欧洲诸民族自家的事，就连东方的基督徒也袖手旁观，无动于衷。另外，这样的分裂在基督教或其他宗教的历史上也并不罕见。将这场伟大革命置于整个基督教历史的长河中，我们就不能说它给人类带来了新的生活准则。不论是好还是坏，它只带来了宗教的变革；但不是新宗教的建立。它自己也并未如此声言，改革者认为，他们只是要恢复那些被遗忘的东西。

[3] 现代科学的兴起就完全不同了，在各方面都与当时宗教运动的发展形成鲜明对照。宗教改革是一场群众性的叛乱，曾使欧洲遭受一个半世纪的腥风血雨。而科学运动的开端只局限在少数知识精英之中。在发生过三十年战争和对阿尔瓦血腥屠杀尼德兰人民起义仍记忆犹新的那个时代，科学家所遭遇的最坏情况只是伽利略在寿终正寝前曾被体面地拘禁并受到温和的谴责。伽利略遭迫害之所以在人们头脑中留下如此的记忆，这本身就是对人类世界观有史以来最深刻变革的平静开端的致意。自从一个婴儿降生在马厩中以来，还真没有哪件大变革是以这样小的动静开始的。

[4] 本系列讲座旨在说明，科学的平静发展实际上重塑了一种心态，致使过去认为异端罕见的思想得以在现今的知识界广为传播。这种新的思维方式已经在欧洲诸民

族中缓慢地发展了多年，最终导致了科学的突飞猛进，并通过对这种思维方式的显而易见的实际运用使其自身得以进一步强化。这种思维方式甚至比新科学和新技术更为重要。它改变了我们大脑形而上学的推测和想象的内容。于是，旧时的刺激就可产生新的回应。也许我用"重塑"这个比喻的说法太重了一点，我要说的是，仅仅是那一点点的心态变化就造成了这所有的不同。这一点可从威廉·詹姆斯公开发表的一封信中得到确切的说明。当这位令人敬佩的天才就要完成他的巨著《心理学原理》的时候，他在写给弟弟亨利·詹姆斯的一封信里说道："我必须面对不可更改的确凿事实来铸造我的每一个句子。"

[5]　现代思想的这一新特点，就是对普遍原则和不可更改的确凿事实之间的关系具有强烈的激情和兴趣。在这个世界上，无论何时何地都有倾心于"不可更改的确凿事实"的实事求是的人，也有致力于构建普遍原则的具有哲学气质的人。正是这种对事实细节的热心关注和对抽象概括的同样热情的紧密结合，才构成了现今社会的新气象。过去，这种情况只是零星出现，看似偶然。而现在，这种心态的平衡已经成为传统的一部分，影响着有素养的人的思维。它已成为让生活变得美好的必需品。大学的主要任务就是把这种传统作为广为流传的遗产一代一代地继承下去。

注释

1. 试比较另一种台湾地区出版的译文"文明的进展并不完全像是渐趋佳境的一道巨流；假使我们以相当大的比例尺绘制成图，也许它会显示上述外观，但是这种宽泛的看法往往使细节模糊，而那些细节却是我们全盘理解文明进展过程之基础"。问题出在大比例尺绘图上：比例尺越大，实际所显示的细节越多，故此汉译不合逻辑。症结在于如何理解 map it on a scale which is large enough. 不是大比例尺绘图，而是将文明史放在一个足够大的背景上观察（而非局部细节观察）之意。
2. 本单元特别提醒大家注意说明、论说文的逻辑层次，我们把它称为 textual profile，也就是语篇逻辑形态。这个自然段可分成两个句群。句群一：共三句，第一句提出观点——第二句提出反面观点——第三句反驳反面观点，从而强化第一句的观点。句群二：起于 New epochs emerge with comparative suddenness..., if...。这一句既承接句群一，又提出了一个新的观点。下面各句都是说明这个观点的具体实例。
3. 仍然提醒大家要注意这一自然段的逻辑形态：前三句奠定了基本观点，以下诸句都是围绕 ... an age of ferment. Nothing was settled, though much was opened... 展开的，是一系列的史实或证。因此，这些史实的翻译都要紧扣这样一个逻辑走向。比如这一句就不宜译为"我们即使把这次大革命投射到基督教的全盘历史中观察，也无法认为它给人类生活创立了什么新的原则"。因为这里的逻辑不是"即使……也"这样的关系，而只

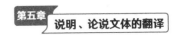

是用于佐证 nothing was settled 的一个事实。
4. 三十年战争发生在 1618 年至 1648 年的欧洲，阿尔瓦镇压荷兰的资产阶级革命的大屠杀发生在 1567 年，到 17 世纪 20、30 年代人们仍记忆犹新。
5. 这里用了 honourable、mild 和 peaceful 等词语，实际上伽利略受到的迫害已经很严厉，只是没有像布鲁诺那样被烧死而已。1616 年 2 月，罗马教廷宗教裁判所宣布，不许伽利略再宣传哥白尼的学说，在教会的威胁下，伽利略被迫声明放弃哥白尼学说。但实际上，他从未放弃自己的信念，一直暗中进行着科学研究。1633 年初，伽利略在罗马被宗教裁判所监禁，被迫在法庭上当众表示忏悔。他的晚年痛失爱女，双目失明，很是凄凉。
6. adorable genius 在此句作定语译出会显臃肿，故移至下句译出，不影响行文逻辑。
7. 资料表明，William 是长子，比 Henry（著名小说家）大一岁，故译为"弟弟"。
8. 这里的 tinge 和上一个自然段的 recoloured—colouring—colour 组成一个连贯的比喻系列，比喻思想方式上的转变。由于汉语不好说"为我们的心态重新着色"，故译为"重塑……心态"。注意下面的译文要以此为准构建："重塑……心态——这种新的思维方式——'重塑'这个比喻"；直到本段的 This new tinge 译为"这一新特点"。

 讲解

语篇形态

注释 2 和 3 都特别提到了语篇形态的问题，这里进一步讨论。

Chesterman 在 1998 年出版的 *Contrastive Functional Analysis* 中这样定义语篇形态："语篇形态指语篇中意义的整体结构形态，也就是语篇中信息推进的模式"（The profile of a text describes the general structural shape of its meaning, the way the ideas proceed through the text.）。也可以说，语篇形态就是信息的逻辑推进模式。先说什么，后说什么，哪里是概括，哪里有转折，等等，作者都必须适当安排，以便把自己的意思阐述清楚。而译者在阅读原文时必须跟上作者的思路，在自己的头脑中建立起清晰的逻辑模式，并按照译语的表达规范清晰地表达出来。说明、论说文的翻译尤其如此。下面我们就来分析几个译例：

(1) For many of these teachers-to-be, the image of the ideal teacher they carried with them into their pre-service course was of one who did not simply "teach" in the sense of "passing on" or quickening skills, knowledge and facts, (2) but one who would "make a difference" "touch lives": (1.1) one for whom pupils' cognitive and affective development was paramount, (2.1) but for whom such development needed to take place within what might

be called a fundamentally pastoral mode of pedagogy. (2.2) For these novice teachers, the teacher they envision eventually becoming is a carer, nurturer and role model as much as an "educator" in the narrower sense of the word, (2.3) one whose *modus operandi* is characterized by personal "performance" and student admiration along the lines described by Harris and Jarvis in their finding from their own research with student teachers (2.4) that "the cultural images dominating the minds of intending teachers are those of charismatic individuals who have changed the lives of those with whom they work".

这个段落摘自一本讨论怎样做一个好教师的教育学专著 *The Good Teacher*，我们先来分析一下它的逻辑形态。作者在一开始便提出师范生心目中理想教师的两个层面（1）和（2）：

For many teachers-to-be:

(1) ideal teacher not simply teach... (2) but make a difference...

接下去，便以第（2）个层面为主线阐述开去（2.1）~（2.4）：

(1.1) for whom pupils'...development was paramount

(2.1) but for whom such development needed to take place within what might be called a fundamentally pastoral mode of pedagogy.

(2.2) the teacher...is a carer, nurturer...

(2.3) personal "performance" and student admiration

(2.4) charismatic individuals

汉语译文要在最大程度上再现这样的行文逻辑或语篇形态。请分析下面译文是否做到了这一点：

在参加岗前培训课程时，许多准教师的心中已经勾勒出了一个理想的老师形象：老师不应该只在向学生"传授"技巧、知识，讲解事实或加快学生对这些内容的理解上进行"教学"，而应该"创造个性""感触生命"。对教师而言，学生的认知和情感能力的发展是最重要的，而这两种能力的发展需要在一种基础性指导教学模式中进行。对于实习教师来说，他们最终期盼担当的教师角色是一个关护者、培养者，一个榜样似的角色，而不单单是个教育工作者，这是"教育工作者"一词的狭义解释。而某个教师的一贯教学作风，正如哈里斯和贾维斯所描述的那样，是由个人的"举止表现"和学生对他的敬佩程度共同勾画而成的。而哈里斯和贾维斯的这个描述是基于他们对实习老师的调查研究得出的，他们的研究结果表明"主宰着这些未来教师的想法的文化形象，即那些有感染力的个人，这些教师认为这些个人能改变和他们一起工作的人的生活"。

第五章 说明、论说文体的翻译

可以看到，译文的后半部分未能沿着第（2）个层面的（2.1）～（2.4）推进，划线部分极大地干扰了原文的逻辑走向，将原文的缜密文理"译散"了。可改进如下：

许多即将成为教师的人在进行岗前培训时心中就已经勾勒出好教师的形象，他们认为好教师不是简单的"教"，也就是所谓的"传递"或者说迅速地传授技能、知识和事实，而应该"产生巨大影响""触及生命"。对好教师来说，学生的认知和情感发展至关重要，而这样的发展需要在以所谓田园式教学模式为基调的情景中进行。在准教师的心目中，教师不仅是狭义上的"教育者"，还是对学生施以关怀和进行培育的人，是学生的楷模。他们还认为教师的普遍特征是"展现"自我和获得学生的敬仰，就像哈瑞斯和加沃斯对实习教师们进行研究后所描述的那样："准教师心目中的占主导地位的文化意象是那些有超凡魅力的人，他们改变了受教育者的人生。"

下面一个译例摘自奥巴马的就职演说：

(1) For as much as government can do and must do, it is ultimately the faith and determination of the American people upon which this nation relies. (2) It is the kindness to take in a stranger when the levees break, the selflessness of workers who would rather cut their hours than see a friend lose their job which sees us through our darkest hours. (3) It is the firefighter's courage to storm a stairway filled with smoke, but also a parent's willingness to nurture a child, that finally decides our fate.

这一段的逻辑形态是：（1）提出观点——this nation relies on the faith and determination of the American people；（2）和（3）是（1）的具体表现，用了强调句式 It is...which/that...。汉译时应该将这种由概括到具体的层层推进再现出来。请分析下面三种译文，看哪一种做得好些。

[a] 因为无论美国政府能做多少，必须做多少，美国国家的立国之本最终还是美国人的决心和信念。当防洪堤坝决堤之时人们善意地收留陌生受难者，当经济不景气时人们无私地减少自己工时而不愿意看着朋友失业，正是他们支撑我们走过黑暗的时刻。当楼道冲满浓烟时消防队员奋不顾身冲进去，还有父母养育孩子时的任劳任怨，正是这些决定了我们的命运。

[b] 因为无论美国政府能做多少，必须做多少，美国国家的立国之本最终还是美国人的决心和信念。于防洪堤坝决堤之时收留陌生受难者的善意，于在经济不景气的时候宁愿减少自己工时也不肯看着朋友失业的无私，正是他们支撑我们走过黑暗的时刻。消防队员冲入满是浓烟的楼梯抢救生命的勇气，父母养育孩子的坚持，正是这些决

329

定了我们的命运。

[c] 不管美国政府能做多少，必须做多少，立国之本最终还是美国人的决心和信念。是防洪堤坝溃决之时收留陌生受难者的善意，是经济不景气之时宁愿减少自己工时也不肯看着朋友失业的无私，支撑着我们走过了黑暗的时刻。是消防队员冲入满是浓烟的楼梯的勇气，也是父母养育孩子的意愿，最终决定着我们的命运。

可以看到，三种译文都基本再现了原文的语篇形态，但逻辑层次和推进力度显然译文 [c] 强于译文 [b]，译文 [b] 又强于译文 [a]。试想奥巴马用他那铿锵有力的语调念出这几句话的时候，是不是译文 [c] 更富于表现力？

下面两个段落摘自学术著作：

(1) So much has been written about the notion of discourse that it is in danger of losing its usefulness as a conceptual framework for social analysis under a welter of debate about what it actually means. I certainly do not want to add to this difficulty, mainly because I take the view that linguistic terms are often—perhaps always—open to interpretation, that this does not generally represent a communication problem, and that readers will be able to work out for themselves from my contexts and usages what I intend the term "discourse" to connote. I don't think we should be too precious about these terms, either. Meanings do evolve, proliferate and expand over time, and I am all in favour of using and reading language creatively. (2) Because many readers will already have definitions of discourse in mind, however, because the subtitle of this book includes the word "discourse", and in order to avoid a debate about the meaning of "discourse" obscuring the issues I really want us to think about, it seems useful to say something about how I am using the term before I proceed to use it.

For the purpose of this book, then, I have adopted a more or less Foucauldian view of discourse, wherein the term is used to denote the constructed parameters (3) within which our perception(s) of the social world and our actions within it are framed—parameters essentially produced and sustained by language and "knowledge" and controlled and patrolled by ideologies (4) that generally serve the interests of the already powerful at the expense of the already disempowered. Describing the way in which all social practice can be perceived in terms of the establishment of and participation in a range of discourses, Foucault has argued that discourses are not about objects, but construct or constitute them and, furthermore, in the process of doing so "conceal their own invention".

第五章 说明、论说文体的翻译

像这样的论说文体的理解和翻译，对语篇的逻辑形态的分析和构建至关重要。我们特别分析一下标上号码的句子。

第一自然段中句（1）so much...that...under... 构成逻辑推进模式，句（2）用 because...because...and in order to... 作状语层层阐明原因。下面译文是否将这种逻辑推进适当再现了呢？

（1）有关话语概念的讨论已经有很多。在对它意义的一番纷杂争议之后，话语失去了作为社会分析概念框架的作用，这是危险的。当然，我不想增加这样的难度，主要因为我认为语言学通常——或许总是——有着开放性的理解，这并不表示有沟通上的问题，读者自己能够从我的语境及用法中推断出我所用的"话语"的内涵是什么。我不认为我们要对这些术语过分究研。意义会随着时间推移而发展、增加和扩展，我赞同创造性地运用语言和阅读。（2）诚然，许多读者头脑中已有"话语"的定义，但是因为此书的小标题包含了"话语"这个词，为了避免让"话语"的意义把我实际想让我们思考的问题搞混，在开始用它之前，先说清楚它的用法是很有帮助的。

译文相应编号即划线部分显然未能恰当再建原文的逻辑形态。句（1）译为两句话，语义连贯受损，最后点出"是危险的"，原文"如此……以致……"的逻辑态势未能准确再现。句（2）"诚然……但是因为……为了……"序列打乱了原文的逻辑走向。试比较下面译文，看如何在汉译文中适当再建相应逻辑形态。

（1）关于"话语"这一概念已有太多的论述，对其确切所指众说纷纭，以致它作为社会分析的概念框架的作用正面临丧失的危险。我当然无意将问题进一步复杂化，因为我认为语言学术语的解释常常——或许总是——有一定开放性，这并不构成交际问题，而且读者也能从我使用这个术语的语境和用法推知我意欲赋予这个词的含义。另外，我认为对这样的术语也不应过分苛求意义的精准。意义总是随着时间的推移在不断演变、繁衍、扩展，我主张创造性地使用和解读语言。（2）不过，由于好多读者头脑中已经有了对"话语"的定义，也由于本书的副标题中有"话语"一词，另外也为了避免让"话语"含义之争淡化了我想让大家考虑的问题，在使用这个术语前把它的含义说明一下还是有益的。

有人将句（2）译为"由于许多读者头脑中已经有了'话语'的定义，而本书副标题含有'话语'这个词，所以为了避免读者在'话语'的意义上面争论不休以致搞不清我真正想让大家思考哪些问题，在我用这个术语之前先谈一下我如何使用它是有用的"。也就是用"由于……而……所以……"重构译文逻辑，同样是可行的。

再看第二个自然段。(3)和(4)标出的划线部分都是定语从句,下面译文采用了拆译方法:

为了这本书,我已或多或少采纳了福柯的话语观点。福柯认为话语是诸多建构因素,(3)通过这些因素形成了我们对人类世界和我们行动的认识。这些因素本质上由语言和"认知"产生并支撑,由思想意识控制并巡查,而(4)思想意识一般来讲会牺牲失势集团的利益而服从于权势集团的利益。福柯从话语的建立和话语的参与角度描述了感知社会实践的方法,并认为话语不是关于客体的,而是关于建构或维持客体的,并且在此过程中,"隐藏了它们的创造"。

所谓拆译就是把定语从句译为后置的并列分句。但这种方法的应用一定要视逻辑推进的走向和力度而定。凡是干扰逻辑推进或使逻辑关系变得松散、不清的,一定要慎重处理。如上述译文拆译出的划线部分就使福柯对"话语"的定义变得模糊不清。论说文中还是设法将逻辑关系紧密的定语从句译为前置定语为好。如:

基于本书的写作目的,我大体采用了福柯关于"话语"的观点,即"话语"指(3)我们用来认识社会和自己的社会行动的一系列已经确立的参数;这些参数本质上靠语言和"知识"得以生成和维系,并被(4)总体上以牺牲弱势群体利益为代价而服务于权势集团的思想意识所左右和监控。福柯描述了所有社会实践都可通过确立和参与某些参数加以认识的途径,指出话语不是在谈论客体,而是在构建或构成客体,而且在此过程中"隐藏了自身的创造性"。

判断语篇的逻辑形态,语篇的整体观念至关重要,而基本语言结构的分析仍是根本。对下面一个句群的逻辑形态的认识,基本句法分析就很有用。

There is nothing wrong, of course, about teachers being remembered or about new teachers wanting to emulate the ways and styles of teachers whom they have previously experienced as successful themselves. Nor, on the evidence of the testimonies of the teachers and students involved in the projects on which this book is based, would many prioritize the charismatic, enthusiastic, caring, inspirational conceptualization of the good teacher to the extent of ignoring or refuting other, less obvious qualities and skills that a successful teacher might require. We might also agree that at a time when technicist models of teaching appear (certainly, to the student teachers we spoke to) to be holding centre stage, the more intuitive, spontaneous, collaborative aspects of teaching need celebrating more than ever.

请对照下面两种译文:

[a] 当然,教师被人铭记或是新教师想仿效自身曾体会过的成功教师的教育方式和风格,

第五章 说明、论说文体的翻译

这本没任何错误。参与研究项目的老师们和学生们的观点为本书提供了依据，该观点认为一个好的老师应优先具备个人魅力、工作热情、关爱学生、启迪智慧等特征，以至于可以忽略或否定一个成功教师可能要求具备的其他略不突显的素质和技能。这也没什么错。我们可能还会同意：当技术型教学模式（当然，对于我们所说的实习教师而言）似乎独占鳌头时，教学中更具直觉力的，更自然的，更合作的方面需要得到空前的赞扬。

[b] 当然，有些教师被人们记住，有些新教师意欲效仿自己以前曾见过的成功教师的风格或者授课方式，这些都无可厚非。根据参与成为本书编写基础的有关研究项目的师生们的表述，他们中有许多人也没有将个人魅力、热情待人、关心他人、善于鼓舞人心列为优秀教师的首要因素，从而忽视了成功的教师还需要具备的而没有受到广泛关注的其他素质和技巧。我们还认为，当技术型教学模式（当然，这里对实习教师而言）占据了中心舞台的时候，更直观、更自发、更要求合作性的教学模式比以往任何时候更应该受到大家的重视。

可以看出，两种译文体现了对划线部分两种迥然不同的逻辑分析，或者更确切地说，句法分析：

(1) Nor is there anything wrong if many would prioritize the charismatic, enthusiastic, caring, inspirational conceptualization of the good teacher to the extent of ignoring or refuting other, less obvious qualities and skills that a successful teacher might require.

(2) Few would (many would not) prioritize the charismatic, enthusiastic, caring, inspirational conceptualization of the good teacher to the extent of ignoring or refuting other, less obvious qualities and skills that a successful teacher might require.

显然，第（2）种分析合乎英语语法。我们也曾就此和作者 Alex Moore 进行过沟通，他说译文 [b] 理解正确，并说：

To put it another way: Some students did like the idea of the charismatic teacher and found it very seductive. However, very few of them liked it so much that they thought it was the single or main answer to successful teaching. They realised that other qualities—the possession of certain knowledge and skills, the capacity for constructive reflection, etc.—were at least as important, if not more so.

逻辑推进模式是作者构建语篇时头脑中的一条思维主线。没有了这个主线，文理就会混乱，思想和事实就会表述不清。译者试图理解原文时，也要以语句为线索在自己头脑中建立起和作者相同的思维主线。这条主线既是理解原文的逻辑框架，又是构建译文的逻辑形态的起始点和依据。译文不是原文的拷贝，原文逻辑模式有时可照样复制，有时要根据中文写作规范做些调整和变通。这时，我们用中文思维写作的能力就是关键了。

小结

英语原文语篇是连贯的，译成汉语语篇也必须是连贯的，但并非必然是连贯的。保证译语语篇连贯是译者的跨语言、跨文化交际使命的重要部分。为什么说原文的连贯并不必然导致译文的连贯呢？原因很明显，英汉两种语言实现连贯的手段是有区别的。首先，在小句级层，英语是"主语 + 谓语"的句法结构，而汉语却可能呈现"话题 + 陈述"的语义结构（参见第三章 Unit Four 的讲解部分）。其次，在句子和语篇层次上，英语重形合，汉语重意合。这就意味着汉语惜用连接词语，且造句谋篇倚重词语而非小句（参见第四章 Unit One、Unit Two 和第五章 Unit One、Unit Two 的讲解部分）。第三，在语境层次，将以英语为载体的信息转换至汉语载体，无异于将一棵树移栽至一片陌生的土壤，这就要求译者充分注意译语读者与源语读者在文化背景上的差异，尽量使译语语篇所承载的信息与译语读者的知识结构相吻合。正因为如此，构建译文必须强调一种译语写作意识，即翻译过程是由原文信息所诱发的译语写作过程。译语读者不同于源语读者，必须保证他们付出合理的努力就能获得想要得到的信息。译者为自己的读者而写作。原文的信息，不是照录、照抄便肯定达意的；原文的语篇形态，也不是照搬、仿造就一定生成连贯、流畅的译文的。译者必须树立为读者进行必要的释义（参见第五章 Unit Eight 的讲解部分）的意识，要发挥自己的译语写作能力，构建合乎译语表达规范的语篇结构和逻辑形态（参见第五章 Unit Nine 的讲解部分）。

练习

1. 翻译下列段落。

(1)

The most serious indictment of the World Trade Center was simply that it was a spectacular waste of government money. The five-building complex, completed in 1977, was erected at the urging of Financial District boosters like Chase Manhattan's David Rockefeller, who, seeing big companies like Mobil decamp uptown, feared lower Manhattan would lose its status as the financial heart of the nation. The Port Authority envisioned the World Trade

Center to be exactly what the name suggested: a haven for shipping firms, importer-exporters, and foreign government officials who did business in the region. Those kinds of business, it turned out, couldn't afford the rents, so the Port Authority went after financial firms, emptying more offices in Wall Street's canyons.

⚠️ **提示**

注意小句间的逻辑关系及翻译。

(2)
The struggle for a tolerant society—not only one in which the big racial injustices are cured but one in which the strong do not prey on the weak, the beautiful do not insult the ugly and the thin do not prevail over the fat—is a worthy goal. But neither resources nor public sympathy is limitless. Treating the discrimination against someone who is fat alongside that of someone who is a paraplegic is part of an effort by special-interest groups in the U.S to make all suffering equal so that all remedies will be. It is a trend that would make the college student who is insulted by a racial joke comparable to James Meredith savagely barred at the door of the University of Mississippi when he tried to register in 1962; rape by a spouse as terrorizing as rape by a stranger with a knife in a dark alley; a *Playboy* calendar on the wall as detrimental on the job as a supervisor who takes away the duties of a clerk who has rebuffed his advances.

In isolation, all of these things—and more—are wrong and should be set right. But in a world of limits, some rights are more sacred than others, some wrongs more deserving of punishment. Not every unfairness derives from the violation of a right. Robert Nagel, professor of law at the University of Colorado, warns, "The rights makers are like children with toys, so delighted and entranced by them they want more and more, heedless of the consequences." Consider lookism, as the practice of preferring the pretty over the plain is called in rights jurisprudence. In the *Harvard Law Review*, Adam Cohen of the American Civil Liberties Union argues that ugly people need to be protected against discrimination too. Cohen says, "People don't realize how pervasive the preference for the beautiful is in our society, starting with teachers who give attractive children better grades." And he adds, "There is nothing wrong with giving these people who have a hard life a legal remedy.

We can always set enforcement priorities later."

There should be a way to recognize that something is too bad without saying it can be fixed. To do otherwise is to fail to protect the truly vulnerable, the truly prejudged, the truly disadvantaged. There is another way to proceed. Let the current trend in America continue until finally, after years of legislation and adjudication, all God's children are found to be aggrieved, and then all, in their need for protection, are equal once again.

⚠️ **提示**

注意长句的翻译。

2. 翻译下列短文。

(1)

A Nation of Hypochondriacs

[1] The main impression growing out of twelve years on the faculty of a medical school is that the No.1 health problem in the U. S. today, even more than AIDS or cancer, is that Americans don't know how to think about health and illness.[1] Our reactions are formed on the terror level.[2] We fear the worst, expect the worst and invite the worst. The result is that we are becoming a nation of weaklings and hypochondriacs, a self-medicating society incapable of distinguishing between casual, everyday symptoms and those that require professional attention.

[2] Somewhere in our early education we become addicted to the notion that pain means sickness. We fail to learn that pain is the body's way of informing the mind that we are doing something wrong, not necessarily that something is wrong. We don't understand that pain may be telling us that we are eating too much or the wrong things; or that we are smoking too much or drinking too much; or that there is too much emotional congestion[3] in our lives; or that we are being worn down by having to cope daily with overcrowded streets and highways, the pounding noise of garbage grinders, or the cosmic distance between the entrance to the airport and the departure gate.[4] We get the message of pain all wrong. Instead of addressing ourselves to the cause, we become pushovers for pills, driving the pain underground

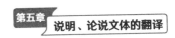

and inviting it to return with increased authority.[5]

[3]   Early in life, too, we become seized with the bizarre idea that we are constantly assaulted by invisible monsters called germs, and that we have to be on constant alert to protect ourselves against their fury. Equal emphasis, however, is not given to the presiding fact that our bodies are superbly equipped to deal with the little demons, and that the best way of forestalling an attack is to maintain a sensible life-style.

[4]   The most significant single statement about health to appear in the medical journals during the past decade is by Dr. Franz Ingelfinger, the late and former editor of the *New England Journal of Medicine*. Ingelfinger noted that almost all illnesses are self-limiting[6]. That is, the human body is capable of handling them without outside intervention. The thrust[7] of the article was that we need not feel we are helpless if disease tries to tear away at our bodies, and that we can have greater confidence in the reality of a healing system that is beautifully designed to meet most of its problems. And even when outside help is required, our own resources have something of value to offer in a combined strategy of treatment.

[5]   No one gets out of this world alive, and few people come through life without at least one serious illness. If we are given a serious diagnosis, it is useful to try to remain free of panic and depression. Panic can constrict the blood vessels and impose an additional burden on the heart. Depression, as medical researchers all the way back to Galen[8] have observed, can set the stage for other illnesses or intensify existing ones. It is no surprise that so many patients who learn that they have cancer or heart disease—or any other catastrophic disease—become worse at the time of diagnosis. The moment they have a label to attach to their symptoms, the illness deepens. All the terrible things they have heard about disease produce the kind of despair that in turn complicates the underlying condition. It is not unnatural to be severely apprehensive about a serious diagnosis, but a reasonable confidence is justified. Cancer today, for example, is largely a treatable disease. A heavily damaged heart can be reconditioned. Even a positive HIV diagnosis does not necessarily mean that the illness will move into the active stage.

[6]   One of the interesting things researchers at the UCLA medical center

have discovered is that the environment of medical treatment can actually be enhanced if seriously ill patients can be kept free of depression. In a project involving 75 malignant melanoma patients, it was learned that a direct connection exists between the mental state of the patient and the ability of the immune system to do its job. In a condition of emotional devastation, immune function is impaired. Conversely, liberation from depression and panic is frequently accompanied by an increase in the body's interleukins, vital substances in the immune system that help active cancer-killing immune cells. The wise physician, therefore, is conscious of both the physical and emotional needs of the patients.

[7] People who have heart attacks are especially prone to despair. After they come through the emergency phase of the episode, they begin to reflect on all the things they think they will be unable to do. They wonder whether they will be able to continue at their jobs, whether they will be able to perform satisfactorily at sex, whether they can play tennis or golf again. In short, they contemplate an existence drained of usefulness and joy. The spark goes out of their souls. It may help for these people to know that in addition to the miracles that modern medicine can perform, the heart can make its own bypass around the occluded arteries and that collateral circulation can provide a rich supply of oxygen. A heart attack need not be regarded as consignment to a mincing life-style. Under circumstances of good nutrition, a reasonable amount of exercise and a decrease in the wear and tear of stressful events, life expectancy need not be curtailed.

[8] Plainly, the American people need to be re-educated about their health. They need to know that they are the possessors of a remarkably robust mechanism. They need to be de-intimidated about disease. They need to understand the concept of a patient-physician partnership in which the best that medical science has to offer is combined with the magnificent resources of mind and body.

[9] We need not wait, of course, for a catastrophic illness before we develop confidence in our ability to rise to a serious challenge. Confidence is useful on the everyday level. We are stronger than we think. Much stronger.

第五章　说明、论说文体的翻译

⚠️ **提示**

1. 这是个长句，如何才能译得条理清晰？
2. 此句如直译为"我们的反应是建立在恐惧这个尺度上的"，则翻译腔十足，亦未必能达意。如何处理为好？
3. 注意 emotional congestion 的汉译的推敲。
4. or that we are being worn down by... 后接三个平行的宾语，结构较长。译文中的修饰语应力求层次清晰、紧凑。
5. 怎样用地道的汉语表达 become pushovers for pills、driving the pain underground 及 with increased authority 的意思？
6. self-limiting 之意如何理解，译为"有局限性的"或"自我局限的"，能达意吗？
7. thrust 意为 the basic meaning or purpose; point (*Webster's New World Dictionary of the American Language*)，其汉译如何定夺？
8. Galen 这一名字为中国读者所熟悉吗？可否采用增译法提供一点儿必要的背景信息？

(2)

[1]　On Ike's huge uncluttered desk in the Oval Office stood a small, black piece of wood bearing the Latin inscription, "Suaviter in modo fortiter in re."[1] It meant, "Gently in manner, firmly in deed,"[2] and it proved, as the president jestingly informed an inquirer, that he was after all an egghead. With his tigerish rages and his chameleon changeability[3], Ike did not live up to either part of this motto, certainly not in the way of Truman, who had proved that the buck stops here. Nevertheless, Ike managed to convey the spirit of his Latin tag. He exuded confidence and optimism. His serene bearing contributed signally to easing the atmosphere of tension generated by the Red scare. Having been coached by the actor-producer Robert Montgomery, Ike was supremely relaxed as a television performer, so much so that he was quite willing to go on the air without rehearsal, though he once remarked blithely that he would probably die of fright. Usually, though, his public appearances were carefully stage-managed, and he resented it when the press revealed details of the elaborate behind-the-scenes machinery which sustained them. Still, the combination of his naturalness and the professionalism of his advisers was highly effective. The president projected

an image of benign self-assurance which was all the more convincing because it pretty well reflected the truth.

[2] The White House staff who knew him best were unanimous in admiring his composure under stress. Arthur Larson was particularly impressed by the deliberate way in which the president took the only time he could find in his crowded day, their speech-writing conferences, to manicure his fingernails—his hands were so large that he employed a paper knife and a foot-long pair of desk shears.[4] Ike was not even flustered by the importunate behavior of some of his guests. When the British ambassador specially requested that Churchill should be provided with his usual midday feast one Sunday during his visit in June 1954, Ike responded to Dulles, suppose we have enough food in the White House to give Churchill his huge luncheon, but I'll be damned if I'm going to change my habits for the Prime Minister—I'll have a light luncheon.

[3] It has been said, of course, that Ike assuaged the febrile temper of the time not just by being unruffled but by being positively torpid[5]. He certainly gave the impression, because of his unabashed need for recreation and vacations, of taking life easy. In some respects he did. Ike was waited on hand and foot and received the best service in the world. His valet even helped him to step into his undershorts. He only had to pick up the telephone to get instant attention—after he left the presidency, like some latter-day Rip van Winkle[6], he did not know how to dial a number. He was surrounded by every convenience and many luxuries. Anthony Eden was amazed, for example, by the remarkable comfort and silence of the presidential airplane, the Columbine, which made it possible for him and his staff to make long journeys and to arrive fresher than when they left. Ike's friends entertained him with a lavishness that was all the more marked for being inconspicuous—Sid Richardson was an exception to the rule of inconspicuousness, and Ike thought it not smart of him to complain,[7] "It's getting to be terrible when a man can't lose ten million dollars without causing a lot of fuss and talk."

[4] Ike himself, though he warned his colleagues never to speak disrespectfully of a billion dollars, was the reverse of ostentatious about his comforts. He put the presidential yacht into mothballs as an economy

measure and rechristened Shangri-la (Roosevelt's mountain hide-away) Camp David, a less pretentious name and that[8] of his father and grandson. Ike did, to be sure, let Mamie go hog-wild over the rebuilding of their Gettysburg farm, a costly and somewhat inefficient undertaking. But he thought she "probably would have a nervous breakdown" without the opportunity to make them a permanent home. Actually, of course, it was impossible not to work hard at Ike's job, and he needed all the help he could get not to exhaust himself. But the fact that he seemed able to relax and enjoy himself as president helped to assuage anxieties about McCarthyism and the Cold War. Others followed his example: the sale of playing cards increased apace and golf boomed as a sport. People swapped unworried jokes about the president's addiction to the game. A favorite quip concerned his request to drive through the four ahead:[9] He was in a hurry because New York had just been bombed.

⚠ **提示**

1. 可否采用拆译的方法，灵活安排汉语句式？
2. 此处应译得言简意赅，符合其文体特点。
3. 对 his tigerish rages and his chameleon changeability 是否可作些表达方式上的调整？
4. 注意对长句的信息单位的分析，句中的定语从句如何翻译？
5. torpid 之意如何根据上下文来定夺？
6. 此处可否考虑加注？
7. 此处可否采用拆译的方法？如可行，如何安排汉语结构为好？
8. 注意分析代词 that 的所指。
9. 此处需了解有关背景知识（高尔夫球的常识），译文中如何处理为好？

参考文献

Baker, M. (2000). *In other words*. Beijing: Foreign Language Teaching and Research Press.
Beaugrande, R. (1980). *Text, discourse, and process*. London: Longman.
Beaugrande, R., & Dressler, W. (1981). *Introduction to text linguistics*. London: Longman.
Bell, R. T. (1991). *Translation and translating: Theory and practice*. London: Longman.
Boase-Beier, J. (2006). *Stylistics approaches to translation*. Manchester: St. Jerome Publishing.
Boase-Beier, J. (2011). *A critical introduction to translation studies*. London: Continuum International Publishing Group.
Brown, G., & George, Y. (1983). *Discourse analysis*. Cambridge: Cambridge University Press.
Chandler, D. (1997). *Semiotics for beginners*. http://visual-memory.co.uk/Daniel/Documents/S4B.
Chesterman, A., & Arrojo, R. (2000). Shared ground in translation studies. *Target, 12*(1), 51-160.
Dollerup, C. (1996). *Teaching translation and interpreting 3*. Amsterdam: John Benjamins Publishing Company.
Faucett, P. D. (1997). *Translation and language: Linguistic theories explained*. Manchester: St. Jerome Publishing.
Gambier, Y., & Luc, D. (Eds.). (2016). *Border crossings translation studies and other disciplines*. Amsterdam: John Benjamins Publishing Company.
Gentzler, E. (1993). *Contemporary translation theories*. London: Routledge.
Halliday, M. A. K. (1985). *An introduction to functional grammar*. London: Edward Arnold.
Hatim, B., & Ian, M. (1990). *Discourse and the translator*. London: Longman.
Lederer, M. (2003). *Translation: The interpretive model*. Manchester&Northampton: St. Jerome Publishing.
Loffredo, E., & Manuela, P. (Eds.). (2007). *Translation and creativity: Perspectives on creative writing and translation studies*. London: Continuum International Publishing Group.
Malmkjaer, K. (2005). *Linguistics and the language of translation*. Edinburgh: Edinburgh University Press.
Neubert, A., & Gregory, M. S. (1992). *Translation as text*. Canterbury: The Kent State University Press.
Newmark, P. (1988). *A textbook of translation*. Upper Saddle River, NJ: Prentice Hall.
Newmark, P. (1995). *About translation*. Clevedon: Multilingual Matters.
Nida, E. A., & Charles, R. T. (1982). *The theory and practice of translation*. Leiden: E. J. Brill.

Nord, C. (1991). *Text analysis in translation.* Amsterdam: Rofopi B.V.

Nord, C. (1997). *Translating as a purposeful activity.* Manchester: St. Jerome Publishing.

Pattison, A. (2007). Painting with words. In E. Loffredo, & M. Perteghella (Eds.), *Translation and creativity.* London: Continuum International Publishing Group.

Pym, A. (2010). *Exploring translation studies.* London & New York: Routledge.

Reiss, K. (2000). *Translation criticism:Potential and limitations.* Manchester: St. Jerome Publishing & American Bible Society.

Schrijver, I., et al. (2016). The impact of writing training on trans-editing in translation, analyzed from a product and process perspective. *Perspectives: Studies in Translatology, 24,* 218-234.

Scollon, R., & Suzanne, W. S. (1995). *Intercultural communication: A discourse approach.* Oxford: Blackwell.

Shreve, G. M., & Erik, A. (Eds.). (2010). *Translation and cognition.* Amsterdam: John Benjamins Publishing Company.

Waard, J., & Nida, E. A. (1986). *From one language to another.* Nashville: Thomas Nelson Publishers.

Wilss, W. (1982). *The science of translation.* Tubingen: Gunter Narr Verlag.

侯维瑞．1988．英语语体．上海：上海外语教育出版社．

胡壮麟．1994．语篇的衔接与连贯．上海：上海外语教育出版社．

李运兴．2003．论语篇翻译教学．中国翻译，24（4），58-62．

廖柏森．2012．翻译教学论集．台北：新悦文创．

刘宓庆．1985．文体与翻译．北京：中国对外翻译出版公司．

刘宗和．2001．论翻译教学．北京：商务印书馆．

彭宣维．2000．英汉语篇综合对比．上海：上海外语教育出版社．

申小龙．2004．语言与中国文化．上海：复旦大学出版社．

王佐良．1987．英语文体学引论．北京：外语教学与研究出版社．